SHIPSHAPE

THE ART OF SAILBOAT MAINTENANCE

OTHER BOOKS BY FERENC MATÉ

From a Bare Hull
The Finely Fitted Yacht
Waterhouses
Behind the Waterfall—a novel
Best Boats
The World's Best Sailboats

Illustrations by Candace Maté

First published in the U.S.A. in 1985 by Albatross Publishing House Inc.

First published in the U.K. in 1986 by David & Charles Publishers plc.

Second printing 1986.

Albatross ISBN 0-920256-12-0
David & Charles ISBN 0-7153-8948-3

Typing by Judy Geib
Set in CG Times typeface by Laffey Type, SoHo, New York City
Printed in the U.S.A. by R.R. Donnelley & Sons

DISTRIBUTED IN THE UNITED STATES
BY W.W.NORTON, 500 FIFTH AVE., NEW YORK

SHIPSHAPE
THE ART OF SAILBOAT MAINTENANCE
FERENC MATÉ

ALBATROSS PUBLISHING HOUSE
VANCOUVER • NEW YORK

DAVID & CHARLES
NEWTON ABBOT LONDON

To the Elmer in us all.

Acknowledgements

Where do you start? On a book like this, where the contribution of so many people was needed to create something of value, it's always hard to give people the credit they have earned. Most often it comes in a small section like this which few people ever read and that is unjust, for not only would this book not have existed without the help of the many dedicated professionals, but the sailing community as a whole would be much the poorer without their years of dedicated work.

I will try and list everyone, and I will list them by no other means than their order of appearance in my life, for some very short encounters left as valuable an impression as some lengthy involvements.

So. Loads of thanks to my old friend Spencer Smith at Book-of-the-Month Club for the pile of research material and the encouragements and for the gems of information and the many laughs when I most needed them; and to Billy Ede who managed the boatyard next to our house in West Vancouver, for his daily visits over the years and endless hints and tips; and to Mel and Chris, and all the others there who always took time the shoot the bull over beers or on the seashore to explain and clarify; and to Rod Fraser, the genius of marine engines, who not only saved *Warm Rain's* diesel from demise, but almost single-handedly furnished the whole chapter on engines in this book; and to Paul Larsen at Hearst Marine Books for his incessant insistence that I get this book done and for keeping me out of the poorhouse all the while. And loads of thanks to "Giffy" Full, the marine surveyor of marine surveyors, for the hours of enlightenment on how to survey your own boat; and to Brody McGregor who owns the legendary Concordia Yard; and to Jerry Smith who runs it, for allowing me to spend the days in the yard photographing everything in sight, and pestering everyone with seemingly endless questions.

So much for the verbal help. The second phase which contributed vastly to the amount of information in this book came from the experts who had mercifully published comprehensive and vital material on their products. At one stage there was a three-foot high pile of leaflets, articles and manuals stacked in my office and I gained some knowledge from most of them, and some were so excellent that I reproduced them in large portion in this book. For the permission to do so, I thank the following:

Nicro Fico and Gary Mull N.A. for the outstanding *Fitting and Rigging Guide*.

North Sails for their essay on *Sail Care*.

Interlux Paints for the mammoth tome on paints, from which much material was used, as were their photos on hull repainting.

Hearst Marine Books for the piece on sail tuning from their book *Looking at Sails*.

Edson International for their piece on *Steering Maintenance*.

And last but certainly not least to British Seagull for their devastatingly adroit book on outboard engine use and care.

And much thanks to all the people who helped with photos and illustrations: Volvo Engines, Garret Wade Tools, Whale Pumps, Shipmate Stoves, Fujinon Binoculars, Johnson Outboards, Chelsea Clocks, Plastimo Compasses, Schaffer Marine Hardware, BMW Marine, and Lewmar Winches.

The biggest thanks as usual goes to Big Red, who has stuck it out for fourteen years and five books, put together in the strangest of places— Phoenix, Vancouver, Newport Beach, Paris and New York City.

Contents

Introduction

Dear Elmer,

I realize that life is complicated, full of gadgets and glitter that beg for our attention, so many distractions that our heads are always spinning, trying to make sure we don't miss out on the fun. And we clutch and grab and twist and turn and spread ourselves so thin that we end up knowing a little bit about a lot of things but when it comes to *essence* we know nothing at all. And with all the grasping, we lose sight of what we really need and want—someone to love and a good boat that will stick with us through our lives. And yet it's to those two things that we pay such little attention, neglecting a kind touch here, a small hug there, except on the days when we need something in return. And when you neglect the small things, they all add up unnoticed, like the years, and then you notice much too late all the damage you have caused.

Both sailboats and people need a little love, and they need it when they need it, not when you decide you have finally time to give. Give it early, by the time you decide you're ready, there might be nothing or no one left to receive.

New York City, 1985   *Ferenc Maté*

SECTION ONE

THE HULL

1

Launching a New Boat

The Bottom

This is as good a place to start as any. We might as well discuss the launching of a new boat, for at least one major future problem can be avoided right now.

With a new wood hull, most bottom paints can be used as their own primers, so no major decisions will be encountered here—see *Painting the Bottom*—but with a fiberglass boat, it's a different thing again.

Some fiberglass boats that have been in the water for a good number of years have developed small blisters on the surface of their underbodies. Controversy goes on as to whether this was caused by something put *onto* the surface after the boat left the builder's yard, i.e. something in the bottom paints, or whether the cause of the problem was more deeply rooted in the hull, i.e. in the gelcoat of the fiberglass under it. These blisters, or osmosis spots, are usually about the size of a lentil, and if you look closely you will see a pinhole in the lentil, and if you press very hard on the lentil, you will find water coming out.

How widespread this problem is, is rather hard to say. First of all, many boat owners don't ever look closely enough to discover the spots; they just keep slapping bottom paint over them. Second, when the spots are being discovered, they are often left as just *being there* and so what. Third, if they *are* discovered they are often left, for they are so numerous that only major surgery will repair them; and fourth, even if they are repaired, the news is usually kept quiet, for people seem reticent to talk about it, as if their poor boat had the zits or some unspeakable social disease.

Anyway, the problem does exist and although it is thought to occur mostly in tropical waters, I can vouch that it happens up north as well. To what extent I can't say for sure, but I can say that in the small yard next to our house, there were only five boats hauled in late October in need of repair, and three of them were there to have their zits removed.

What, you may rightly ask, does this have to do with the launching of my new boat? The answer is that perhaps preventive steps should be taken at this time to avoid major surgery later on. Just how major this surgery is can be simply told. A thirty-foot boat next door had about eight hundred little zits, all of which had to be ground out one by one with a grinder, then filled by hand with epoxy putty, then faired in one by one. This took about forty

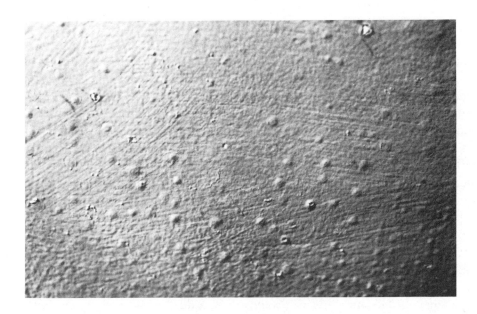

No, Elmer, this is not a closeup of the moon—it's the bottom of a boat with a bad case of the zits. Each of those little lumps is a gelcoat blister with water in it. The only way to fix a blister is to grind it out, fill it and sand it.

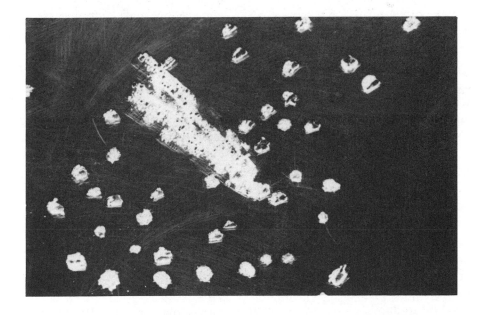

When you pop a blister you'll create a good-sized hole with rough edges. Sand there fair before you fill.

man-hours. If you multiply that by twenty-five to thirty-five dollars per hour, depending on where you live, you come up with one very expensive outbreak of acne.

The prevention is, as usual, much less painful than the cure, consisting of the application of two coats of a good epoxy primer which will seal any minute flaws or pores in the relatively porous gelcoat, and thereby eliminate the potential problem of blistering. This task if no big deal. A couple of gallons will cover a thirty-foot fin-keeled boat. The preparation of the surface will take a little elbow grease, but you are well advised to do this even if you are just applying ordinary bottom paint, for the new gelcoat has on it a layer of mold-release wax, which allowed the hull to slip easily from the mold without damaging the surface. This should come off to create a better base for the bottom paint.

First, wash all dirt off the hull with detergent and water. It would be ecologically ethical to be accustomed to using a dishwashing liquid like *Joy*—it sudses in salt water— for any washing operations around a boat, since it's one of the few that contain no phosphates. Now I'm not entirely certain what phosphates are, I just know that they're bad news because they do something unspeakable to sea life, and will in time turn the whole ocean into ditch-slime. Now you wouldn't want *that* on your conscience with all the other horrors, would you?

So wash down your sweetie with *Joy*, then wash her down with fiberglass solvent to remove the afore-discussed mold-release wax. This does not mean you should slosh the stuff all over the place as if you were bathing some elephant, but it means soaking a rag, then wiping the hull with it. Rotate your rag often and change rags often, otherwise all you'll end up doing is pushing the wax around from one part of the hull to another.

Next, sand down the bottom with 120 grit sandpaper. Don't overdo it. You're only trying to take the sheen off the gelcoat, not bore a hole to China. Now that you've created all that dust, get rid of it. First, brush the brunt of it off, then wipe off the stubborn stuff with a rag dampened with solvent. Now, tape off your boot stripe, and you're ready to apply the primer.

Epoxy primers are a two-part thing that should be mixed according to the directions of whichever brand you choose. Do follow the directions carefully unless they sound dumb. Application is usually best accomplished with an airless sprayer. You can rent one of these for about ten dollars a day, so you might as well do that and put on a couple of nice even coats, Some manufacturers recommend more. Read the can.

If at all possible, do spray this on—don't roll it. Save your strength for the bottom paint—you'll need it. When you do spray, take all the precautions recommended by the paint manufacturer, or you might end up with totally waterproofed lungs.

If however, you are into body-building or some other depravity, by all means roll to your heart's content, but make sure you use a roller made to withstand the onslaught of the solvents in the epoxy primer. Some have in them solvents that dissolve the glue that holds the furry part to the cardboard tube. I speak from experience. I once used the *wrong* kind and the glue dissolved and the fur unwound, and there I stood on a late Sunday afternoon with my hull just started and the stores all closed and with this thing in my hand that looked like a wet dead cat. So beware.

Pre-Launch Survey

When you mention this notion to most people they usually laugh so hard their tonsils show, yet through experience of having spent a year at Westsail as a consultant to builders and owners, and after witnessing some emergency haulouts directly after launching—the most embarrassing of course being our very own—I've concluded that the foundation of good seamanship must be laid just before the time of launching of a new boat.

The expectations and excitement in most of us reach a high point when our new boat rolls into a boatyard, and we can hardly wait until she's in the water with sails billowing and spray flying, with us behind the helm, feet planted, and hearts pounding almost as hard as when the love of our lives staggered us with her first kiss.

But the greater our expectations, the greater our disappointments, and with a thing as complex as a sailboat, both in its construction and in its function, it would be naive of us to expect everything to work perfectly the first day. Hundreds of parts are assembled in her from a dozen different manufacturers, all of whom employ ordinary mortals, all of whom commit ordinary errors; and if you consider all the hours involved in the building of your boat—not just the construction and tacking on of hardware and mechanicals and sails, but consider too all the hours spent in the making of that hardware—you might come up with a number close to four or five thousand. And if you reflect back on your life over the last five thousand hours, and consider for one honest moment the hundreds of mistakes you've made in that time—the astounding oversights, the laughable stupidities—then perhaps you'll allow for a few mistakes made by the builders of your boat. For although they may each be dedicated and caring and meticulous in their work, they too—I hope to God—have greater weights upon their souls than the tightening of screws and the spreading of some putty. So expect them to lose their concentration once in a while, when it all comes over them, and expect a few mistakes, and expect some imperfections. If you do, your disappointment will be less and your enjoyment greater, and you won't be roaring through the yard upon the great day of your launching, snapping and cursing and demanding, accusing everyone in your path of cheating you and neglect

ing you and conspiring against you.

Take it easy. Even a perfect boat won't do you much good when you lie dead of a heart attack. Have a good time. You may never get another chance to enjoy a good boat launching again.

And the first thing you should do is a complete survey of your boat.

'Giffy' Full of Marblehead, Massachusetts, who has spent thirty years on sailboats as crew and skipper and the last twenty-five as surveyor, has had enough bad experiences with new boats to believe they all merit a survey before launching. In the time I spent with him while he surveyed a fine wooden ship, he impressed me as one of those few who really do care about others, who loves nothing more than going through a boat he's hired to survey and coming out without finding anything wrong at all. But that seldom happens. What too often happens is that he finds so many things wrong that he barely has the heart to tell the anxious owners who are waiting with their champagne bottle and bright eyes full of stars.

His stories include everything from giant voids in the laminates of brand new hulls—including one "you could crawl inside and spend the winter in"—to a boat that had thousands of small pinholes, and another that had the chainplates installed with the bolts in place but not a nut in sight. So. It might be worth your while to hire an experienced surveyor.

But be careful who you do hire. Many surveyors, most of them in fact, are self-appointed and unlicensed, for there is no real licensing system, and according to Giff—who is considered a genius by craftsmen who know his work—too many surveyors hurry through a boat at a ridiculous pace, sometimes in a couple of hours, and call the thing done. Meanwhile, Giff—whom I have seen scramble all day with the speed and thoroughness of a squirrel gathering its winter stores—takes a good two days to do a thorough survey on a forty-footer. So if you are to choose a surveyor, go on

"Giffy" Full, master surveyor, doing a biannual survey of a meticulously kept wood boat. Fiberglass boats don't need to be reconnoitered quite this frequently but should be done just prior to their baptism. You never know.

some strong recommendation or reliable reference, for two or three hundred dollars is a lot of money to flush down the drain. And an even greater shame is that if a small problem goes undetected, it will only get much worse and cost a bigger bundle to repair.

If you have the confidence and the time, by all means do your own surveying; you'll never get a better chance to get to know your boat first hand. Besides, now is the time to find out where everything is, and how everything works, from bilge pumps to stoves, from seacocks to fire-extinguishers, *now*, not when you're out at sea and a hose bursts and water starts pouring in and you're running around all aflutter as if you mistook a chili pepper for a suppository, looking for seacocks and bilge pump handles but ending up with spare socks and spaghetti.

Get to know your boat. It's not underwear that you just step into and forget about; its a very complex machine and you should know how it's put together, and you should know at least in theory how it comes apart, and if you say, "I'm a toughguy,

I can take my chances," then you're not really a tough guy but a mindless fool, because it's not just your life you're putting in danger, but also the lives of those who are fool enough to sail with you, as well as the lives of the poor bastards who have to come and rescue you when you finally bugger up and go running to your radio whimpering for help.

So go through your boat inch by inch before you launch her, and get to know her inch by inch. Not just like some tourist who opens a door to some magic land, peeks in and thinks he's seen it all— because he hasn't, he hasn't seen a damn—and he'll go away more confused than before he came. So find everything and check everything, and twist knobs and turn levers and find out what they do and how, and once you've gained some familiarity, *then* you have earned the right to go aboard and ask her to take you places. For knowledge and awareness is what makes a sailor, not a pair of white-soled shoes and a stupid cap.

So much for the moralizing—let's go and do a survey.

2

Pre-Launch Survey

The following is a modest outline of what needs to be done. It is by no means a complete *How to Survey a Sailboat*, for that would take a book on its own and a lifetime of surveying experience, but it covers the major problems and will at least keep you from sinking the first time out.

Rod Stevens, one of the finest yacht designers of our time, has a personal checklist for sailboats before launching and I respectfully used many things from his list as a skeleton for the following.

The Hull

1. Voids

The first thing to do is check the hull. Take a small mallet—Giff uses a four ounce plastic one—and go tap tap tap every square inch of the bottom and topsides. What you're looking for is voids in the fiberglass hull, voids caused by air being trapped between the laminates. To find them, you have to listen for a hollow, lifeless sound, instead of the firm solid sound you hear when you hit good glass.

If you find a void, get hold of the builder and have him repair it. If the void is of any size, that's a major structural flaw and should not be treated as a cosmetic repair. Some builders tend to favor

a quick-and-dirty repair, which involves drilling two or three small holes into the void spot close to its edge, then injecting epoxy into one hole until it squirts out the other. While this may be an almost acceptable procedure if the void is small and located in something non-structural like an icebox liner or a shower pan, it is *not* acceptable on structural components like the hull. The problem occurred in the first place because something stopped the two layers of glass from sticking to each other—something like moisture or dust or oil having been on the surface—and if they couldn't get the damned thing to stick under ideal conditions when everything was exposed and easily accessible, then how the hell will it stick now with some feeble resin trickling through a feeble hole?

Anyway, if the void is of any depth, you'll be creating a layer of unreinforced resin with no fibers in it, and that's about as strong as hardened caramel candy. But all this is irrevelant because the damned thing won't stick anyway.

Giff told me a story that proves this notion perfectly. He surveyed a brand new forty-footer—a respectable craft built on the east coast by a company that had been building boats for over a decade—and found sixteen voids (heart attack city), each a good foot around. Giff told the owner

This is not a loincloth for a ladder, but a very good way to keep boatyard grit off your decks.

to tell the builder to take the boat and shove it where the sun don't shine. But this was in June and the owner was anxious to go sailing, and the builder swore on all the Bibles in Utah that he'd do a perfect job of fixing it, with a lifetime warranty. That's worth a lot all right, when the guy might go out of business in the next twenty minutes. Anyway, the builder sent down some poor clown with a drill and a jug of resin, and on he went and drilled the holes and filled the voids as best he could. So off the owner went sailing for the season and in October he called Giff back to look at the hull again. Well, Giff started tapping with his little hammer, and sure enough, he found the voids again—good as new, bigger than ever, and as a bonus he found five more to boot.

Giff drilled a few of his own holes to see what was going on inside, and from each pocket they

had filled with resin, he found water trickling out. To make a long story short, the boat ended up being returned to the builder who in turn sent a new one to take its place. No voids.

The proper way to repair these voids is to have them ground out completely, and filled in with the proper layers of cloth and mat or whatever the layup schedule calls for. The only problem with this is that it's difficult at best to achieve a perfect finish without the use of a mold—anyway, who wants a boat that's been patched with bits and pieces?

If you do decide you can live with it, make sure you get a good discount. There was nothing in the shiny brochure about the voids.

2. Hard spots

When you've done that—and it should take you a couple of hours go first to the bow, then to the

It's dumb to haul your boat to paint the bottom only to destroy the top. Pad the ladder and save the caprail.

stern, and sight along the surface of your hull. Look for any sudden breaks in the reflections that you see. Do this on a bright day if you can, when the reflections are strong and clear. What you're doing here is looking for *hard* spots on the hull that may be caused by a bulkhead improperly forced or bonded into place. Such a hard spot must be remedied right away, for once the boat is launched and sailing, the fiberglass skin will work and bend around this hard, sharp edge, and cause delamination or fracturing of the skin.

If you think you've found a potential problem spot, go up to it and close your eyes and run your palm flat over the surface and try to *feel* the spot. Do this even if you only vaguely suspect a spot, for reflections can often fool you. If you're still a bit uncertain after you have felt it, get a good straightedge like a yardstick and try to get a good sharp reflection of it *across* the suspected hard line.

Now look at the refection closely; if the reflection of the straightedge smoothly follows the curvature of the hull, then you have no problem, but if there is a sudden *break* in the reflection, you'd better do some more research. Go below and have someone tap on the outside of the hull where the suspected hard spot is and go around until you can find the spot on the inside of the hull. It there is indeed a bulkhead or other likely culprit where the suspected spot is, then get hold of the dealer or the builder and—what the hell—do a little yelling, it'll help to take the pressure off your chest. Just don't take it too seriously. It's not worth dying over. It's only a boat.

The surveyor's best friend. "Giffy's" plastic hammer to tap-tap out rot in wood and delamination in fiberglass.

3. Through-hulls

Check all through-hulls for cracks around them where caulking had been used in the seam between the hull and the bronze. Have someone open the seacocks inside and push your finger up there to make sure bits of wood or woodshavings or fiberglass haven't gotten stuck up there during construction. Make sure the valves open and close smoothly.

Now take a small ball peen hammer and give each seacock a firm but solid tap. This is not a game of golf so don't tee up and try to whack the seacock over the horizon. Just tap it gently and listen for the sound of an existing crack. You want to know what a cracked seacock sounds like? It goes 'Clung.' You happy now?

Doing this test is not overkill, for a seacock could easily have a flaw from casting that might give way under the torque of being wrenched tight,

or from something heavy being dropped on it during construction. If you launch with a cracked seacock, the first good plunge down a wave could blow the thing apart, especially if it's closed and there's no place for the pressure to be released, and down you'll go like a lead balloon.

You might do well to close all seacocks for the launching itself, and then once the boat is in the water—but before the slings are released—open each one and check for leaks. Check the hoses and hose ends too, just to be sure. It's not impossible that a hose might have been unwittingly slashed during construction. If you decide not to close the seacocks, at least check to see if you *will be able to close them* when the time comes. With space being as precious as it is in boats, and with assembly coming at all odd stages, a seacock may be installed long before the cabinet is built around it. One will find too often that there is simply not enough room to turn the seacock lever from the vertical *open* position to the horizontal *closed* position. If this is the case, don't take chances. Have the thing altered before you launch. Often the seacock can be simply turned 180 degrees which will require recaulking, etc., but if you are lucky you'll have the type of seacock where the handle can be shifted from one side to the other. Take a good look to see what you have to do, but whatever you have to do, do it now.

4. Propeller and shaft

Check to see that the propeller and shaft turn free and fair. Even though they may have been in perfect shape when the boat left the plant, they could have been damaged or bent during transport. Most truckers slip a chain or strap right through the aperture, or around the aft end of a fin keel, to keep the boat from sliding backwards in the cradle during transport. This is when something could have gotten torqued out of shape.

Check the crown nut behind the prop to make sure it's snug, and check the cotter key that is through it to make sure it is bent enough that it won't slip out on the first spin.

Check the stuffing box. That's the fat-looking bronze thing around the shaft inside the boat where the shaft comes through the hull. Make sure the nut on it is tight. Don't overtighten it or you'll crush the packing material inside it and it will then leak. If it feels tight, leave it.

5. Transducer

See that the speedometer transducer is properly aligned. It should be perfectly parallel to the centerline, otherwise it will give a false reading. It you have the most common type with the paddle wheel, then give it a spin—it should spin freely and stop smoothly.

6. Centerboard

If you have a centerboard, make sure it operates freely and smoothly. You might take a long stick and feel up inside the centerboard box to clear away any old building materials. Wood shavings or pieces might be in there causing no difficulty while they're still dry, but once launched they could swell and hamper a smooth operation.

7. Rudder

The rudder should turn without binding or rubbing on anything. If there is a bit of binding now, it could get worse once the thing is loaded with the pressure of the water as you're surfing along at nine knots. Then again, the pressure of the water may just free the bind. Who knows. Check it anyway.

8. Zincs

Make sure all sacrificial zincs are in place and make sure they're tight, especially the zinc collar on the shaft. If this little sucker comes loose, it can slip along the shaft and bind and prevent you from going into reverse when you're coming full-steam into the dock after your first flawless outing. Ever hit a cement wall at five knots? Makes a hell of a noise when the bow cracks like an eggshell.

On Deck

1. Voids and hard spots

Get out your little four-ounce plastic mallet once again and repeat the procedure as described in *Voids* and *Hardspots* above.

2. Stanchions, pulpits and lifelines

Make sure the stanchions are secure, lifelines tight, and for godsake, be sure all the pins in the lifelines have cotter keys or spring-rings in them, or as soon

Check your prop, crown nut and cotter key before launching; saves playing Jacques Cousteau after the prop drops off.

as you lean against the thing, the pin will fall out and the lifeline come loose and there you'll be in the water wondering who pushed you in. It was you, Elmer, because you didn't check the lifelines.

3. Lifesaving gear

This equipment should be in place before you launch. Sure you're only going for a quick spin in the harbor, but you'll be in a state of frenzy during all that time, for everything will be new and strange, and that's when you're most likely to make mistakes and end up playing kissyface with the harbor seals.

4. Steering wheel

Mark the wheel now, indicating which rudder is parallel to the centerline.

5. Odds

Secure anchors, boat hook, reaching pole, etc. so they won't get underfoot when the crane lifts the mast in place and you're scrambling about trying to find the hole.

6. Fenders and docklines

These should be aboard and ready, and that means not packed away in some obscure locker still in their plastic bags. You'll look mightly foolish coming smartly into your slip and stopping her up perfectly only to be blown into the boat next door for lack of mooring lines.

Down Below

1. Plumbing
All hoses should have double hose-clamps at each end. Don't take anything for granted. Take a screwdriver and check each one to be sure it's tight, especially the hoses that fit onto through-hulls. And do check both ends of a hose. Water is very democratic, it doesn't care which hole it has to use.

2. Bilge pumps
First clean out the bilges of any shavings and bits of crap—this is the most likely place for garbage to accumulate. Make sure the screens on the end of your bilge pump hoses are clean too. First, of course, make sure you have screens on them; if you don't, go get them now and put them on. You might think it a funny time to mention this, but do get a powerful vacuum cleaner and clean out, then wipe out with a wet rag, all your lockers and all your bilge areas. *Get rid of all the crap now.* More boats have sunk because of inoperative bilge pumps than almost any other thing. This is inexcusable. Most bilge pumps are so simple they seldom break down—I'm talking of course about the manual, diaphragm kind, They fail because something got stuck in them, and the little flaps won't close and the pumps won't pump. While you're at it, you might as well open up the pump and make sure that there is nothing to it. On pumps like a Whale 25, this is a simple task; you just turn the two black knobs and open up the sides. On other pumps, you might need a screwdriver to loosen a few screws, but I assure you it's worth the trouble.

When you've done all that, throw a couple of buckets of water into the bilge and test the pumps now, before your life depends on them.

3. Floorboards
This might sound overcautious, but Rod Stephens suggests that the floorboards be checked to be sure they're not too tight, and that a nice ten-degree bevel is put on them. Once the boat is in the water, in a humid environment, the boards can swell shut in a few days to the point where you'll never open them again without an axe. This swelling of floorboards seems to be an unending event, for in each of the last seven years I've had to plane *Warm Rain's* every season, only to find them tight the following spring. Then one day I went berserk with the plane and took off three pounds of wood and I haven't had a hint of trouble since.

4. Hatches and doors
Make sure they all work loose and smooth. Know how to unlock all hatches quickly from the inside in case you sink or burn. (That's it, Maté, don't candycoat it, give it to them straight.) Anyway, you'd feel like a fool if you went for your first sail and ended up being trapped in the head by an ill-fitting head door.

5. Fire extinguishers
Find them. If you don't have them, get them and mount them. Have one readily accessible from the cockpit, without having to go below into the fire to get it. Have one beside the galley stove; most fires start there. Have one that's rigged so you can spray into the engine room without having to open anything, thereby feeding air into the fire.

Engine and Mechanical

1. Emergency tiller
The emergency tiller should be in its place— just in case.

2. Lightning gear
Check your lightning ground installation and all wire connections.

3. Engine oil

Check engine oil level and gearbox oil level and coolant level, if engine is freshwater is cooled.

4. Batteries

They should be completley filled with water.

5. Seacocks and valves

Open engine intake seacock and valve on exhaust hose—if you have one, and you should. (I mean if you have a valve, not a hose, for I humbly assume that you have a hose.) Open these now, for you might forget to open them in the heat of the moment when the hoist is about to turn you loose and you're busy trying to start the engine. If you do forget, the water pump on the engine will run dry and burn out the impeller. And that's just the beginning.

6. Tools

Do have decent tools on board for your engine in case something does go wrong out there, especially, if for some reason, you don't yet have your sails aboard.

Rigging—Before Stepping Mast

1. Chainplates

See if you have nuts on the chainplate bolts. Remember old Giff's story.

2. Turnbuckles

These should be in place, right hand thread down, which means they tighten and loosen the same way as a bottle top, which tightens and loosens the same way as most other things in the world. This is not some quirk, for few things are more frustrating than trying to set, tune, or repair the rigging, only to tighten something every time you want to loosen it, and loosen something when you're trying to make it tight.

3. Pins and keys

Have all toggles, clevis pins and cotter keys in place, the lower ones with the cotter keys bent, the upper ones ready to receive the rigging. Put a little lube on each pin to make sure they won't bind when you're busy trying to step the mast. Have a few spare pins and keys handy in case you drop some overboard.

4. Swedges

With a magnifying glass, look over all swedged wire terminals to make sure there are no cracks in them. A friend didn't do that, and he happened to get a bad batch, and all his rigging had to be changed after the mast was stepped, and what a pain that is, shimmying up the mast a hundred thousand times, taking off rigging shroud by shroud, then taking each piece to the rigger, etc.—a true and thorough horror compared to doing it while the mast is still lying horizontally on a pair of sawhorses.

5. Mast

Take a hard look at your mast. Sight along the track to make sure *it* is straight. Run your finger inside the track to make sure there are no loose or askew rivets (if it's the rivetted-on kind) and to get out any obstructions if it's the slot-in-the-mast kind. Then take a damp rag and wipe out the inside of the track again. On the rivetted type track, run your finger along both ends of the track gate where it adjoins the solid pieces to make sure the ends have been rounded and will cause no obstruction to the sail. It might behoove you to grease the track with Vaseline for those impressive mainsail dowsings.

6. Spreaders

Take a hard look at the spreaders to see if there are any dimples in the extrusion. Nothing can bring a mast down as quickly as a failed spreader. Check spreader-to-mast attachment. Check and eliminate any sharp edges. Wrap the spreader ends with

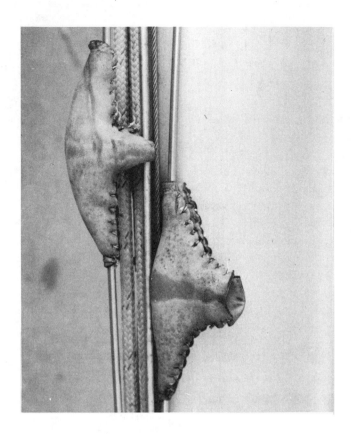

Handsomely sewn leather spreader ends. Better than the wheels or the bulky rubber ones, because those effectively lengthen spreaders and thus chafe the headsails more.

leather or tape to eliminate possible sail chafe and tear. Most sailmakers agree that damage by spreader ends is one of the leading causes of tears in headsails.

7. Bosun's chair

Have a bosun's chair aboard right from the first time you go sailing. If a halyard jams or a sheave jams, you should be able to go aloft to free it and not have to leave a two-thousand-dollar sail hang ing there half hoisted, beating itself to death while you putter back to your slip.

Also have aboard a decent ditty bag with bits of line and rigging tape and some rigging wire and a handful of shackles and pins. Just in case.

8. Mast gear

Have mast wedges and mast collar handy.

9. Mast wiring

I've left one of the most important things until last. Check the wiring in the mast. Get a battery and hook up each mast light to it one by one, and make sure they all work, and make sure the bulbs are tight and secure and the covers or lenses tight and waterproof. Again, it's much easier to make repairs

A fair bosun's chair with a stiff seat—padded at that—and good baggy pockets that won't go flat and tight when the chair is loaded with your weight. A belt fits around your midriff to keep you secure.

now than to do it later dangling from a bosun's chair.

Once the wiring is found to be okay, see it there are any wires that can slap against the side of the mast when the boat is rolling in an anchorage and you're trying to sleep while the wire is playing bongos right beside your ear. If there are loose wires—belatedly installed coaxes and wind instrument wires are usually the culprits because most self-respecting boat builders put all their mastlight wires into a PVC tube which in turn is riveted to the mast wall—do something about them now. The simplest thing is to get some hunks of foam rubber from the local foam rubber scrap pile, and tie them on the spare line that should be in any decent mast. Tie one every five feet or so and make sure they fit snugly into the mast to inhibit wire movement.

10. Mast bottom

If your mast is keel-stepped or stepped in a base on deck—as opposed to a tabernacle mast which sits free and clear above the deck out of any standing water—I think it a very good idea to coat the bottom few inches of the mast—inside and out—with a well built-up coating of epoxy. Make it a good heavy coating, for it will take some beating being put in place, and usually undergo movement under sail. Both can cause some wear, resulting in bare aluminum which is just sitting there waiting to corrode as soon as it can find itself some nice standing water to help it out.

On any mast a small limberhole should be drilled near the base to allow accumulated water—which comes in through the masthead and halyard openings—to drain freely away. Drill the hole

A couple of layers of epoxy resin and cloth, both inside and outside the foot of the mast, keep it from corroding in the dark dank bilge.

before you do the epoxy coating so that the sides of the hole can receive the coating too.

Rigging—After Stepping Mast

1. Sharp things

Tape or cover all sharp edges in the rigging. There will be bent-over cotter keys everywhere, with ferocious ends just waiting for an unsuspecting sail to come by. Tape them now, or put on those molded rubber things that look like undernourished zucchinis—North Sails advise against these, for they effectively extend the length of the spreaders—or if you are really classy, you can do what I saw on a Baltic 50.

The owner or the yard or somebody, had cut some beautiful gray elkhide—stiff stuff that had considerable body—and tailored it to fit over the turnbuckles right from the deck up. They had put Velcro along the long edge to allow quick access to the turnbuckles, which is a commendable thought but flawed because Velcro has a fairly short life aboard a boat—what with salt and sun eating away at it—to the point where those bizarre little tentacles turn to dust. A better solution would be to just stitch along the long edge with a good strong thread, then cover the stitching with a couple of coats of Seamcote, the stuff sailmakers paint over the seams of sails to increase the resistance of the stitching to chafe. To get at the turnbuckles, you need not undo the seam. Just slide the whole thing up the shroud and *voilà*; now you don't see it, now you do.

2. Sailbags

Mark all your sailbags. They should come marked from the sailmaker but if they don't, mark them or you'll look mighty strange hoisting a storm jib in a three-knot breeze.

3. Spreaders

Get out you bosun's chair and do your first shimmy-up-the-mast exercise; you don't have to go far, just up to the spreaders. This is not a sightseeing trip; you're going to set the spreaders at the proper angle to the shrouds. Some people think this is overkill, for you can sort of adjust them before you step the mast, but that just isn't good enough, for once the shrouds are torqued against them, the whole thing suddenly changes. So go and reset them. If you have single spreaders, raise them so that the angles the spreader makes with the shroud are equal, that is, the angle above the spreader is equal to the angle below it.

4. Lastly

Tie knots in the ends of the halyards or bitter-end them to cleats, then go ahead—crank her up and leave the dock. Good sailing. Oh yes, I almost forgot, do look over the side to make sure there is water coming out through the exhaust through-hull. If not, shut her off and go investigate.

Note exhaust gushing cooling water. Peek over the side once in awhile to make sure your intake hasn't gotten plugged up.

3

Hauling Out for the Winter

To Haul or Not to Haul

For sailors who live in climates where the waters freeze in winter, or even if the winters are only too cold or too wet for sailing, storing the boat on land should be considered. In icy waters this is very strongly recommended, for ice can cause damage to hulls—if not structural, at least cosmetic. In places where the ice problem is negligible, you should still consider hauling out for the winter, and if you ask, "Why?" I'll answer, "Why not?" You'll have to haul out in the spring anyway, so there is no extra expense there, so why not store her on land and save a lot of wear and tear and potential problems.

If you smile patronizingly at this and mumble something about a boat belonging in the water, then I'll have to say to you, "True, but not tied to a dock." First and most obviously, a boat in the water left unattended—and too often forgotten for the winter—can one day decide she's had enough and sink. Whether because of a failed seacock, or a slow leak, or through theft or vandalism, makes little difference, because sunk is sunk and that's all there is to it. And even if she doesn't in fact sink, the thought of her sinking will often cross your mind and you'll worry, whether in the mid-

dle of the night, or on Christmas eve, or halfway through your holiday in Rangoon, and that's a waste of time, for life's too short for that.

Even if you are among the blessed who never spend a moment fruitlessly worrying, you should still consider chafe. Chafe comes long and often during winter storms when the boat is nudged about, straining lines and cleats and fenders. Not only will the lines and fenders chafe, but the dirt and grit that build up on the fenders and the hull will, very neatly, be ground into the gelcoat or the paint, and leave some very deep scars that will too often be reparable only through re-painting or re-gelcoating.

Now you can say that you'll be down once a week to wash all the grime away, but deep inside you know you won't, so why kid yourself.

If you don't care about the gauges then think about theft. It's much easier to empty a boat's contents by stepping nonchalantly over a lifeline than to have to scramble up and down a tall ladder with both arms full of goodies. And by the same token, I would venture to guess that it's measurably easier to slip the mooring lines of a boat and vanish with it in the night than it is to put the sucker on your

A fleet of Concordia yawls tucked in for the winter. If you're not going to use your boat for a few months, you might as well haul her and save her from chafe and theft and sinking.

back and tiptoe down the lane.

But then it's your boat; do what you want. Pleasant dreams.

If I still haven't managed to put the fear of God into you, then think about the money. It is normally much cheaper to store a boat on land than in the water, especially if you have the old dear moved into your own driveway. Not only will she then become an instant topic of neighborhood gossip, but you will be much more likely to do maintenance and repairs and modifications if she is out there staring at you through the bedroom window. And not only will you save on your moorage but you'll save on your insurance, for the boat can often be included under household furnishings, or personal items, or pets.

When I was in South Dartmouth, bleeding everyone dry at the Concordia boatyard for infor-

mation for this book, I was astounded at the number of driveways that were winter homes for boats, and I don't mean daysailers—I mean, Boats. Them yankees know the value of a buck.

If you do store your boat on land all winter and are lucky enough to be in an area with semi-protected waters—ones that are safe enough in the summer blows but unsafe in winter storms—you can dispense with marina fees altogether by keeping your boat on a buoy during the sailing season. Or you can just launch her in the spring and get the hell out of there and go cruising, which is what you ought to be doing anyway.

Now back to winter hauling.

Dragging the old dear home can be done in three ways. The cheapest is buying an old boat trailer of some sort, or a flatbed trailer which you can convert yourself, and having the hoist plop her

One of the best winter homes for medium-sized boats is your own driveway or backyard. A trailer like the one shown can be put together fairly cheaply and best of all you can work on your boat all winter long without deserting your loved ones or your wife.

If you live close enough to the boatyard, you can just ask the machine operator to take a little drive and stop off at your house.

The finest hybernatoriums are nice old sheds. Whatever happened to them all?

onto it and then dragging the whole show home.

The second cheapest method might be having the hoist itself saunter down the street, if you live close enough and the wires are high enough.

The third and most likely method is having a boat mover come and take you home. This is the most costly method of the three, for it involves transferring the boat from the hoist to a truck, and every time you involve another machine and another worker, up goes the cost, but don't just shovel money at everyone—barter. Don't be shy. You'll be surprised how flexible they can be that time of the year when so few boats are being delivered.

Cradles and Blockings

The nicest way and ultimately the safest way to store a boat for long periods—or for any periods for that matter—is to have a cradle built for the specific boat, a cradle into which she'll fit like a glove. This can be made of wood or metal. The wood one is not only cheaper to build, since any old wood beams can be used, but it is infinitely more suitable for home construction, since no welding will be required. The steel one does, however, have one redeeming factor in that, with the installation of adjustable screwpads, it can be made to fit almost any boat and thus permit re-use if you buy another boat. Or it can allow you to recoup a good part of your investment through resale for use with almost any other boat. In most cases, a custom-made wood cradle is recyclable only as much as kindling.

But, as in most cases, the best system is the most expensive system, and so it is with cradles.

More flexible and cheaper than the cradle, and requiring much less metal to fabricate, are the bizarre but ingenious tripod things that I discovered in the Concordia yard. These creatures, that can be made of steel tubing as light as one inch in diameter, are made as independent pieces that can be set at any chosen distance from each other, thereby enabling them to accommodate anything from a dinghy to the Queen Mary. Do note however, that even though the tripods and the nose piece are freestanding, they are joined together by

A steel cradle is hard to home-make but is adjustable to suit almost any boat.

A good old-fashioned wood cradle and a set of hoity-toity tripods. The tripods are costlier to make but they are adaptable to any boat and *they store with relative ease.*

A close-up of the independent tripods. Note single one under bow—the boat is a short-keeled Swan—and note also the chains holding the tripods together, keeping them from "kicking" out.

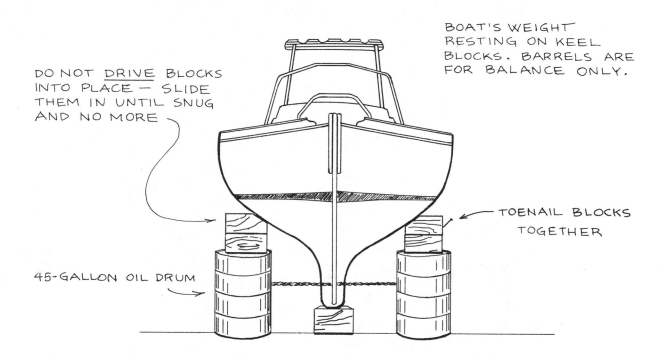

BOAT'S WEIGHT
RESTING ON KEEL
BLOCKS. BARRELS ARE
FOR BALANCE ONLY.

DO NOT <u>DRIVE</u> BLOCKS
INTO PLACE — SLIDE
THEM IN UNTIL SNUG
AND NO MORE

TOENAIL BLOCKS
TOGETHER

45-GALLON OIL DRUM

- CUT KEYHOLE SLOT IN BARREL.
- PASS CHAIN THROUGH ROUND PART
- AND LOCK IT IN VERTICAL PART

<u>THE POOR MAN'S CRADLE</u>

lengths of chain, slipped into slots, to keep the tripods from being *pushed* out by the weight of the boat. This may seem to you like overkill, but don't forget that even though the boat may sit as steady as a rock when first landed in the autumn, the ground may become soggy with winter rains, and the blocks under the keel may sag, and the weight of the boat may shift, and thus try to push out a tripod. So don't argue, dammit! Use the chain.

If you think this system is a bit more chancy than the cradle then you're right, but don't overlook one great advantage, which is that these things can be stacked and stored out of the way. Few things are harder to store than some great ungainly cradle that has the weight and manageability of a hard-frozen elephant lying on its back.

The cheapest way to shore up a boat is on forty-five gallon steel drums. These you can usually get free from an oil company or a disillusioned steel band. The drums can be made to be *adjustable* by using a series of blocks and wedges on top of them, which can be made secure by tacking them to each other with long spikes. The drums, in turn, can be attached to each other, and thus made secure, in much the same way as the freestanding tripods described above. Holes can be drilled in the sides of the drums to accommodate chains, allowing for the same system as the tripods. The holes should in reality be slits, shaped as the drawing, so that the chain links can be freely inserted through the wider top part, then slipped down to the narrower part to be made secure at the desired link. Oh yes, just for safety, I think I would add some extra lengths of chain, two diagonally between barrels, and two more lengthwise between barrels just to be sure.

There is no need to invest much money for this, for old chain is cheap to buy, or if you are more nautically inclined and love feigning self-reliance to boot, then you can use your anchor chain for this purpose. No, Elmer, that does not mean taking your hacksaw and cutting the thing into bitty

lengths—it means simply that you take your anchor chain, leave it in one piece just like the Good Lord meant for it to be, and slip it into the barrel through the hole on one side, then out through the other side through the large hole there. Then you go to the next barrel like a good boy, and do the same thing there. My God, Elmer, what would you do without me?

Blocks, Screwpads and Wedges

Although I include this discussion under long term winter storage, it applies equally even if the boat is on land only for the day. Care should be taken with the blocking of the boat both for its safety as well as your own, for a boat toppling over can suffer substantial damage at the bilges, as well as make a pancake out of you, as you innocently fumble around below it.

1. Blocking the keel
The most important blocks will be the keel blocks that you will set directly on the ground if using tripods or barrels, or on the cross-members of the cradle if one is to be used.

I say the most important, for if done properly *all* the weight of the boat will be carried by these blocks that sit under the keel. The four cradle arms, or tripods or barrels *should not carry any of the boat's weight*; they are there only as things to keep the boat balanced, keep it from falling over to one side or the other. Many people forget this simple fact and proceed to either crank madly at the levers that raise a steel cradle's screwpads, or drive wedges between bilge blocks and the hull with enough force to wedge the earth in two, with the predictable result of virtually driving the pads or wedges right through the bloody hull. Merciful-Mary-Mother-of-Jesus! Think, Elmer. Think!

If you're standing somewhere and you slightly lose your balance, you put your hand out and lean

BLOCKING A LONG-KEELED BOAT

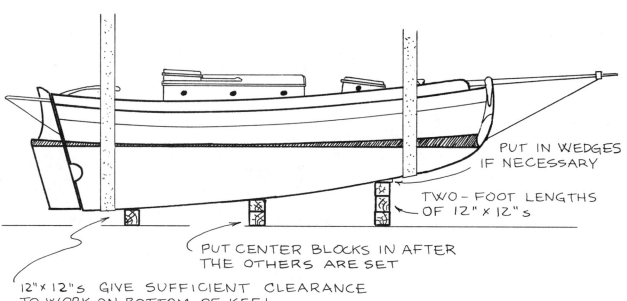

PUT IN WEDGES
IF NECESSARY

TWO-FOOT LENGTHS
OF 12" X 12"s

PUT CENTER BLOCKS IN AFTER
THE OTHERS ARE SET

12" X 12"s GIVE SUFFICIENT CLEARANCE
TO WORK ON BOTTOM OF KEEL

BLOCKING A FIN-KEELER

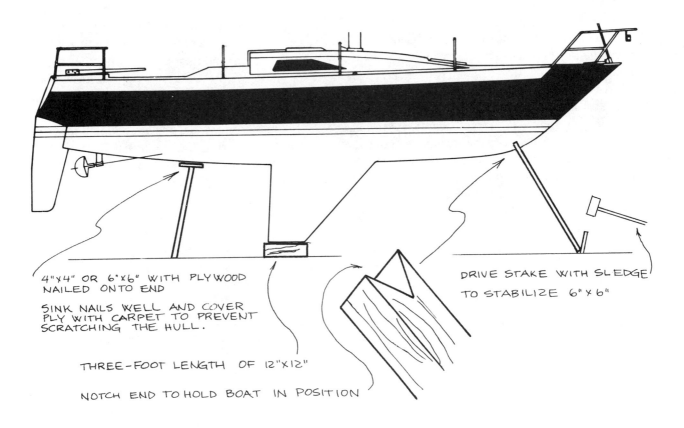

4"x4" OR 6"x6" WITH PLYWOOD
NAILED ONTO END

SINK NAILS WELL AND COVER
PLY WITH CARPET TO PREVENT
SCRATCHING THE HULL.

THREE-FOOT LENGTH OF 12"x12"

NOTCH END TO HOLD BOAT IN POSITION

DRIVE STAKE WITH SLEDGE
TO STABILIZE 6"x6"

THERE WILL BE SIDE SUPPORTS AS WELL.

lightly against a wall, but almost all your weight remains on your feet—right? You *don't* try to drive your nails into the wall and try to raise yourself up, do you? Or do you? If you do, you might as well go ahead and drive the wedge right through the hull, because with the major problems you've got upstairs already, this one will seem blessedly minor.

Now that I have impressed upon you the importance of these blocks, let us discuss just what they should look like. They can be summed up by the old American adage, "The bigger the better." A good size that is manageable by hand without necessitating trusses and hernia operations, is a nice hunk of twelve-by-twelve, about two feet in length. The twelve inches of width will nicely take up the boat's weight without digging into the keel, and along with the two feet of length, will help distribute the load over the ground without the block being driven down through the surface. The block's twelve inches of height raises the keel sufficiently high above the ground to enable you to get at most of the keel's bottom for cleaning, repairing and repainting.

Do not try to use pieces of bitty two-by-fours to make up one big block, especially in height, for the stack of sticks can buckle with the least movement, and the whole can thing slide forward and fall onto its side, creating the aforementioned bilge damage and human pancake. If you live in the desert or the Arctic where large wood blocks are sold by the ounce, fine, I give in, use the smaller sticks, but use at least two-by-tens and *do* tack them all together with spikes, and do have the spikes near the ends of the planks and not in the middle, at least in the topmost board where they could surreptitiously work themselves up into the keel.

In case of the blocks on the ground, it is usually enough to use two with a fin-keeled boat and three with a full-keeled one.

If a steel cradle is used, so that the keel sits directly on a cross-member of the cradle, put a

piece of plank in there as padding so the keel is not set directly on the steel.

On a wood cradle, the wood cross-pieces normally suffice as the base, with blocking needed only to make up for the rising of the keel toward the bow.

Whichever method is being used, be sure the ground under and around the block is solid, and make sure the drainage through the winter will be good, otherwise if the ground gives and the blocks sink in, the four pads or wedges under the bilges will get the whole weight of the boat, and very possibly cave in or dent the skin. The damage they may cause to fiberglass boats may never be discovered, for the glass may pop back out once the weight has been removed, but delamination of the glass layers may have already occurred.

If you do come down one day and find the pads bearing an abnormal load to the extent of actually making some sort of dent in the hull, first put in two new blocks on either side of the old one to shore the boat, then back down on the screw or back out the wedge, but slowly and gently, to make sure the whole boat doesn't come after it. Then take a small plastic mallet and tap the affected area inch by inch, tap by tap. Tap and listen well; listen for a flat, lifeless sound that indicates delamination. If you don't know what a flat lifeless sound sounds like, then tap a part of the hull that you can assume to be undamaged first, to get your ear accustomed to what a good sound sounds like. If you find no difference between the sound of the good part and the potentially damaged part, then either there is no damage or you're tone deaf.

How you block the keel will determine how level the boat will sit, and while this is not critical for a boat that will be stored for a few days only, I think it important if it's to be left all winter long. Most boats have deck drains somewhere near the aft end of the deckhouse, and the decks are so designed that all water runs off them and drains out through there. Now then. If you block your boat

Adjustable screw pads on steel cradle or tripod balance *the boat, Elmer, they don't* lift *her off the ground. So to set them, don't just keep cranking 'til she topples—make them fairly snug and that's all.*

unlevel, you will change the plane of the deck so that it won't drain completely. Instead it will leave a little puddle standing somewhere. Over the course of the winter, all sorts of dirt and grime will gather and settle there, since this now is the new-found low point of the deck, and by springtime you are likely to end up with a nifty swamp of black crud.

In case of an all-fiberglass deck this might result in no worse than a virtually unremovable stain, but on teak decks it will turn the pink wood black. Only some very deep scouring, which will result in actual loss of wood, will bring this deck back to new. A waste of time and a waste of deck, both easily preventable by taking thirty seconds to check the waterline with a common level.

If you own a wooden boat, this is all the more critical, for standing water will freeze and thaw, freeze and thaw all winter long, and if a minute crack existed in a seam or canvas covering, the ice will make it wider, and a minute leak may begin and, in no time at all, rot out the plywood or solid wood below.

2. Pads and wedges

What pads and wedges should *not* do was discussed above, so all I'll say here is that both of these should be made tight only after the boat has found its final position on the keel blocks. But before the wedges or pads are made tight (relatively speaking), the straps on the hoist should be slacked until they bear no more weight—until all the weight is resting on the blocks, and all that the straps are doing is keeping the boat's balance. Now that should give you a clue as to the next step, the next step being tightening the wedges or the pads. Since the straps are now only balancing the boat, the pads and wedges will need to do exactly that and no more. So. Check to make sure the boat is sitting upright—that is, not heeled to either port or starboard—then one by one tighten the pads or tap, in the wedges, *but gently*, and when you meet resistance, give another gentle tap then stop. That's it. When you've done all four like that, the straps can go.

Pulling the Mast

The Concordia Boatyard, which stores over seventy large boats on land each winter, pulls the mast from each boat before hauling. The masts are then stored in long sheds all winter long. Some of you might think that this is too much trouble, but I was told five good reasons why this was done and of the five, four are enough to make one consider pulling and storing a mast even if the boat is left in the water.

1. Chafe and weathering

Both will be eliminated. Some of the worst mast damage can come from halyards and running backstays which become slack over the winter and chafe against the mast and spreaders. Chafe will easily wear through the paint or varnish of a wood mast and continue right down into the wood. An aluminum mast is not much better off, except that it might not chafe quite as deeply.

Weathering on most masts occurs in the cold and rainy season when the moisture can cause rot in wood and oxidation in aluminum. If freezing is encountered, the problem is worse, for small cracks will become larger and varnish or paint will lift easier.

2. Checking mast and rigging

Each year I spend half a day shimmying up the mast, with magnifying glass and tools and cleaning things in hand to check all fittings, wash down mast and rigging, and do whatever repairs or touch-up painting might be needed. Needless to say, all this could be made much easier if the mast lay in some warm shed where more time and care could be taken with its maintenance. Repairs aloft are difficult at best and seldom thorough enough, not to mention the fact that all this work can be done in a warm shed during the winter months instead of being delayed until the weather warms, when the time—were the boat in shape—could be spent sailing.

3. Checking the base of mast

There is no other truly satisfactory way to check the base of a mast than by pulling it from its step. Both rot and corrosion are the most severe down here—mostly on the inside of the mast—and unless you're very slim and very slippery, you will find great difficulty in getting in there to look.

4. Boat protection

Most skippers attempt to install some kind of winter cover on their boats to save hatches and woodwork, and the whole boat in general, from the ravages of winter. On *Warm Rain* we have a great, vast cover made of so many pieces and flaps and zippers, holes and strings that it takes Candace and me a whole day to decipher and install the sucker. Although Gary Storch, our sailmaker, did a superhuman job in laying out and fitting all these bits to sheer perfection, we have found that it's impossible to keep all water out when a mast and a whole slew of rigging have to pass through the cover. The point here is this: A simple holeless, flapless awning, without all the jigsaw pieces, takes one-tenth the time to make and install than the Rubic's Rag we own. The time and money saved is almost indescribable, for don't forget, a cover won't last forever and a new one will have to be made every few years at yet another horrendous expense.

As mentioned before, such a cover cannot be made to fit perfectly, thus it will always allow in enough water to stain the fiberglass and lift the varnish, whereas a simple one-piece winter cover that lies like a blanket over the entire boat will act as a good boathouse to keep the whole boat dry.

5. Strain on fittings

If you have ever watched a sailboat with her sails down in a wind, you will have noticed that the simple pressure of the wind against the mast and rigging arc quite enough to push her a ways over. Now as you can imagine, it must take quite a bit of

Late autumn in Massachusetts. Note number of boats hauled in background and some still in the water, and most of them without masts. Not only is it easier to check and work on masts and rigging this way, but a complete awning can be fitted more easily and much *more cheaply.*

torque to move the keel of a boat around that much. Now, when a boat is sitting on land, it cannot roll when hit hard by a gust. Instead, the rigging and chainplates have to absorb all the shock. Although I don't believe that this strain is anywhere equal to the brutal force of a good gale battering even reefed and shortened sails, it does seem that the boat and her fittings are subjected to a lot of unnecessary strain if the boat is hauled and the mast left in.

So for all the above reasons, one should pull the mast and tuck it away until the cherries bloom.

The poor man's boathouse. It stows all summer nicely tied like a stack of kindling, then abracadabra...

...it turns into a little chalet with a view until...

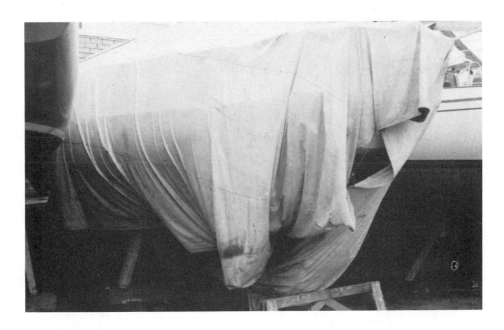

…you throw a big canvas blanket over it and make it into a giant tamale.

Pad the feet of the tamale with canvas, otherwise they might scrape the bejeezus out of your deck.

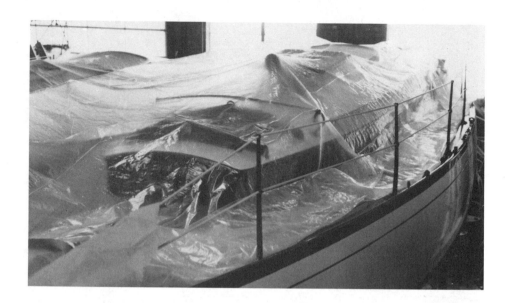

How to spoil a boat rotten. Put her inside a warm shed for the winter and *cover her with poly. Might as well bring her a hot toddy; then sing the little bitch a lullaby.*

Storing the Mast

Once the mast is out, check it over completely (see section on mast maintenance and repair) and replace all cracked fittings, and sand and clean off all chipped or cracked paint and varnish. Don't leave this last until spring, for if there is corrosion or rot under the paint, it's best to find it now, for both of those conditions are likely to deteriorate even though the mast is under cover. The deterioration will of course be slowed considerably, but the moisture in the air will slowly keep it going. Anyway, it's best to gauge the depth of these things now, just to assess the extent of repairs to be done.

At Concordia, they like to put a couple of coats of fresh varnish on the wood masts for the winter, and after having touched up aluminum masts, they like to clean and then wax them before they're put away. Giff, the master surveyor, strongly recommends covering the mast with brown paper or poly, to keep it clean and cozy and looking sparkl-ing fresh for spring.

Giff also cautions about handling of the rigging while the mast is out. All rigging should be tied to the mast—tied, not taped—for the tape will take paint and varnish with it in the spring. This is not for some obscure aesthetics, but to keep the turnbuckles and rigging from dragging on the ground while the mast is being moved. If you do drag it, you'll pick up bits of dirt and sand that can grind and abrade and bind expensive, vital fittings.

Anyway, as I said, there is lots more of this stuff—very important stuff that you should not neglect—in the section on masts and rigging, pertaining to masts, whether standing or lying down, so read it and heed it or wear a hardhat on your boat in case the mast comes down and tries to part your hair.

And as for how the rest of the boat should be handled, read the chapter on winterizing.

One of the coziest places I've been in lately was the mast shed at the Concordia yard. It was late autumn and late afternoon and the sun was low and the place was quiet and there were all these beautiful old varnished masts snuggled in, telling each other stories of what they'd done all summer.

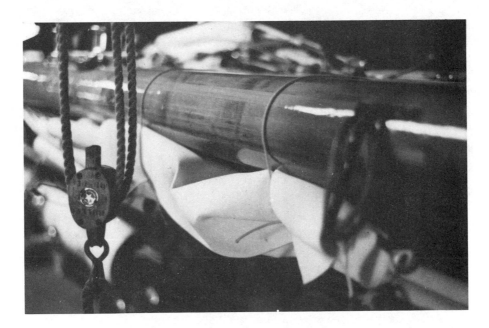

When you're moving your mast about, tie all your rigging—don't ask me what the sail is doing there—to your mast so you don't drag your turnbuckles through the dirt and sand.

How not *to leave your boat for the winter. Everything will weather and fade and be filled with dirt and grime unless some merciful soul comes along and "liberates" them and moves them to warmer climes like* his own *basement. Strip her before somebody else does.*

The worst place to leave your sails for the winter is aboard. Take them home and store them and pull them out some quiet night and spread them on the floor and have the whole family gather round and do some sleuthing to see if they can find worn stitches or some chafe. Beats the hell out of watching Morgue *and* Windy *on the tube.*

4

Spring Haulout

To Haul or Not to Haul

Almost every spring, depending on the condition of the bottom paint on *Warm Rain*, I go through the week-long exercise of trying to decide whether to haul or not to haul, and if to haul where to haul.

The first part of the dilemma should never even come up, for most sailboats, whether made of wood or fiberglass or aluminum, could use a hauling every year, not only to have the bottom cleaned and repainted but also to give the entire hull the eye, to see what on earth is going on down there anyway.

1. Wood boats

With wood hulls the number one menace one should be on guard for is rot, while the other number one menace is corrosion of fasteners. The latter is not a serious problem on new wood boats, most of which have been fastened by very stable monel or bronze fasteners, but on older boats the potential is great enough to warrant a vigilant eye.

Some wood boat owners shrug and say that they have no need to worry because bronze was originally used to fasten their hulls, and no matter how old the boat the bronze fasteners will retain their soundness. This is true enough in most cases, for boats up to fifty years old have been found with com-

pletely sound fasteners, but according to Giff that is more the exception than the rule. Many old boats were fastened with bronze all right, but a bronze fastener is only as stable as it is pure, and it is only as pure as it was made. If it was made impure, then the impurities in it can be leached out through galvanic action and weaken the fastener to the point where it will fail. Giff showed me a beautiful looking fastener he had recently pulled from an old ship he had surveyed, and to the naked eye it looked to be in flawless shape, but when he gave it a moderate whack with his ball peen hammer, the fastener cracked in half like candy cane.

Somehow for some reason the bronze had *hardened* and lost all its malleability and with it most of its resistance to sheering forces.

Aside from the hardening, the aforementioned electrolysis could be setting up in all but the purest of fasteners, and electrolitic action promotes rot in the wood immediately surrounding the *hot spot*. What all of the above means is that you should haul your boat once a year to see what's going on.

2. Aluminum boats

These are such gluttons for electro-galvanic (I didn't

The first of twelve thousand shots of hoists. This one is here for no particular reason other than that it looks good.

No matter how perfect a shape your topsides seem to be in, the bottom—where leak-water settles—might develop pockets of rot. This fine varnished beauty had to have five planks removed.

even know I knew that word!) action—aluminum being one of the top conductors, very near to copper and hence its appearance in wiring as of late—and although very fine systems can be set up to protect aluminum hulls from electrolysis, if I owned an aluminum boat, I'd still feel better if I took an ogle at the underbody once a year.

3. Fiberglass boats

Fiberglass is moderately safe from most diseases except for the little osmotic (I think I just invented that one) zits which were discussed in the section on launching a new boat. Yet the fear of its occurrence—for the little zits get larger with time as more water is absorbed around each infected spot—should motivate one to haul once a year.

What's the big deal anyway? Money certainly cannot be used as an excuse, because most yards will haul a thirty-foot boat for about a hundred dollars, and on most boats, cleaning and painting and inspecting the bottom can be done by two people working their behinds off in one long day. Even if you don't haul, there is work to be done on the bottom, like changing the sacrificial zincs—and if you don't change these then you had better shake your head, for you'll be sure to be changing something much more expensive, like an eaten away prop or a shaft next year—and if you intend to sail faster than four knots, then you'll have to have the slime and crap scraped off the bottom no matter how expensive and technically wonderful a bottom paint you use. Both of these tasks will require a diver and divers cost money—if they do a thorough job probably a hundred bucks—and then you still won't have inspected the bottom or checked the seacocks or spent a perfectly great day in some sunny boatyard grunting and sweating and complaining to the other inmates about the horrors and indignities of owning a boat.

So haul.

Where to Haul

Once I have surrendered to the inevitable, the next point of tedium is deciding which humble boatyard we will honor with our presence. If you're lucky, this decision will be pre-empted for you by the fact that there exists only one yard in your vicinity, but let me be the devil's advocate even if that is the case, by telling you that one of the best times Candace and I had hauling out was when we cruised to a little distant island and hauled out in a small old shipyard there.

Apart from the romance of the place—and it had a lot of that, being in a sleepy bay formed by rocky islands of gnarled arbutus trees and old sheds and old orchards, which was more than reward enough—there was the money.

The old boatyard, being out of the way of big demand and not having great mortgages to pay like its city cousins, could afford to charge thirty percent less for its services. Now we didn't end up actually saving much, because we had such a good time messing with the boat on that old marine railway that we decided to spend a couple of extra days poking about, but each moment we spent there felt as much a holiday as some cruises we've taken.

Added to all that was the reward of knowing that we were helping a fine old yard survive.

How to Haul

1. On your own legs

The least expensive and the most frantic way to haul a boat is the way many people still do in small harbors world wide—using the tide. This system is of course totally useless to those near the equator where a spring tide has a range of about two feet, which is barely enough to decently scrub your bootline, but anywhere else where the tide drops

If you're going to haul, you might consider hauling at some fine little yard away from the city. It's better for the soul.

ten feet or more, you can—with some fancy footwork—re-do your whole bottom without paying a cent.

This method involves first of all finding a completely quiet bay (I don't mean noise, Elmer, I mean the water), for if there is any wave action—and what's usually worse, any wake action from half-wits thrashing powerboats—then you'll probably suffer more damage on a tidal grid than you're trying to repair.

The bottom should be good hard sand with no rocks of any kind. If the bottom is of very, very fine pebbles, that's all right too, but in that case you would be well advised to set a solid two- or three-inch thick plank, at least as long as your keel or even longer, underneath the keel to fend it.

Getting the plank under the keel will take a bit of doing. First, nail a couple of two-by-two's to the top edges of the plank—see drawing. The two-by-two's will serve as guards to keep the plank from sliding out from under the keel. Next, with the plank in the water, load it up with a few rocks—

not too many, just so it starts to sink—then dive down (you'll need some weights yourself to get down there) and carefully take the plank with you. I say carefully, so you don't spill the rocks and have the plank shoot upward like a bat out of hell. Now slip the plank under the keel and remove the stones one by one until the plank slowly rises and snugs itself under the keel.

If you do use the tide, you'll have to tie your boat to pilings or a sea wall or use poles like the old French fishboats to try to keep her upright. All sailors with fin-keeled boats take heart, and don't think for a minute that this activity is restricted to boats with full keels. Most modern fin-keels have fairly long, flat bottoms, and most of them are close to the geographical center of the boat, so setting a boat on a decent fin-keel should be no great problem—the older scimitar-shaped keels of course notwithstanding. I saw many a Beneteau and Dufour tied to the old sea wall at La Rochelle with the help of some good solid fenders for protection, and with the help of good solid mooring cleats for

The cheapest way to haul is using the tide and your own peg-leg. But I beg you; don't beach your boat on the year's highest tide or she'll be there until next Christmas.

support, and not a single one did I see suffer any damage.

If you harbor fears of falling on your nose hauling your fin-keeled boat, then you can make a simple bow-crutch to ease your mind. This need be nothing fancy; an old four-by-four will do. A nice hunk of old oak that lies around in boatyards—the remnant of old cradles—would be an ideal choice. Anyway, once you have it, cut a notch in the top end and simply wedge it under the bow. See illustration. If the bottom of the place you're hauling in is a bit soft, then put a plank flat below your bow-crutch to distribute the load. To be really safe, tie a rope to the bow-crutch about midway up and double it around the back of the keel and back to the

crutch to help keep it from *kicking* out.

An alternative to the *tie-to-something-solid* system is the use of the *legs* you see on the French fishing boat in the photo. This will give you the ultimate freedom of hauling anytime, anywhere, pilings or no pilings, sea wall or no sea wall. If you do decide to use the *legs*, you should definitely use a bow-crutch, and on a boat of twenty-five feet or over, you might be well advised to use two legs per side. One caution: Don't put the legs too far forward or aft; keep them close amidships where the beam of the boat is the greatest, hence the lever arm of the support system, the longest.

Two caution: For extra security row out an anchor about a hundred feet on both the port and star-

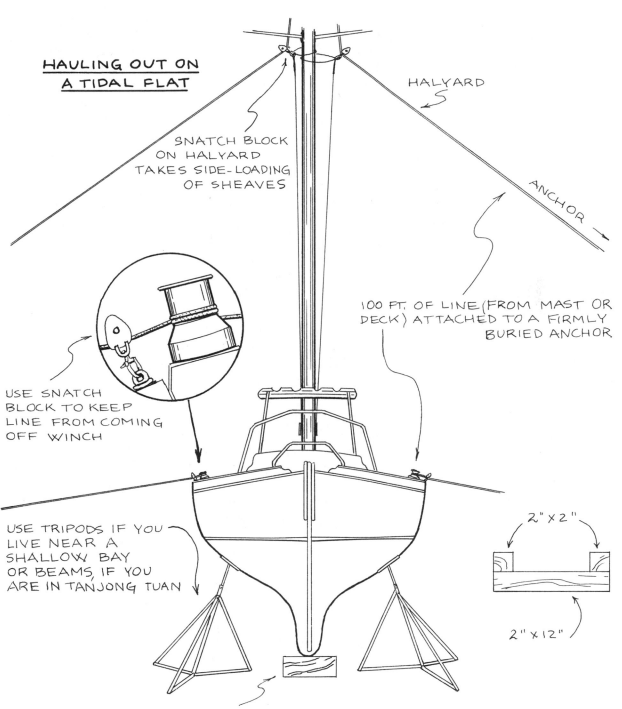

HAULING OUT ON A TIDAL FLAT

SNATCH BLOCK ON HALYARD TAKES SIDE-LOADING OF SHEAVES

HALYARD

ANCHOR

USE SNATCH BLOCK TO KEEP LINE FROM COMING OFF WINCH

100 FT. OF LINE (FROM MAST OR DECK) ATTACHED TO A FIRMLY BURIED ANCHOR

USE TRIPODS IF YOU LIVE NEAR A SHALLOW BAY OR BEAMS, IF YOU ARE IN TANJONG TUAN

2" X 2"

2" X 12"

IF YOU CAN FIT IN A COUPLE OF BLOCKS TO WORK ON BOTTOM OF KEEL, SO MUCH THE BETTER

board sides, set them and bring the lines back to the boat and tie them to your halyards and pull them tight with your halyard winch. To take the side loading off your sheaves, use a snatch block as shown in the drawing. Take it easy. You're trying to keep the boat upright, not topple her, so once the lines are taut, leave them. The trick here is to tighten the lines completely evenly, one gentle pull per side per time, or you will indeed bring the poor thing down.It is best to do this when the boat is still just barely afloat, for then you can tell readily by the waterline which side is too high and which too low, and if you pull too hard on one line the boat will simply heel a bit and not fall over. So take it easy and pull gently and don't break anything.

Now for the frantic part. This is so embarrassingly obvious I'm almost afraid to say it, but for godsake, Elmer, don't put your boat on the beach on the highest tide of the year, or I promise you, you'll never get her off there in one piece again. Look closely at the tide book and make sure you compensate for daylight saving time, and try to haul on an eight-in-the-morning high tide so you'll be refloating well before dark. And make sure that the evening tide is at least six inches higher than the morning one. Even then, have everything ready to go in the evening as the water rises: anchors off the sides, with one of them reset aft as a potential kedge; legs loosened off as soon as the water hits the bootstripe; and generally all things ready to shove off. Now take it easy; I said *be ready*, I didn't say, *panic*.

Once high tide does come, you usually have half an hour of slack tide before the water begins to fall once again, so *don't* panic.

Anyway, now that we've discussed the end of this topic we might as well go back and say a few things about the beginning.

First of all, once the boat settles on her keel, start adjusting and setting your *legs* right away; if you dally, and the boat starts to heel in one direc-

tion, then it's already too late to maneuver the legs. You may be able to bring her back by winching in on the opposite winch—the high side—but don't try to do this if the boat is gone more than an inch or two or you'll break something.

If you are caught in the predicament of not being able to bring her back, don't yell for the coast guard. Get the *legs* out of the way and just let her go gently over as the tide falls. Nothing serious will happen if the bottom is sandy and you close all your hatches and your portlights. Most decently designed boats will go delicately over and end up sitting on the bilge, not even coming near to the topsides. You might do well, once she's about to touch, to check to see that there are no rocks beneath where the bilge will settle, then once she has settled down, don't just stand there feeling sorry for yourself, get out your brush and start scrubbing down and cleaning the high side of the bottom that's exposed.

If it's hard going, dip your brush into the sand and use it as a scouring compound. It works great and it's as cheap as hell. When the bottom is clean, let it dry, then paint it. Sure you'll only have done half the job, but half the job is better than none. You'll only have half to do tomorrow and you won't have to fool around with the legs again. Just run a single anchor from the mast where the lower shrouds join, out the side you painted the day before, and set her on her keel again and haul in on the halyard to make sure she goes over on that side. It's not much use scrubbing and painting the same side twice in two days.

One small trick: Once she is almost touching, give her a little help with the halyard to get her to lie hard on her bilge instantly without mushing about and bouncing and scraping off the paint you put on so carefully yesterday.

2. Against pilings or sea walls
This isn't half as demanding physically as the *leg* trick, but you'll have to get up just as early in the

WHEN FENDING OFF A PILING
DON'T RELY ON STANDARD
RUBBER FENDERS. CUT A GOOD
LENGTH FENDER BOARD —
ABOUT 3' — AND USE SOLID
RUBBER FENDERS SHOWN.

FENDER BOARD

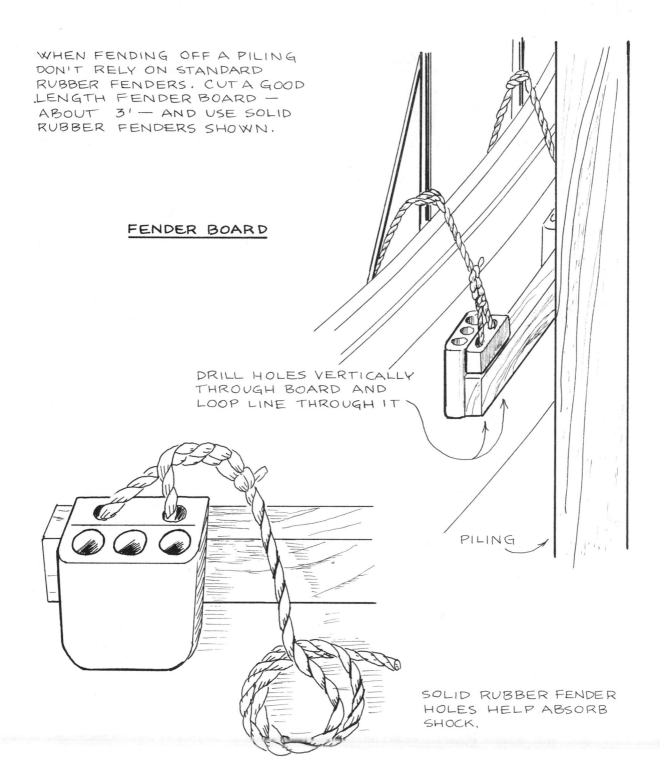

DRILL HOLES VERTICALLY
THROUGH BOARD AND
LOOP LINE THROUGH IT

PILING

SOLID RUBBER FENDER
HOLES HELP ABSORB
SHOCK.

morning to get the job done.

Tying to pilings is just like tying to a dock, except you'll have to loop your line around the piling and keep paying attention to it as the tide falls to make sure the line doesn't get caught up on the piling and yank your cleats right out of the deck. The only other thing you'll have to do is either hang your fenders—the bigger the better—by both ends so they lie horizontally, i.e., at right angles to the piling, to allow for some forward and aft movement, or make yourself a quick fenderboard—see drawing—to do the same thing except a little better.

Tying to a sea wall requires exactly the same caution, with the added attraction of not being able to hang a loop of line around the piling to allow for slippage. You'll have to be a bit more attentive and let out line as the tide falls, that's all. Watch your fenders to be sure they don't wedge and ride up above the gunwale.

So, there are the two least expensive and, as usual, most exciting ways to drydock your boat. Anything in comparison is super safe and super predictable. Sounds like life to me.

3. Tips for tide hauling

From the time you touch bottom to the time you float free you'll have about twelve hours. You won't be able to do much for the first and last two because the water will be too deep around the boat, so you can see that you'll have a lot of work to do in the remaining eight hours. A few tips in that regard:

a) As soon as the water falls a few inches, get out your scrubbing brush and get into the dinghy and start cleaning the boot stripe. It will generally be covered with bits of oil residue and desiccated dead things, so have some non-abrasive cleaning compound ready, something like Fantastic, and remove all the goo.

b) As the water falls more, start checking the hull and your seacocks and changing your zincs. Don't leave these things until the end when you're exhausted by the long day—you might

forget them.

c) Scrub the bottom as soon as the water is shallow enough to stand in. Do the side in the sun first, for it will be the first to dry, and the scum and stuff is much easier to remove when it is still wet. Another advantage of starting on the sunny side is that it can dry nice and fast, and by the time you finish the shady side, it will be ready to paint and you won't have to stand about waiting.

d) For scouring compound use sand. Right below your feet. It will remove not only the growth but also the softened old paint, or at least it will roughly feather in the edges.

e) Once the bottom is clean and rinsed off, don't wait for the last spot to dry before you start painting. I'm not saying to paint *over* the wet spots, I'm saying to paint *around* the wet spots and come back to them later.

4. Marine railways and floating hoists

Both of these are ideal, or at least sufficient, if you want to haul your boats for a day just to clean and paint the bottom and change zincs. The problem is that in the busy season they charge an arm and a leg for any extra days you want to spend out of the water. This is understandable since a yard usually has only one machine and they make their money hauling and launching boats, not by having people parked on it.

There are no particular precautions to take here except for one, and this one applies to the Travel-Lift type hoists as well—the ones that pick you up in a sling and tote you about a parking lot. Do have a profile drawing of your boat handy with the underbody clearly drawn, so the man working the slings (Travel-Lift) or setting the blocks (marine railway) will know exactly where to put them to get the best set for your keel, without damaging the rudder or propeller.

Oh, one other thing. The pads that steady a boat on a marineway are usually covered with some kind

The old-fashioned marineways are good for short haulouts just to paint the bottom, but usually cost too much to tie up for a number of days.

No matter how you haul, it's always advisable to shore up the bow.

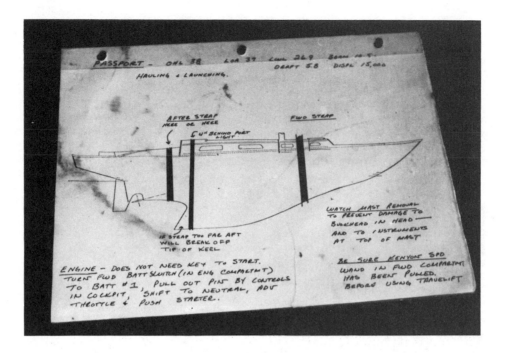

It shows good seamanship to have a profile sketch of the boat aboard to help the hoist operator set his straps. If you will be absent while the boat is being hauled or launched, leave a few instructions pertaining to starting of engine, cautions to be taken, etc.

of padding—often carpeting—to keep the topsides from being marked up by the hard, wood pads. Yet many of these pads have collected dirt and grit in them, which can badly mar your gelcoat or paint. To be safe, have some thick rags handy—old towels would be perfect—and slip them between the pads and your hull. If the operator gets insulted, that's tough—it's your boat and you're entitled to your own paranoias.

5. Travel-Lifts

If you want to haul out for a few days, weeks, or months, you can't beat the *sticks on wheels.* The great advantage is that they can haul you out and cart you to some obscure corner of the boatyard

and deposit you there in a cradle or on tripods or on barrels—see *Winter Haulout*—and within twenty minutes return to haul another boat. This of course means that you're only charged a relatively short machine time-—average about $100 for a thirty-foot boat; that's in and out—and the rest of the time you are charged only storage which is usually whatever you can haggle the boatyard down to.

This method of haulout is very straightforward. The only precaution to be taken is that which I already mentioned with marine railways: Be sure to have an underwater profile of your boat available for the machine operator so he can figure out where to place his straps. Have this handy each time you haul even if you use the same yard; you can't ex

For a long haulout, the travel hoist is the most economical to use, for it can put you in the back corner of the yard, where you can putter around to your heart's content.

pect the poor guy to remember the underbody of every boat he hauls. As proof of that, I can hardly remember my own—in a general way sure, but not to the point of knowing exactly below which stanchion the bottom of the rudder lies.

If you live in the Virgin Islands, where you can see twelve thousand feet into the water, don't worry about the drawing, just look over the side.

Do read carefully the section under *Winter Haulout* so you'll know all about the pratfalls of cradles and barrels and blocks and wedges.

Profile Drawing of Your Boat

5

Cleaning the Bottom

The Scraper

The scraper is the *second* tool you'll use after your boat has been safely yanked from its comfortable womb by a couple of suspenders and flung gracelessly into some dirt lot. The *first* one is your mouth. As soon as the boat stops swinging in the slings, grab the little guy who has been yanking the levers on that rickety machine, and beg him to take his pressure hose and pressure-blast the bottom of your hull clean. Now most yards have these pressure hoses and most willingly use them to blow away the barnacles and seaweed that droop like an inverted jungle where your keel used to be, but when the little guy has finished with the worms, plead for him to tarry a while and in the name of Saint Buhla the merciful, the patron of our bottoms, would he kindly blast away the worn and flaky bottom paint, now, while he's still at it. Bless his heart.

This request is not an unreasonable one—nothing like say the emperor of Rome asking Androcles to take a walk in the Forum Sunday afternoon and pet the gentle kitty cat—for all you're really asking is that he stand a little closer to your hull with the little squirter that he's choking by the neck, and squirt nice and hard and blow away the old paint. And when he's finished with what he thinks is a perfect job, *that's* when you will need to drag out the old scraper because now, old lion heart, you'll have to scrape the rest. So. Drag out the scraper with its fine edge and start scraping. Don't hurry. Enjoy yourself. This is the moment you will realize the extent of your great wealth, for all this time you had thought you owned a tiny little tub, when in fact here you are scraping the Titanic.

So, for now give thanks—in a while you will be cursing the hour of your conception.

Anyway, the scraper. The best one to use is a wooden handled one with removable blades. They come in all sorts of widths but get a three-inch one; anything narrower will chain you forever to this already interminable job, and anything wider will prove not only useless but even harmful, for the corners of a very wide blade will tend to catch and leave deep gouges in the sides of concave hollows where the keel fairs into the hull. In convex areas like the turns of the bilges, a wide blade will prove unnecessary, for only the central couple inches will be touching the surface anyway. So don't waste your precious strength by toiling with a tool of needless weight. Get a three-incher and scrape

When you haul, get the boatyard guys to blast away most of the flora and fauna with their pressure hose. Saves a lot of scraping which usually entails lots and lots of slime trickling down your arm into your armpit.

If the wildlife gets stubborn, you'll have to persuade it with a long-handled brush. You don't need fancy-assed scouring compounds; use the sand and dirt under your feet.

To clean off ornery barnacles and old paint, your best friend will be a wide scraper with a replaceable blade. Have a narrow one as well for the hard-to-get-at places. Have a fine file along to keep the edges sharp.

away.

Many bottom paints become obligingly brittle after a year—most of them aren't great adherers anyway—so you will be able to make fairly decent progress. But don't fool yourself. I've scraped *Warm Rain's* bottom a number of times, and each time it took a good half day, and at the end of each half day my arms felt like lead. Granted she is a full-keeled thirty-two-footer with more wetted surface than a comparable fin-keeler, but then this is no time to nitpick. What the hell is a *nit* anyway?

Back to scraping. Wear a mask. Sure you're only scraping, creating mostly flakes and not dust, but then bits of the stuff can still head for your lungs, and it is poisonous. Why do you think worms avoid it? So be as smart as the worms. Wear a mask.

Scraping is such an embarrassingly simple pro-

cess that I can't believe I did it wrong for three years before I learned it. You need only look at the blade to realize that it has a single edge designed for *pulling* toward you—*not* for pushing away. If you try to scrape while pushing, all you'll do is dull the blade to the point where it won't scrape even on the pull. So don't do it!

If the blade does become dull or nicked or both, sharpen it. For this use a fine file. Unlike chisels, the edges of scrapers should be slightly curved to help keep the sharp corners from damaging the surface. Some people advocate grinding the corners round to render them harmless, but I feel that would be destroying a useful part of the tool which allows you to work very close to an edge and do a remarkably accurate scraping job. If, however, you are a total klutz and don't trust yourself with sharp

When you go to scrape, don't just sit down and move the scraper back and forth as if you were stroking your cat—put some weight into it.

corners, by all means grind them off before you make your hull look like a freshly plowed cornfield.

Whichever way you sharpen it, use it only pulling, with long firm strokes—not a bunch of nervous little short ones. No one has ever hit a home run tap-tap-tapping the ball out of the park. The long firm strokes do it. So do it. And home run hitters don't use just their wrists; they use their

weight, so don't be shy, lean on the sucker—might as well take advantage of your flab.

There are many who feel scraping to be primitively slow, who seem to feel lost without some sort of power tool roaring in their hands, who insist on using a grinder to take off old bottom paint. With some of the ultra hard bottom paints you might just have to do that, but for most of the

After the long vertical strokes, you'll have to do some shorter clean-up ones to get the stuff that was left behind. Take care not to gouge the gelcoat or tear up the wood.

softer paints I'd avoid the grinder like the plague. Not only is it noisy and heavy and prone to leaving great round gouge marks in your hull if you lean too heavily on it, but worst of all, any decent-sized grinder will throw the most vicious cloud of poison dust you have ever seen and only the most expensive of painting masks will reduce the dust intake. The good ones—made out of rubber and metal that look like a gas mask—work well but the little paper ones don't do much except make you feel better until you go blow your nose and find a half a pint of bottom paint. Then you start wondering how much is in your lungs. So scrape, dammit—scrape!

If you have re-ground your blade so often that there is too little left to use, don't throw away the handle, just unscrew the old blade and put in a new one. Oh, yes. You might find a very small scraper like one with a one-inch blade handy if you're stripping trim pieces of wood or working in tight areas around skegs and propellers.

Do keep that fine-toothed file with you to touch up the edge when it starts to dull.

Removing Old Bottom Paint

If you are changing the type of bottom paint you are using, or if the old paint has begun to flake off in some parts or is coming easily off some parts while sticking like the proverbial to a blanket on others, you might as well roll up your sleeves and get ready to strip the bottom.

This should be done, for not only do ragged edges look ugly even when covered with new paint, but all those ragged edges will certainly slow your

Now I know you're not about to enter the America's Cup, but that's no reason to have ten thousand tiny sea anchors—in the form of old paint ridges—on the bottom of your boat.

boat. How much exactly is not the question—even if it were, I wouldn't know the answer—but ask any racing skipper if he would be caught dead sailing on a bottom like that and see what he says. Sure you're not a racer, but then you don't want to be named turtle-of-the-year either.

1. Chemical paint removers

The easiest way to get old bottom paint off a hull, whether it's wood, fiberglass or aluminum, is to soften it with a chemical paint remover, then scrape it off, first with a broad putty knife, then a scraper. But *don't* for godsake stop reading now and rush out to buy the first remover you come across, for if you do, you might end up by turning your fiberglass hull into jello, or your aluminum hull into a giant sieve.

Paint removers come in two types: the ones that destroy fiberglass by softening it and the ones that don't. Get the ones that don't.

Only very few manufacturers supply this stuff and it is very clearly marked e.g., The Interlux one is subtitled *Fiberglass Paint Remover*, so don't let some clown of a clerk talk you into taking the wrong stuff.

As Bob Wilkinson, the resident genius at Interlux explained to me, both paint removers are of the same base—methylene chloride—but the one for fiberglass hulls has simply been *weakened* to a point where it won't attack gelcoat but will still make mincemeat out of an average bottom paint.

For aluminum hulls, a different rule applies. Aluminum can easily withstand a methylene chloride type paint remover which is what you encounter in most hardware stores, but it reacts violently—in point of fact it gets eaten up to nothing—by industrial type paint removers such as caustic soda or any paint remover with an acid base. So beware lest you buy the wrong stuff and end up with nothing but a fully rigged deck and some plywood cabinetry.

Back to the good news. According to Dick the painter, who has been scraping and cleaning boats at the Concordia yard for sixteen years, the new paint removers aren't nearly as strong as the old ones, which gave off viciously toxic fumes upon application. The toxic stuff has now been banned by the environmentalists who seem to have this incurable phobia about keeping people healthy and alive. The new stuff that's out is a little weaker and it will only soften up one old coat of paint at a time, but it still beats grinding, so have patience and scrape coat by coat.

Do not get over zealous when applying paint remover. The active substance in it evaporates quickly, and the paint *redries* and then it will be almost as hard to remove as before you applied the stuff. So. Cover only a small surface at a time— say four square feet. The Interlux manual says to "lay on a thick coat in one direction only. Do not brush back and forth."

As soon as the paint is soft—sometimes you can see it curdle or bubble—take your four-inch putty knife and gently scrape along (pushing) to peel off the bulk of the soft *skin*. And it is a kind of skin, like the thing you get when you over-boil milk. Don't use the blade type scraper yet, for first of all it's not wide enough, and second, there is only a small clearance between the body of the tool and the hull and this small clearance will quickly get clogged up by the reams of paint, which you will then have to clean off with your fingers. So use the putty knife first and then use the scraper to get the stuff that the putty knife missed.

After you have scraped, you'll find smudges of the paint and paint remover left on the hull. I think it good practice to hose down the hull and scrub off the smudges with a stiff brush, otherwise the paint you will be putting on might get infected.

Use care when you are using the scraper so you don't gouge the fiberglass. On wood boats use even more care, for the sharp blade of the scraper tends to tear up the surface of the wood if you go against the grain. This problem seems to affect wet wood more than dry, so if you can afford the time to let the wood dry out a little, so much the better. If not, use care.

2. Dry scraping and sanding

Taking off old paint by either of these methods is a mean and ugly task recommended only for those who like to suffer. The disadvantages have already been discussed under *Scrapers*, so I'll just mention a few things here.

Scraping dry, that is without paint remover, requires no skills—just a lot of muscle and stubbornness. Go to it.

Grinding off old paint with a power grinder— and that is what you'll have to use, not some tiny block sander that will do little besides massaging you hands—especially bottom paint, takes nothing but muscle and a mask and a few loose screws upstairs.

First, use only a proper grinder which has lots of power so its motor won't burn out, and a second handle coming off the motor at right-angles enabling you to use both hands. In an hour or two you'll be wishing you could use your feet. Another good aspect of the grinder is that it comes with a foam rubber padding—to which you normally attach sandpaper with adhesive—and it is this padding which makes the grinder a somewhat forgiving machine. If you lean too hard on it, the foam rubber will collapse, keeping the sandpaper flat against the hull, instead of digging savagely into it with the edge, as a foamless disk would tend to do.

Using a belt sander to remove paint from a hull

is a mild form of suicide. A belt sander is made for *flat* surfaces and if the surface isn't flat before you start, I tell you brother, it sure will be by the time you finish. A belt sander cannot *give* or *conform* to the curves of the hull like a foam-disked grinder can, hence it will sand into the hull a small flatspot every time it moves. If you do your whole hull with it, you'll end up with the only boat that has ten thousand chines.

While grinding, wear a professional painter's mask with the replaceable cartridges, not the cheapo paper kind. Use as coarse a paper as you dare, for then the ground particles will be fairly large and they'll fall almost straight down, instead of floating into your eyes and ears and whatever other orifices you may have left uncovered. *But* be careful to hold the grinder flat against the hull and move it around instead of holding it in one spot too long or you'll end up looking at the insides of your lockers. And beware not to grind off any of your gelcoat. Start with eighty grit paper. If you find it too slow going and you're not causing any damage, then go coarser. If you find the eighty too coarse, i.e., it digs in before you get a chance to move it, then get some one-hundred grit, but make sure you bring lots of food and a blanket because you'll be there a good, long time.

3. Using heat
Open flame is not recommended for bottom paint removal, for the fumes emitted by the burning paint will be toxic. But for removing paint from the topsides of *wood* hulls read the following.

Bill Ede and I have been pals for years, ever since we built our house next door to the small boatyard he managed in Fisherman's Cove, and once we moved in, I'd see him every day coming through the garden, more often than not shaking his head in disbelief, and bringing a story about what some poor boat owner had done to a boat this time. One of the worst ones was about a man who used a small propane torch with the wrong kind of tip on it, and ended up scorching the wood of his whole topsides with little tiny scorch marks that made the boat look as if a million red-hot earthworms had just finished a stampede.

How the man kept from burning the whole thing to the ground I'll never know.

Anyway, we had an old cedar dinghy that was built by an old shipwright, who by then had such poor eyes that he built more by feel than by sight, and after a few years of use, that old dinghy had so many layers of varnish and paint on the bottom that we could hardly lift her anymore. One day Billy came and said he had a spare couple of hours and he was going to go and strip the boat. I laughed. The paint on her was like armor, and there was no way on earth you could get it off fast unless you used dynamite. But Billy insisted and we took the dinghy into the shed and flipped it upside down, and he brought out a small propane torch with a wide flared fitting on the end that made the flame fan out instead of making it into a pin-like hot spot, and he lit it and went at the dinghy, holding the torch a few inches from the surface, moving the flame constantly back and forth over an area of about one foot square, and when the paint lifted lightly—but before it scorched—he quickly ran the scraper over it and the paint came off like snow off a windshield.

And with his skill the dinghy was stripped completely in less than two hours.

The one thing that stuck out more than anything was that the paint should never be over-heated. If you run the scraper over it and find only the surface layer of paint coming off, just pass over it again with the torch. It is better than heating the paint too much and causing it to bubble and burn and mark up the wood and burn down the shed. Some marking of the wood will be inevitable, because as soon as you scrape the paint, some flakes or strips will stand on edge and catch fire the moment the flame comes near them. This is normal. Just scrape the burning stuff away quickly. If the wood scorches slightly now and then, just dowse it with a damp rag. A slight scorching is no great problem, for with the heat the grain will be raised anyway to the degree that you'll have to sand everything lightly, and the slight scorching will come off at that time.

Never try to use heat on a fiberglass boat, for not only will the gelcoat be damaged but the heat build-up can also delaminate the whole hull.

The same thing goes for aluminum, for it is such a good conductor and can absorb heat so rapidly, that the relatively thin skin of a hull may deform before one notices the paint lifting or bubbling. Once a plate of aluminum buckles, it's Katie bar the door, for it's not something you can correct with a little sanding or painting. Aluminum hulls should probably be sanded for best results, but a common caution that every paint manufacturer subscribes to, is not to use sandpaper that contains metal in the grit, for small bits may stay behind on the hull, creating a miniscule electrolytic environment (now there's an impressive phrase) which will result in the aluminum pitting.

Infrared heat lamps are safer to use than open-flamed torches, but somehow I fear them more than I fear open flames, for the heat build-up in both aluminum and fiberglass will occur much more stealthily without the fine warning system of the open flame—a fire.

If you are ultra attentive, then perhaps you *can* use it, but I'm not sure how you can properly see the paint lift, since to be effective, the lamp has to be held no farther than an inch from the surface.

Heatguns are glorified hairdryers, and if you are inclined to use a heat system, they may be the safest choice.

Irons—you got it—especially the old kind you heat up on a stove are sometimes recommended by old-timers for removing paint from canvas but I cannot see any advantage to using these instead of heatguns or paint removers.

4. Sandblasting

The least painful way to clean the bottom of an aluminum or steel boat is by sandblasting. A large portable unit which comes attached to a truck will sandblast a thirty-foot boat in about an hour, costing you no more than about a hundred dollars. And the best part is that all you have to do is sit there and watch.

With an aluminum boat, be sure they use only white silica sand, for other grits may cause corrosion due to contamination by impurities which are often found in blasting grit used for steel.

5. Bronze wool

Notice the intentional absence of *steel wool* here. Steel wool is bad news anywhere aboard a boat, for it rusts and leaves horrendous stains in wood and paint and fiberglass. Using it to scrape away bits of old paint is even more dangerous, for it breaks into tiny filings that stick in the paint or wood, which you then unsuspectingly paint over. The tiny filings will then rust and bleed right through the paint. Use only *bronze wool* and keep the damned steel wool off the boat.

Well, I don't know about you but I've had enough of this paint removal stuff. All we left out were tweezers and dynamite. Time for a beer.

To remove old paint from wood boats use a small propane torch. But make sure you have a nozzle that produces a broad easy flame, not one that gives you a fine blue tip which will burn right through your hull. Do not use an open flame to remove bottom paint; the fumes produced are toxic.

6

Painting the Bottom

Surface Preparation

Most of the ardent ones of us spend hours reading and pondering about what *type* of bottom paint to use to get the best—or at least better than the present—results. But all our strutting and fretting won't matter a damn if the surface of the hull isn't prepared properly, for then *no* paint will stick to it no matter how expensive. And strangely enough the most expensive two-part ones are the most fickle of them all and will stick the least.

So.

Interlux puts out a great reference manual of some three hundred pages which discusses everything you ever wanted to know about painting and varnishing. The problem is they give these only to their dealers for their personal use so that most of us are still left in the dark. I read through the manual. The whole thing. It was thorough. Mindbogglingly thorough. Up to page two I was fine; page four I started scratching; page five I was twitching; page six I was pacing; and by the time I reached page seven, I was praying for a fire or an earthquake or a flood, so I could run out into the street and die happy in the gutter.

But it was a great experience finishing that manual. After a mere five hours I had a total com-

prehension of both Purgatory *and* Eternity.

But dull as it was, it had excellent hints and ideas worth using as a skeleton for discussions on painting.

Previously Painted Bottoms

Most conventional bottom paints—ones that are *not* the two part types or vinyls—can be applied over existing antifouling paints if the old paints are in good condition. Good condition meaning that the paint is still firmly adhering and shows no sign of physically breaking down, that is cracking, checking or alligatoring. (Alligatoring? Is that like the Samba?)

If the paint is in good condition, just clean it and let it dry before applying fresh paint. The old bottom paint should be rough-sanded to remove the top layer of old, spent antifouling paint, which has leached and lost its active properties. The leached bottom paint is usually too weak a surface to hold the new.

Wear the kind of mask mentioned under grinding in *Cleaning the Hull*. After sanding, wash down the hull with soap and water to remove all the dust.

If the surface is not in frighteningly bad condition, you may try removing the dead paint with some dedicated hand sanding. If you're not getting anywhere, use the grinder.

If your new paint is going to be of the vinyl variety and your old paint is vinyl—no problem. But if your old paint isn't vinyl, you'll have to go down to the gelcoat.

Once the bottom is cleaned as above, you are ready to paint.

Bare Surface

1. Fiberglass

Before painting a new fiberglass hull, you can prepare the surface by two different methods: sanding or priming.

If you decide to sand, wipe the gelcoat down with a fiberglass solvent wash to remove the mold-release wax. Change rags frequently and turn the rag frequently, otherwise you'll just end up pushing the wax from one place to another. Sand the hull lightly with 80 grit sandpaper. Sand thoroughly until all gloss has disappeared. Brush the hull down with a rattail brush to remove the brunt of the dust, then wipe down with a rag and an acetone-type thinner—one that leaves no oily residue. Then paint.

If your paint fails after you have sanded the hull, then you either hadn't sanded well enough, or you didn't clean up well enough after the sanding. Try again.

Priming starts the same as the sanding. The mold-release wax has to be washed off with solvent using the same caution as above. Apply one thin continuous coat of fiberglass primer. Don't worry about looks. Do not spray and do not sand.

Most antifouling paints should be applied within a two- to three-hour period. The vinyl paints are an exception—the primer should be allowed to set

overnight before a vinyl is painted on.

Allow overnight drying of the antifouling paint, then apply a second coat.

The Concordia yard always puts on two coats of bottom paint over fresh wood or fiberglass, and the Interlux people recommend the same thing.

The reason the overnight drying is recommended when you are putting vinyl paint over the primer, is that the solvents in the vinyl may *resolvate* the primer, in which case the primer will bleed or blend into the vinyl antifouling paint. If this happens, an adhesion failure will probably result.

2. Bare wood

Wood boats should be sanded clean with 80 grit to be sure of cleanness and smoothness. Dust with rattail brush, then wipe down with a thinner.

There are three ways to ready a wood hull for bottom paint: one, using a 10 percent thinned coat of the bottom paint itself to ensure good penetration into the wood; another, using a thinned down coat of red lead; and the third, using a layer of Cuprinol wood preservative. The first two can be painted over the next day, but if Cuprinol is used, it must be allowed to dry completely; dry until the oily surface has completely disappeared. This may take a good long time and is not recommended if an early relaunching is anticipated. If, however, you are hauling for the winter, you can apply the Cuprinol in the fall and let it stand until spring before you paint on the antifouling paint.

If you use the thinned down antifouling paint as the primer system, it's best to put on two full coats of bottom paint after the primer one. Let each dry overnight between coats.

Planked hulls require a seam compound to fill in the seams you opened up as you scraped the bottom. If the cotton caulk came out, replace it with a small piece of cotton and tap it home with a caulking iron. Don't try to ram it through the seam— just tap it. You can use two types of compound to fill the seams; the first is the *white lead* type which has been in use for many decades, and the other is the polysulfide variety which has become *the* underwater compound on wood as well as fiberglass and aluminum boats.

Preparing the seam for the two types of compounds requires diametrically different approaches. If you are using the white lead type filler—both Interlux and Woolsey have ones called Underwater Seam Compound—then you'll have to prime the seam with a prime coat of the antifouling paint you'll be using *before* installing the seam compound. If this is not done, the seam compound may not adhere properly and may fall out.

If, on the other hand, you are using the polysulfide, you will have to clean the seam *completely*; that means of all paint, oil and dirt. Next, using cotton swabs dipped in acetone, give the seam a final wipe and when that is done fill in with polysulfide.

The question of which to use will of course arise, and there is only one way that I know of to make a meaningful choice, for both products work very well, and both dry only on the surface and remain supple for years, which is a long way of saying that they will move with the planks without separating from the wood. So. If the seam already has one type of compound on it, use the same stuff again. Most people, yours truly included, have had problems with mixing different types of caulking. If you are refilling an entire seam, you might consider switching, but why you would bother is beyond me, because next time you'll have to have both compounds handy in case some patching is to be done.

3. Aluminum boats

Most antifouling paints used for aluminum boats require special methods of application because they involve catalyzed epoxies that should be sprayed to a prescribed film thickness, and under pretty severe temperature restrictions. Aside from that,

you have to sandblast or grind the entire hull, then dust it completely clean, then apply a barrier coat primer the same day. And aside from *that* you have to spray on five different layers of barriers and tarryers, and aside from that they want you to spray the antifouling paint, which as you know is poison so they recommend a sprayhood, and complete skin coverage—in other words, forget it! It's a great protection system but leave it to a boatyard expert to apply.

Sounds like panic city to me.

Interlux does however capitulate and recommends one of their systems for the amateur and it goes like this:

Wipe surface clean of all contaminants with an acetone type thinner.

Thoroughly abrade clean aluminum with medium grit emery cloth to a bright metallic surface.

Wipe again with acetone to remove residue.

Apply one thin coat of *Vinyl-Lux Primewash 353/354* (a two package Interlux product; other brands are available), which is a metal surface prep allowing for the adhesion of subsequent coats of paint. This material when applied properly will be greenish-yellow and transparent. It should not be applied like paint. Only a very thin coating of between three and five mils thickness is required.

The best way to apply it is by spray. If you spray you'll have to reduce the *Primewash* with a special thinner they make: four parts of mixed *Primewash* to one part thinner.

If brush application must be used, reduce the mixed *Primewash* with the thinner to the point brushing is eased. Lay on the stuff quickly without overbrushing.

Primewash dries rapidly and can usually be over-coated in an hour or two, or as soon as coating is hard.

Apply two coats of a vinyl bottom paint that does *not* contain copper. The Interlux paint specifically formulated for aluminum hulls has tributylin fluoride as a poison instead of copper. (Have you got a sense of Eternity yet, Elmer?)

Paint manufacturers discourage use of bottom paints containing copper—most of the common ones do—for they fear that, "If electrical contact is made between the aluminum hull and the copper antifouling paint then galvanic corrosion will occur."

4. Steel boats

Here again, to do a proper job you should have the hull sandblasted, then cleaned of all grit and residue with a broom and air hose. Then—and here I quote from the manual, with my blurbs in parentheses added—"*Immediately* (before the thing begins to rust again) apply three or four coats (you'll have an arm like Popeye's) of a silver metal primer."

"If brush or roller-applied, allow an overnight drying between coats. (Sounds like a week in the yard just to paint the bottom. I knew there was a reason I've always shied away from steel boats.) If spray applied, it's possible to coat much faster. However, if time is not a problem, it is best to allow overnight drying between coats to be assured of full solvent evacuation. (Now *that's* dramatic writing.) Overcoating too quickly when the weather is cool may lead to solvent entrapment and possible blistering when the boat is put in the water."

"The anti-corrosive barrier coat primer has two main functions. First, it must protect the steel from salt water corrosion. To do this properly, a total film thickness of eight to ten mils is required. Second, it must isolate the antifouling paint containing cuprous oxide from the steel, so that galvanic corrosion will not take place. Because of these two factors, it is essential that sufficient barrier primer be applied." (And you thought they had you putting on four coats just so you'd use more of their paint. Shame on you.)

7

Bottom Paints

I'm sure that an hour from now I'll be sorry I ever started this chapter, for opinions range so widely and wildly on what constitutes a good bottom paint and which of the many dozens actually work, that to arrive at any worthwhile conclusion is almost impossible. But I don't want to give up without trying.

Things You Can Grow On Your Hull

As most of you know, the oceans of the world are teeming with tiny things called *plankton* which interestingly enough comes from a Greek word meaning "to wander." Now, you cannot see plankton because they are microscopic, but you can see them at night in the form of phosphorescence.

Now you may say, what do these tiny creatures have to do with the forest of seaweed and the herd of barnacles that grow on my boat? The answer to that is that all things must start small. To clarify, most of the tiny critters that you see—or rather *don't* see—floating around, are actually spores of plants and the larvae of animals.

The most typical of these are the great variety of seaweeds and sea grasses and the many shells like barnacles and tube worms and mussels. Now of course you never see a herd of mussels backstroking up to your hull and staking out the bottom like the pioneers, but they do come as tiny guys, one at a time (like orphans) and glom onto you and grow into big and healthy mussels to which you can add a nice white wine and some parsley and some spices.

So anyway, there are all these orphans wandering around out there looking for a place they can call home, where they can settle down and raise some children and grow old in dignity and peace, and there you are with your shiny boat worrying about how much slower you'll have to go now that a family of sea-squirts has begun homesteading on your keel. The answer of course is, quite a bit slower, which perhaps is a small price to pay for having your own sea ranch full of soggy livestock, but you are probably a city boy and don't much care for barnacle round-ups and tube-worm rodeos, and you want them critters off your property and you never want them settin' a foot on it again. Okay, Elmer, okay. I know just how you feel. But it's gonna cost ya plenty.

Keeping Out the Orphans

The best way to keep these kids from glomming onto you is to outrun the little buggers. In other words, throw away your fenders and your bumpers and your shorepower cord, and quit being a breakwater for the dock and go the hell sailing. Of course to that you'll say, "Sure, but I'll still have to stop sometime." To which I'll say, "Who says?"

Anyway, I know you're not about to go and do laps around the globe, and you know you're not about to do laps around the globe, and we both know you want to keep your bottom clean and shiny, so the only other solution is to plop down a hundred bucks and get yourself a gallon of anti-orphan paint.

These paints function by repelling the spores and larvae through the release of toxic substances into the layer of water adjacent to the hull. That said, it is obvious that bottom paints are not like other paints which are designed to remain stable in their state of newness come hell or high water; on the contrary, bottom paints are made to break down, or leach out or whatever your choice of words. Once all the toxins—or at least so much of the toxin that it cannot leach at the rate necessary to keep the settlers off— have leached out, a new layer of paint will have to be applied.

What a paint must therefore do is maintain an adequate rate of leaching for as long a period as possible, and of course it has to fulfill basic requirements such as sticking to the hull and spreading in decent fashion.

You can look at bottom paint as a reservoir of poison, and the deeper—or in this case thicker—the reservoir the longer it will be effective. It follows then that a thin coat of bottom paint will leach out sooner than a thick one, yet you can't in turn build up a ten-layer coat of paint and reason that it should leach forever, for as the toxic leaches out, it leaves behind a layer of neutral or dead stuff—all those things in the paint that held the tox-

ins in place and let the paint smooth etc.—and once this layer of dead stuff becomes too thick, the toxins can no longer penetrate it, or *leach* out.

Cuprous Oxide and metallic coppers have been used as repellents for over a hundred years and still remain as the base of most bottom paints. Mercury and arsenic bases were tried for a time but mercifully banned, for they became a danger to a wide range of marine life.

Choosing a Bottom Paint

When I tried to take the easy way out of this dilemma by asking Brody McGregor, the owner of the Concordia yard, which bottom paint works best, he answered without a moment's hesitation, "None of them. Not one of them is worth the powder it takes to blow them to hell. None of them can really keep the scum from forming over them, and once the scum comes and settles over and isolates the poison, all the other growth comes anyway, so what the hell is the use." And that from a man who has used up a few thousand gallons of the stuff.

Another thing which complicates the problem even more is the fact that boats move around from one body of water to another, and a paint that lasted fine in one location may not be as effective someplace else. The density of marine organisms is greatest in coastal waters that are 48 degrees Fahrenheit or warmer. Add to this the fact that runoff from the land brings a wealth of food on which plankton exist, making harbors and estuaries virtual breeding grounds, and you can see the problem obfuscating itself. So, it's always advisable to ask people in your local yard what they have found to work over the years, and then if they give you a Brody McGregor reply, you just go to the marine store and play Pin the Tail on the Donkey.

If you haul your boat for the winter, don't waste

good money on expensive paint. Get something that lasts as long as your boat is in the water and no more.

The plot thickens. though, when you intend to keep your boat constantly in the water.

In fresh water the only thing that will grow on your boat is algae which is generally known as *scum*. Paints using an organotin base instead of the copper associated ones, seem to have proven best here. The old bronze bottom paints you see on old lake-racing boats have built a great following.

For salt water, generally speaking, the higher the cuprous oxide content of a paint the more effective it will be. Hence a paint containing 25% cuprous oxide will be effective only half as long as a paint containing 50% cuprous oxide. A difference here of course could be made by the *binders* used in the two paints. If one paint has a *binder*— the sticky stuff in the paint that holds the copper together and sticks it to the hull—that allows slow leaching, and the other a binder that *dumps* the copper out, then obviously that will affect the length of time a paint will remain active.

For boats that will be hauled for the winter, get good fast leaching paint. These are generally soft and wash away during the season instead of building up and forcing removal by scraping or other drudgery.

If you want bright colors, you'll have to pass on the copper paints and use something like Trilux which is designed for aluminum boats, thus instead of the copper it has a tributylin floride base.

The only difference we have so far neglected is the *hardness* of the paints, which doesn't necessarily determine how effective they are, but will determine how slick they are and racers do put emphasis on this.

Conventional bottom paints are the softer paints which leach out at a relatively fast rate, wear away so there is less to remove next season. They come as weak or as potent as you like.

Vinyls are the harder paints ideal for racing,

for they form a very smooth bottom. They tend to build up over the years, although they can be more effectively sanded for overcoating with new paint.

Copolymers are the new kids on the block. They are very durable, not significantly affected by exterior weathering, so the same coat can be used for two seasons and paint won't break down if the boat is out of water for winter. These are said to release the toxin (organo tin) at the very surface of the skin, so they wash away very evenly, thus being always effective and never *trapping* usable toxin under dead layers. This even wearing is an important factor, for there will never be a build-up of old coats which take much time and grief to remove. But even this stuff—which costs an arm and a leg—does not prevent slime growth, and as I said in the beginning, a thick layer of slime will nicely isolate the toxins and the settlers will move right in. So you will either have to have a diver clean the bottom from time to time or haul and power wash or scrub down. Sounds ideal for those starting a circumnavigation.

One tip. When buying bottom paint and comparing brands and prices, compare the percentage of the active toxins in the can. They usually say what the percentages are. If they don't, you can tell by lifting them up. The more copper or tin, the heavier the can.

Painting Tips

1. Stirring

Most paints contain cuprous oxide which is very dense and will settle to the bottom of the can like packed mud. To mix, get a clean paint bucket and pour half of the paint into it. Now stir and scrape the copper until it breaks up and moves. Then mix and pour back and forth between the two cans until all the paint in both cans is equal in density and color. If the copper is spread through the paint unevenly, then the paint will leach unevenly and

If you insist on spraying bottom paint, use the cartridge type mask this guy is using. Don't grumble, just look hard enough and you'll see it. And if you look hard enough you'll also see that he's wearing a pair of goggles.

function unevenly, to the point of some parts failing to repel anything but the dumbest or weakest settlers.

2. Thinning

It is recommended that you never add anything but a suitable paint thinner to bottom paint or you'll upset the binder and screw up the leaching process. They warn you vehemently against the use of thinners period, for you might create too thin a coat which will be next to useless.

3. Rolling

Regardless of what people may tell you, do *not* use a great hairy roller for applying bottom paint. This is most important with paints that have a lot of copper in them. These will be so dense and heavy that if you soak a hairy roller with them, you won't be able to lift the thing, never mind use it. If you don't believe me try it but have a spare arm handy.

The long-haired rollers have another disadvantage. As the roller gathers speed—which it will hopefully do or you'll be pussyfooting there all night—it will start spraying little specks of paint, like rain, all over your arms and face and hair. I ruined a fine pair of sunglasses that way once.

The last reason to use s short-haired roller is a matter of economy. With a long-haired roller you won't just be wasting the paint you spray all over yourself, but you'll throw out about half a pint when you throw away the roller.

4. Spraying

Spraying bottom paint is sometimes done by the racing fraternity to achieve a smoother finish. If you do spray don't forget you are spraying liquid poison, so wear the cartridge-filter-type face mask. Cover all your skin and hair and be prepared to throw away whatever clothing you are wearing.

Keels and other metal parts should be primered and then painted with a non-cuprous bottom paint. Any paint with copper in it should not be used on metal because it can cause electrolysis.

5. Painting through-hulls, shafts, etc.

I was surprised at the quantity of barnacles on propellers and shafts of boats at Concordia, boats that had been in the water less than six months. Bottom paints that contain no copper can be used for underwater metals without fear of setting up electrolysis. You'll have to use a metal etching primer before you apply two good coats of bottom paint. The disadvantage here is that most bottom paints come only in quarts and you will probably use about half a pint for all your metals, so it's advisable to team up with others in the yard and split a can.

One warning: Paint the shaft *after* the sacrificial zinc collar has been put in place. If you paint the shaft beforehand, you will isolate the zinc from the shaft, making the sacrificial system less effective.

6. Painting under pads and wedges

A predictable ritual goes on in the boatyard next door to where we used to live. Almost every day, Mel, the resident mechanical genius who has forgotten more about boats in his fifty years of working around them than I will ever gather, roars out at the top of his voice like a maddened bull. This is not to scare the sea gulls or signal closing time, but it's a warning roar to some poor fool or other to stop loosening the screw pads on the cradle his boat is sitting in or the thing will topple over right after the next half turn.

It's frightening to see people risk having their boats topple just to get a swab of paint in under the pads. Don't even think of it. Wait until the boat is back in the sling and *then* you can paint the bare spots. Most good boat yards know you'll have to do this and they allow time on the machine for you.

Well, that's the end of that. I swear that if I had to put as much effort into actually cleaning and painting the bottom as I did writing about it, then *Warm Rain* would have sunk years ago from the weight of all the barnacles hanging on her keel.

Don't try to paint under cradle pads or wedges by temporarily backing them off or pulling them out. Wait until you're back in the slings and then paint those areas.

8

Checking the Wood Hull

Too many people assume that just because they haven't run into a rock at full speed all season long, the hull of their boat is in pristine condition. Not so. First of all, there is rot that could have started without the boat ever moving. If she did move, then her hull underwent tremendous strain each time she sailed hard, for, in a manner of speaking, the sails are doing all they can to pull the mast out of the boat rigging, chainplates and all. Add to that the beating the poor boat takes every time it pounds into a wave, and you'll readily agree that checking the hull thoroughly each time you haul is not really being overcautious.

How Rot Starts

Although the most common cause of rot is freshwater leakage, it can come from such unsuspected sources as electrolysis in metal parts and fasteners, or spilled battery acid, or almost totally unpredictable sap-pockets in the wood that can nurture rot in a boat only a few years old.

I hate to sound frightening or pessimistic, but this *is* a book about the problems boats encounter and how these problems can be prevented or repaired, and if I just skimmed over the things that

may cause you anguish for fear of upsetting you, then the whole book would be worthless. So brace yourself.

Rot Prevention

Rot is the most dreaded of wooden boat diseases and unfortunately sometimes even perfect maintenance doesn't insure one against the possibility of it occurring, but I promise you, brother, it can go a long, long way.

1. Leaks
The entrance of fresh water is the primary cause of rot in a wood boat, and that is good news, for all leaks are preventable or at least readily reparable. Although the leaks that cause the rot are often in the deck or the coachroof or around hatches, it is often the hull that suffers the rot, for that is where the water most often ends up, either in the bilge or else trapped in small undraining pockets around frames and bedlogs and floors.

Thus it should be obvious that in a wood boat no leak can be shrugged off as being minor, for even the most innocent leak, in the least important seeming place, can end up attacking a vital

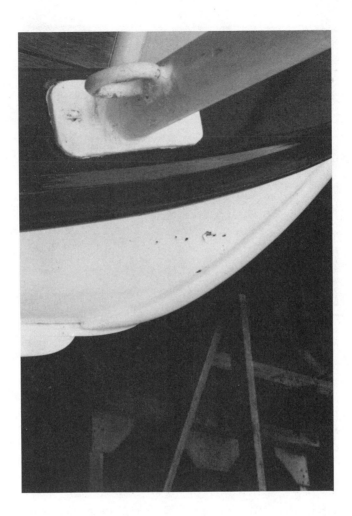

Sadly enough, even aboard the most meticulously-kept boat—and the one in this photo certainly is that—rot can develop. In this case it was in the end of a plank— see deep holes left by awl—either from a deck leak or a sap pocket in the wood.

structural part.

What is even worse is that there are such things as internal leaks, leaks that travel between pieces of wood, or between wood and canvas and never actually surface to become noticeable—they stay humbly out of sight and rot the boat away from the inside. I guess what that means is that you've got to stop leaks before they start or at least very soon thereafter.

So inspect your boat often, especially around the bases of hardware like chainplates, cleats, blocks, stanchions, windlasses and winchpads— things that undergo great strain, strain that can break the seal between a piece of hardware and the wood it's mounted on.

Look for even the tiniest of cracks, for a tiny crack can open wide once the fitting is loaded with the strain of sheets and halyards, and let in substan-

Where hardware is fastened to a hull or deck, much loading will be transmitted and the boat will tend to "come apart." This is true for both wood and fiberglass boats. If a small crack in a seam is discovered, it should be checked and sealed off right away or rain water can lodge in the crack and set up rot or delamination.

tial amounts of rainwater or washdown water. It takes very little moisture to get rot going and even less to nurture it once it has begun.

After having checked around hardware, check around things that move: hatches, skylights and portlights; for considerable load can be put on these by an off-balance crew member. If they do somehow break the bedding seal, a leak can begin.

Then look closely at all the so-called *trim pieces* that have been bedded in caulking and screwed to the hull or deck or house—things like caprails, rubrails and eyebrows, and especially ledge-like things that tend to hold water.

Lastly, check everything else: the corners of cockpits, the bases of bulwarks, the seams in canvas decking and the caulking in teak decking. Any crack anywhere must be considered a potential starting point for rot.

Any seam aboard a boat will be subject to some movement, especially if it is as loaded as a winch base. Check for rot and reseal right away before the thing gets worse.

Even fiberglass boats have wood parts—both this photo and the one before are of fiberglass boats, this one, a Westsail, the last one an Ohlson—and wood aboard these needs just as much care as wood aboard a wood boat. Than photo proves that painted wood will not suddenly become infallible.

Where hardware has been removed from a boat, the fastener holes should not be forgotten or water will get in them and rot will begin.

Deck seams open up where the caulking comes away from a deck plank. Spots that remain wet after the rest of the deck has dried indicate a broken seam that needs repair.

Once a crack is discovered, it should be opened to be sure no damage exists below it. Then it should be cleaned with acetone and filled with whatever bedding compound was originally used. Or if that compound seems to have failed, then scrape it all out and clean whatever is to be bedded with acetone and re-bed it with a new compound. Generally speaking, use a polysulfide caulking for hardware and Dolfinite for bedding wood onto wood.

2. Acid

Spilled battery acid can set up wood rot very quickly. Batteries should be stored in heavy-duty plastic containers, or in wood boxes completely lined with fiberglass. Do not assume for a moment that your battery is different from all others and will never spill a drop of acid, for it will, or you will when you're filling it up.

3. Electrolysis

An electric current can be set up between dissimilar metals connected by the moist wood of the hull and, according to Giff, this can also begin rot. Thus, avoid having potentially dangerous combinations like bronze fasteners and steel floors.

4. Poor ventilation

Water need not pour like Niagara onto a surface for rot to begin, it can very nicely start in wood exposed for long periods to very damp air. Mildew will be the first step and from it rot can begin.

Do whatever you need to do to insure that each part of a boat is totally ventilated. Your doors should have louvers or cane, or at least a series of round holes drilled into them for ventilation. Have substantial cowl vents all over the boat to keep air moving inside even if the boat is otherwise locked up.

If you leave the boat for any length of time, for godsake open all doors and lockers and icebox lids and engine room hatches before you go and *leave*

them open. It might not look too shippy but it will allow the air to move about and keep the boat mildew free.

5. Dirt

Dirt can be a direct accomplice of water in causing rot. First, it can dam up limberholes, preventing water drainage, creating nice wet pockets for rot to start; and second, it can act like a sponge and hold moisture longer than it would normally take to evaporate, and thus aid in the forming of rot.

6. Poor drainage

Sooner or later all boats will get fresh water in them through portlights that were left open, or water tanks below being filled, but in a boat where limberholes were installed and maintained this should cause no problem.

So go through your boat and clean out all your limberholes. Take a piece of wire and poke it through each limberhole to clear it. If you have never checked before, check now to see if all the places that you think should have limberholes— places like ledges or pockets that *might* hold water if it should enter into the area— do in fact have them.

If they don't, get a drill and drill them now. Be sure to drill as low as possible in the pocket, so all the water will drain out. One caution: Do not drill the hole so close to the edge of a structural piece that you create a *break* in the piece, for then you are weakening the member substantially. It is much better to drill a hole higher in the piece, for then it will retain its strength, much like the reinforced truss of a roof retains its strength even though it is hollow in the center—much like the hull of a fiberglass boat that's cored with foam or with balsa—both of which are about as strong as a hamburger bun—retains its strength, even though there is no strength in its center.

Drilling a limberhole not quite at the bottom edge of a piece will of course create somewhat of a pocket which could hold water, but the pocket can be eliminated by filling it right up to the edge of the limber hole with either epoxy or with melted pitch. This of course can only be done if the wood to be covered is completely clean and dry, for you are trying to create a perfectly sealed bond. If the bond is less than perfect, then you'll cause more damage than you're trying to prevent, because water will seep into the imperfect seam and sit there, unable to drain or even evaporate away. So, as with any other gluing—clean and dry and then apply.

Checking for Rot in Wood Hull

Checking for rot in the hull is a very simple process requiring only time, patience, a four ounce ball peen hammer with a plastic head and a small pocket knife or an awl.

Start at one end of the boat and with the plastic hammer—whose edges should be somewhat rounded to avoid leaving dents or marks—tap each square inch of the boat. Don't pound or bludgeon with the hammer—you're not breaking rock, you're just listening for soft spots. If you do find a spot that doesn't have the healthy sound of solid wood, go over it again with the hammer to determine how large the unhealthy area is, then start poking the suspected area with the point of the pocket knife. If the wood is healthy, the blade of the knife should penetrate no more than one-sixteenth of an inch into planking of hardwoods like mahogany or teak, and only a little more into softwoods like cedar or pine. In the case of oak, which is used extensively for frames, knees and floors, penetration should be next to nothing.

You will of course instantly demand to know just how hard to push. Well, Elmer, it's like this. You have to use more force than you'd use to pop a birthday balloon, but less force than you'd use to stop a charging rhino. The best thing to do is to find in the boatyard an old piece of wood with

some rot in it, and practice on it with both the hammer and the knife so you can grow accustomed to the difference, both in sound and in feel. Take note particulary at how marginal wood—one that is not obviously rotten—feels and sounds. You'll find this around the edges of obvious rot. This is particularly important, for it will allow you to detect rot early and correct it early before it spreads and causes major damage or even worse, a major disaster at sea. But back to the hammering.

While you are hammering thoroughly but gently along, don't let your gaze wander away constantly to all the bronze flesh strutting and jiggling across the yard, but keep it riveted constantly to your hull. You will often find visual clues of either rot, or open seams which may eventually cause rot or corroding fasteners which leak rust through the skin of paint. Any of these things are a sign of trouble that should not be neglected but looked thoroughly into.

I was shown one sign of rot by Giff that I for one would have surely missed. He pointed out hardly noticeable wet streaks in the obvious pattern of woodgrain showing through the otherwise completely dry old bottom paint of a boat that had been hauled for some time. What was happening was that the softer grain—the sappier part of the wood—was being attacked by rot and had become so pulpy that it was now holding water. Although this is rather an esoteric and very early sign of rot, anytime you see a wet patch on an otherwise long-dry bottom, you can be sure something is wrong.

Open seams, either at plank ends or along joints like the stem or gunwale, should be thoroughly inspected for rot. Even if soft spots are not found, the seams should be dried, cleaned and filled, but filled completely, not just surface-filled, for water may travel into the pocket you've created, through an opening other than the one that you've just closed off, and it will be trapped there and begin to rot the wood.

Underwater seams are not as prone to rot as

In a wood hull, wet-grain marks that read through the bottom paint mean that moisture might be trapped by the softening sappy grain. Keep an eye on it for rot may be on the way.

Definite sign of a bad seam. Clean it out and investigate. Check the inside of the spot as well.

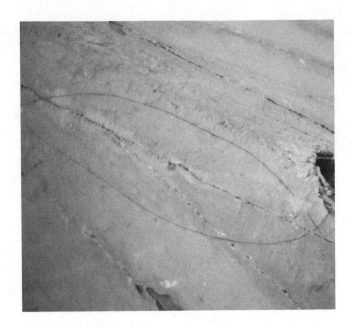

Even a minor crack means swollen and moving wood. Investigate.

If a plug is swollen and pushing through the paint, it might mean a fastener rusting and swelling below it. Pull the plug and check the fastener.

A boat rots inside as well as outside. Check all bulkheads, especially where they join the hull or the deck. Check any pockets where water may be standing.

above water ones, for the underwater wood is generally well pickled by the salt water. The exception of course is the boat that is hauled for the whole winter, in which case the bottom becomes almost as vulnerable as the deck or topsides.

Cracks in the paint are good indicators of swelling of the wood. Protruding bungs over a fastener, or rust leaks through paint are signs that somehow the fastener is being reached by water and is rusting out. In bronze-fastened hulls, dark green stains coming through a crack or seam indicate the same problem. None of the above insinuates even for an instant that you should check only the common danger spots mentioned, it merely urges that you check them with even greater care than you check the others.

When you are checking your wood hull for rot remember one thing: Your hull has an inside as well as an outside and the inside is even more prone to rot than the outside, for the inside has an infinite number of small *pockets* where fresh water can pool and rot begin. And if you ask where this freshwater is supposed to come from, then I'll tell you it comes from all those little deck leaks that you haven't bothered repairing just because the water didn't drip directly on your face while you were asleep.

While you are checking the inside, clean the inside.

While inside the hull, look over your frames for delaminations or cracks, and if anything seems out of the ordinary, investigate.

This internal checking of the hull need not be done, or rather should not be done during a spring haulout, for usually you will be wasting precious cradle time, but is best done in advance of hauling

Rain water that leaks into a boat often ends up in a pocket in the bilge. Check these with great care and if possible fill potential water traps with either pitch or epoxy.

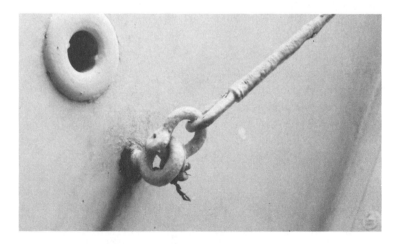

Where there is rust there is moisture and where there is moisture there can be rot. Check and repair.

so that if any major problems are discovered, they may be corrected later when you do haul. Finding the problem early can allow you to prepare and make arrangements for repair, whether it means reserving a shipwright or just getting hold of materials or even just thinking the problem through.

When working the inside of a hull, you will often not have enough room to swing a hammer so you will have to use the point of your knife to check for rot.

One last thing. Rot is not a plague that sneaks into boats through the chimney like a ghost; it is something that can in large be prevented by keeping fresh water and moisture away from wood, which can very possibly be done be keeping the boat tight and well ventilated and in good repair.

Rust

One major problem source on older wooden boats has been the use of galvanized, or even worse, ungalvanized iron parts. This was always done as a matter of economy that unfortunately backfired in the long run. Iron fasteners, iron floors, often knees, and too often iron exterior fittings were used instead of bronze, all resulting in many hours of frustrating maintenance and many hours of frustrating and expensive repair.

1. Floors and knees

The major problem is that rust forms with frightening speed in a salt environment and even the most meticulous sailor will have problems staying ahead of its onslaught. Rust usually reaches epidemic proportions in a boat because it is either not detected early enough, or if detected, it goes ignored. This is especially true in the case of floors and knees where the appearance of rust is too often assessed as a cosmetic nuisance that really is of no consequence because it is mostly out of sight.

This has always amazed me, for it should be obvious to all that iron was chosen for these parts because of its strength, therefore any weakening through rust—which occurs as soon as the oxidation penetrates the surface—jeopardizes the structural integrity of the whole boat.

Granted, most iron parts have a lot of "spare" metal in them and most will not fail immediately after the loss of the first millimeter of metal, but rust seldom arrests itself when fed constantly by salt water and air—in fact the porous oxidized layer will hold water better and longer, thereby lending a hand to its own destruction. This must not be allowed to happen. The first appearance of rust should be treated as a serious event that needs immediate attention and correction.

2. Fasteners

Fasteners fall into an even more sensitive category, for they are usually not as "overbuilt" as frames and knees, and once they go they're gone. By the time their rusting is discovered, usually with the help of a wood plug that's pushed through the paint by the expanding of the rust in the fastener—and notice I say *in* the fastener, not *on* it, for rust is caused by the breakdown of the metal; it is not something that fell *onto* it like snow from the heavens—or streaks of rust running out through the paint, it is usually too late to do anything but change the fastener. Unless the rust is a completely isolated case, one should probably consider having the whole hull refastened within a few years. How many exactly is impossible to say without seeing the extent and gravity of the corrosion, so the best thing to do is take out a few sample fasteners from different parts of the hull, and ask a knowledgeable surveyor or a good shipwright to have a look at them and give you an opinion.

3. Removing and replacing old fasteners

To extract a plug from a wood hull is not a difficult task as long as the extraction is not put off too long. If it is, then the whole head of the fastener may be so weakened that it will fall off as soon as removal is attempted, resulting in so much extra work that you'll curse yourself for having left the job until now.

Anyway, to remove a loose plug—one that is already forced partway out of the hull—use an awl. Just tap it into the center of the plug and give your wrist a twist and normally the plug will pop. If not, take a drill—not too big a one, one whose diameter is about a third the size of the diameter of the plug—and drill a pilot hole into the center of the plug. Drill all the way in until you hit the fastener You'll find out why in a minute. Next, take a sheet metal screw and screw it into the plug until it hits the fastener—that way the threads will be able to grip most of the plug when you're trying to pull it out. If you don't drive the screw deep enough, you might only pull part of the plug out with the screw, leaving a little disk at the bottom of the hole. The little disk will be a true bastard to get out without damaging the edges of the hole, meaning further repairs still.

Once the plug is out, take the awl and clean out the slot in the screw to create a good grip for the screwdriver, then slowly, and with even force, turn the screw. Keep lots of pressure on the screw, for the head is likely to be fragile and you may damage the slot and then it will be extra-work-time again.

Most old timers suggest giving the screwdriver a solid tap with a hammer to loosen the grip of the threads, but care must be used if the screw is badly corroded, for what sometimes happens is that half the head falls right off. So use your judgment and if you are unsure try tapping and see what happens.

If you destroy the head of the fastener, you have two routes to follow. First and easiest is to abandon the fastener and drill a hole right above or below it—not beside it, Elmer, or you'll probably miss the frame—and put in a new fastener and new plug. If there is a decent part of the head still left on the old fastener, just leave it as is and plug the hole. But if there is no head at all, then take a countersink tool—that's the one with a little dimple in the end as opposed to a centerpunch which has a pointed end—and with it and a hammer, bend what is left of the fastener to give it a grip on the wood.

If you don't want to abandon the broken fastener, then by all means try to drill it out. First, take a centerpunch and set a dimple in the center of the shank of the screw—a nice little dimple into which you can set the tip of the drill bit with which you will be drilling out the fastener. If you don't set the dimple, you will find the drill slipping forever from the screw and gouging the bejeeezus out of the wood around the fastener. For drilling, use a bit about the same diameter as the shank of the screw. Once you have all the metal out, set a new fastener of silicon bronze, monel or stainless steel in place of the old, and cover with a new plug. If you have gouged up the edge of the hole, don't despair. Simply get a drill bit the next size up and clean off the edges by drilling a new counterbore, then use a suitably larger new plug to fill the hole. New plugs are best set in epoxy or waterproof glue for a sure hold.

4. Rust repair

If the piece of iron that is affected has enough body left to remain structurally safe, then it should be treated to prevent any further rusting. There are products that are actually called *rust arrestors* which one can theoretically paint right over the rust. They soak into the rust and seal the metal below from all air and moisture. I somehow greatly mistrust these things for two very good reasons. First, you cannot properly assess the extent of rust on a piece of metal unless you *remove* all the rust from that piece of metal, to see just how much of the piece of metal you actually have left. I see little use in soaking a piece of structural metal with a rust arrestor when all that's really left of the metal is a loosely held mound of rust dust. Second, if the layer of rust is of any depth, it is very difficult to get it to dry completely, hence, when the rust arrestor is applied, you might be trapping moisture inside. The moisture will cause more rust still and expand and crack the rust arrestor and then you'll be back where you started from.

So. Don't fool around—if you can remove the piece of metal do so and have it sandblasted. If not, get out your little hammer and start chipping off the rust. Some people foolishly hold back from using a hammer, believing that with a decent blow they might crack the old metal. And you know what? They are right—or at least half right—for they may truly crack the old fatigued piece, but then better to crack it now than to have it crack at sea when the sails are tugging and the keel torquing. So don't be shy—hit the bastard! Then take a chisel and scrape off what rust is left, and then put a wire brush on a drill motor and wirebrush the piece until it shines. Then immediately wipe it with an acetone-like solvent to remove all dust, and still *immediately* paint the piece with a first class metal primer, followed by at least three coats of the best metal paint you can get.

The best method of cleaning and rust-proofing a piece of rusty fitting is to take the thing right out of the boat and go and have it sandblasted and re-painted. This way, all parts will be totally clean and totally recoated and that is what you want, for all rust needs is a tiny foothold and it will spread like the plague all along a piece.

Once the piece is out and then found to be in not the best of shape, don't throw it away, take it instead to a good caster and have it recast out of bronze. This will cost you a little more than having it recast of iron but think of all the future headaches and worries you'll be saving yourself.

The only time a decision of some gravity will have to be made regarding the substitution of new bronze for old iron is when floors of a wood boat are being replaced. If the boat's hull was original-

ly fastened with iron that is still there, then perhaps one should think twice before changing to a bronze floor, for a nice "battery" may be created by having the two metals in such close proximity. Giff told me that he has encountered many problems that involved boats that were carefully bronze-fastened but thoughtlessly equipped with iron floors; this caused electrolysis, which in turn induced rot in the surrounding wood.

In closing, let me emphasize the need for thorough maintenance of iron parts. Never neglect even the smallest scratch—sand it and paint it, otherwise it will spread, and not only will it stain the paint around it hideously, but it will begin a rampage of rust that will be very difficult and disheartening to try to stop.

Electrolysis

To describe as simply as possible, electrolysis is the process whereby one type of metal gives up electrons or even atoms to another type of metal nearby. For this to occur, an electrolyte—a substance that connects the two metals, in the case of boats the salt water they're immersed in—has to be present. The degree to which this will occur will depend on a number of factors, the leading of which is the difference in the *activeness* of the metals. The stable metals are gold, silver, bronze and stainless steel, while the most active ones are metals like magnesium and zinc. It is for its *activeness* that zinc is used as a sacrificial anode on boats. When a current has begun, zinc will happily surrender great chunks of itself to feed the current, thereby protecting the more stable metals around it.

If the zinc is not present to sacrifice itself, then the most active of the metals present will have to give up some of its electrons—in other words, some of itself. For example, if you have bronze through-hulls and a bronze shaft and propeller, but for some

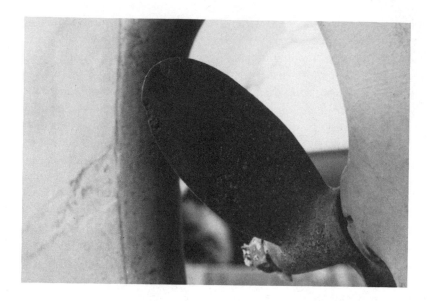

Electrolysis can start fine pitting in a metal, and eventually will eat it completely away. Look at the tip of this propeller where it looks as if the termites got it.

incredible reason iron gudgeons and pintles, then the iron—being the less stable of the two—will begin to give up its electrons and erode. The first sign of this is a *pitting* of the metal. Pitting is easily visible on an affected surface, for it looks as if it had been sandblasted. If the pitting is extensive, the thinnest part of the affected metal will eventually get holes right through it and if left uncorrected, the entire piece will eventually vanish.

Electrolysis in a wood boat is an even more serious problem than in a fiberglass boat, for in a wood boat not only will the discrepant metal parts be affected, but so will the wood surrounding them. As mentioned in the section on repairing rusted parts, electrolysis can set up rot in the surrounding wood.

So. Check all your zincs carefully at haulout to make sure there is still some anode left from the season before. If the zincs have vanished, then check all your metals closely—with a magnifying glass if need be—to make sure they did not suffer

from electrolysis themselves after the zinc took a walk.

If one of a number of zincs is more affected that the others, then check for an electrical *leak* close to that piece. To avoid this, one would be well advised to connect all underwater metal fittings with a common copper strap and connect this strap to one good-sized zinc.

Conversely, if one zinc of a number of zincs is *not* at all worn, or noticeably less worn than the others around it, don't just smile and think yourself lucky, but rather assume that somehow the zinc was at fault and had failed to perform the required sacrifices. Check the metals that the zinc was supposed to be protecting to make sure they didn't suffer, then throw away the zinc and get another one.

On a wood hull, it is best to have a zinc attached to the hull itself as well as the metal parts, for don't forget you have metal fasteners in the hull which need just as much protection as the shaft or the gudgeons.

A zinc collar will sacrifice itself to electrolysis, thereby protecting the metal it's attached to. Imagine if your shaft was as chewed up as this zinc is.

Zincs should not be allowed to be eaten completely away, for then action will begin on the more expensive surfaces. Note pitting at the tip of lower blade.

A zinc that has done its job with some reserve still left.

A zinc that was left too long. There is nothing left but a clump of white powder. That it was left too long is obvious from the fact that the forward nut has been eaten away as has a part of the bolt itself.

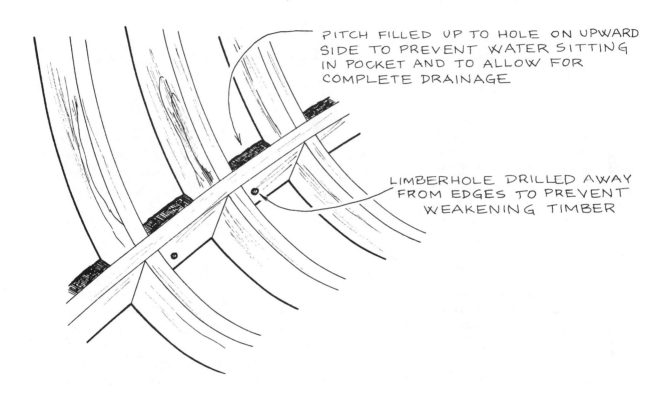

PITCH FILLED UP TO HOLE ON UPWARD
SIDE TO PREVENT WATER SITTING
IN POCKET AND TO ALLOW FOR
COMPLETE DRAINAGE

LIMBERHOLE DRILLED AWAY
FROM EDGES TO PREVENT
WEAKENING TIMBER

DRAINING POTENTIAL ROT-POCKETS

9

Checking the Fiberglass Hull

The major symptoms of fiberglass hull failure were covered under *Launching a New Boat*. Each spring when you haul, go through the list step by step, for almost all the things mentioned there also apply to a boat hauled every year. But of course with a boat that has just gone through a season of hard sailing, there will be even more opportunities for failure that could arise from exterior damage like grounding, or wear-related failures like bulkhead separation or hardware fastener destruction.

After each haulout, the exhaustive *Pre-Launch Survey* should be done, as should the following.

Keel and Ballast

1. Keels and keelbolts

The most common problem, and the most frustrating one in terms of incessance, has to do with the keel-to-hull attachments, namely the keelbolts, which seem often to leak for inexplicable reasons at inexplicable times, and the most frustrating part is that no matter what you do, the damned things keep leaking, sometimes one at a time and sometimes in harmony.

Attempts at sealing keelbolt leaks from inside the boat are usually futile, for you can't get the thing dry enough long enough to caulk it. Besides, the proper way to re-caulk the bolts is to remove the nuts and backup plates and re-bed the whole thing.

Now, Elmer, I plead with you on bended knees, *please* don't try to do this while the boat is in the water for you will be courting the ultimate disaster. Let me, as a deterrent, relate a story I heard in a logging camp some summers ago.

It was up north in the middle of nowhere in a small floating camp, that late one afternoon a sailboat pulled up along the cookhouse and the crew asked if they could tie up for the night for they had some repairs to do. Loggers, being friendly and hungry for strangers, told them to go ahead; so they tied to a log. Two women sat on the deck and told a logger fishing from the log that the men below were fixing a leak. Well he heard tools rattling and then curses and then more tools rattling and then a great loud scream and then, the logger said, the boat jumped out of the water as if some giant had kicked it in the ass, and as soon as it fell back in, it rolled over on its side and sank.

Well, it seems the boys below had started with a little leak at a keelbolt, so they poured themselves a couple of stiff scotches and went to work. They took off one nut to do a proper re-bedding job. That was fine, but with one nut gone the neighboring

Keel bolts can be re-sealed—in a fashion—from the inside, if the boat is hauled and keel propped up and the nuts removed and bolts dried and cleaned and caulked.

bolt began to leak, so the boys went and pulled the nut off that, and then the next one and the next one until half the nuts were off, and you guessed it Elmer, the last few bolts carried all the load, but that small spot in the bottom couldn't take it all and it gave, and the keel tore part of the bottom out and sank. Then with the weight gone, the boat popped out of the water and then it sank too and hung there by its docklines.

So, don't do it! Temporarily caulk the thing as best you can, then do a thorough job when you haul.

Even if there are no apparent leaks, check the joint between the hull and keel to make sure the seam hasn't opened.

If there is an obvious leak or even no leak but an obvious opening of the seam, then the best thing to do is to drop the keel and re-bed the whole thing. This is an arduous task that you should leave to a boatyard, for the keel has to be blocked, then chained so it will stay upright once the bolts are free, then the hull has to be raised screwpad by screwpad—not the keel allowed to come crash bang down from some dizzying height—then the top of the keel should be faired for a perfect fit, then the keel covered with polysulfide, then the boat lowered onto it again. Not a quick hour's work for you and the missus.

Anyway, check for the slightest crack and investigate.

If the boat has grounded during the season, then clean out any damaged area in the lead and fill with epoxy and grind fair.

2. Keelboat corrosion

With high grade stainless steel being used on most good quality modern boats, the threat of keelboat corrosion is not as grave as it used to be. But one can never tell exactly what quality the thing really is, so for the few seconds that it takes to check the bolts, go ahead and do it once in a while. All that's involved is tapping each bolt with a hammer. If it gives a nice solid sound and nothing happens, then you're okay. If it gives a sickening crack and rolls away into the darkest recess of the bilge, then, Elmer old chum, you've got yourself a situation.

3. Internal ballast

The danger of leaks starting from stress in the hull of an internally ballasted boat is rather less than on an externally ballasted one. But there is a slight chance that leaks will occur either through the rudder attachments, or more often from the inside through the bilge, when laminates that were installed to seal the ballast from the bilge fail.

a) Rudder Leaks. The hardware holding the rudder in place often undergoes so much stress, especially in heavy seas, that the seal around the rudder fails, and water can get into the internal ballast.

Giff told me a story about surveying a just-launched boat. He opened up the floorboards and stepped onto the laminate covering the ballast, and he jumped right back out in fright, thinking he'd just stepped on someone's waterbed. When he looked back down, the whole thing was undulating slowly, back and forth. Well he went and got the dealer to come and look at the phenomenon, and the dealer glanced down and smiled wryly and said, "No problem, Giff, that's an internal water tank."

When Giff informed him that his "watertank" had no inlet and no outlet and no vent, the dealer looked up a little shaken and said, "My God, Giff. Do you think we have a leak?"

It can happen. So once in a while step on top of the laminates covering your ballast, and if you don't get seasick, put your floorboards back in place and forget about it for a few months.

If a problem is found, haul the boat and remove the rudder to let the water out the same way it went in, only a little quicker. The problem will of course be to reseal the thing so it won't happen again. Since there are so many ways the original design could have been done in the first place, I'd hate to speculate on how to repair it except to say that whatever fittings there are should be isolated from the major portion of the hull. See illustration. Once that is done, clean off with acetone the area where the bolts are to go, fill the holes with polysulfide, and then install the bolts.

b) Laminate leaks. If the water in your bilge vanishes without your pumping it, then something is wrong. It's a known fact that putting a laminate over the ballast while hanging upside down in the bilge is no easy task even for Indiana Jones, so don't get emotionally overwhelmed if you do discover a leak.

The first step in repairing it will be to get the water out. This cannot be done by hauling the boat and pulling the plug as above, but it can be done while the boat is still in the water.

First, find out from the builder where you are likely to get a clear shot at reaching the bottom of the keel without any interference from the ballast or the filler around the ballast. Once you've determined that, cut a hole in the ballast covering laminate and get out all the water. You may be able to pump out the brunt, but then you'll have to get the rest out with a sponge or cloth tied to the end of a stick. When you've sponged out all you can, cut a hole a few inches in diameter in the other end of the ballast covering laminate and put a lit-

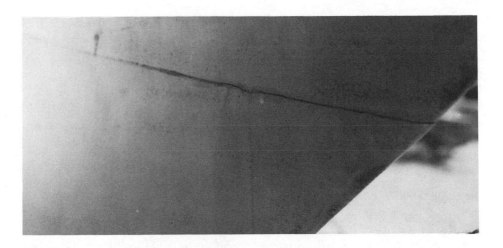

The outside seam of the keel-to-hull attachment is where the water should be stopped. The only real way to re-seal a crack like this is to drop the keel and refit the surfaces and re-seal the whole thing.

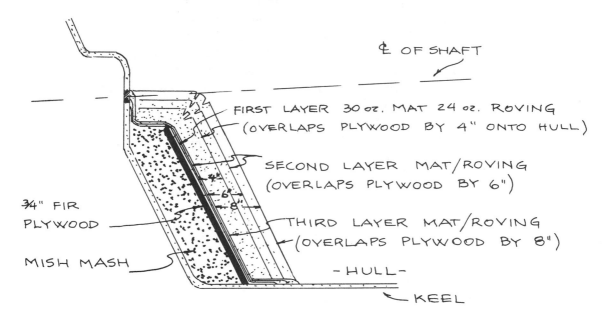

If you discover a leak into the ballast, coming in through gudgeons, then the best way to eliminate it forever is to isolate the aft part of the keel as shown in the drawing.

tle electric heater with a great big fan, so it blows right into the hole. A vacuum cleaner, with the hose reversed so it blows instead of sucking, would be good too. Blow the sucker dry. It might take a day or two. Then re-seal your holes. See *Fiberglass Repair*.

Rudder

The rudder on a sailboat undergoes as much strain as almost any other part and, as most of you have read, in hard racing it is often one of the first things to fail. Now most of the reason for failure is the design or construction of the beast, but every once in a while failure does come through wear which should have been detected and corrected under normal maintenance.

The first thing to check for is corrosion of bearings or gudgeons and pintles. If there is no obvious corrosion, check for wear. This is simply done by grabbing hold of the rudder and jiggling it back and forth and up and down, to see how much play the fittings have in them. Now of course it is impossible to say how much play fittings *should* have in them, so your best reference here is, "Is it worse than last year?" If it is, have it checked out. On the other hand, if you simply have a gut feeling that the play is too much, then by all means have it checked, for you'll probably be right. If there is any visible wear such as grooves or gouges in

the metal, get ready to replace it.

Scrape and scour the space between the rudder and skeg, or rudder and keel, for the barnacles can get so thick here that the rudder may actually bind. Speaking of which, swing the rudder back and forth to check it for binding. Even if it's a minor thing, investigate, for it may be an indication of something bent. A free-standing spade rudder is always more vulnerable to bending, so check it with great care.

Next, lock your wheel or have someone hold your tiller with all their might, then hold the trailing edge of the rudder and try to move it. If you can move it without the tiller or rudder moving, then something is either loose in the steering or the tiller box, or worst of all the rudder stock might be loose inside the rudder. Look at everything carefully.

Lastly, look over the rudder for any drips of water or any wet spots that linger after the rest of the rudder has dried. If you find any, then water has somehow gotten into the rudder. Check the laminate seams or bolt holes, or the point where the stock enters and leaves the rudder. The first step in any rudder repair is to drain the rudder. If the rudder is hard to remove, drilling a hole in its bottom to achieve drainage is a pardonable sin, as long as the hole is small, and as long as you don't just plug the hole later with a dab of epoxy but actually do a standard and proper fiberglass repair job. See *Fiberglass Repair*.

At each haulout, check to see if the rudder stock has been bent. To check for wear in the rudder shaft bearing, try jiggling the shaft back and forth. If it's loose that's bad news.

Through-Hulls and Seacocks

Check all exterior portions of through-hulls for broken bedding seams. Next, open up all the seacocks and poke your finger inside as far as you can to be sure nothing has drifted up there and stuck inside.

The next step is to go down below and grease the threads on the locking arms to make sure they'll continue to operate easily. Then grease the balls or drums of the seacocks themselves. Unthread the grease plug bolt in the seacock, and with the seacock closed squirt in some grease. Now close the seacock so the lever is 180 degrees to what it was before, and squirt in another shot of grease. Now turn the handle back and forth a few times to work the grease around.

One caution. If at all possible, do *not* use a crescent wrench to open the grease plug, for the plug is bronze and can be fairly easily rounded and thus ruined. Use a box wrench or fork wrench of the exact size.

Giff had a great idea that most boat owners should incorporate into their boats: the self-greasing seacock. This can be had by removing the grease plug and replacing it with a threaded grease cup. With a grease cup storing the grease, all you'll have to do to grease the seacock is turn the cap of the cup slightly tighter once or twice a year. Be sure the grease cup and its base are bronze—this is no place to start electrolysis. And be sure you get a *grease cup*, the kind that has the thread-on cap, and not a *grease nipple* with an open end made for grease guns, because the pressure of the water will just blow the grease right out of those, and after the grease comes out, "here come de ocean."

Check through-hulls for electrolysis and check the caulked seams for cracks.

CHECKING A SEACOCK

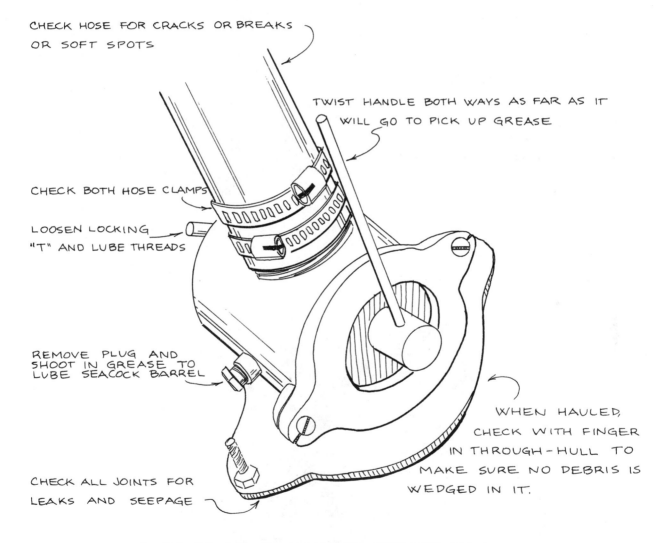

CHECK HOSE FOR CRACKS OR BREAKS OR SOFT SPOTS

TWIST HANDLE BOTH WAYS AS FAR AS IT WILL GO TO PICK UP GREASE

CHECK BOTH HOSE CLAMPS

LOOSEN LOCKING "T" AND LUBE THREADS

REMOVE PLUG AND SHOOT IN GREASE TO LUBE SEACOCK BARREL

WHEN HAULED, CHECK WITH FINGER IN THROUGH-HULL TO MAKE SURE NO DEBRIS IS WEDGED IN IT.

CHECK ALL JOINTS FOR LEAKS AND SEEPAGE

NOTE: GREASE-PLUG MAY BE REPLACED BY THREADED GREASE CUP WHICH WILL HOLD GREASE FOR FUTURE LUBES.

Cutlass Bearings

Listen to what I tell you about cutlass bearings, because I *know* about cutlass bearings, because I have *paid* four hundred dollars for a cutlass bearing that wore out in record time. Before we delve too deeply into how to *save* the cutlass, maybe we should talk about how to *find* the cutlass, for if you're half as ignorant about your cutlass bearing as I was about mine, then you will have trouble figuring out whether to start looking for it at the top of the mast or in the sink.

To put it technically, the cutlass bearing is that serrated rubber cookie-cutter-looking thing with a brass sleeve around it, that your propeller shaft sticks through out of the hull. The water is supposed to go through the teeny little grooves to *lubricate* the rubber and cool it. *But.* With all the turbulance around the propeller, the water is often too busy churning and thrashing to bother threading itself into the teeny grooves, so the rubber heats up and hardens and wears out much quicker than it should.

To insure that adequate water is reaching the bearing, the type of systems shown in the photo should be installed.

Anyway, to check wear in the cutlass bearing, stand below your prop and grab it and jiggle it from side to side. If it doesn't move inside the bearing, then you must live right; if it moves a sixteenth then it's getting worn; if it moves an eighth, brother, get out your handkerchief. Although you may be getting no water into the boat—the stuffing box should hold it out—that is no reason to ignore wear in the cutlass bearing, for you can encounter many more problems if you do.

If the bearing is worn, the shaft will vibrate and can put your engine out of alignment, and cause a vicious vibration in the whole boat that can wear and fatigue everything from fittings to bonds.

So if the thing is worn, have it replaced. If it's not worn but you do have bad vibration in the whole boat, then either your engine is running badly or it is out of alignment. See *Engine Maintenance* for those ailments.

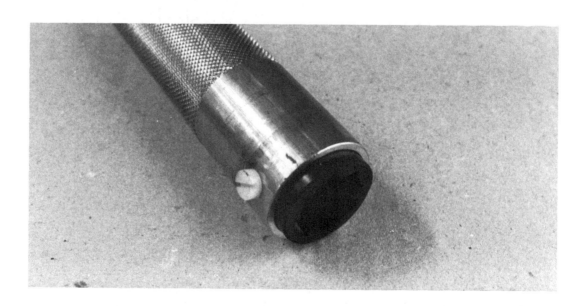

This is one good system that feeds the water into the front of the cutlass bearing. The water then circulates through the bearing and comes out of its aft end.

An independent bearing casing that again allows for good water circulation.

Knotmeter Transducer

It is completely annoying to start off on a cruise with the bottom all slick, the rigging tuned, the sails bulging with wind, and you certain that you're sailing faster than you ever have before, until you look down at the knotmeter and the bloody thing reads zero. Well, Elmer, nine times out of ten it's not its fault; it's yours. When the boat is hauled, either pull the transducer out or leave it in, it makes little difference, but whichever you do, take a sharp and pointy knife, and thoroughly and patiently scrape away all the calcium and crap that has built up around the paddle wheel and its shaft.

Spin the little bugger and make sure it spins freely and stops evenly. If you want to make sure it works, just turn it on and spin it hard by hand. It should read over four knots.

If you pulled the transducer, do make sure you re-install it with the shaft of the paddle wheel perfectly at right angles to the boat's centerline, otherwise you won't get a full reading because the water will be hitting the paddle wheel on an angle.

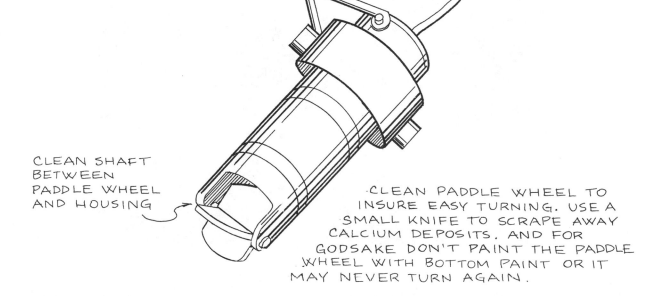

PADDLE WHEEL TRANSDUCER

NOTE! BE SURE TO ALIGN TRANSDUCER SO THAT THE PADDLE WHEEL SHAFT IS PERPENDICULAR TO CENTERLINE OF BOAT

CLEAN SHAFT BETWEEN PADDLE WHEEL AND HOUSING

CLEAN PADDLE WHEEL TO INSURE EASY TURNING. USE A SMALL KNIFE TO SCRAPE AWAY CALCIUM DEPOSITS. AND FOR GODSAKE DON'T PAINT THE PADDLE WHEEL WITH BOTTOM PAINT OR IT MAY NEVER TURN AGAIN.

Notes

SECTION TWO

TOPSIDES AND DECK

10

Cleaning

Gelcoat and Paint

I am absolutely flabbergasted by the inexplicable inconsistency most of us seem to practice, one which allows for, or actually demands, that we spend hundreds of hours and thousands of dollars a year on washing and cleaning, waxing and waning, tinkering and tuning, our precious four-wheeled rust-buckets, which in about four years' time are as likely to be fruit juice cans as cars, while our poor sailboats, that are often of ten times greater value—and that's only financially; what they do for our souls can't ever be measured—sit leashed to the dock, buried under layers of salt and grime and sea gull shit.

Ridiculous.

Not only is a well-kept boat a pure joy to behold, but in almost every instance cleanliness aboard will extend the sailboat's life, whereas the time and money we save by being slobs to start with will come back to cost ten times more in money, time and grief.

So get the soap and bucket, Elmer, and let's have ourselves a good time.

1. Washing
First of all get yourself a nifty boat brush that you've seen in all the movies, with the long handle and round head. Don't get one with a head that has corners because the thing is usually too big to get into all those nooks that hold the dirt so well. Besides, the corners might damage screens or even gelcoat.

To continue this fascinating discussion on scrub-brushes, let me say that the *real* ones with the real bristle are the best, because they are softer and hence easier on gelcoat and varnished areas than the nylon ones, which have been known to scratch. But enough already! If you want to know more about scrub brushes, ask your mom.

The only other thing you'll need to wash your boat down is some soap and some fresh water. Many of you will say, 'What about a bucket?' Well, I'll tell you. The purists insist on never using a bucket to wash a boat, for a bucket gathers all the grit that's rinsed out of the brush, only to have the brush pick it up again the next time it is dipped, and proceed to grind the recycled grit smartly into the gelcoat. Sounds a little farfetched even to me, but it makes wonderful sense if only because it means no bucket to buy and fill and clean and kick over.

The logical thing to use is a mild dish soap that can be squirted directly onto the boat. Use *only* soaps that contain *no phosphates* for phosphates do cruel things to sea life and you wouldn't want that on your conscience on top of all your other evil deeds. (Rerun.)

To keep paint and gelcoat and varnish in good shape, you should wash the boat down every time you come back from a sail. If you leave the salt water on the boat to dry, the water will evaporate and the salt remain, and the salt crystals together with the bleaching rays of the sun will bleach the bejeezus out of everything in sight. If that weren't enough, the salt that stays on board will keep absorbing moisture from the air, and it will hold the moisture and with it dirt, and together they will drool and dribble and stain everything, especially unprotected teak.

When you're cruising, and fresh water is too dear to waste on washing down the boat, don't despair, for there is usually rain and if there is no rain, there is dew. Don't count on the rain to do a perfect job without you, get out your brush or rag and loosen the dirt for the rain to rinse away.

If you get up early enough to catch the dew you'll have all the fresh water you need. Just get an old towel and wipe the boat dry, but turn the towel often, and shake the salt out of it often, or you'll just end up with it in little piles everywhere.

If you think this is absurd procedure, just think of all the times you've shammied down your dumb car.

The most important time to do this is right after a hard sail in good weather, especially windward, for then the boat will be covered from stem to stern with salt that will dry immediately to crystals in the sun, and suck up and hold the next batch of spray that comes aboard. After one particularly hard twelve hours on the wind we accumulated almost half an inch of the stuff in a baggy corner of our reefed main.

When we were sailing off the Mexican coast

and there was no rain and no dew only lots of sun and salt gathering on board, Candace used to slosh the whole boat down with buckets of salt water to rinse away the crystals, then she used to wipe it dry. Although a thin film would usually remain, it still beat the hell out of the carpet of salt that we had before.

If you have left your boat for a few weeks between sails, it is good practice to wash her down before you go out again, for much dirt will have accumulated, all of which will be ground into the gelcoat by feet and bodies and even sheets.

2. Fenders

The number one damage-causer aboard most boats are fenders. These are usually of fairly porous rubbery stuff which holds grit so well you'd think that was its main job. As soon as the boat undergoes some movement from wind in the rigging or a wake of a passing boat, the grit is ground into the gelcoat with great efficiency.

The best solution is to try and tie the boat away from all docks, but since that's seldom possible, the second best thing is to keep both hull and fenders clean. *Do not* use abrasive cleansers to clean your fenders because not only will the abrasives remain in the rubber to grind away the hull, but the little grooves they cut into the soft rubber will now trap grit ten times better than before.

One fine solution that seems to work is making little dresses for the fenders out of something like terry towels which will act as a cushion between the grit and the hull. These of course will have to be washed thoroughly and often.

3. Stains

Most good glossy paints won't stain as badly as the more porous gelcoat, especially if the gelcoat is older, for then it sucks up stains like a thirsty sponge would water.

The first thing to realize is that your boat is not a toilet bowl whose stains should be attacked with

The best way to avoid having the fenders abrade the hull over the winter is to tie the boat away from the dock.

all kinds of abrasive cleansers and much muscle. Take it easy. Most stains are soluble with either simple solvents like alcohol or kerosene, or non-abrasive cleaners like *Fantastic* (which really is) and sometimes even lemon juice—although with the price of lemons nowadays, I would avoid forming a habit. If you do use any kind of solvent on gelcoat, be sure to wash it off right away, for some may stain, while others may actually soften the gelcoat.

If the above stuff won't work, that means the dirt has gone deeply into your gelcoat and you'll have to send somebody in there to get it out. More often than not, you will have to abrade a layer of dead gelcoat and get the dirt out with it. The lightest stuff is the wax-and-clean rubbing compound made for fiberglass. A stronger abrasive is straight fiberglass rubbing compound which will take off any amount of gelcoat given enough time and muscle. If you want to do a quick-and-dirty job on some intransigent stain, get some cut polish used for cars, a polish made for the hard baked enamel, not the soft and porous gelcoat.

If that doesn't work, get the axe.

The ultimate stain remover.

Waxing

This is not a hobby on a fiberglass boat, but a necessity if the gelcoat is to last a decent length of time. A well waxed hull sheds water and with it salt and grime, and the reasons to keep a boat free of those have already been described.

Apart from dirt-shedding, the wax will act as a barrier against salt and sun and dirt, a barrier that will have to be eroded before the gelcoat can be touched. And lastly, a good wax will help in keeping away the stains. Oh, I almost forgot—a well-polished hull with the reflections dancing on it is almost as good as the light-show at Limelight.

So, wax her until she's squeaky slick, and most importantly, wax her before you put her away for the winter to protect her from all harm. There is no need to rub her to a high gloss at that time, just put on the wax and buff lightly.

Don't think that only the hull needs the protection of wax. The house gets even more sun than the hull, so it needs waxing too. Try not to get wax on areas where you walk, or you'll be doing somersaults forever.

Cleaning Metals

As you'll have found out after owning your boat a few months, stainless steel is anything but stainless and the poorer quality the steel, the less stainless it is. So be prepared to wipe it once in a while. The quickest and cheapest way is using the same rubbing compound you use on the fiberglass. You don't need to use a thick coat, just put a bit on a rag and it will do wonders. This is perfect stuff for stanchions and chainplates; *however*, I would not use it on things like turnbuckles or tangs or around swedged-fittings or stainless steel wire. Maybe this is just a personal paranoia, but I dread getting the granular stuff in between things that move, just in case it could

somehow grind or bind up something. In these touchy areas we use a thing called *Neverdull*, which is far from the truth, but it does take the surface rust off well. This is one of those cotton-in-a-can things that is impregnated with some polish or something. Anyway it works well on all metals, even badly darkened brass, if you have the fortitude and biceps in your fingers.

Painted metals, like masts and booms, need cleaning and waxing too but here again I would stay away from abrasives just in case the grains find their way into blocks. The same wax that you use for fiberglass should do fine here. I'm not a believer in having a thousand different compounds and goops on board.

Cleaning Woods

Varnished surfaces should be washed often with mild detergent if they are to keep their shine.

Oiled teak is a difficult thing to keep clean, mostly because there is so much resin in the oils that are available—the resin lets the oil harden so it doesn't just turn tacky and gummy—that once the resin turns dark, which it inevitably does, there is little hope of bringing the wood back to life again without removing all the resin from it by sanding or with TSP.

Uncoated teak is simpler to maintain, except that it stains every time you turn around, and unless it is always kept clean, it will usually look grey and dull and lifeless.

Anyway, for both oiled and bleached woods, the best *and* the cheapest cleaning compound you can buy is TSP. That is short for Trisodium Phosphate and I haven't the faintest what that is, I only know that my mom used to use it on everything and that nothing in the world gets wood as clean as *it* does. I think it works by dissolving everything that's

Stainless steel is anything but. A light rubbing compound brings it to shine in no time. Chromed metal—the light—should be washed of salt often and waxed often to seal the metal from the corrosive salt. This one has been neglected and spots of corrosion are everywhere.

oily, for if you put it on teak you can actually see the oil being sucked right up, and if you leave it on in a strong compound, you can see it turn reddish-brown as the teak oil rises into it. As it lifts the oil it also lifts the dirt, and the teak will glow a beautiful pink when you're done.

The stuff is available in hardware stores and drugstores and it's ninety cents a bag, and in a bag there is at least a pound of crystals, of which you put a couple of spoonfuls in a whole bucket of water, so you can imagine how long it will last. Now, if you went and bought some fancy-assed marine product to clean your teak you'd probably get a bottle with a cute nautical label that would cost you five bucks and last you half a deck. Forget

it. It's probably diluted TSP.

But as I said, this stuff is very strong, so use it in moderation. If you're not getting the results you want, thicken up the brew.

Also remember that as it takes the oil it takes some of the soft parts of the wood too; it is therefore actually wearing the wood away.

I mention this, for it's very easy to let your bare teak go for a year or two, then get some TSP and keep strengthening it until all the dirt is out, and end up with a piece of teak with wildly raised grain. There is nothing wrong with that initially I suppose, for it makes excellent non skid, except that eventually you will have no wood left at all between the screws. So use the stuff sparingly but often and don't let stains get too deep.

A mistake I've seen many people make is to let the TSP do all the work for them. In other words, they just slop the stuff on and let it sit there. That's bad. First, rinse the wood down so that the grain is soft and the dirt somewhat loose, then take a little of the TSP and water solution and spread it over an area no more than a couple of square feet. Without waiting, start scrubbing with a stiff brush across the grain and with the grain. Put some effort into it. You'll live longer. Then as soon as you can see the first tint of redness or darkness come into the by now almost foamy stuff, get the hose and rinse it and scrub it all off. Don't leave any TSP in the grain or it will keep sucking out the oils.

Now I know all the above sounds as scary as hell, but it isn't really. I just stressed its corrosiveness because most modern teak decks start out only one-half inch in thickness, which doesn't leave you much wood in a plug that covers a screw head, so you can't afford to blow away an eighth of an inch of deck too many times.

Maintaining Wood

There are basically four things you can do with exterior teak: You can varnish it or oil it or paint it or leave it. With other woods, like mahogany or oak or fir used on the exterior, your choice is blissfully limited, for if you don't varnish or paint, the thing will look like hell in no time and then it will rot.

1. Varnishing

Warm Rain has all her exterior wood varnished— except her teak decks, Elmer, because then she'd be a skating rink—and without doubt it is the best way to preserve teak as well as keeping it looking its best. Admittedly it takes some sanding which is a pain and some varnishing which is great fun for it goes fast and the results are truly fine, for few things look as beautiful as richly glowing varnish.

It's true that you don't have to do much work if you just leave the teak bare, but then it always looks pretty dull. Oiled teak looks good for a couple of weeks but then it begins to get dark. Varnish on the other hand looks good for months at a time, and even after that you'll only need a couple hours of light sanding and one new coat to make her glow again.

The problem with varnish arises when it's not looked after enough, for then cracks can form in the varnish where a joint or seam moves in the wood, and if the crack is not re-sealed early, then the water that gets in through the crack will get into the wood and cause the varnish to lift more and more. If frost comes into the picture as well, then the lifting can become epidemic. To repair such an occurrence—especially if a good six coats of varnish are in place everywhere—is a major task indeed, for the peeled stuff has to be removed and the remaining edges carefully feathered in, and the crater you've created has then to be filled to bring the level of protection up to the other six coats.

Perhaps the best solution is to varnish only areas where there are very few seams, for on solid wood good varnish lasts a long, long, time. So. Varnish easy stuff, like handrails and eyebrows and coamings and caprails and rubrails, but don't varnish hatches made of narrow strips, where for every piece of wood there is an equal length of seam.

How to strip and varnish will be covered later.

2. Oiling

Oiling allows you more flexibility. Unlike varnish, which looks great while it's good but once it peels it's had it, oil deteriorates with respectful graduality until one day it turns quietly black.

The same problem occurs here as with teak left bare: each cleaning, whether with sandpaper or TSP, will take with it a bit of teak, until one day the plugs will fall out and will have to be replaced. With varnish, this problem won't have to be feared.

3. Painting

As mentioned, most wood on the exterior—other than teak—will need the protection of either paint or varnish if it is to survive. There is nothing wrong with painting wood; it's usually a quick job often requiring only two coats instead of the six required for varnish, and it certainly does protect the wood impeccably from salt and sun and wear. The one complaint I have is that if anything, it hides the wood too well, and signs of rot are very often difficult to detect. With varnish, one can always see what is going on below. This is doubly a problem since most cracks—hence leaks, hence rot—take

place near fittings that move under strain, meaning they're carrying some load, meaning if the wood rots and the fitting goes flying then something important might go flying with it. But if you promise to keep the paint in fine shape all the time, then by all means get out the brush and bucket and slop the stuff around.

More on painting later.

4. Leaving wood bare

As I said, this can be done only with teak, whose oil content keeps it from rotting. If this is your choice, fine. Just sit back and watch it turn gray, then scrub it with bleach or salt water often to get it looking clean.

11

Repairing Fiberglass

Surface Scratches

Okay, so you scratched the fiberglass; it's not the end of the world. If the scratch hasn't penetrated the gelcoat then first of all try to take the scratch out with rubbing compound. If it proves too deep for that, don't start filling yet, for you might be able to *sand* out the scratch.

First clean the area off with acetone. Don't forget you have to remove all the wax you've just put on there via the rubbing compound, as well as the old mold-release wax that might still be there. Now get a small block, and with 400 grit sandpaper wet-sand the scratch out. Once it has disappeared, switch to 600 grit and wet-sand over the whole area. Do all this with patience or you'll go through the gelcoat. Once done, go over the whole thing with rubbing compound. Now that wasn't so bad, was it?

Deep Gouges

I have taken out the odd piling and grounded on the odd rock in my day—what fun would life be if you always played it safe—and at the sound of each contact I prepared myself for going down with

the ship, envisioning the water pouring in through a gaping hole, but each time I would seek out the damage and find nothing but a gouge.

A gouge is different from a scratch only in that it's deeper, so you'll have to go to the store and get yourself a handy little gelcoat repair kit. This consists of either a clear resin and something to thicken it with and some pigment, or—especially for white hulls—a putty with the pigment already in it, so all you need to do is add the hardener. That last one sounds good to me. Who needs all that fooling around?

But if you want to mix your own—then you're probably the type who makes his own granola that almost always comes out tasting like old sawdust—the first thing to do is to make a putty by mixing the resin with the filler stuff, and then play around with the pigment until the color is close to the piece being repaired. When you get bored with that, put it down and prepare the surface.

First, widen the gouge so the putty will have a decent surface to grab onto. This you can do with a screwdriver or a juice can opener or a nail, or if you have one of those little drums with sandpaper on it that fits into a drill motor, then you can

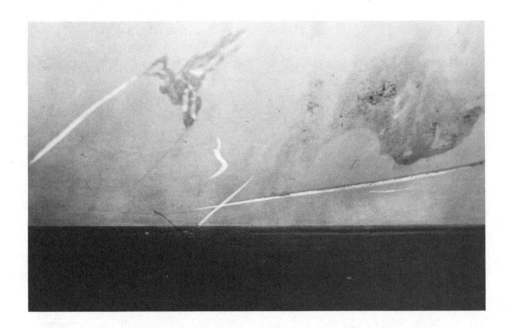

Deep gouges that have gone through the gelcoat have to be cleaned out and filled and faired in or water will soften the unprotected fiberglass.

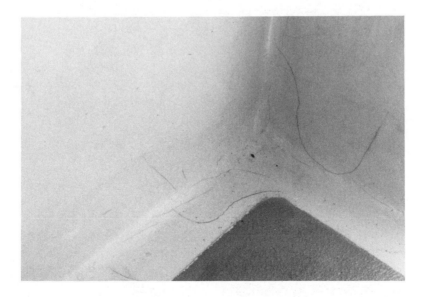

Crazing may look innocuous but it should not be ignored. First, it can let water into the fiberglass, and second, there is obviously some movement below that caused the crazing. The movement will have to be halted or things will only get worse.

use just the very edge of that. But stay loose and don't go doubling the damage—you're trying to widen the gouge, not deepen it. If you're using one of the pointed tools above, *pull* the thing toward you evenly and smoothly. Don't push it with a jerky motion or you'll chip out the edges, and then where will you be? So once you've gouged the gouge—if the edges are smooth—clean out the area with acetone.

Next, take the putty and add the catalyst, then take a very clean and small putty knife and ram the putty in there. Keep the knife nice and flat, and as you press and move along you'll find the putty behind the knife bulging a little from the groove. That's okay because it'll give you something to sand and fair in.

Once the stuff is down and looks not bad, you'll have to seal it from the air so it can harden. Weird, but true. If you're a big spender and have bought some of that green slop called polyvinyl alcohol, then spray it over the fresh gelcoat now—that's what it's for. If you didn't buy the stuff, don't start whimpering, just get yourself a sandwich baggie or a piece of cellophane and put it over the patch. Tape down one end and roll the air out with the bilge pump handle, then tape down the other end so the wind won't blow it away. Big deal.

When the filler has hardened, peel off the baggie, or wash off the green slop with water, and then get a small block and sand the whole thing down with 220. Be sure you've let the filler harden completely or even the 220 will pull some of it out. Then switch to 400 and wet-sand, then switch to 600 and wet-sand. Buff with rubbing compound and that's it. Now stand back and enjoy your masterpiece. So the color doesn't quite match— what did you expect? Your mamma didn't name you Elmer instead of Leonardo for nothing.

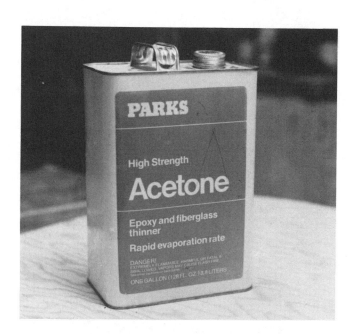

The best thing to wipe fiberglass with before filling or painting. It removes oils and leaves none of its own behind. Wear rubber gloves to avoid contact with skin.

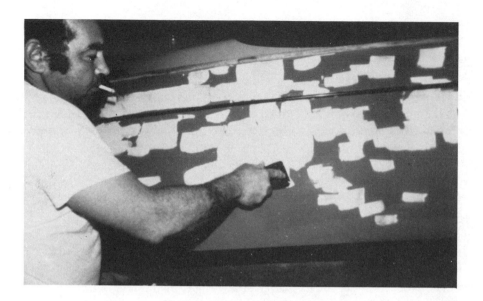

After you've cleaned out each scratch and gouge, fill with gelcoat putty if the dings are shallow, and with epoxy filler if they are deep.

Sand all filled spots completely until the filler is "ghost feathered" in. Any poorly sanded spots will look ten times worse after painting.

Holes

1. Single-skinned hulls

Even though we have the best intentions and the clearest of minds, the Elmer in us all may some-day break through and we'll find ourselves on a rock with a hole in our boat. And somehow it seems the bigger our boat, the bigger is our Elmer, and the harder we will hit and the larger will be our hole.

All in all, fiberglass is pretty tough stuff, and to hole a well-constructed boat takes a lot of force, so much force in fact that the damage is usually many times larger than the actual hole itself. So the first thing to do is to assess just how much *delamination* the impact has caused. There are usually torn layers of delaminated fiberglass all around the hole, so you might as well begin by cutting these away with a sabersaw. No, Elmer, you can't just glue them back together and hope for the best.

To cut away the broken stuff takes some fortitude, for you will be increasing the size of the hole and, as you know, in a boatyard the bigger the hole the bigger the crowds and the louder the snickers. Tell them to get lost or they might make you nervous, and you might slip with the sabersaw and accidentlly chop down their masts.

Use a coarse, metal-cutting blade. Don't rush. I know you want to get the torture over as soon as possible but fiberglass is tough stuff and if you rush, the blade will heat up and break. Take your time. Enjoy yourself. Pretend you're hacking someone else's hull.

Do *not* cut a neat square or rectangular hole. Avoid creating any corners or odd shapes, for you will ultimately be creating weak spots. Cut nice clean circles or ovals—these will have no weak spots and will fair in nicely. When you think you've cut out enough of the damage, take your four-ounce plastic mallet, and tap and sound all around the hole to be sure you haven't missed any spots.

Unless it is absolutely impossible, the hole should be repaired from the *inside*, for then a well-fitted template can be used on the outside to create the new contour. If you work from the *outside* you will end up with a rough, shapeless exterior, the fairing of which will take forever, involving the grueling job of endless filling and sanding.

If you have any cabinetry or liners in the way, cut them out. I know it sounds like a lot of work, but so is grinding and filling, and you'll get a much better job at the end to boot.

Now that you have a nice even hole, you'll have to bevel the edges of the hole with a grinder *on the inside*, to create lots of adhesion surface for the new laminates that you'll be putting in, laminates that will increase in size as you go.

The amount of beveling necessary will be determined by the original thickness of your hull. Hulls up to ¼-inch should be beveled about 10:1. In other words, a hull with a ¼-inch skin should have the laminate around the hole beveled 2½ inches. On thicker hulls, the proportion of bevel-to-hull thickness should be increased to 15:1. Hence a hull of ½-inch thickness will have to have the edges of a hole beveled 7½ inches. Remember the bevel does *not* depend on the size of the hole but on the thickness of the hull.

Given the above, you will readily see why I said before that it is much better to bevel and fill the hole from the inside of the hull, for something as small as a 3-inch hole in a ½-inch hull, will have—with the two 7½-inch beveled edges added—an affectively destroyed surface 18 inches in diameter. (7½+3+7½=18). And that isn't really all, for the repair laminates are usually allowed to run well past the beveled edges and onto the full thickness portion of the hull.

When you have beveled the inside, go back outside and check the edges of the hole to make sure

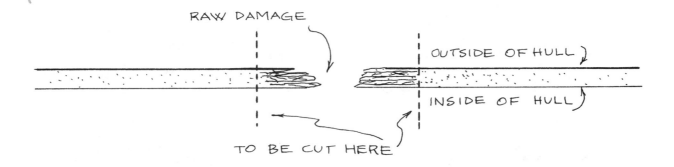

RAW DAMAGE

OUTSIDE OF HULL

INSIDE OF HULL

TO BE CUT HERE

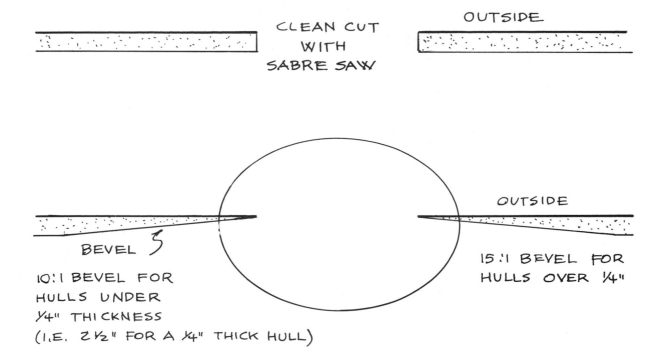

CLEAN CUT
WITH
SABRE SAW

OUTSIDE

OUTSIDE

BEVEL

10:1 BEVEL FOR
HULLS UNDER
¼" THICKNESS
(I.E. 2½" FOR A ¼" THICK HULL)

15:1 BEVEL FOR
HULLS OVER ¼"

A small puncture in a single-skinned hull should be repaired from the inside so that the bevel you'll have to put on the undamaged skin will not increase the size of the damage on the boat's exterior.

The first step in repairing a puncture is to ascertain how much delamination has occurred beyond the hole itself. The second step is to cut away all the damaged laminates with a saber saw. The third is to bevel the edge of the hole.

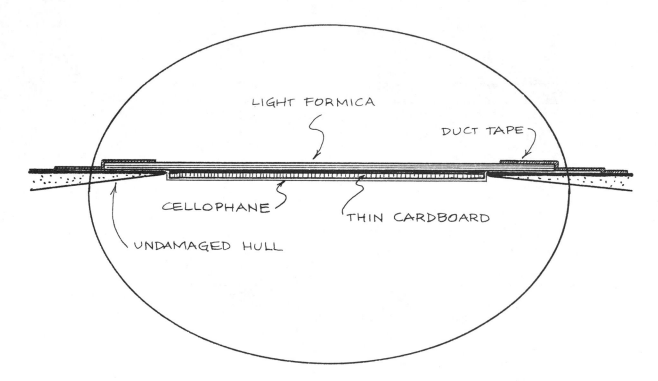

The fourth step is to lay on a mold as above. The formica gives the form its strength while the cardboard—the thickness of a paperback cover—creates a slight hollow that you will later fill with gelcoat filler. Lay in the same laminates as in the original hull layup schedule, then add 20% just for good luck. Make each layer slightly larger than the preceding one.

there are no chips or cracks.

The next step is to vacuum everything clean and then wash it down with acetone.

Now comes the tricky part; you will have to make a decent mold on the outside to replicate the curvature of the hull. It the hole is not too large—not more than about 5 inches—then a firm but flexible thing, like thin formica, can be used. Cut this with a sharp knife so it's about ½ inch larger all around than the hole. Glue it temporarily to the hull with duct tape all around the edge. Now go inside and cut out a piece of thin cardboard—the thickness of a paperback book cover—to be as large

as the hole. Put some rubber cement on this and glue it to the inside of the formica. This *padding* will in effect create a very shallow hollow in the hull, a hollow which you can later fill in with a thickened mixture of gelcoat to achieve a thick waterproof surface.

Now go back out and take the *mold* off and line the inside of it with cellophane—smooth please, no wrinkles. This will allow you to pull the mold away after the laminates have set. Now, tape the mold back in place carefully so the cardboard fits nicely into the hole. This time do a perfect job with the duct tape so everything is tight and stable.

Now go to it. Brush on a good layer of gelcoat and let it cure. Next, lay in two layers of one ounce or 1.5 ounce mat, depending on whether your hull is under or over ¼ inch. Let it cure before you go on or you'll trap too much heat in the laminates. Finally, lay in alternate layers of mat and cloth—cloth is stronger than roving and easier to work with—making sure that each layer is progressively larger than the preceding one. Let the builder's original layup schedule be your guide as to how many laminates you put in, and then add another 20% for good luck.

When everything is set, go outside and take off the tape and peel away the formica. If there are any voids, fill them in now with putty. Next, mix a thickened batch of gelcoat and fill up the dip left by the cardboard, plus a little more. The extra will be sanded down when you do your final fairing.

Remember to cover the gelcoat with cellophane or the polyvinyl alcohol we talked about in repairing cracks, or the gelcoat won't set.

When it has set, fair everything in, starting with 180 grit, then 220, then 400, then 600, then rubbing compound.

Well, that's it. That was a high price to pay for Elmering around, and don't try to tell me that it wasn't your fault. Like my dear old granny used to say, "There are no accidents; only stupids."

Amen to that, Nana.

Thoroughly wetted out surface.

2. Cored hulls

Cored hulls should be treated in the same fashion as single-skinned hulls as far as the beveling proportions and laminates are concerned, but a major difference exists in procedure, for both skins will have to be beveled and repaired individually.

The added attraction in cleaning out the damaged parts in cored hulls is determining whether, and how far, water has penetrated into the core, and whether or not the core has delaminated from the inside skin.

If there is no damage to the core or the inside skin, then proceed to repair the outer skin as you would a single-skinned hull. Unfortunately you'll have to work from the outside, which means you'll have to enlarge the hole by beveling the outside, and you'll have to lay up your laminates in reverse order—that is, from the inside out with the gelcoat going on last. But look at the bright side. At least you don't have to build a mold.

If the core is damaged, you'll have to dig it out and replace it. Cut the new piece on a bevel, then glue it into place with epoxy paste—see drawing. Beveled as it is, it adds a bit of extra resistance against the loading on the hull. Almost all the loading comes from the outside, either in the form of the boat pounding against waves, or the rigging trying to 'straighten' the curvature of the hull by pulling upwards on it.

If it has been determined that there *is* damage to the inside skin, cut the damaged area away and then bevel both inside and outside layers as shown in the illustrtation. Wedge the coring as above, for the same reason. This means a slightly larger hole on the outside than otherwise, but I think it's worthwhile, so don't argue, just do it.

One last point. Some people advocate that it is quite all right to try and repair a cored hull that has both skins damaged, by working from the outside only. This to me seems totally absurd and I'll tell you why, but it's best that you look at the illustration to follow along.

Say you have a nice even hole 2 inches in diameter, in a hull whose skins are ¼-inch thick each. If you were to work from the inside *and* outside, then the total surface diameter that you'd have to destroy (beveling included) would be 2½-inch bevel, plus 2-inch hole, plus 2½-inch bevel, or a total of 7 inches. *But* if you work from the outside only, then you'll have to have beveled the *inside* skin to the 7 inches *as starters*, meaning you'll have a *7 inch diameter hole* (before beveling) in the outside skin. You then have to bevel this 5 more inches in total. If you have followed along, you'll have noticed by now that the hole itself in the outer skin had to have been enlarged from 2 inches in diameter to 7 inches in diameter, just to give you the privilege of working from the outside only without disturbing a bit of cabinetry. Well, Elmer, if you are willing to do that, then I suggest you count your cards again, because I tell you Son, you ain't playin' with a full deck.

Whew! I'm glad that's over with. I don't much like talking about holes in boats. Gives me the shivers.

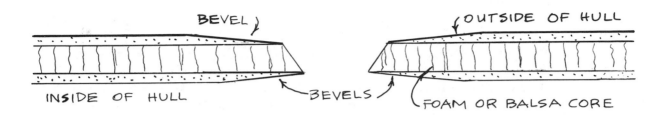

BEVEL

INSIDE OF HULL

OUTSIDE OF HULL

BEVELS

FOAM OR BALSA CORE

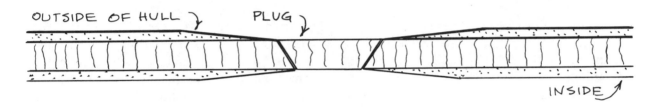

OUTSIDE OF HULL

PLUG

INSIDE

PLUG MUST BE SAME MATERIAL AS CORE TO AVOID DIFFERENTIAL HEAT EXPANSION PROBLEMS.

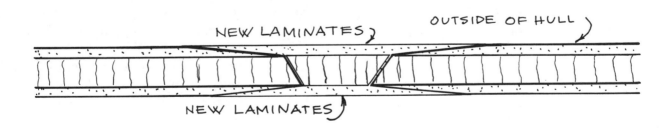

NEW LAMINATES

OUTSIDE OF HULL

NEW LAMINATES

A puncture in a cored hull should be repaired from both sides so the beveling of one surface will not necessitate the creation of a giant hole in the other. If you can't quite follow that, then read the text; it will either clear things up or totally confuse you.

Repairing Nonskid Areas

Having a good nonskid deck and house top is essential to the enjoyment and safety of any boat. If the nonskid is applied after the deck is out of the mold, either in the shape of some high friction rubber sheeting or just a painted surface that contains skid-inhibiting granules, then repair to a damaged or worn surface is relatively easy, involving only removal of the old stuff and resurfacing. If the non-skid is actually a pattern molded into the deck at time of lamination, then a simple and proper repair is next to impossible.

1. Small repairs

On a molded nonskid, if the damage is very small—maybe a couple of square inches—you can try *sculpting*, which is exactly what you think it is. It involves grinding down the damaged surface to make sure the wax and cracked material is removed. Do not grind any farther than you need to, for it's good to retain at least the base of the pattern of the nonskid for you to begin rebuilding on. Rebuild the pattern using epoxy putty and a small knife. Make sure to thicken the epoxy to the point where it will sit up well so you can work it. Take it easy on the hardener—you may not be as great a sculptor as you surmised, and if the stuff sets before you add the final touches, then you'll have to grind the whole thing off again. If you are uncertain of your abilities, practice on some playdough.

When you're done, you'll have to cover the repair with gelcoat, and here you will again have to use care. You will need a good quantity of it to stand up to the wear and abrasion a normal deck receives, *but* you will also have to make sure that you don't use too much gelcoat or you'll fill up the tiny grooves that make the nonskid non-skid.

If your nonskid surface is painted on—sprinkled with silica or crushed walnut shells—then I suggest grinding away the old stuff until the surface is smooth, and re-painting and re-sprinkling. I have seen too many attempts where the correction was made right over the old surface without any prior grinding, and the result was a sad looking little mound covered by paint, that not only looked bad, but was a perfect little thing to trip over.

2. Large areas

As you can guess, the same method of repair applies no matter how large the damage to a surface that has the nonskid sprinkled into it.

One caution: Use only the very best sandpaper to grind down nonskid, for as I told you before, the stuff is either silica or ground walnut shells, both of which are harder than hell and both of which will tear weak sandpaper to shreds.

Oh yes, another caution: Some manufacturers advocate mixing the nonskid granules into the paint and then rolling the mixture onto the deck. That's just bad news. First of all the granules sink toward the bottom making for a very inconsistent density, and second, the roller will be so full of the stuff in no time that it will no longer turn but merely skid along. A genuine horror show. So just roll the paint on first—a nice thin even layer—but do it quickly for you'll have to sprinkle the granules on before any of the paint loses its tackiness. Don't worry about sprinkling on too much—put on reams of the stuff, for anything that doesn't come in contact with the paint will remain loose and can be brushed off. Now let it all dry over night. Do not think of *pressing* the granules into the paint or doing anything of a similar nature—after you've sprinkled it on, leave the stuff alone. Take a walk. The next day, brush off all the excess granules with a stiff brush, then apply a coat of paint over the ones that stuck. *Do not* sprinkle anything into this.

On molded nonskid, attempting to repair a large area with the sculpting method could lead to a lifelong undertaking. The only real solution is to grind out the whole of the affected area, and replace it with some of the molded rubber nonskids now available in sheets. These are without doubt the most non-skid of nonskids—with perhaps the exception of teak—so if the rest of your nonskid is not particularly effective, perhaps you should consider resurfacing the whole deck.

If your molded non-skid is badly damaged—or not worth a damn because it was badly done to start with—you may think of resurfacing the whole thing with sheet rubber non-skid. The stuff is so good it's almost too good—it's hard on bare feet and knees. Some of the London police boats have been using a type called Treadmaster for twenty years. It seems to outlast the boat.

Notes

12

Repairing Wood

Shallow Dings

These often occur in wood caused by dropped winch handles, or sometimes *thrown* winch handles that missed the head they were aimed for.

If the dent is truly minor, you may be able to *raise* the wood by soaking it judiciously with water, then aiming a hairdryer right at it on full heat. To keep the heat in and the moisture going, drape a soaked towel over the nozzle of the dryer.

If the damage is on a flat surface, you can get a wet towel and set an ordinary iron, good and hot, on top of it. The heat from the iron will create steam you can get a wet towel and set an ordinary iron, good and hot, on top of it. The heat from the iron will create steam, drive it into the wood and raise the grain.

Plugging

If the above won't work because the fibers are too badly damaged, and if the damage is smaller than an inch in diameter, then get out your drill. You'll have to do some plugging.

You can repair the wood by drilling a shallow hole—no more than ¼ inch—with a drillbit large enough to remove all the damaged wood. Then simply get a suitable sized plug—of the same wood as the damaged piece—from a marine store and dip the tip of it into clear epoxy, line up the grain of the plug with the grain of the wood being repaired, and tap it into place with a mallet.

Before the glue has set, get a fine sharp chisel and with the bevel part down, skim a little off the top of the plug to see which way the grain breaks. If you go and try to take the whole thing off at once, you may get the grain breaking away from you, hence you may just take a good part of the whole plug right out. Once you have found the direction of the break, move the chisel to the *lowest* part of the plug and finish taking off the rest. Be patient—do it bit by bit. What's the hurry? You're only doing a plug, not a whole teak deck.

One caution: It might behoove you to go to the hardware store and sample the plugs in stock, for you might find that they don't have the exact size you want. If such is the case, don't despair, get a plug slightly larger than the one you need, and drill your hole to suit.

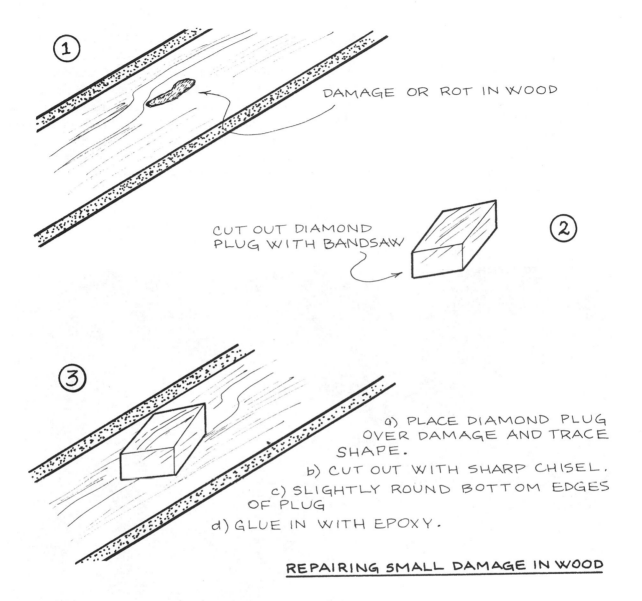

① DAMAGE OR ROT IN WOOD

② CUT OUT DIAMOND PLUG WITH BANDSAW

③ a) PLACE DIAMOND PLUG OVER DAMAGE AND TRACE SHAPE.
b) CUT OUT WITH SHARP CHISEL.
c) SLIGHTLY ROUND BOTTOM EDGES OF PLUG
d) GLUE IN WITH EPOXY.

REPAIRING SMALL DAMAGE IN WOOD

Inlaying

If you have big dings or small rot, meaning that the damaged area is larger than an inch, don't get nervous and start thinking about replacing the whole piece of wood—you can do a very simple *let-in*.

This requires a very sharp wide chisel and a mallet. If the wood is to remain exposed to the eye—varnished or oiled but not painted—then a very clean and good looking job needs to be done, one that will *not* require eight gallons of wood putty to fill in the mistakes. So, first decide on some nice looking shape that you can incorporate into your woodwork. A diamond looks clean and traditional besides being nice and easy to cut.

Determine the approximate size of the plug you need to cut, then get hold of a piece of wood of the same variety and approximately the same grain as the damaged piece. With the aid of a bandsaw, cut out the shape you need. Clean off the bottom edge with sandpaper but don't round it. Not yet anyway. Now take this piece, and use it as a template to mark off the damaged piece. With your sharp chisel, cut out the damaged area. Start chiseling well inside the lines, so that if you make a mistake there will be no need for instant hara-kiri of the abdominal variety. Once the bulk of the damaged wood is out, clean out the hole. Next, slightly round the bottom edges of your plug so it will slip into place without buggering up the edges of the hole, then put epoxy on the bottom of the plug and tap it in place with a mallet. Plane or Sureform off the extra wood. There…you're ready to go into the parquet business.

To repair rot in a plank, it's often easiest to change the whole plank. Don't just hack out the old plank—try to get it out in one piece so you can use it as a pattern. Dry-fit new one with clamps and braces and wedges before you fasten it to hull.

Check all frames. If you find a bad one, then either sister it or replace it.

Treat the inside and the edges and the ends of each new plank with Cuprinol or similar wood preservative—that's the stains that you see. The outside you can either prime or preserve later.

13

Varnishing and Oiling

Varnishing is an art. Many books have been written on the fine points and procedures, including a thirty-seven chapter manual by Frederick Oughton, called the *Complete Manual of Wood Finishing*. A warning: DON'T READ IT! If you do you'll get hooked and you'll spend all your time trying to convert your boat into a violin, and you'll never dare step aboard lest you mar the varnish.

For those who want varnish on their boat but also like to sail, I shall give you a condensed version of Mr. Oughton's manual:

a) Sand wood.
b) Slap on varnish.
c) Let dry.
d) Hoist sails.
e) Piss off.

Now back to reality. If you really do want a jewell-like finish on your wood, read Mr. Oughton. His book is the most comprehensive there is. For all you other dilettantes, here's what you do.

New Wood Preparation

Sand thoroughly with 100 grit sandpaper. When I say thoroughly, I mean thoroughly, I don't mean stroke it as you would your dog and call it done. If you do, the grain will remain high and the whole thing will look like hell even after eighteen thousand coats.

Always sand with the grain except on end grain where it makes no difference. Use nice even pressure and do use a sanding block, otherwise you'll end up with tiny hills and gullies.

Once you've sanded, don't wander off like Cain, but put on the first coat, or a quick rainfall or even the moisture in the air will raise the grain again. Plan to finish sanding by noon at the latest, so the dew won't turn your varnish dull. Actually this is no big deal with the first coat for it will be thinned down a bit and it will soak into the raw wood, but it will be a big deal on the coats to follow.

Now take your rattail brush and starting on the *upwind-most point of the boat* sweep off every last speck of dust. Do not limit the sweeping to the parts you've just sanded, but sweep the whole damned boat, or the wind will simply blow the crap all over your varnish, and if you don't know yet, you will soon learn that dust sticks to varnish almost as well as the proverbial to a blanket.

Next, wipe all your sanded surfaces with a barely damp cloth to get out the tiny critters. Some people use a storebought tack cloth. Others make it

If at all possible, masts and hatches and such should be taken indoors for the winter and varnished there.

themselves by soaking a cotton rag in warm water, wringing it out, pouring on a trickle of turpentine, then laying it on some newspaper and sprinkling about a tablespoon of varnish over it. Then you wring out the cloth to distribute the varnish evenly, and hang it up to dry for a half hour. It is supposed to pick up every last speck of dust. I wouldn't know. Like I told you, I use a damp rag. Oh, yes, when you're finished with your tacky cloth don't throw it away—you're supposed to shake it out and store it in a covered mason jar like Granny did with fruit, so you can use it next year. Of course when you go to use it next year, you'll find it turned to stone. But don't get upset. Take the rag out of the jar, lay it on a good hard surface and beat it with a hammer until it's soft. *Then throw it away.*

Choosing a Varnish

There is really not much argument here. At the Concordia Boatyard, which looks after a whole slew of old Concordia yawls, each of which has an acre and a half of varnished surface, they use nothing but good old-fashioned spar varnish. So do we. We use McCloskey's—I probably spelled that wrong but I'm in the middle of Manhattan and it's the middle of the night and there is no one to ask—Man O'War, which is a beautifully rich varnish that is full of ultraviolet filters so your wood doesn't bleach out, and it's beautiful stuff to use and it doesn't come off in great sheets like varethane and it comes in a really pretty can. What more can you ask for?

Varnishing

After wiping with the cloth, let the surface dry, then go and put on the first coat of varnish thinned down with 10 percent paint thinner. Over oily woods like teak, some people recommend going with 15 or 20 percent thinner to make sure the first coat soaks well into the wood and gets a good foothold. Let it dry overnight, then sand lightly with 220. Sweep the whole boat again, wipe, and put on your first full coat of varnish. Let it dry overnight and put on at least three more coats. Sand with 220 between each coat. Don't gasp. We have more varnish on *Warm Rain* than the rest of the boats on the west coast combined, and we can do a complete sanding and varnishing in about four hours. But then we're a good team—Candace works and I read the directions.

Interlux, the paint people, have compiled a list of do's and don'ts that you should consider. The stuff in parentheses is my humble contribution.

a) Don't use varnish out of its large original can, but pour only what you'll need into a small clean container. (That way when you kick the thing over you'll still have a little left.)

b) Don't use varnish that has sat open in a can for some time. It probably has picked up dust. Strain it before you use it.

c) Use high density nylon stockings for straining. (Make sure your lady has stepped out of them first.) Do this with new cans of varnish as well as old ones, parts of the the contents of which may have gummed up. (May as well strain new varnish too. What the hell.)

d) Don't stir or shake varnish. It will cause air bubbles which will be trapped in the varnish forever. (Pretty dramatic stuff.)

e) Use only good quality varnish brushes. The pros use short bristled, natural hair ones. A short bristle brush enables the applicator to spread the varnish quickly without flopping and allows more time to *tip off* before the varnish starts to set.

f) Be sure the bristles of the brush are completely wet before you start varnishing. Failure to do so will cause bubbles.

g) Never apply varnish in the full sun. It will be almost impossible to brush and may blister. (This is communist propaganda. We always apply varnish in the full sun because that's when it's the most fun and we haven't had a problem yet. Of course you'll need to use more varnish so it doesn't dry before you get a chance to spread it, which is great because it comes out like a sheet of glass.)

h) Reserve the varnish brush for varnishing only. (Amen to that, Brother.)

i) Don't varnish something in a cool shaded area, then move it into the sun to dry, or bubbles may form because of the expansion of air in the pores of the wood caused by the heat of the sun.

j) Avoid varnishing on windy days, for not only will all sorts of crap (paraphrased) be blown onto the varnish, but the surface of the varnish may set too fast and a smooth coat will be hard to achieve.

And the Eleventh Commandment—which when not followed, sends Candace into a (for once) justifiable tizzy in which she screams her red head off and waves her skinny arms around—tells you to clean your varnish brush *thoroughly* after each day's use. Thoroughly means with paint thinner first, then with soap and warm water. Then hang it up to dry or at least lay it flat. Leaving the brush in thinners overnight is a bad idea even if you hang it in the thinners like the pros recommend, for you are no pro, and you might decide to do something else tomorrow, or the weather may decide for you, or your dog may stop a truck, or it may kick the thinners over, or a war may break out, and by the time you've pieced your life together again, your brush will have gone dead dry. So be a good boy;

The best paint or varnish bucket is the disposable paper kind that fits into a nifty little metal bracket. The bucket can be heaved after each day's use, obviating cleaning and avoiding the chance of old dried stuff getting into next day's varnish.

wash it and rinse it and lay it flat. We don't want Candace angry. Do we?

Re-varnishing

If the old varnish is dull but solid—no peeling, no dark spots, no milky areas—then just get out your 220 and sand lightly and sweep and wipe and var-nish as above. If you have bad spots—which you probably will along seams which tend to swell and move—then scrape the ruined varnish off (don't try to sand it for it will take forever), and feather in the edges, *to perfection*, with sandpaper. Be careful not to hollow out the bare wood or you'll have a dimple forever. Take it from one who has them. Unfortunately, if you have left the bad spot bad too long, then the wood will have darkened. You can

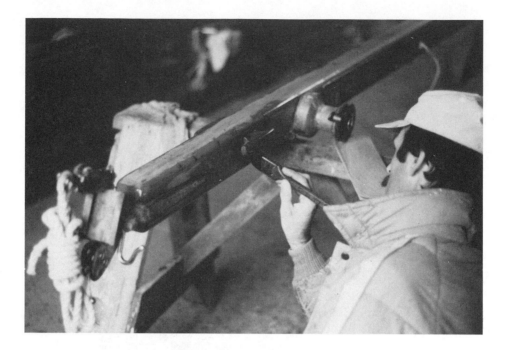

Sand between coats with 200 grit. Use lots of varnish in and around joints to prevent cracking. Above all, enjoy yourself; varnishing can be one of the most rewarding tasks aboard.

try to bleach it out with oxalic acid, which you can buy in a hardware store, but if that doesn't work, you'll just have to sand it and live with the dimple.

To use the oxalic acid, dissolve the crystals in warm water, until it will not dissolve any more crystals. Apply the solution outdoors in the sun until the desired bleached effect is reached. Once attained, you'll have to neutralize the stuff, or it can result in a complete breakdown of the varnish you put over it. To neutralize the oxalic acid, use a solution of soda ash and water. Soda ash is also obtainable from most hardware stores. Once the neutralizer is dry, you will see that the grain has been raised somewhat. Sand it smooth with 80 grit.

Once you have brought the darkened wood up to snuff, put on a thinned primercoat. Don't forget you're dealing with raw wood. Put at least three coats on the spots before you go and put a full coat on the whole boat, otherwise the bad spots will be bad spots every year.

Stripping

If the varnish has been let go for some time, and you judge attempts at patch repair futile, then by all means strip the whole thing off and start again. The chemical varnish stripper and a scraper is the simplest team to use. *But* you must use the stripper with caution aboard a boat, for there will be painted wood or gelcoat everywhere, and if you spill the stripper or inadvertently brush it onto a painted or gelcoated surface, or if you scrape the thick gummy layers of dissolved varnish onto a painted or gelcoated surface and just let it sit there, you can cause a lot of damage.

If you are going to strip, it might behoove you to tape off all surrounding areas with masking tape, and cover any areas that might be endangered with a few layers of newspaper or one layer of cardboard.

No matter what you do, pick up the dissolved curls of varnish right away, and have a bucket of water and a rag handy to wash off areas that have gotten affected.

A few pointers:

a) Wear rubber gloves. The stuff burns skin like crazy.

b) Don't be skimpy with the application of the remover. Use a thick coat.

c) Blunt the edges of any scrapers or putty knives you may use or you may gouge the wood.

d) Start scraping as soon as the finish starts to crinkle. Don't let it dry on the piece.

e) Bronze wool is often the best to use with the remover in the last stages. In addition, a wood dowel cut on 45 degrees is excellent to use in corners or near edges where the point of a metal may cause damage.

f) After you think you have removed all the old finish, wipe the piece down with a rag soaked in lacquer thinner. Wipe only in one direction, turn the rag over and wipe again. Unfold and wipe again. This will not only remove any residue or surface barrier agent, but will assist in removing any silicones present.

g) Once you've done that, sand lightly with 80 grit and treat it as new wood.

A couple of last notes on varnishing. The whole process becomes a chore only if done with such irregularity that major repairs are constantly necessary. If you touch up small damages when you spot them you will prevent them from becoming big ones. And no matter how lazy you are and how unrewarding it seems, *do* repair all small damages and cracks in the fall, or they'll get ten times worse

through the winter. If you do varnish, prepare to have a good winter cover over the boat, one that keeps all water off all varnished areas. Nothing does more damage to varnish than water that enters small cracks.

If you have never varnished before, try it. Most modern boats have so little wood trim that such minor varnishing will be fun, and the results a joy to behold.

Oiling

As I mentioned earlier, this is definitely a second-best system for preserving exterior teak, and—with the exception of some of the polymerized oils which produces a harder, more durable surface—next to useless for exterior anything else. But it seems to be the most popular method among sailors, so we might as well talk about it.

New wood should be sanded with 80 grit, then 100 grit to achieve a fine finish. Sweep all areas of the boat totally clean and wipe areas to be oiled with a good tack cloth to get out all the sawdust. If the sawdust remains in the grains, it will turn black upon the application of the oil.

Cut the first coat drastically with mineral spirits 20 to 50 percent—depending on the product—to have it absorb well into the wood, and act as a firm base for following coats. Let it dry completely, then apply the first full coat. There are two different schools of thought on oil application, one advocating the use of a cloth, the other a brush. The cloth people say they use less oil since they don't leave excess oil on the wood which will just have to be wiped off later. This has to be done with brush application. They also claim that they effectively *rub* the oil into the wood.

The brush people say their system is better for the very reason that it allows the extra oil the brush leaves to soak deep into the wood. So take your pick. If you do brush on the oil you will have to remove all excess by wiping vigorously with a cloth—turning the cloth frequently *before* the oil becomes tacky. If tackiness persists, simply wet the surface with more oil and wipe immediately. Allow each coat to dry overnight and then buff lightly using very fine brass wool.

If you get small damage spots, use the bronze wool to clear them up, then re-oil.

1. Choosing an oil

There are so many oils available that one really is hard pressed to choose, so let us just differentiate between two basic types: those using linseed oil as a base, and those using Tung oil.

The traditional base is linseed oil, and it is a good wood preservative, and has the advantage of being much less expensive than Tung oil. Most linseed oil products have had resins and driers added to make them quicker drying and more durable, but unfortunately some of the resins tend to turn dull and dark in time.

Tung oil is very fine stuff, in that it does not turn into a dull dark finish but will retain its clarity even though it contains UV filters and anti-mildew retardants. Make sure you get only oils marked for marine or at least exterior use, otherwise they will not contain either of the above, and thus offer the wood very little protection. Pure Tung oil finishes provide a tough, hard surface that is said to be absolutely waterproof and impervious to dust, alcohol, diesel fuel, as well as fruit and vegetable acids—but not Italian salami. A small company called Sutherland Welles makes a good marine grade Tung oil that is highly recommended by many users, and the only hitch is that it costs $70 a gallon.

An oil sealer will not last or protect the wood as well as varnish but it is a lot less hassle to apply.

Notes

14

Painting

Okay, let's lean on the manuals again to see what to do and what not to do.

Basic Application

Trying to describe how to brush on paint is like trying to tell you how to stroke a woman's body. You have to *feel* it in your fingers and your heart; otherwise you might as well forget the whole thing. But to be blunt and to the point, probably the most essential requirement is that the paint be spread evenly as quickly as possible to a uniform film thickness. One of the most common mistakes is to apply the paint too thickly—particularly on horizontal surfaces. If this is done, problems which can occur are incomplete drying and consequent wrinkling, solvent entrapment and resultant blistering, and sagging or running of paint on verticals. Don't try to hide things by applying too much paint in one coat. In most instances two relatively thin coats are much better than one heavy coat. On the other hand, very thin paint coats are also a no-no because you'll get uneven flow and uneven gloss and brush marks.

Weather

Try to pick a shirtsleeve day with no threat of rain. Try not to paint on a hot day under the direct rays of the sun—brushing will be harder and you might get blistering to boot. Pick a day with little wind or the wind will blow dust and flies and leaves and feathers all over your new paint, as well as cause the paint to set up so quickly that it cannot spread evenly. The perfect day may be hard to come by, but if you do get it, you're also likely get the best paint job with the least effort.

Surface Preparation

Nowhere does the saying "You can't make a silk purse out of a sow's ear" apply more than here. How well you prepare the surface will determine how well your masterpiece will look. An uneven surface will not only *not* look more even when painted, but can often look *worse* when glossy paint is used, for then every imperfection will show twice as much in the reflections.

There are such an infinite number of products for painting, bedding, etc. that one has no excuse for using something that isn't ideal for the job. Take a little time and ask a few questions; it might save you a lot of labor and money in the end.

Obviously the surface must be dry and clean, but that is just the beginning. Certain surfaces require special prime coats or build-up coats prior to the final coating of enamel. Don't skimp on the primer. Normally they fill better, dry faster and sand much easier than the enamel. Sanding between every coat, whether primer or enamel is a must if you want a good finish. Pay attention to the grades of sandpaper recommended; if you don't, you may scratch the surface so badly that it'll show through the final coat.

Thinning

There are no enamels that go on perfectly under all weather conditions as they come in the can. The ability to modify the enamel to weather conditions of a particular day is one of the factors that often separate an Elmer from a professional. How intelligently you thin the paint will determine just how smoothly it will flow on, which in turn will determine just how well the brushmarks will be hidden, and just how mirror-like your finish will be.

There is no great mystery to thinning paint to suit the temperature. So long as you are aware of the need to do so, you are more than halfway there. The best thing to do is to leave yourself a bit of time before beginning and try a few brushstrokes on a disposable but very smooth surface—at least as smooth as your hull—to see just how well the paint is spreading and how well the brushstrokes are blending together.

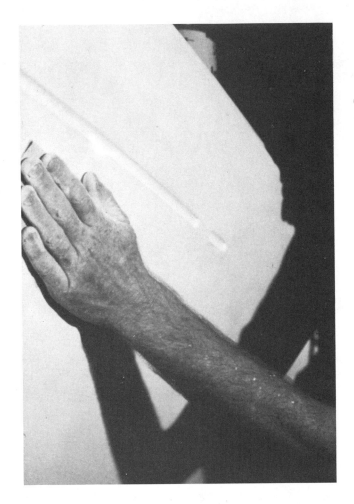

Every professional will tell you that surface preparation is 90 percent of the job in painting or repainting. All small flaws will show up much more once the shiny new paint is applied. So fill and sand and sand again.

Spraying

Most modern paints brush so well that there seems to be little point to indulge in spraying where the nerve-wracking possibility of equipment failure exists. Besides, it takes much more experience to achieve a flawless finish than with a brush. But if you insist on spraying, take a few precautions.

The modern polyurethanes are particularly finicky products requiring scrupulous cleanliness in lines, guns and pots. Air compressors must be adequate in size and in good order. Oil and moisture contamination in an air supply is an immediate disaster. Too often will you see a sprayer looking dejectedly at his spray gun and his drooling paint job, wondering out loud, "What the hell went wrong now?"

Presuming that the equipment is first class and in good condition, thought must be given to setting up the pot and atomizing pressures. For most enamels a pot pressure of 8-12 p.s.i. is adequate. Atomization pressures will usually fall into the 45-55 p.s.i. range, although some people apply paint at much higher atomization pressures, in order to get a very fine breakup of paint. Higher atomization should be avoided because of the large amount of overspray and consequent waste of paint.

In order to get better breakup, three things can be done.

a) If very low pressures are being used, the atomization pressure can be increased.

b) All enamels require thinning when being sprayed. Breakup of paint can be improved by adding additional thinner.

c) The pot pressure can be decreased so that more atomization air is available per unit of paint being atomized.

A viscosity cup is very useful to have. By using it properly, you will maintain exact viscosity regardless of temperature and application conditions. The paint of one manufacturer will not necessarily have the same viscosity from batch to batch. You cannot expect to thin enamel the same way, day in and day out and have the same results. Cold days will require more thinner than hot ones. As with brush application, the correct use of thinner will be the difference between a poor result and an excellent one.

Once the equipment is checked and the enamel thinned to approximate spray viscosity, it is best to test spray on a clean smooth surface that has approximately the same porosity as your boat. Tape whatever you will use onto a wall and give it a few shots of spray and look for proper breakup of the paint. Adjust the gun for fan size and paint flow. When it seems to be spraying well, spray a small surface area on the boat. Do the smallest independent area possible like the transom that way

you'll get a chance to get used to the whole procedure without buggering up the whole boat. First check to be sure the paint is laying out properly. If it's not, wipe the transom clean, make the necessary adjustments, and try again. *Do not start to paint the entire boat until you are sure the equipment and paint and you are all performing well.* If you get flustered, don't start blasting away in fury as if the spraygun were a flamethrower. Take it easy. Sit down and have a beer. You'll feel better and calmer and the whole world will be brighter.

When you have everything working well, continue onto the whole boat using smooth, even arm movements. Keep moving and spray light. It's always best to spray light for you can easily go back and give it another shot, whereas it's a true sonovabitch to have to stop and wipe off a run. When you have finished a job you are happy with, write down the important facts, like type of paint, temperature, amount of solvent, pressure settings etc. so you'll have some terms of reference the next time you paint.

Finally—although perhaps it should have been firstly—be sure to use the correct safety equipment. Solvents, by way of evaporation, and the paint particle itself when atomized as an aerosol, represent serious potential health hazards. Each product has its own warning statement that should be read and understood thoroughly. It's always nice to know exactly what you're dying of.

When two-part epoxies or polyurethane paints are being used, it is particularly important to use proper breathing apparatus. Both of the above products, if used improperly, can cause irreversible death.

A good spray finish requires proper materials, an experienced, *logical* applicator and professional equipment. When you can bring these together you will get fine results. If any of the above is lacking you better just get yourself a brush and start stroking.

Previously Painted Surfaces
(For Conventional Enamels)

If the existing paint is in sound condition but is beginning to show wear due to loss of gloss, chalking or color fading, it is time to apply fresh paint. On a wooden boat, this type of condition will usually be noticeable after one season's use.

To refurbish, all that will be required is a good sanding of the old paint with 120 sandpaper followed by two coats of enamel. Sand between coats with 220 grit. The Concordia yard, as well as most old painters, recommend two coats of enamel, but if the coat beneath is truly in good condition so that no parts will have to have been sanded bare and retouched with primer, and if you really are going to paint every year anyway, you'll probably get by with just one coat. If, however, you do have primer spots, then you'll either have to cover each spot with a coat of enamel before the final coat, or surrender to the notion of two full coats.

If the hull is scratched, or just not as smooth as you would like, don't try to use the enamel as build-up coats over the blemishes. As I mentioned before, enamels neither build fast, nor dry fast, nor sand well. Use an undercoat that excels in all the above things. Allow to set overnight, then sand with 120 grit sandpaper.

If the hull has deeper blemishes than just a scratch, use a trowel cement instead of trying to fill in with nine thousand coats of undercoat. If you are using trowel cement it's best to apply a coat of undercoat over the old paint after it has been well sanded, for then all the bad spots, including rough wood grain, will show up for you to repair now. If you don't use the undercoat, the bad spots might not show up until after you have laid on the first coat of enamel.

So do the undercoat first, then apply trowel cement, then sand with 120, then apply two coats of enamel. You can skip the second coat if you're willing to spot-paint with enamel over the patches of trowel cement, and then sand with 220 before you apply a complete coat. If you don't spot-paint over the trowel cement, you might get a thing called "flashing," which is not what you think it is, but simply a duller sheen over the spots in the final coat.

A word of caution about painting over old paints. Some paints are rather antisocial and don't mix at all well with previous coats of paint. Vinyl, epoxy and two-part polyurethane are among the rudest of them all. If you are about to use these over an old coat of paint, check with the paint dealer first. If you get a shrugged shoulder, keep investigating because some of the solvents of the above three can often dissolve the old coat of paint below them, lifting and bubbling the whole finish. If you think your paint looked bad before, just wait until your whole boat turns into a warty toad.

Bare Fiberglass Boats

I'm not sure why anyone would bother painting a fiberglass boat with enamel, when the new two-part polyurethanes are now available for brush and roller painting. These paints—Awlgrip by Grow and Interthane by Interlux—are infinitely tougher, hold their gloss much better and look a hell of a lot glossier to start with than enamel. Sure their application is a lot more demanding in money, time and gray matter, but once done, you can have a few years' respite, for the stuff stands up better than even gelcoat.

But if you insist on using dull old, paint-again-soon enamel, here is what you do.

First, no matter how old your boat, assume that it still has mold-release wax on it, and if not, you'll probably have waxed it a few times yourself. In any case, paint won't stick to wax, so get if off with a fiberglass solvent wash. Keep the rag good and wet and turn it often, then wipe with a clean dry rag.

Gelcoat is smooth and slick and not very porous. Paint does not stick well to this type of surface, so you'll have to either roughen the surface by using 100 or 150 grit sandpaper until the gloss of the gelcoat is removed—to establish a good foothold for the paint—or use a special primer which will soften the gelcoat slightly and at the same time chemically unite with it. If you use the primer you won't have to sand.

The no-sanding system is said to be the superior system that supports better adhesion. Interlux conducted some tests using both systems and after three years of immersion found the primed, non-sanded panels standing up better than the sanded ones.

1. No sanding
a) Wipe with solvent.
b) Apply full thin coat of fiberglass primer. Don't spray; don't sand.
c) Let set but not too long. Most primers need to be painted over within a specified time frame, e.g., no less than two hours, but no more than three. Put on first coat of enamel. Let set overnight.
d) Sand with 220 or finer paper. If bits of the primer stick through, sand those smooth too.
e) Wipe off sanding residue with thinner.
f) Apply second coat of enamel.

2. Sanding
Same, except you'll sand the gelcoat with 100 or 150 grit paper. If you have deep scratches, you might need three coats, in which case you should wet-sand between coats. If you do wet-sand, you'll have a coat of muck left when you're done. This won't wipe off with a dry rag like dry dust would—you'll have to hose it off and give it some help with a rag.

Bare Wood Boats

From the paint maker's point of view, three different types of wood exist. One includes woods such as mahogany, whose deep short grains have to be filled before a true yachty paint surface can be achieved.

Another type is a flat soft-grained wood like fir, whose soft summer grain must be stabilized by applying a good sealer directly to the wood. This is done to stop the soft grain from absorbing the final coats at a greater rate than the harder winter grain will. The sealer should be applied until the soft, lighter, summer grain produces a glossy surface. Usually at least two coats will be required. When you see a gloss, that means that the soft grain is saturated with sealer and the wood is ready for finishing.

The third group is made up of the greaseballs like cedar and teak, that have so much surface oil that the paint will hardly stick to them. These will have to be wiped down with a rag, rich in a powerful oil-less thinner like acetone, to dissolve and remove the surface oils prior to painting.

1. Short grain
a) Woods like mahogany should be sanded with 80 grit.
b) Apply one coat of a full-bodied primer or "sanding surfacer". Allow to dry overnight.
c) Sand with 120 grit to as thin a film as possible *without* breaking through to the wood. Properly sanded, the paint film will be translucent in many areas. Remember the purpose of the sanding surfacer is to fill up the deep grains in the wood. There is no purpose to building up a thick coat of the stuff.
d) Apply another coat of sanding surfacer and sand. Be sure the surface is clean after sanding and before applying surfacer. The best way to clean the surface is to wipe it with a clean cloth

dampened with thinner.

e) Surfacer should be applied and sanded until all the small grain marks vanish, and the surfacer surface appears as one smooth coat. As mentioned a hundred times before, it's much easier to sand down these primers than to try and fill the grain with enamel, and try to sand that down.

f) Again, wipe the surface clean and apply first coat of enamel. Allow to set overnight.

g) Sand with 220. Rewipe to remove dust.

h) Apply last coat of enamel.

2. Paste wood filler

As with most things to do with boats, there are alternate methods. A paste wood filler can be used instead of the surfacer. Use of the wood filler eliminates sanding. Most paste wood fillers are made to be applied with a putty knife, thus have to be reduced with thinners to the consistency of thick paint to be used on a large surface like a hull.

Brush the reduced stuff onto the bare wood. Then wipe with a rag *across the grain* to remove any excess material. Continue wiping until the grain of the wood is no longer streaky or smudgy looking. Any clean natural fiber material can work as a wiper. No, Elmer, don't use corn husks. No.

By thorough and even wiping you should be able to achieve a uniformly smooth surface ready for painting.

3. Trowel cement

If you do the first route, using the sanding surfacer, you might notice after the first coat of it has been put on, that what you previously thought to be a perfectly smooth wood hull now shows patches of rough grain structure, or small dents, or surface scratches. If you want to avoid putting on another full coat of sanding surfacer, you can just go over these areas with trowling cement.

Troweling cements usually are of two types: a quick drying one—dries in an hour, ready for sanding—and regular trowel cement, which needs to set up overnight. The first has the obvious advantage of not delaying painting for a whole day, but it has a disadvantage which it shares with most quick drying products, in that it has a tendency to shrink and crack. The regular slow drying one will shrink only an imperceptible amount. On very shallow fills, or where a rough grain is being leveled, I think it would be all right to use the quick dryer and get the damned thing over with. If however, you are talking about a groove of $\frac{1}{16}$ of an inch or deeper, then use the regular stuff or you'll still have a dip after the quick-dry stuff quick-dries.

Never use either of these trowel cements on bare wood. The wood must always be primed. Trowel cements can be used at any step of painting *except* as the very first coat and the one-before-the-last coat. If it's used just before the last coat, it will soak up too much paint and flash through.

4. Seam Compounds

These will be required on flush planked boats. They should *never* be applied directly to fresh wood, but should be preceded by a primer filler coat. The exception to this is of course, the polysulfide compounds which must *always* be applied to very clean, very bare wood—except if polysulfide is to be used on teak, for then the oil in the teak must first be isolated from the polysulfide by a teak sealer. When polysulfide is used to fill the seam of a hull, it should be gunned into the seam and drawn flat with a putty knife.

Brushing

One of the keys to how good your paint job will turn out is just how well the paint flows onto the surface. The two factors controlling that are the quality of your brush and the consistency of your paint. Everyone always talks about how you should have exotic bristles for varnish to get a glass-like finish, all the while ignoring the subject of brushes for paint, as if any old white-wash broom or coarse-as-pigs-hair bristle would do. It won't. For a good finish, get a natural bristle brush—about three inches wide if you are painting the whole hull—and make sure it has a decent thickness so it will carry a nice amount of paint, giving you a good-sized patch to work on at a time. If the ends of the bristles are split, you will get an even finer finish.

When joining a new patch to one you've just finished, start the brush from the new patch and fair toward and into the previous one. Finish the stroke by lifting the brush smoothly out of it. Don't start fairing by jabbing the brush into the older patch. It could have begun to set and then your jab marks are sure to show.

To get a good overall finish, my good friend Spencer Smith, who has been around wood boats all his life, suggests using a light oil called *Penetrol* mixed in with the enamel. This, in minimal quantities, will help the paint flow together much more smoothly. He said that, whereas he always had brushmarks no matter how much care he used, once the *Penetrol* was added, the paint would flow and fill in the brushmarks and form a glass-like finish.

Two-Part Polyurethanes

As of the past few years, a new product has become known to the world of boat painting to the delight of all, especially to owners of fiberglass boats whose topsides have been badly marred by years of salt and sun and smashing into wharves. The new paints, unlike the dear old enamels, finish to an incredibly smooth surface whose shine far surpasses even that of gelcoat. And best of all, the surface will last for years with virtually no maintenance, except regular rinsing down with fresh water and timely washings with a mild

detergent.

Just how tough is this paint, you ask. Well, according to this morning's *New York Times*, the U.S. Army is spending millions of dollars to repaint all its vehicles with it, for polyurethane fulfills "a need for a new paint that would resist chemical warfare agents better than ordinary enamel paint." How is that for a bonus? Not only will you not have to wax your boat like you did previously with your gelcoat, but if you find yourself in the middle of a chemical war, you can be sure your hull will come out unscathed. Of course you'll be crumpled up like a dishrag, deader than a doornail, but my gosh is your boat ever gonna shine!

Anyway, before you get so excited you embarrass yourself, let me give you the bad news. The stuff takes nerve-wracking meticulousness to apply, and it's dangerous to use if sprayed. So, if you're a nervous gadfly, whose attention span has not yet conquered the thirty-second T.V. commercial, then by all means just keep thumbing through the book, and find a nice long page number to lose yourself in.

For all you others who thrive on suffering, lean back in your chairs—I'm about to show you a real good time.

To thrill you from the beginning, let me say that if you spray the stuff and inhale it…well…you die.

If you don't die but you make a mistake and cause runs or drips, the only way to correct them is to sand them out with very fine paper and buffing—see *Correcting Runs*—in which case, "Due to the change in the integrity of the paint film which may take place as a result of this process, the buffed area may not maintain the same level of gloss as long as the remainder of the boat." Or in plain English: It'll soon look like shit.

There is hope however. Whereas only a few years ago this stuff had to be applied by no method other than spraying, the addition of new brushing liquids will allow almost anyone with a bountiful supply of patience and a modest amount of com-

The two-part polyurethane paints give a virtually maintenance-free finish that is glossier than gelcoat. They can be applied with brush and roller. All you have to have is the patience of a saint while you prepare the surface.

mon sense to achieve a beautiful mirror-like finish, *providing* that the hull has been prepared with the meticulousness of a brain surgeon.

The two-part polypaints can be applied over bare fiberglass, aluminum, wood or steel, as well as surfaces previously painted with two-part polyurethane.

For boats already painted with a conventional enamel, there are primers available to cover any surface imperfections or hairline cracks, and to act as direct *conversion* coatings prior to the application of the polyurethanes. This conversion coating is a must, for the two-part polyurethanes contain some very aggressive solvents, which can soften or lift old coats of paints other than epoxy, gelcoat, or catalyzed polyurethanes.

1. A Warning

As mentioned before, these paints are very dangerous if sprayed, for a highly toxic substance called hexamethyline is in the stuff, which if inhaled during spraying can cause very terrible respiratory disorders. The simple dustmasks are useless, so much so that the only thing the U.S. Health people actually approve is a thing called a " positive pressure mask," which means that you need to use *outside air* or air uncontaminated by the spray. In other words, a full-fledged pressurized oxygen system, like you use for diving or high altitude soaring, one where the pressure of the air will keep out the surrounding air, which is contaminated by the atomized hexamethyline. So don't fool around!!

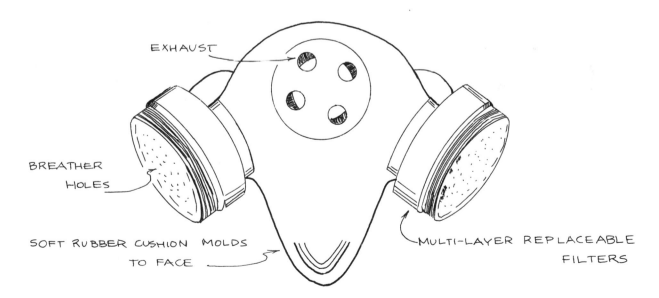

This is not *a sophisticated jockstrap. It's a very effective mask that you should wear when spray painting or sanding.*

The best solution of course is not to spray the stuff, for although it is a much faster way of applying paint than using a roller or a brush, the time you save just simply isn't worth it if you spend the time you saved lying in an iron lung.

So roll and brush it on, but even then use a mask in case you begin to roll too fast—which you should never do if you want a good paint job—and the small particles of paint start to fly around. Even if you're just rolling and brushing, do cover up all your skin, for as I said before, two-part poly is highly resistant to chemicals, and that includes solvents, and once it kicks off (sets) on your skin, you'll have one hell of a time getting if off. Wear good thick rubber gloves, and tape around your shirtcuffs, just to be sure. Do wear goggles. If you spray, wear a spacesuit.

If after all that, you still get some two-part poly on your skin, whatever you do, *don't try to wash it off with soap and water*. Water kicks off (causes to set) two-part polyurethane and how you'll get it off once it is set is beyond me. If you do get some on your skin, wipe it off with a rag wet with solvent.

2. Surface preparations
Remember that surface preparation is 90% of the job. Polyurethanes require a flawless surface, as their ultra high gloss will *highlight, not conceal* underlying imperfections, to the extent where a gnat's shorthair when painted with poly can come out looking like a boa constrictor.

3. Bare fiberglass (gelcoat in good condition)
If the gelcoat is in sound condition without scratches or gouges or crazing, requiring only sanding but not filling to bring it to a paintable condition, then here is what you do.
a) Wash down hull with a solvent wash to remove all waxes, silicones and grease.
b) Sand the whole hull with 100 to 150 grit production paper, depending on the condition of the gelcoat. If one area is more deeply chalked than another then this area will suck the paint in more and give you an uneven finish. So sand until the hull seems of even texture.

Great care should be used when sanding gelcoat. Too coarse sandpaper can produce scratch marks that may show through the finished coat. A good anchor pattern is important for good adhesion, but it must not be so good as not to be obliterated by the final coats. The choice of sandpaper will depend on how hard the gelcoat is.
c) After sanding, brush off the whole hull with a rattail brush and then, just before you paint, wipe down the whole hull with a solvent wash to remove all the fine residue, including whatever settled on the hull since sanding.
d) If the polyurethane, as it is being applied, begins to *crater* that means the gelcoat is too porous. To test to see if the gelcoat is too porous, just apply any paint to a small area of the gelcoat and check for cratering, then wipe the surface clean with the appropriate solvent before the paint dries.
   If cratering is present, you will have to apply a prep coat of epoxy primer.
   Sometimes porosity can be confused with an unclean surface. Wax residue from an improperly cleaned or sanded gelcoat will cause *fish eyes* which resemble gelcoat porosity.

4. Bare fiberglass (gelcoat in poor condition)
If the gelcoat has scratches or crazing or other atrocities, you'll have to use a surfacer to fill them in.
a) Wash hull with solvent. Don't argue.
b) Using a three-inch putty knife with a soft flexible blade, fill all dents with an epoxy surfacing or fairing compound. Let it dry thoroughly before you go on.
c) Sand the repaired areas smooth with paper no coarser than 80 grit, then sand the whole hull down with 100 to 150 grit.

d) First, brush off the whole hull, then wipe off the entire surface using the thinner that is used in the epoxy primer you will be next applying.

e) Apply one coat of epoxy primer. Let set completely, then sand with 120 grit.

Usually only one coat of the epoxy primer will be needed, but if a second coat is warranted, repeat steps d) and e) before you begin to paint on your two-part polyurethane.

5. Bare wood hulls

To have a clean, dry, well-seasoned wood hull before applying paint is an important point no matter what paint you use, but very much *more* vital when you are using two-part poly.

You should not attempt to paint unseasoned wood; if you do, you'll get blistering and severe paint failures.

a) With an epoxy surfacing and fairing compound, fill any gouges and holes. Once dry, sand these areas smooth with 80 grit.

b) Sand the whole hull with 80 grit.

c) Brush, then wipe area with a clean cloth dampened with a thinner appropriate for the two-part poly-primer you'll be using in the next step.

d) Apply a full coat of two-part polyurethane primer and allow to dry overnight.

e) Sand with 120 grit. As with sanding a primed wood hull for regular enamel, you should sand the primer here to as thin a film as possible without breaking through to the bare wood. When properly applied, the paint film should be translucent in many areas. Remember you're trying to fill up the grain in the wood, not build a bulletproof coating over it.

f) Repeat steps d) and e). Be sure the surface is clean after sanding and before applying the surfacer, by wiping down as above.

g) Depending on how thorough a job has been done, it may be necessary to apply a third coat of primer—repeat steps d) and e)—until the

small grain marks are no longer visible.

h) Again wipe the surface as clean as possible, before putting on the first coat of the two-part poly enamel.

6. Previously painted surfaces

As I said before, because of the solvents in the two-part poly, you can't paint it directly over conventional enamels. So you need to apply a *conversion* coat over the old stuff, before the two-part poly is applied. The conversion coat has to have very specific characteristics, in that it cannot have solvents strong enough to attack the old coat of paint, yet it must be stable enough to withstand the solvents in the two-part poly which will be coming over it.

a) Make sure surface is free of moisture.

b) Sand entire surface with 120 grit.

c) Brush, then wipe with clean cloth and thinner.

d) Apply full coat of conversion coat—with Interthane it's called Polythane—and allow to dry overnight.

e) Sand conversion coat with 180 grit paper. Be extremely careful not to break through the conversion coat.

f) Wipe clean with cloth and brushing liquid, then allow to cure completely—preferably three days—before applying two-part polyurethane enamel.

If the old enamel surface is in poor condition, then an appropriate primer—check with your paint dealer—should be used as a conversion coat, and sanded and reapplied as often as necessary. When you are sanding, remember not to sand through this coat either, or there is a very good chance the original enamel will lift in the spots where the conversion coat had been sanded through. If you do break through, retouch these areas.

A last note on preparation. Be sure you use only the proper primers and surface preparations, ones that are compatible with the two-part polyurethanes, or you'll be guaranteed that the whole thing

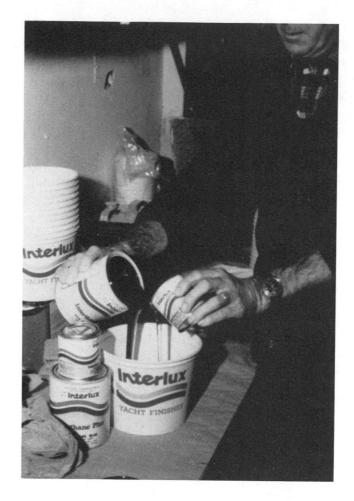

The two-part poly must be mixed in exact proportions to get a proper finish. If you mix it wrong, the thing will never dry and your hull will just become the world's largest flypaper.

will fail and peel and lift and God knows what else.

Applying Two-part Polyurethanes

1. Mixing
This is a most important part of the process, for not only will you have to mix the two parts of the paint—enamel with reactor—but you'll then have to add the appropriate type and amount of solvent. The amount will depend on whether you are spraying or brushing or rolling. So question the dealer thoroughly and read the labels thoroughly and be exact with what you do. I told you that this stuff was only for those who like to suffer.

2. General hints

Two-part polyurethanes are moisture sensitive products that cure by chemical reaction, which is triggered and accelerated by temperature and humidity. So apply it on a good, dry, calm day to get best results. Because the stuff will show any imperfections, it's a good idea to wet down the ground around the boat to keep down the dust. Do this wetting down *before* the final wipe down, for the wetting itself can raise some dust. Jeeezus what a production! I get worn out just writing about it.

Anyway, the best temperature for painting is between 50 and 80 degrees Fahrenheit. Pot life expectancy, once you mix, is only eight hours, so mix only what you'll use that day.

It's safe to apply a second coat of the two-part poly, without sanding in between, up to forty-eight hours after the previous application. However, the pros do sand in between coats for the best results. If you are wet-sanding, remember you'll have to wash off all the scummy stuff with lots of water and a rag, then let dry, then wipe with cloth and thinner.

3. Spraying

If you are in doubt as to the safety precautions you have to take when spraying two-part polyurethane, read the *Warning* in the beginning of this section. Then read over the general comments under the heading *Spraying* in the section on *Conventional Enamels* and then read the following.

a) Apply a mist or tack coat and allow to tack up for ten to fifteen minutes, or until the coating passes the thumbprint test. When the thumb can be pressed—don't try to play little Dutch boy; press gently—on the paint film, leaving a print on the coating but *not* paint on the thumb, then it has tacked up sufficiently.

b) Apply a full-flow coat over the tack coat. Using this procedure, one coat may be satisfactory depending on the spray technique used and the surface preparation. If a second coat is required:

c) Wet-sand first coat after letting it dry overnight, with 340 grit—or finer—wet-and-dry paper, to remove any surface imperfections such as dust and fruitfly footprints. Be sure all sanding residue is removed by flushing the surface with fresh water.

d) Apply second coat of two-part poly.

Interlux makes some specific recommendations regarding pressures and equipment used, as follows:

Manufacturer: De Vilbiss, or comparable equipment.

Equipment: FX nozzle and needle, 704 air cap (or equivalent .003 nozzle and needle).

Pot pressure: 10-12 lbs.

Atomization pressure: 40-50 lbs.

Suggested viscosity spray for Spray Application: 19-21 seconds, No. 2 Zahn Cup, or 13-14 seconds, No. 30-16393 Sears Cup.

Specifications: Wt/gal. reduced for spray application, 10.5 lbs.

Flash point: 74 degrees F.

Cure time: Touch-dry - 1 hour
Hard-dry - 10 hours
Overcoat - Overnight.

4. Brushing

a) Apply in very thin coats to prevent sags.

b) Use quick, even strokes and always maintain a wet edge. Never cut back into the paint once it has begun to set up.

c) "Gang painting" is recommended for boats over 30 feet to maintain a wet edge and avoid lap marks.

d) After the previous coat has been allowed to dry overnight, wet-sand with 340 or finer, wet-and-dry paper. Flush with water to clean all residue.

e) Make sure all brushes and equipment are cleaned every night. Use only a very high quality, short natural bristle brush, such as a pure Chinese bristle brush.

If you brush, touch-dry will take two hours and hard-dry about ten.

5. Foam roller

For a very even coat that goes on rather faster than the brush-only system, use "gang painting," with one person on the roller, and the other on the brush. Use the type of brush described before. As for a roller, use one that is guaranteed to withstand the solvents of two-part polyurethane, otherwise both the foam and the glue holding it to the roller may dissolve and, I tell you, Brother, you ain't seen a mess until you've seen a rotted apart roller stuck in bits and pieces all over a half-painted hull.

a) The guy—or guyess—on the roller should roll a thin coat in one direction with a minimum amount of overlapping. Do not load up the roller with paint; it should be free of excess paint to insure a thin coat.

b) Have the brushperson follow behind, "tipping off" or leveling any air bubbles. Be sure to always maintain a wet edge. Use one or two even strokes, brushing back in the direction of the previously tipped wet paint. Once you've smoothed the paint *don't* go cutting back into it, for it's a very quick drying paint and you'll just bugger it up.

c) After an overnight dry, wet-sand with 340 and flush with water as above.

d) Repeat steps a) and b).

Some of the lighter tints and whites may be rolled on *without* tipping off with a brush. You'll get a good finish but it will look a bit orange peely. If you have a friend left, you might as well have the thing tipped off. If you don't have a friend left, then maybe you should be out finding one instead of fooling around here, painting some dumb boat.

For troubleshooting polyurethanes look in the *Index*.

If I never have to write out the word 'polyurethane' again, it will be toooo soon.

"Gang painting" (sounds rude to me) is suggested for best results. The man on the roller applies the paint while the brushman comes behind him and tips off to get a glossy, non-orange-peely finish.

15

Patching Caulking Seams

On teak decks or caulked hatches, the caulking will eventually give way, if not everywhere at least in spots. It seems that no matter how well the original compound was placed, there appear weak spots where the wood may have moved or an airbubble burst or something. On *Warm Rain* we did the original seams with utmost care but still a few spots showed loose in the first three years, and since we repaired those, no new ones have appeared. In most decks these spots are easy to find for they remain wet long after the rest of the deck has dried. If left uncorrected, the spots are guaranteed to get bigger with frost, or even from deckshoes tugging the loose rubber.

Since the caulking is the first—and often only—line of defense that keeps water out of parts of the boat that are vulnerable to rot—in case of fiberglass boats the plywood or balsa core of the deck, in the case of wood boats the whole damned thing—one should repair the seam breaks as soon as they're discovered.

1. Cleaning out

First, get a very sharp knife—the kind with the removable blades which are narrow and sharper than hell would be best here—and cut a nice bevel in the caulking seam, a good two inches from each end of the suspected delaminated caulking. I say two inches past, just to be sure you get not only everything that's bad now, but even the parts that are *thinking* of being bad in the future. Now, take the knife and run it along right beside the wood, *but don't nick the wood*, on each side of the seam. If your hands are shaky or you don't trust yourself, then skip this step and go on to the next.

Now to scrape out the caulking. For hundreds of years shipwrights have used a variety of simple handmade tools. The tail of an old file can be heated and bent at a 90-degree angle and ground to sharpness along the edges to the shape of the seam, or an old good quality screwdriver can be thus sacrificed.

Whatever you use, bear down on the thing—you don't want it jumping out of the seam gouging a little trench in your deck. Push the blade down all the way to the bottom of the groove and pull toward yourself. Get every last bit out or you may as well forget the whole thing. If you find a few stubborn suckers sticking to the sides of the groove, take a square file and turn it on edge and run it smartly along the sides until there's nothing but bare wood. Leave no burrs or splintered wood.

Now, get yourself a vacuum cleaner strong enough to suck the chrome off a doorknob, and

Black stains next to the grooves in teak decks indicate a separated caulking seam.
Repair the seam before it gets worse and causes rot below it.

get every last bit of crap out of that groove. And I don't mean *maybe*. When that's done, get one of those cotton swabs-on-a-stick that you clean your ears with, and dip it into the primer that comes with the two-part polysulfide that you use to fill the seams.

2. Caulking

First let us not get into a discussion here as to what to use. *There is no choice!* Either you use two-part polysulfide or you might as well just ram a stick

of black licorice in there—it will be at least as useless as the other things you have in mind. So. Mix the hardener into the black goop with a nice slow motion—you don't want to go fast, because if you go fast you make air bubbles and the bubbles stay in and burst later and then you're back where you started from. So mix nice like a good boy.

Oh, I almost forgot: You best tape off the edges of your wood so this stuff doesn't run over onto

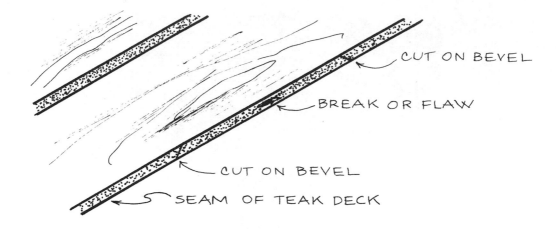

CUT ON BEVEL

BREAK OR FLAW

CUT ON BEVEL

SEAM OF TEAK DECK

PATCHING A CAULKED SEAM ON DECK OR HATCH

it. If it does, then you'll have to sand it off and if you sand it off, that little area will be a little deeper and a different color than the rest of the deck. If you say, "So what?" then I say, "You're right," because if you don't care, I sure don't; I mean after all, it's your deck.

Anyway, fill your empty cartridge, and cut only a modest hole in the tip of it—you don't want to re-create the last days of Pompeii, you just want a nice little flow of black goop. Fill the groove from the bottom up. Overfill a little and leave the excess there for sanding later. If you're not going to

sand—if it's taped off—leave a slight bit over the deck surface, then hold a putty knife almost horizontally and pull it along the filled seam with a slight downward pressure. This will allow a slight extrusion of material behind the blade, so a slight convex (sticks up) surface will be left. The convex will allow for minor shrinkage during curing. The stuff sets up pretty fast so get the masking tape off pronto. If you don't, then get your sharp knife and cut the excess along the edge of the tape and then pull the tape off.

There; good as new.

Notes

16

Care and Repair of Canvas Decks

Care

On old wooden boats, canvas decks lasted many years, and somehow I suspect that they would last a long time now, were they well kept up. They do require meticulous maintenance, that is true, but the amount of work involved is so minimal, that deterioration of a deck for lack of upkeep is inexcusable.

The key to canvas survival is protection and that protection can come only from the paint that covers it. First of all, do everything you can to keep the deck clear of bits of stones and sand that get tracked aboard from ashore. Nothing will abrade the paint faster than a nice sharp little stone being ground into the deck by your three-hundred pound lady friend doing pirouettes.

Paint over canvas cannot be let go like paint on some surfaces, because as soon as the first crack opens, rainwater will get into the canvas and stay there, and rotting of not only the canvas but also the wood below it, will begin. The argument that the canvas has been soaked with paint upon application, therefore offering protection to the canvas until infinity, simply doesn't seem to be true, so don't depend on it. "Giffy" the master seaman and surveyor left no doubts, saying that as soon

as a crack is spotted in the canvas, even a hairline crack, it should be fixed immediately before worse things happen.

Touch-Up

Dabbing a bit of paint onto the crack is a temporary solution at best, for the solid, and often thick, pieces of paint on both sides of the crack will keep moving independently of each other, and the crack will reopen in no time.

The thing to do is to get a bit of paint remover and a scraper with an old blade and do a proper job. First of all, *dull* the blade itself, then round the corners of the blade so it will not catch and tear the canvas. Then apply the paint remover, covering a good couple of inches on either side and either end of the crack, and get down to bare canvas. You are doing this to give the new paint a decent-sized surface to cling to, instead of some pathetic little crack. Next, lightly sand the area *outside* of the area you have just removed the paint from, to reduce the thickness of the paint there, so you can *fair in* the new paint gradually. Now,

Painted canvas decks can last a long time if well kept, like the top of this house, or...

...they can look like this if neglected. Keep the seams tight and well painted and the deck will last for many years.

paint with a good quality enamel.

If you have conentional enamel on the rest of your canvas, don't try to get fancy and use epoxy-type paints, for you'll just end up lifting all the old paint off with the powerful solvents in the new paint.

When repainting an old deck, you can't just add on paint indefinitely, for the thicker and older the paint, the more likely it is to crack. So you will have to strip the paint off occasionally. When you do, don't sand—it's too easy to tear up the canvas. Use the paint remover and scraper as described above. Take it easy with the blade—you can play *Three Musketeers* some other time.

Patching

If you get a tear in the canvas, the proper way to repair it is not by stapling the edges down and painting over them—that's next to useless. To repair a tear you'll have to make a proper patch.

First, cut out the torn part. This is best done using a very sharp knife and either a metal straight edge or a tin can. With the straight edge, you'd be cutting out either a square or a rectangle, and with the can you'd be cutting out a circle. The circle is perhaps the better solution, for you won't be leaving any corners which are always the weakest points, hence the most likely to tear. When cutting, be sure to cut with a very sharp blade. Never pull or tug at the canvas, and especially don't try

to pull out loose threads like you do with your socks, for you'll stretch the canvas, and it will be almost impossible to lay it flat again.

When the torn patch is cut out, lay it over the new piece of canvas and draw an outline for the new patch, *one inch larger* all the way around.

Next, lift up the edge of the canvas around the hole you have cut and run a piece of sandpaper over the *underside* of the canvas all around the hole. You are doing this to ready the old canvas for the patch, which you will be putting *under* the old canvas. If you put a patch with corners on top of the old stuff, the fine corners of the patch can come loose and turn upward. If you put the round patch over, you'll have a larger circle with more edge to be kicked up.

Make sure there is no moisture anywhere in the area before you place the patch.

Now, put paint on the outside inch of the patch, and over the entire bottom of the patch, then let it touch-dry. Then put a second coat over the one-inch perimeter of the patch, and also the sanded perimeter of the bottom of the old canvas, and slip the patch under the old canvas with the paint still wet. Fit it into place. No wrinkles please.

Now gently tap around the edges to get a good adhesion between the two canvasses, then dab paint onto and into the patch and let it dry. Add a couple of coats of paint over the whole thing, including the top perimeter of the hole where you sanded the old paint, to help it fair.

REPAIRING A SMALL TEAR IN CANVAS DECK-COVER

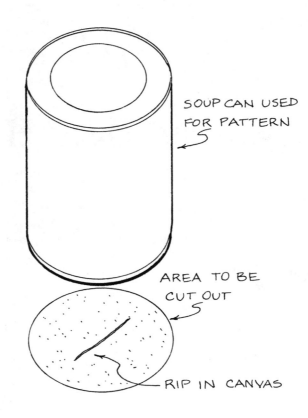

SOUP CAN USED
FOR PATTERN

AREA TO BE
CUT OUT

RIP IN CANVAS

NEW PATCH SLIPPED UNDER
OLD CANVAS

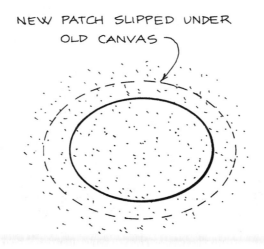

17

Rebedding Deck Hardware

It's safe to say that most leaks aboard start around hardware which carry enormous loads, loads that are trying to tear them out of the boat. If the boat was poorly built to start with, or if the skipper is among the more mentally disorganized, or—God have mercy—if the two manage to find each other, then hardware will be a-poppin' and a-flyin' faster than champagne corks on New Year's Eve.

Check the base of all your deck hardware for leaks at least twice a year, for although you may not be getting a leak inside the boat, you sure might be getting one into the core of your deck. On too many modern boats with complicated liners and insulation and wallpaper—you may laugh, Elmer, but I swear I've seen it lately—you never know just what the hell is really going on in the deck or the hull. So you have to get down on your hands and knees and scurry from block to cleat like a little mouse, and take with you a hunk of stainless wire. If you suspect a crack in the caulking under a piece of hardware, then scrape away at it with the wire, and if you scrape out some dirt, then pardner, you just went and found yourself a leak. Very seldom will there be a void in the caulking that doesn't go right through to the fastener, so you might as well assume that what you've found is indeed a true-blue, certified dripper.

Go below and take the nuts right off the piece of hardware and yank that critter out of the deck, and scrape off all the old goop from both the hardware and the deck. Wash everything down with acetone, then caulk the bejeeezus out of everything in sight; and I mean the base, the deck, the bolts, the hole—everything—with polysulfide. Caulk the bastard until you can't even see the pieces for the caulking, then put it back in place and slip on those nuts and crank them and squeeze them until the little suckers scream.

But, if you have some itty-bitty washers inside there, the size and bulk of a gnat's left titty, then you've just gone and gooped yourself all up for nothing, because that hardware's going to come loose as soon as a mosquito lands on it for a rest.

The prudent skipper will not be caught in this predicament, will he, Elmer? No. He wouldn't have bought a boat made for a Barbie Doll in the first place, and in the second place, he would have evaluated the strength of his washers *before* he spread all that goop and turned himself into human flypaper.

If the washers are undersized, then change them now and give yourself a fighting chance. When are they undersized? When they look like washers instead of backup plates. Ideally the best thing to have

PROPER BACK-UP PLATES FOR HARDWARE

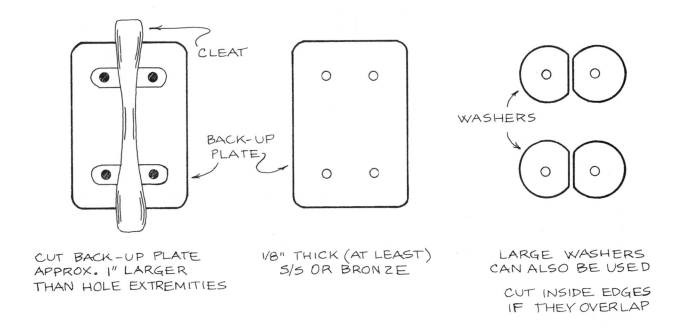

CLEAT

BACK-UP
PLATE

WASHERS

CUT BACK-UP PLATE
APPROX. 1" LARGER
THAN HOLE EXTREMITIES

1/8" THICK (AT LEAST)
S/S OR BRONZE

LARGE WASHERS
CAN ALSO BE USED

CUT INSIDE EDGES
IF THEY OVERLAP

under cleats and winches and windlasses and turning-blocks and chainplates are solid one-piece backup plates, that start at $\frac{1}{8}$ of an inch in thickness for small boats, and go up from there. Their size should be larger than the base of the hardware itself—as much as an inch larger all the way around, to distribute the load over as wide an area as possible. If you don't want to mess with having a special plate made, then that's too bad—at least I warned you. Second best is a set of washers of the above-mentioned thickness, washers that are as large as possible without overlapping each other. Actually it's better to get ones that would overlap, for then you can usually trim one side with a hacksaw to make them fit beside each other, while the uncut sides are out there still, spreading the load.

18

Care of Windlasses

Few things on a boat work as hard and get as much abuse *and* as little care and maintenance as a windlass. One of the most common abuses comes at anchoring. First, Elmer unloads the anchor over the side and lets out line after it until the line goes slack. Then as he stands there gazing into the water, totally uncertain whether he has actually just anchored or not, for something to do he throws a couple of loops of anchor line around the windlass. When he finally decides that he can't stand there all day looking like a fool he goes and cleats the line, but at the same time leaves the loops wrapped around the windlass. This is just plain abuse, for if any kind of blow comes up and the boat tugs at her line, the windlass will bear the brunt of every tug. Sure it's strong and built to take it, but imagine how much more wear it can thus undergo in a single night, compared to your smoothly hauling the anchor for two minutes a day.

Worse still is the ardent cruiser who uses all chain, and leaves the chain on the windlass overnight. In a blow, every jerky tug will be transmitted to the windlass. Don't do it. It's a windlass, not a shock absorber. Have a length of good anchor line handy with an eye spliced in it and a good D or harp shackle as well. Get one that has the pin that can't fall out even when unscrewed. When you've set the anchor, attach the shackle to the chain and let out both chain and line—about twenty feet is fine, although the more the better—and then cleat the line and let the chain go slack some more. The line will now act as the shock absorber, and not only will you save the windlass, but you'll also sleep a hell of a lot better, for the grinding sound of the chain won't be transmitted directly to your skull.

On boats that are sailed hard, windlasses get more than their share of salt spray. This salt should be rinsed off as often as possible, and the insides should be often flushed *and* greased to protect the gears and the bearings from the salt. They should be torn down and checked, cleaned and greased once a season *if* they are the types where very little water penetration to the inside is possible. But if they are of the older variety whose gears are exposed, then cleaning and greasing—not oiling, but greasing with good grease—should be done at least twice a year. Some of these you can actually grease without tearing down, by using a solvent-soaked rag on a stick to clean the gears through the opening, then dabs of grease on the stick to grease them. You don't need to worry about greasing each tooth separately—just place dabs here and there and pump the windlass a few times to have the grease spread to all the teeth.

Even though this windlass is normally under a fiberglass hatch, it still gets a good-ly amount of salt, so flush it often.

19

Fenders

It's ironic that something like fenders, which are supposed to offer a boat protection, can do so much damage. Now I'm no fool, not a big one anyway, yet through sheer lack of experience I did over one winter cause bad fender abrasion to *Warm Rain's* topsides. She was in a small marina next to the house and although she was protected well against the southeast where most of the bad weather blows from, she was a little open to the west from where the winds often build up after a storm, bringing with them a goodly swell. Whereas most of the people in the bay were aware of this, I being new to the area wasn't, and made no provisions to tie the boat across to another boat away from the dock. When the swells did come, she pitched and bucked for a day and a half—not violently, but just enough to grind the dirt on the fenders and the hull deep into the gelcoat. Dumb.

To a lesser scale, most boats suffer this fate, for there is always some movement, and the only way to avoid all abrasion is to cross-tie to another dock or another boat. Now granted this is a genuine pain if you happen to be using your boat frequently, but if it stays in the water over the winter when boat-using becomes sporadic at best, nil at worst, then there is really no problem, so tie the damned thing across.

For the summer months, do get a good system of fenders. Four is not too many for a thirty-foot boat. If you have only two, and one happens to deflate while you are absent, then you could suffer some bad abrasions on your hull from the dock. Don't skimp on fenders—get decent-sized ones, for the larger they are the more air they have in them, and the more air they have, the more give they have and the less likely they are to scratch the gelcoat.

Whatever fenders you get, keep them clean and keep the hull beneath them clean too, for then there will be nothing to be ground into the gelcoat. Don't use abrasives to wash the fenders, because abrasives leave deep scratches for the grit to lodge in.

Perhaps making little dresses out of terry toweling is a good solution, for it adds an extra cushion and makes for less friction than a rubber fender does.

If you have any swell where your boat is docked, you might be wise to hang the fenders horizontally from the side of the dock, instead of hanging them from the boat. Leave enough give in the line to let the fender *roll* up and down a bit with the movement of the boat. Rolling will reduce abrading. You do however have to make sure that the fender can't roll up enough to end up on the dock and be of no use at all.

Four hefty fenders are not overkill for any boat over thirty feet. If one deflates you'll still have lots of protection. A single healthy fender can do sweet zip on its own.

Two last points. First, never let your fenders dangle into the water. Barnacles can grow on them in no time, and if the fender ever rises up in a swell or blow, the barnacles will put a nifty gouge into your hull.

Second, most of the deep gouges occur as you come into the dock at an angle, either because of cross-winds or cross-currents or a short circuit in your mind. In these instances, the fenders amidships are totally helpless, and the topsides just aft of the stem take a beating. Two things can be done to avoid this. First, you can put a small rubber wheel on an axle on the corner of your dock. If you don't want to spend that much money—about $50—then just get a molded rubber corner piece for the same spot. Either of the above will eliminate the most gruesome gouging weapon. Second, some castoff fire hose, gathered and pleated and tacked to the side of the dock, will help cushion blows farther in. Neither of the above will of course be of any help to you in foreign ports, so upon entering those, pay extra attention to your telltales to check the wind, and do look over the side to see which way, if at all, the water is moving. Once you know what's going on around you—compensate.

It's a great idea to cover your fender with terry toweling but the thing is useless if allowed to dangle there empty of air.

Oh, one last thing. I have seen much damage to wood caprails and rubrails caused by fender lines. This seems to occur when the fender is trapped hard between the hull and the dock, and as the line goes tight it chafes hard on the caprail or the rubrail. The only solution I can think of is the one I mentioned before, where you tie the fenders horizontally to the dock instead of dangling them from the boat. This will also prevent the fenders riding up onto the dock in a swell or wake, leaving the hull unprotected.

The two best protectors: A hefty fender with terry toweling around it to cushion abrasive grit between the hull and the fender, and old fire hose gathered and pleated and tacked to the edge of the dock to protect the hull in case fender deflates or rides up onto the wharf.

20

Portlights and Windows

Opening Ports

Opening portlights have a habit of leaking after a few years, especially in hot climates where the neoprene gaskets inside them harden and crack and become as useless as titties on a bull. These have to be replaced by a new gasket. When you are replacing them, watch for three things. First, clean out the old gasket *completely*. If you leave even a little piece of the old stuff in there you will run into the problem of having a small highspot once you put the new gasket in, and this will invariably cause a frustrating little leak. Use the end of a square file to clean out the groove. Second, cut the gasket on a bevel so you don't create a straight path for the water. Put the joint in the gasket up at the top of the portlight, where it's least likely to leak. And third, get the right gasket. You can talk yourself into believing that any size will do, but it won't. If the thing is too small or just barely sufficient when new, then it will soon compress into never-never land and leak like a sieve. If it's too large, you'll massacre it trying to get it into the too small groove in the first place.

Windows

The good fixed windows aboard are of lucite, the less good of plexiglass of some variety. Lucite is infinitely harder and more scratchproof. Whichever you have, be careful with them for they can become so scratched that every time you look out through them you'll swear you've been engulfed by a permanent bank of fog. *Never* wipe a non-glass window with a dry rag. Either crystals of salt or grains of dirt will scratch it instantly. Always hose or flush the window first, then wash with a soft clean cloth, not one you've already washed the deck with, for it may have grit on it. Don't use the deck brush to wash down windows as you scrub the deck. A brush with hard plastic bristles is guaranteed to scratch, and even a natural bristled one may trap grit among the bristles and scratch the window. After hosing, chamois down the windows, then wipe down with McGuire's plexiglass compound to take out minor scratches and to give it some protection.

Ports or windows that use plastics for frames are bad news to start with, for they can be chipped or cracked by winch handles or reaching poles, and even more so once they become more brittle with age. Most of the brittleness comes from the sun, so if you have plastic frames, you might con- sider either putting on a few layers of varnish with some very good UV filters in it or you can paint them with a good paint made for plastics.

One of the best protectors you can get for a canvas deck is a fine macraméd mat to clean shoes of all small stones and grit so they won't be ground into the canvas.

21

Compasses

Installation

It's no use installing a compass on board if you can't see it. Make sure the helmsman can see the lubber lines from any position.

You have to keep a compass at least three feet away from large metallic masses like the engine, and at least two feet away from another compass, repeators of electronic instruments, electrical circuits—that means all wires—and things like fire extinguishers with metal cases.

Don't forget to keep non-fixed metallic and electronic objects such as tools, radios, cameras and even knives away from the compass.

Light alloys, brass, copper and stainless steel are generally considered non-magnetic, but just to be sure check them with a magnet.

When you get a new boat or a new compass, or even if you get a used boat, you are well advised to have your compass swung to correct any *built-in* magnetic deviation of the boat. A very good description of how to swing your compass is in the *Boatman's Manual* by Carl D. Lane. If you feel too incompetent to do it yourself, hire a pro, and be ready to pay up to $150.

Maintenance

The rays of the sun will not only discolor compass cards to the point where you won't be able to *read* the numbers, but they will also turn the transparent dome so hazy that you won't even be able to *see* the numbers. So when not in use, always keep the compass covered with a canvas cap.

The transparent dome or surface of the compass is usually Lucite, thus vulnerable to scratching. Never try to clean it with a dry cloth or you are guaranteed to scratch it. Rinse with lots of water to remove dirt and salt or clean with McGuire's plastic polish. If you have external gimbal screws, grease them periodically.

When laying up for the winter, it is most advisable to remove the compass, clean it, and store it in a clean dry place away from magnetic influence. Remember, it's an instrument not a shotput—don't heave it about.

Some common problems.

If you have two compasses on board that show different readings, then either one of them is too near something magnetic, or the two compasses are too near each other.

If the card swirls about, then the vibrations in the boat are too strong. A thin layer of foam between the compass and the boat should help absorb vibrations.

If the card no longer moves, or moves too much, then the pivot is worn or broken. Have it fixed. It won't get better.

If you have an air bubble in the compass, then it has a leak. Take it out and have it fixed.

Don't forget, a compass is the single most important instrument aboard. Don't mess with it or neglect it or you'll be a sorry Elmer.

Handbearing Compasses

The single biggest piece of preventive maintenance you can do for your boat—the one that will save you the most work and money and agony—is keeping the poor dear off the rocks. One of the best ways of doing that is by doing your coastal navigation frequently and accurately. For this, your best friend will be a handbearing compass. Not only are these extremely useful for navigation, but they also look beautiful both in the box and in your hand, and they look so authoritative that they can make the most simple-minded bimbo look like a real sailor.

To use it, you should have two, or better yet, three recognizable landmarks or points of land whose bearings you can sight, then plot onto a chart. Where the lines intersect, that is where you are. Just like magic, ha Elmie?

First, stand away from magnetic masses such as steering compass, etc. Of course you have to have the handheld compass with you, otherwise you can stand wherever you like. Now take the compass and hold it at eye level. Frame the object in the V sight. Slightly turn the compass so that the object and the lubberline are perfectly aligned with the bottom of the V. In a rough sea this is next to impossible, for the boat will be bucking and the compass card swinging, in which case you'll just have to do your best to try to establish the mid-point of the swing. Note the bearing either on paper or if you have a compass like the Plastimo, then you'll have internal rings to note each sighting. When you've *shot* all three, plot them and find yourself.

The Plastimo manual points out an interesting way of using a handheld compass to prevent a collision at sea. First take successive bearings of the vessel which appears to be on collision course for about five minutes. If during the five minutes you haven't yet collided, and the bearings that you've noted have become smaller, then the vessel will pass ahead. If the bearing widens she will pass astern. If the bearings stay the same, GET OUT OF THERE!!

22

Docklines

I never cease to be amazed by the lack of reverence most people exhibit toward their docklines. They are, after all, the yacht's only contact with dry land, and if well handled they can assure us—at least most of the time—that our vessels will be found in roughly the same place as we left them a few days back, instead of having drifted away, into or under something mean and heavy.

Although docklines seem to be undemanding bits of common rope, they do require a few minimal courtesies, like proper storage and handling.

Nothing destroys docklines as quickly as chafe. Never use docklines without chafeguards. These should be of a decent-weight leather sewn onto the line wherever it is in constant contact with hawse pipes or fair leads. Make the chafe guards at least ten inches long, to allow for variation of onboard attachment. Docklines, as all lines on a shipshape yacht, should have their ends whipped.

Stowage of docklines on many vessels is a disgrace. They are heaved into dinghies, lashed onto dogs, or thrown into the lazarette among oily cans and dripping diesel containers, then hurriedly yanked out as the boat roars up to the dock. Sacrilege. Docklines are the simplest things to stow. First, coil them smartly. Candace has been trying to teach me how to do this for fourteen years. A waste of time. I'm still trying to learn how to tie a tie.

On the bow you can slip it around the samson post or put it in the anchor well, and in the stern you can *hang it in*, not throw it into, a cockpit locker. They will then be readily accessible, obviating the need for stuffing the dog into the icebox while his leash is hurriedly used to tie the boat up to the wharf.

To relieve the wear not only on docklines but mooring cleats as well, a rubber snubber should be incorporated into the lines.

One caution. In a sincere attempt to better protect their boats, many skippers use springlines run from amidships or from cockpits. The notion of springlines is commendable indeed, *if* you have a proper place to spring them from. Running them from sheet or halyard cleats only leads to abrasion of innocent areas of paint and wood or gelcoat. Beware. If any line in tension from boat to dock or piling is touching a part of the boat, you will certainly get wear where you didn't want it.

Docklines will in time become as stiff as wire rope. Their revival is simple. Once a year, put them in a bucket of warm water with some mild detergent and slosh them around and squeeze them like you would a sweater. If you're too lazy for that, then throw them into an old pillow case, tie it shut and

PALM AND NEEDLE WHIPPING

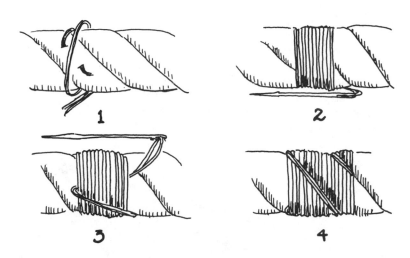

As you can see in the drawing, the whipping needed to prevent the end of a line from fraying is frightfully easy to do. You have no excuse for having your lines looking like old floor mops.

Springlines are a commendable idea but not if they chafe the hell out of the fiberglass. Note nice deep gouge worn into the turn of the coaming between the springline and the winch.

RUBBER SNUBBER SHOCK ABSORBER

SNUBBER ABSORBS SHOCK AND
SAVES LINES AND FITTINGS
FROM WEAR AND FATIGUE

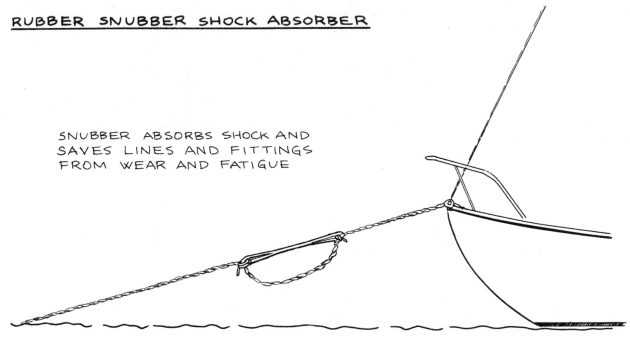

IN ANCHORLINE, LASH SNUBBER TO
ANCHOR RODE WITH LIGHT LINE.

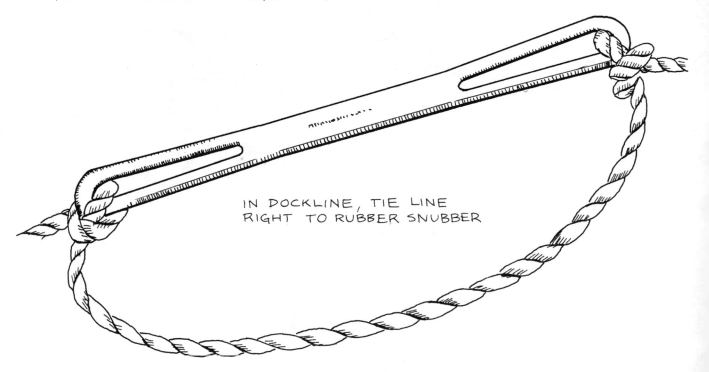

IN DOCKLINE, TIE LINE
RIGHT TO RUBBER SNUBBER

Chafe gear is vital anywhere dock lines ride. Note fairlead and bronze strips either side of the caprail.

heave it into the washing machine—because if you don't put it into the pillow case, Elmer, then you'll end up with your washer blades hog-tied and your motor burning, that's why. Anyway, you'll be shocked at how soft and manageable the old ropes will turn out.

23

Blocks and Other Hardware

It's not really our fault if we mistreat blocks. They ask for it. They're heavy and hefty and are built of plastics so tough that a bazooka couldn't scratch them, so how can we help but assume that they can live quite nicely without our love and care. The funny thing is that most of the time they can, and we need to do something pretty ignorant to really damage them, but certain simple things can be done to appreciably extend their life.

The most important thing for us to understand is that most blocks, most of the time, are loaded with salt. This is of course obvious after a day of heavy sailing when we ourselves are wet with spray; but even on an average day, bits of salt will work their way into tiny spaces between bearings and the narrow slit between the cheeks and sheaves, and our quick occasional hosedowns of the boat do pathetically little to remove it. So the first thing to do is to flush blocks often to remove the salt, dirt and grime. Don't be frugal, use lots ot water.

Most blocks will get dull and whitish-looking as the surface oxidizes slightly, and here a bit of wax will do wonders. But refrain from using *any* rubbing compound, for the grit from it can get into those critical tight places and cause binding or wear. Keep all blocks well lubricated. Any decent white grease will do, although some people say that yacht grease is essential. You couldn't prove it by me. I've used everything from duck fat to olive oil. Why should a crummy block eat better than me?

Check the blocks occasionally for any bent or cracked parts and replace them immediately. Most come in pieces, and if you catch a small failure in time, it may save you having to replace the whole block. Besides, if a damaged block is allowed to keep working until it fails totally, you may just end up getting the whole force of a whipping sheet or a flying block in the back of the head.

When stowing blocks for the winter, wipe them and grease them and wrap them in cloth and keep them in a dry place.

Snap shackles, cam cleats, mainsheet traveler cars, spinnaker pole ends, sheaves in masts and booms, quick-release pins, as well as all tracks on the mast and the deck should be regularly washed and wiped and greased; not only to give them longer life, but also to make them much easier physically, and less frustrating mentally, to use.

One note on blocks. Never overload them. It's always best to check with the designer or builder or with good rigging guides—see *Index*—to be sure to select the ideal block.

And remember, the loading on any block is proportionate to the angle of the line that passes

TYPICAL CONVENTIONAL BLOCK CONSTRUCTION

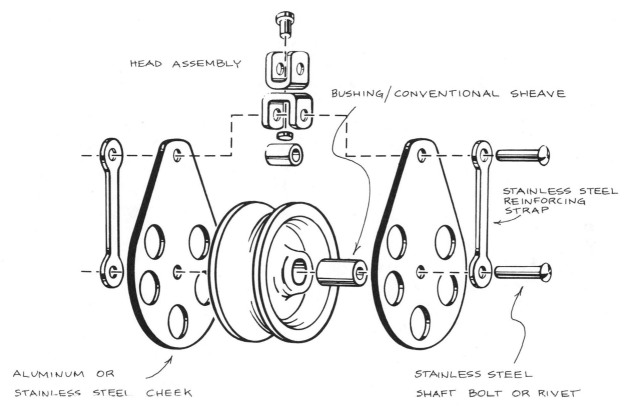

HEAD ASSEMBLY

BUSHING/CONVENTIONAL SHEAVE

STAINLESS STEEL
REINFORCING
STRAP

ALUMINUM OR
STAINLESS STEEL CHEEK

STAINLESS STEEL
SHAFT BOLT OR RIVET

NOTE: FLUSH OUT BLOCKS THOROUGHLY TO
REMOVE SALT. OIL REGULARLY.

through it. A block deflecting a line 45 degrees or less, carries less load than the total line tension. But if you increase the angle, you'll increase the load, to the point where on a turning block—where the line is turned 180 degrees—the load would be nearly twice the load in the line itself. If that sounds bizarre to you, join the crowd.

So think well about how and where to use blocks and, as for their maintenance, think of them as little machines, for that's exactly what they are.

SCHAEFER MARINE BLOCKS

TURNING BLOCK (FOOT BLOCK)

USED FOR TURNING SPINNAKER SHEETS AND JIB SHEETS. WHEN TURNING JIB SHEETS THE BLOCK SHOULD BE USED IN CONJUNCTION WITH A FAIRLEAD BLOCK. USUALLY MOUNTED NEAR AFT END OF BOAT, ALONG THE RAIL.

TWIN SHEET LEAD BLOCK

FOR USE WITH GENOA AND STAYSAIL SHEETS. WIDE MORTISE CONFIGURATION ALLOWS TWO SHEETS TO BE LED THROUGH THE BLOCK AT ONCE. DESIGNED TO LEAD AS CLOSE AS POSSIBLE TO DECK LEVEL FOR MORE TRIMMING FLEXIBILITY.

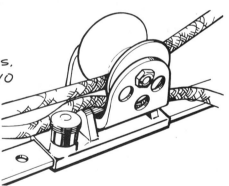

FAIRLEAD BLOCK

FOR USE WITH GENOA SHEETS AND HAL-YARDS. BLOCK IS SHOWN IN USE WITH GENOA SHEET AND IS MOUNTED ON A SLIDE. BLOCK SHOULD BE USED IN CON-JUNCTION WITH A TURNING BLOCK IN GENOA SHEET APPLICATIONS. WHEN USED FOR LEADING EXTERNAL HALYARDS AFT FROM THE BASE OF THE MAST, NO SLIDE IS USED.

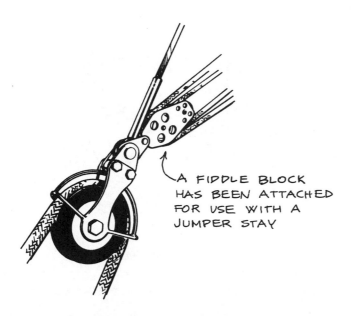

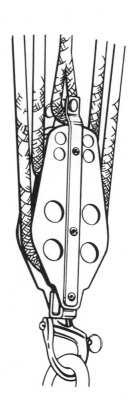

A FIDDLE BLOCK
HAS BEEN ATTACHED
FOR USE WITH A
JUMPER STAY

RUNNING BACKSTAY BLOCK

A LIGHTWEIGHT BLOCK OF MAXIMUM
STRENGTH FOR USE IN MAKING MAST
ADJUSTMENTS.

FIDDLE BLOCK

FOR USE IN MULTIPART SYSTEMS SUCH
AS MAINSHEETS AND BOOM VANGS. HAS
TWO OR MORE SHEAVES.

STAINLESS STEEL SPRING MOUNTING HOLDS
BLOCK UPRIGHT WHEN NOT IN USE.

SWIVEL FAIRLEAD BLOCK

A PATENTED SCHAEFER DESIGN, THE BLOCK SWIVELS AND TILTS IN ALL
DIRECTIONS TO ACCOMMODATE SHEETS OR LINES, BUT IS PREVENTED FROM
MAKING CONTACT WITH DECK.

A CURVED PLATE IS
USED TO MOUNT BLOCK
ON MAST OR BOOM

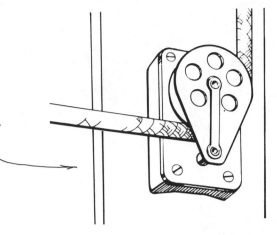

CHEEK BLOCK

USED FOR TURNING SHEETS AND
HALYARDS. WITH FLAT PLATE, MOUNTS
ON DECK, DECKHOUSE OR COAMING.
A SCORED ALUMINUM SHEAVE IS
USED FOR ROPE AND WIRE COMBINA-
TIONS.

SMALL HALYARD LIFT BLOCK

FOR USE WITH HALYARDS
AND TOPPING LIFTS. SIMILAR
IN APPLICATION TO A FIXED
FAIRLEAD BLOCK BUT ON A
SMALLER SCALE.

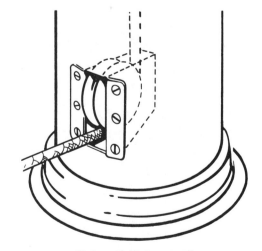

EXIT BLOCK

LEADS INTERNAL HALYARDS OR OTHER
LINES OUT OF MAST, BOOM OR SPINNA-
KER POLE. A V-GROOVE ALUMINUM
SHEAVE IS USED WITH ROPE AND WIRE
COMBINATIONS.

STRAP EYE ALLOWS SHOCK CORD
ATTACHMENT TO LIFELINES →

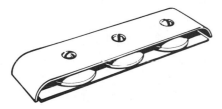

MULT-LINE CHEEK BLOCKS

ACCOMMODATING FROM 2 TO
6 LINES OR HALYARDS, THESE
LOW PROFILE "DECK ORGAN-
IZERS" PROVIDE A BETTER
AND STRONGER WAY TO LEAD
LINES AFT.

SPREACHER BLOCK

FOR USE WITH SPIN-
NAKERS, BLOOPERS
AND REACHING SAILS,
BLOCK PERMITS FASTER,
MORE EFFICIENT SHEETING.
CONFIGURATION PREVENTS
SHEETS FROM CROSSING AND CHAFING
WHILE CONSTRUCTION IS ABLE TO
WITHSTAND EXCEPTIONALLY HEAVY
SHOCK LOADS.

BLOCK AREA OPENS SO THAT LINE
CAN BE INSERTED EASILY WITHOUT
THREADING FROM ITS END

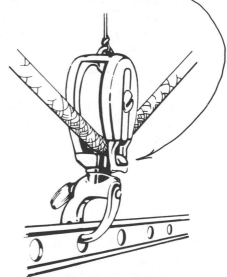

RATCHET BLOCK

USED ON MAINSHEET SYSTEMS, THE
MULT-SHEAVE BLOCK PROVIDES THE
NECESSARY MECHANICAL ADVAN-
TAGE. THE RIBBED AND RATCHETED
CENTER SHEAVE (WHICH CAN "FREE
WHEEL" WHEN THE RATCHET LEVER
IS RELEASED) TRANSFERS SOME
OF THE LOAD FROM THE USER'S
HAND BACK ONTO THE BLOCK.

SNATCH BLOCK

DESIGNED FOR A MULTITUDE
OF USES (WHEREVER THERE IS
AN ATTACHMENT POINT) SUCH
AS SHEETS, FOREGUYS, CUN-
NINGHAMS, PREVENTERS ETC.

24

Going Aloft

Each spring I look forward to going up the mast. It's the last thing after painting the bottom and cleaning the topsides and varnishing all the wood, so perhaps I like it so much because I know that after this there is nothing left but sailing. Or maybe I just like dangling from a rope.

I go aloft instead of Candace who weighs fifty pounds less than I do, because I'm stronger so I can pull myself up easier—that's right Elmer, I'll tell you how in a moment—and because I have a longer reach, and because I worry too much and I couldn't stop worrying for a minute if she was up there with her skinny arms and legs swaying in the breeze. But before we start for the heights, let's talk about what to take.

The Bosun's Chair

A good bosun's chair aboard any boat is a must, for not only is a good chair—with a solid wood bottom, strong canvas sides, a brace across the back and side pockets for tools—much safer to be in, but it makes you more relaxed and calm; and when you're relaxed and calm you don't make as many mistakes and when you don't make mistakes it's pretty hard to fall. Unless whoever is hauling you up decides you're better dead.

Anyway, get yourself a good bosun's chair and load it up with everything you need, because then you won't be hanging up there yelling your fool head off about things you've left behind.

Tools

Take a good six-inch crescent wrench—a hateful tool but handy for the odd-sized nuts aloft on spreaders and mastheads. Don't just slip it into a pocket like you would a salami sandwich, but tie it to a short line, about four feet in length to give you enough reach—and tie the line to something on the chair. This way if you drop it, you will neither kill anyone below nor put a deep mean dent into your deck.

And while we are talking about dropping things from aloft, we might as well lay down a simple physio-economic law about falling objects: All things cheap and heavy, like pliers and wrenches will *always* land on the deck or house top or on someone's head where they cause much damage. *But* all the expensive, light things like rings and watches and pins and blocks *always* fall overboard. Onward.

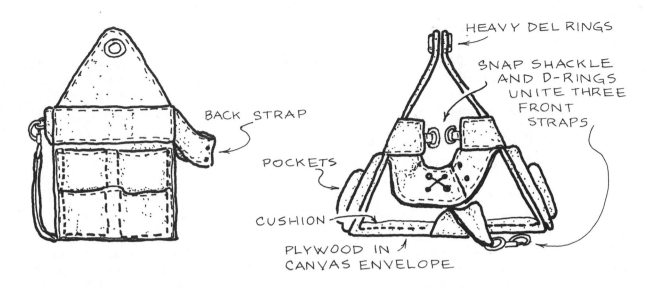

HEAVY DEL RINGS

SNAP SHACKLE AND D-RINGS UNITE THREE FRONT STRAPS

BACK STRAP

POCKETS

CUSHION

PLYWOOD IN CANVAS ENVELOPE

SIDE VIEW   FRONT VIEW

A SHIPSHAPE BOSUN'S CHAIR

As frustrating as this sucker is to use because it never sets at exactly the spot you want, it's still nice to have aloft with all the varied nuts and bolts to tighten. Be sure to have a little lanyard on it so you don't bean the loved ones down below.

Take a small pair of pliers for cotter keys and rings; take a screwdriver for scraping loose paint or varnish and fixing mast lights; take a small piece of sandpaper for cleaning off light bulb ends and sockets and sanding away loose paint or varnish. Take some rigging tape to tape off cotter keys which may tear sails.

Tie a small plastic pail with about three inches of water in it—if you put in any more you'll just spill it anyway—and put in it some mild detergent and a good cotton rag. Take a plastic bottle of Fantastic to clean off bad spots. *Never* use a scouring compound on rigging or fittings because the stuff can get in between moving parts like sheaves or toggles and either bind them or abrade them.

Tie the handle of the bucket to the chair with a light line as tall as your mast. Use line no heavier than ⅛ inch, otherwise it will weigh a ton and its bulk will always be in your way. You'll use the line to haul up fresh water, of which you'll need a lot to clean the mast and rigging, and to haul up things you need aloft like clean halyards and parts.

Take with you also a small mirror encased in plastic. This you'll need to check rigging and fittings right next to the masthead where the space is too small to fit your head. Tie it to something; you don't want seven years of bad luck.

If your eyesight isn't what it used to be, take a magnifying glass. Hairline cracks are a bitch to find even at the best of times with the best of eyes.

Last but not least, if you have external rope halyards which you have removed for the winter to clean and to keep clean, then take with you an old wire coat hanger—with the joint unraveled—for you'll need somehow to feed the soft rope over the double masthead sheaves. If you have single sheaves, forget the hanger.

Parts

Take spare lightbulbs, a few clevis pins, cotter keys,

and the chafe guards for the spreader ends.

Put tools in one pocket of the chair and parts in another. With your weight on the chair, the pockets go tight and it's a hell of a job rummaging around in there. *Don't* put anything in your jeans' pockets; you'll never get it out.

Going Up

Unless you're a total sissy, go barefoot. The grommets in deckshoes can scratch the hell out of anodizing, paint or varnish.

Tie a good bowline into the rope that is to haul you. If you're using a shackle, tape it after it's shut.

Get a foot off the deck and test the chair and gear with all your weight. Jump up and down a bit. Have your hauler cleat the halyard once your feet are a couple of inches off the deck, so that if somehow the halyard comes off the winch and you take the big dive, the rope will go taut just as your feet hit. You hope.

Now, as I said before, the best way to go up the mast—the safest and the fastest and the easiest for your hauler—is to *pull* yourself up. This entails simply pulling down with all your weight on the free end of the halyard you are tied to. With your weight now out of the chair, all the hauler has to do is pull the empty chair up to your waiting butt. Use your feet on the mast to help you. Climb like you climbed trees when you were a kid.

Have your helper put as few turns as possible on the winch—three is tops—otherwise the thing will foul and you'll have to hang by your hands with your weight off the halyard until she can correct it.

If you have internal halyards, don't worry your fuzzy little head—haul a block aloft to the masthead with the standard halyard, with a nice ½-inch line *twice* the height of the mast rove through it. You now have yourself an *external* halyard.

Unless you have some irresistible urge for doing otherwise, go up the aft part of the mast. This

Take a few cotter keys—or rings if you prefer. The rings are easier to put in and take out but then of course they can also take themselves out with greater ease. Nothing is more frightening than sailing along quietly at night only to hear a gently "ping" and find a ring lying on the deck. Merciful Mary Mother of—now where did that come from?

is where the mainsail track or groove is and it will need close inspection and cleaning. Now quit dawdling. Get up there. Rest at the spreaders

Neither of you is as tough as you think. Enjoy the view.

25

Checking Mast and Rigging

Generally

The best way to check the mast and rigging and affiliated hardware is to wash down every square inch as you go. First, removing all the dirt will enable you to see cracks and failures better; and second, no matter how hard you try, it's just too difficult to keep your visual concentration on a forty-foot mast unless you're involved in something tangible like wiping off the dirt.

Masthead

After washing, check all the tidbits on top of the mast: windspeed indicator, antennas, lights, etc., to see if there is any sea gull damage or corrosion. Put a little grease over cable fittings to protect them. Have your mate turn on the masthead light, then if it works, give it a few taps with the screwdriver handle to make sure there is no loosening connection. Check for condensation under the cover of the light. If there is some, take off the cover and clean it and put in a new gasket. If you don't correct condensation now, the light will surely fail soon, usually when you most need it and are least able to repair it.

Look inside the masthead and check the sheaves for cracks. See if you can turn them and see if there is grit or wear anywhere. If a sheave doesn't turn as freely as you'd like, don't panic, it might just be your off-center weight that's causing it to bind.

Now check all around each fitting for corrosion or rot. Remember, any bubbly surface in an aluminum mast means corrosion, and any blackening in a wood mast means that rot is very near. On a wood mast, check the joints of the boards to see if the glue is beginning to fail anywhere. If you find rot or corrosion, repair each and paint or varnish right away. Be sure to remove all oxidation or rot before you paint. If the damage is deeper than the surface, have an expert check it—you may have to pull the mast for major repairs. If the damage is minor, sand and clean it out, wipe with acetone, fill with epoxy putty, then paint.

Now check all of your tangs and fittings and swedges. This is where you'll need the help of a little mirror, for not only won't you be able to see the parts between the tops of the shrouds and the mast, but you'll also find that it takes a superhuman effort to get around to the front of the mast to check the headstay fittings. If there is a fitting you can't

Check the masthead for corrosion—all those little blisters that you see in the paint—and sand it out and paint it. Check all your pins and cotter keys and lights and instruments. Check too your halyard sheaves and all swedged fittings.

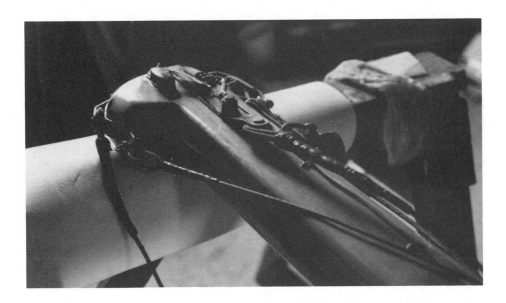

On a wooden mast the menu is much the same as above, except of course you'll check for rot instead of corrosion. If you see any blackening of the wood around and under fittings, for heaven's sake pull the fitting now and see what needs to be done. If the wood is black, the rot has begun.

Now I know this is no award winning photo, but if you look closely at the throat of the swedge, you will see a definite blistery crack. The fact that it's hard to see is good practice for you, because that's about how hard it will be to find a cracked fitting aloft. And what's worse, I won't be there to hold your hand and point things out.

get a clear look at, run your fingernail carefully over it in both directions—if there is a crack, your nail will slightly catch. Check the thinnest part of each fitting the most thoroughly. Remember that the weakest part usually goes first. Check the throats of swedges nearest the wire and check the ends of eyes or the joints of tees on turnbuckles.

To check the wire rigging, take a few layers of toilet paper and wrap it around the rigging and run it up and down. A frayed or cracked wire will catch a piece of the paper, and *flag* the problem for you.

If you have to remove a shroud or a fitting to either re-bed it or paint under it or whatever else, for godsake don't just loosen things up and pull the pin; for the weight of the shroud will just yank the thing right out of your hand and that'll be that for the caprail, or the gelcoat, or the wife. Before you loosen anything, tie a line tightly to the piece and lash it to the masthead, then lower the piece down slowly and carefully using a halyard.

Check cotter keys or rings to make sure they haven't been partially cut through by the movement of the rigging. If they show even a nick, change them.

Tape up any sharp pieces or your spinnaker can catch and shred itself.

Okay, now you can go down about three feet. Most civilized people prearrange a couple of simple signals to be used between them, such as tapping on the mast twice to begin lowering and once to stop. Yelling back and forth, especially in a breeze, with each bout full of, "What did you say?" and, "What do you mean by three feet?" and, "Don't call me an imbecile or I'll leave you up there 'til you rot!" is enough to drive both you and the poor neighbors half out of your minds.

A couple of notes of import here. First, be sure to remind your mate to lower very smoothly and gently, not to just uncleat the line and let it go. It's good for a laugh once in a while, but generally

Disconnect all the cable fittings and clean them off with sandpaper; then spray them with a moisture displacer like WD 40. Then recaulk all the holes where the cable etc. penetrates the masthead.

speaking you just freak out and swallow your tongue and die. Smooth starts, smooth stops. After all you *are* the love of her life, not a sack of fertilizer.

At your next station, wipe down and check everything you can get your eyes and hands on. If you have a sail track, check every inch and every rivet. If your eyes are feeble, run your finger up and down inside the track and feel for loose or sharp things. If you say that's not important, just wait until you're out in a gale and the mainsail won't come down.

Proceed similarly down the rest of the mast, making prolonged stops at all fittings and a major stop at the spreaders. Don't forget all the lights

along the way.

Lights

Check each light as you come to it by having the hauler turn them off and on. Don't just say it's too bright out to see the feeble lights, cup your hand around the damned thing and have a real look. Light failure will normally be a result of the neoprene gasket under the lens going hard from the sun, and once it hardens it cracks and then moisture gets in the light and then it's Katie bar the door. If the light has failed, or if there is

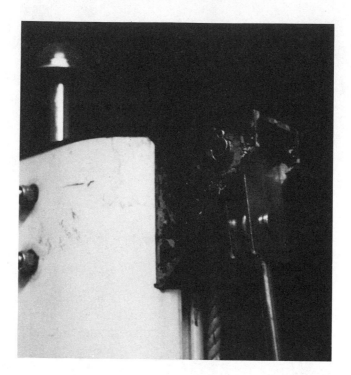

You'll need your little mirror to get a look at the parts of the fittings that face the mast. Have a look at the cotter key in the picture. Some people aren't happy unless they make a pretzel out of it, while others swear that the legs should be spread no more than twenty degrees. Take your pick. But I must tell you that the pretzel is a true bastard to remove.

Check your sail groove for wear. If you leave chafe and corrosion marks like these unrepaired, they'll just get worse until the sides of the grooves become so pitted that you'll have a hell of a time raising and lowering sails. This chafe was caused by a snap shackle in a halyard being left in the main's headboard overnight. Bad, Elmer.

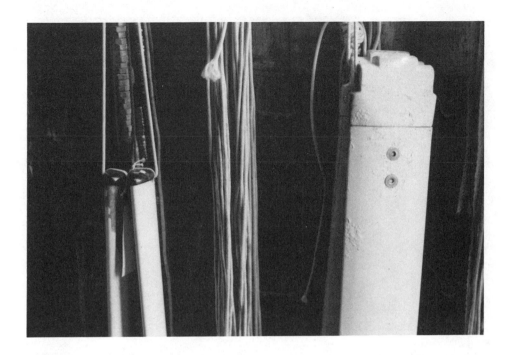

I have no idea why spreaders corrode so much faster than the rest of the mast, but they do and that's that. Sand them down to the bare aluminum, and primer them and repaint them with a good two-part polyurethane.

moisture built up, change the gasket as mentioned above and take out the bulb and, with the sandpaper, sand off all corrosion from it. Then sand the inside of the socket as well. Check the light again; if it still doesn't work, heave it.

Spreaders

Spreaders are most vulnerable because of the number of fittings on them. Each of these can either fail or trap moisture and cause corrosion or rot. As above, clean out and re-seal any suspected areas. The most vulnerable spots are the spreader-to-mast fittings and the spreader tips, both of which undergo small but frequent movement. While you are here, check to see that your spreaders are at a proper angle. Be sure to remove whatever chafe gear you had on your spreader tips during last season and check underneath for any corrosion or rot. Put on new chafe gear. North Sails, who probably repairs as many spreader-torn sails as anyone, cautions against the use of wheels or molded rubber chafe guards, or for that matter anything that may extend the effective length of the spreaders. They recommend either sewn on leather or just tape. But do make sure you put on something because most sailmakers will tell you that spreaders are one of the leading sail-killers.

When you finally get down to the boom, check it closely too, especially if you have slides instead of a bolt-rope in the foot of the mainsail, for every time the main slats in light airs, those awful little slides make an awful little noise as they hit the

Check each and every tang, swedge, pin, and bolt for cracks. Check the base for the spreader, rivet by rivet, to make sure nothing is loose.

boom and take out another smidgen of paint or anodizing.

Waxing

The paint on a mast, unless it's two-part polyurethane, will last much longer if waxed with a standard automotive wax. Don't, however, use any rubbing compound, because rubbing compound has abrasives in it and if they get between the mast and fittings, they'll chew the hell out of the soft aluminum. So, get an automotive wax and wax away, for not only is the wax going to save the   paint, but it can get into little cracks between the mast and fittings or the mast and the track, and seal nicely against moisture, hence, stave off corrosion.

Rigging

As mentioned above, the rigging should be wiped down thoroughly. This is no problem on the shrouds, for you can do them as you descend the mast. Although it will involve a bit of swinging from side to side, by this time that should be just sheer fun to you. The forestay and the backstay present another problem, for unless you are terribly gifted in the bicep department, you're going to have trouble pushing yourself the ten to fifteen feet necessary to reach them. So perhaps using the little system shown in the drawing might be the simplest method of getting at least the brunt of the dirt off the stays.

The turnbuckles should be flushed out well and sprayed with something like WD 40 or greased lightly for protection. Just because they are down

Take all the old tape off the turnbuckles and check everything for wear, cracks, and balling, then put in new cotter keys, and go tune the rigging. Don't forget to put new tape over the cotter keys when you're done.

on deck and easily accessible doesn't mean you should neglect them or delay inspection until a later day. Check them now. Go over everything with a magnifying glass. It will take less than half an hour and it's time well spent. If you have a boomkin or a bowsprit, check the stays and fittings supporting them with extra care, because somehow it appears that these are the first to go, possibly because they get more salt than the others, but perhaps even more

because of the oils—and God knows what else— they collect from the surface of the water.

Eye your toggles closely to be sure they are aligned and not bound somehow. On a boat, any binding or misalignment can lead to failure by loading the fitting with side forces for which it was not designed.

When everything is cleaned and checked, tape all the cotter keys over with some rigging tape, and

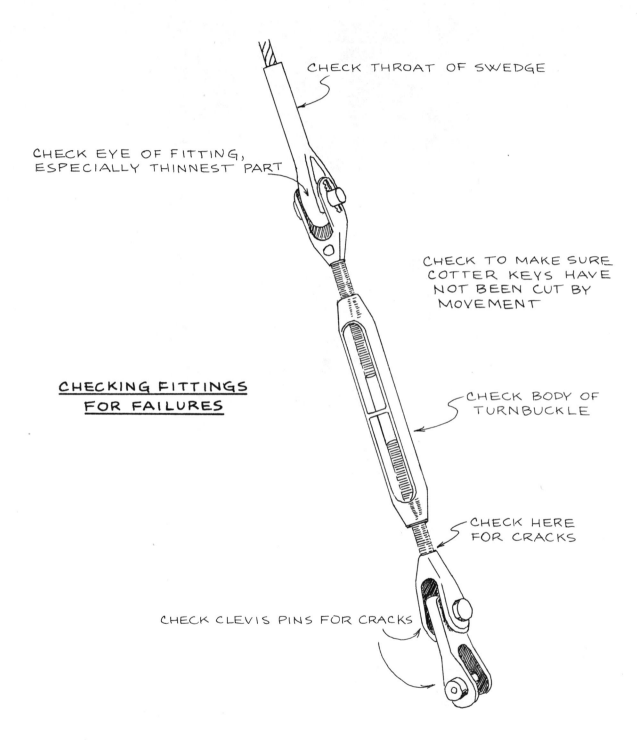

CHECK THROAT OF SWEDGE

CHECK EYE OF FITTING,
ESPECIALLY THINNEST PART

CHECK TO MAKE SURE
COTTER KEYS HAVE
NOT BEEN CUT BY
MOVEMENT

**CHECKING FITTINGS
FOR FAILURES**

CHECK BODY OF
TURNBUCKLE

CHECK HERE
FOR CRACKS

CHECK CLEVIS PINS FOR CRACKS

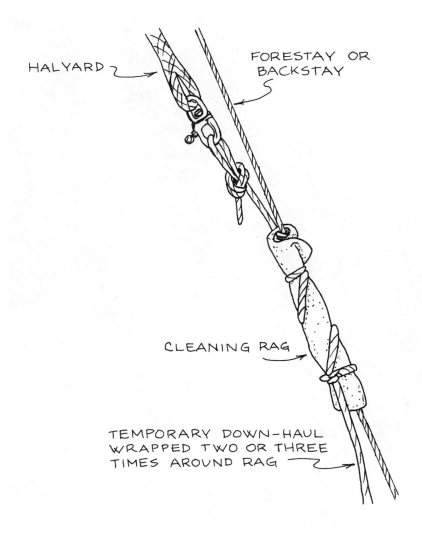

HALYARD

FORESTAY OR
BACKSTAY

CLEANING RAG

TEMPORARY DOWN-HAUL
WRAPPED TWO OR THREE
TIMES AROUND RAG

YANK RAG UP AND DOWN A FEW TIMES TO CLEAN
STAYS THAT ARE TOO HARD TO REACH FROM
BOSUN'S CHAIR.

REMOTE-CONTROL STAY CLEANER

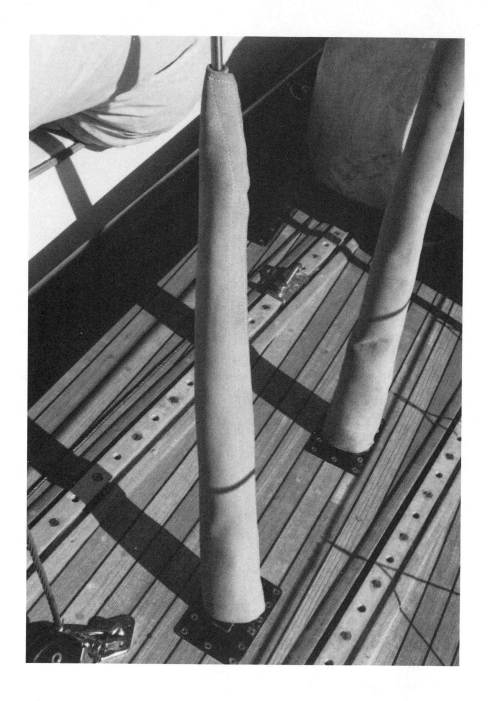

The best way to protect your sails from the sharp things on your turnbuckles is to cover them with elegant elkhide stockings. La di da.

If you're a peasant who can't see his way clear to an elkhide wardrobe for your hardware, then you can get these imitation sewer pipes and stick them on your turnbuckles.

Spinnakers and gennys are often the victims of sharp things around the pulpit. Tape over lifeline turnbuckles and pins and cotter keys or you'll be a sorry Elmer.

if there are any sharp or dubious edges, tape those as well. Anything that a sail can catch on, it will, sooner or later.

Don't forget to check the lifelines too, and tape their sharp points.

When you've finished washing the mast and all the rigging, give the boat a good wash or the dirty stains that have dripped from above will eat their way into the gelcoat or the teak decks.

The Mast Step

The base of the mast, whether it's stepped on deck or down below, is prone to corrosion or rot. If stepped on deck, it will encounter some movement, and if stepped below it will get more than its share of bilge water which, combined with some backed up dirt, makes a perfect environment for storing moisture for a good long time.

The best defense I have seen against this was in a small boatyard in France, and later I saw a more crude version in the Concordia yard. Both defenses consisted of a number of coats of epoxy being applied to the bottom six inches of the mast, both inside and out and right around the bottom edge. The French version could not have been more than about three thin coats, but the Concordia version had the stuff packed on thick. I don't think that more than three coats is necessary. Anyway, it seems like a very fine solution to a nagging old problem.

De-rigging and Re-rigging

If you have to change the entire rigging, it is best and fastest to pull the mast and remove the rigging and take it to the rigger so he can use the old rigging as templates for the new ones. To try to measure each piece individually is not impossible, but it can be an arduous undertaking if there is any wind, for the tape measure will be blown all over the place. Do not use string to measure rigging, because string that's fifty feet long stretches a ridiculous amount and you'll never know exactly what you measured no matter how hard you try.

If you have a lot of time to waste, you can pull half the rigging down at once and have the rigger replace those pieces. Then put those back up and pull down what's left. A decent sequence goes something like this. First batch: upper shrouds, staysail stay, backstay. *Set both running backstays first.* Second batch: all lowers and forestay.

Whichever system you use, do a quick tuning of your rigging first. This may sound odd, but it's the only way to find out exactly how the old stretched rigging fits. Once the rig is tuned, go around to each turnbuckle and make a written note of what's going on *in* it. You should make adjustments to the measurements to get the proper fit. The new rig should tune out so that each turnbuckle is at least half open. In other words, half of the threaded part should be out of the body when tight. This is to allow for stretching of the rigging, which is bound to occur with use. Rigging, unlike a wool sock, seldom shrinks.

26

Tuning the Rigging

A boat that is poorly tuned is a boat that will sail poorly, regardless of how clean the bottom or how new the sails. And a boat that is *really* poorly tuned can easily lose a mast in a stormy sea, for lack of uniform and consistent support.

Tuning a rig is a simple although time consuming task, requiring only a couple of good fork wrenches to loosen and tighten turnbuckles. This is no place for substitutes. Don't use adjustable pliers or channel locks on your turnbuckles, for the teeth of those tools will chew up the expensive hardware. A crescent wrench is acceptable but only if you set it very carefully, so you don't round off the corners.

Okay, let's tune.

As the yacht headsail is so important, let's start there, marrying the mainsail to this as we proceed. In anything other than light winds, the forestay, however tight, is going to sag to leeward due to the weight of the wind in the sail. However, it soon reaches a point at which a considerable increase in load is necessary to make it sag further. The sailmaker can calculate and allow for this initial movement when cutting the luff of the sail, but from that point on, correct flow in the foresail will depend on the tension to which the forestay can be subjected.

On most yachts, the conventional method of tensioning the forestay is by moving the masthead aft, via the backstay. However, it's impossible to exert sufficient tension to limit sag to a constant and acceptable degree in all wind strengths, if the mast is allowed to develop any degree of sideways bend. Further compression will simply increase the bend.

It is therefore essential that the mast be free from lateral bend at all times. Achieving this condition is what is basically meant by tuning the rig.

At the Dock

While still moored, trim the boat to its designed waterline. if the mast is keel-stepped, remove the chocks at deck level and slack off all the shrouds. Now center the mast athwartships by adjusting the cap-shrouds (uppers) only. At this stage, do not harden them down. Measuring the distance between the masthead and equal points either side of the boat with a steel tape measure hoisted on the main halyard is a good way. Be sure that the main halyard is in the center sheave in the masthead, otherwise you'll get two varying readings. Also, try to pick not too blustery a day, since the wind will catch the tape and blow a goodly belly in it and you'll

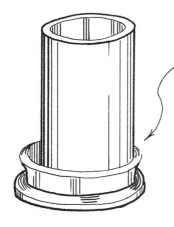

A KEEL-STEPPED MAST, WHEN UNDER
WORKING TENSION, SHOULD BE IN FIRM
CONTACT WITH AFT EDGE OF THE PARTNER
HOLE AT DECK LEVEL.

FULLY TENSION CAP SHROUDS WITH EQUAL
TURNS ON BOTH TURNBUCKLES UNTIL TAUT
THE MASTHEAD IS NOW IN POSITION.

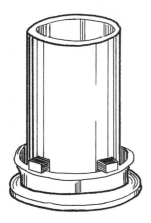

AT THIS STAGE, FIRMLY CHOCK SPAR INTO
THE CENTER OF THE HOLE AT DECK LEVEL.
THIS ACHIEVES A SLIGHT BOWING
EFFECT IN THE SPAR WHICH IN FACT
MAKES IT MORE RIGID.

HAND TIGHTEN ANY SLACKNESS.

SETTING THE SPAR RAKE AT 2°-4°

have a hell of a time trying to get exact readings.

The forestay and backstay can now be adjusted to position the mast in the correct fore and aft plane. The amount of rake depends on personal preference, the balance on the helm while sailing, and whether or not the boat is equipped with a backstay which can be easily adjusted while sailing. This is usually accomplished either by a wheel device, a hydraulic ram, or a system of pulleys.

The stays should be adjusted so that when they are at working tension, mast rake is between two and four degrees. These degrees of travel become limits of travel if the backstay is easily adjustable—the spar being more upright for off the wind sailing and raked aft under tension for windward work. If the same working tension is used on all points

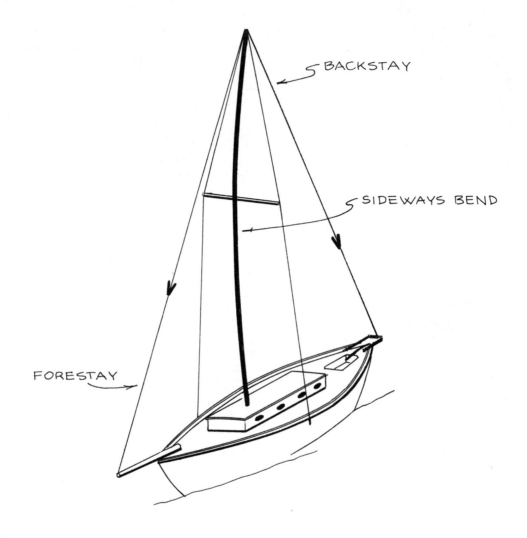

ON MOST YACHTS THE CONVENTIONAL METHOD OF TENSIONING THE FORESTAY IS BY MOVING THE MASTHEAD AFT, VIA THE BACKSTAY. HOWEVER, IT IS IMPOSSIBLE TO EXERT SUFFICIENT TENSION TO LIMIT SAG TO A CONSTANT AND ACCEPTABLE DEGREE IN ALL WIND STRENGTHS, IF THE MAST IS ALLOWED TO DEVELOP ANY DEGREE OF SIDEWAYS BEND.

of sailing then the degree of mast rake must be fixed within these limits. A keel-stepped mast, when under working tension, should be in firm contact with the *aft* edge of the partner hole at deck level.

If not, the mast heel position will have to be adjusted until it is.

The cap shrouds can now be fully tensioned with equal turns on both turnbuckles until they are

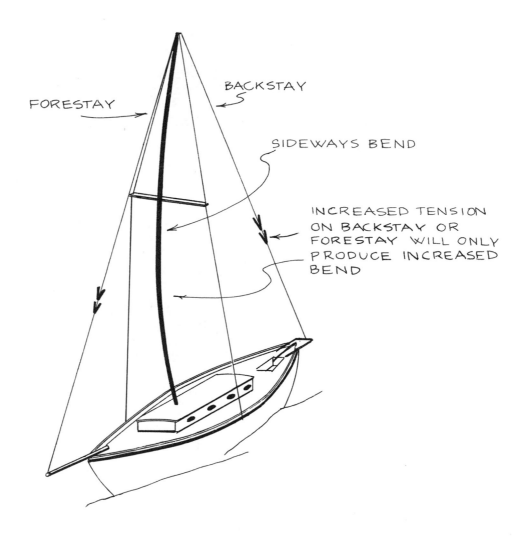

FORESTAY

BACKSTAY

SIDEWAYS BEND

INCREASED TENSION
ON BACKSTAY OR
FORESTAY WILL ONLY
PRODUCE INCREASED
BEND

IF MAST IS ALLOWED TO DEVELOP ANY DEGREE OF SIDEWAYS
BEND, FURTHER TENSIONING OF STAYS WILL SIMPLY INCREASE
THE BEND. THE MAST, THEREFORE MUST BE FREE OF LATERAL
BEND AT ALL TIMES. THIS IS BASICALLY WHAT IS MEANT BY
TUNING THE RIG.

really taut. Check athwartship position of masthead again with the steel tape measure. The masthead is now in position. At this stage, the spar is chocked very firmly into the *center* of its hole at deck level. This achieves a slight bowing effect in the spar which in fact makes it more rigid. Hand tighten any slackness out of the lower shrouds and, if fitted, intermediate shrouds, and we are ready to go sailing.

BOAT SHOULD BE HARD ON THE WIND HEELING ABOUT 20°-25°
SIGHT UP MAST TO ASCERTAIN ANY LATERAL BEND
IF CENTER IS SAGGING TO LEEWARD TIGHTEN LOWER WIND-
WARD SHROUDS UNTIL SPAR STRAIGHTENS.

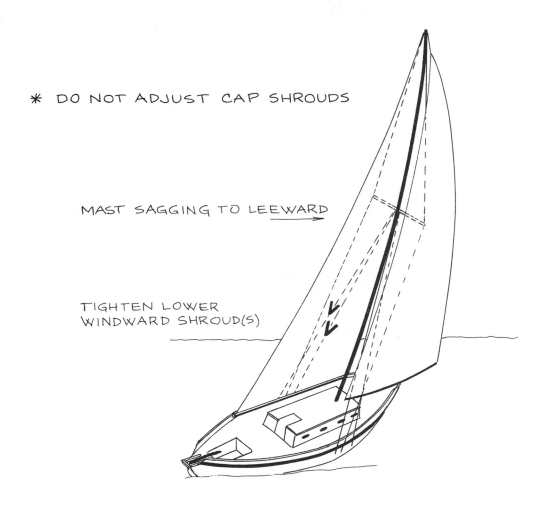

✳ DO NOT ADJUST CAP SHROUDS

MAST SAGGING TO LEEWARD ⟶

TIGHTEN LOWER
WINDWARD SHROUD(S)

Under Sail

Put the boat hard on the wind under full sail in sufficient wind to make it heel between twenty and twenty-five degrees.

By looking along the main sail track or groove, you can certainly ascertain any lateral bend that might be developing. If the center of the mast is sagging to leeward, then tighten down on the windward lower shroud or shrouds until the spar straightens. If it's bowing up to windward, then slacken off on the windward shrouds. Masts with

BOAT SHOULD BE HARD ON THE WIND HEELING ABOUT 20°-25°
SIGHT UP MAST TO ASCERTAIN ANY LATERAL BEND.
IF MAST IS SAGGING TO WINDWARD SLACKEN LOWER WIND-
WARD SHROUDS UNTIL SPAR STRAIGHTENS.

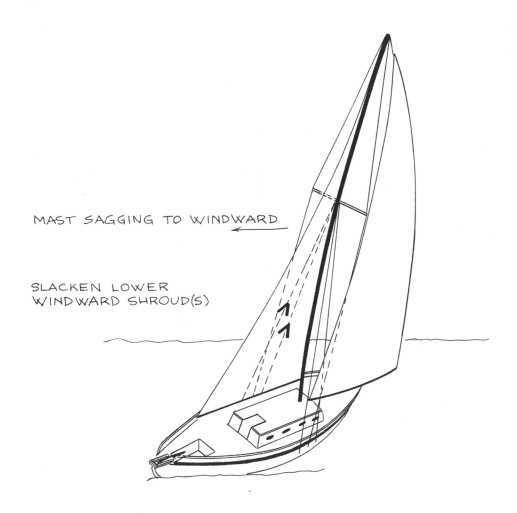

MAST SAGGING TO WINDWARD ←

SLACKEN LOWER
WINDWARD SHROUD(S)

MASTS WITH MORE THAN SINGLE SPREADERS COULD EXHIBIT
A COMBINATION OF BENDS EACH OF WHICH MUST BE ADJUSTED
WITH RELEVANT LOWER OR INTERMEDIATE WINDWARD
SHROUD. WORK FROM TOP DOWNWARDS.

BOAT WITH TWIN LOWER SHROUDS

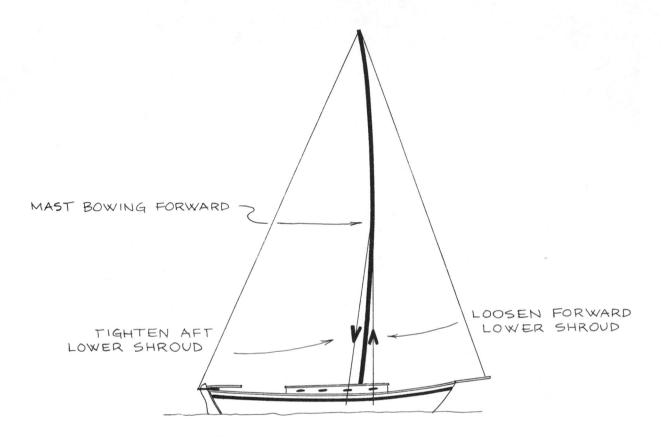

MAST BOWING FORWARD

TIGHTEN AFT
LOWER SHROUD

LOOSEN FORWARD
LOWER SHROUD

LOOK UP THE SIDE OF THE MAST. IF IT IS BOWING FORWARD
AT SPREADER HEIGHT, SLACK OFF ON THE FORWARD AND TAKE
DOWN ON THE AFT LOWER UNTIL THE SPAR IS STRAIGHT.

more than single spreaders could, of course, exhibit a combination of bends in either direction, each of which must be adjusted out with the relevant lower or intermediate windward shroud. In this case always work from the top downwards, getting the intermediates right before tackling the lowers.

However many spreaders are fitted, one principle remains—do *not* adjust either cap shroud.

On boats rigged with twin lower shrouds, you now must look up the side of the mast. If it is bowing forward at spreader height, slack off on the forward and tighten the aft lower until the spar is straight. Reverse the procedure if the mast bows

BOAT WITH TWIN LOWER SHROUDS

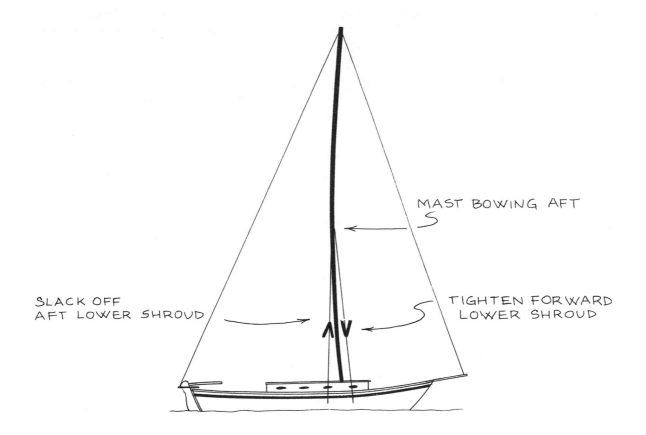

MAST BOWING AFT

SLACK OFF
AFT LOWER SHROUD

TIGHTEN FORWARD
LOWER SHROUD

IF THE MAST IS BOWING AFT AT SPREADER HEIGHT, SLACK OFF ON THE AFT AND TAKE DOWN ON THE FORWARD LOWER SHROUD UNTIL THE MAST IS STRAIGHT.

aft. Check to see if these adjustments have affected lateral bend, and if so, straighten the spar out again by equal amounts of adjustment on both windward lowers.

On boats with single lowers and a baby stay, the job is somewhat simpler. Leave the baby stay off until all lateral bend has been eliminated. Then

it can be used to prevent the mast flexing as well as for small fore and aft adjustments.

Once you are satisfied, tack the boat and carry out exactly the same operation on the other side of the rig. Unfortunately it is only after all this effort that you will be able to see if the cap shrouds were tensioned sufficiently before you left your mooring. If, with the windward rigging nicely holding the mast straight, the leeward shrouds are excessively floppy, then Elmer, you are unfortunately back to square one. Tighten down on the cap shrouds by the same number of turns each side, and then start all over again to balance the lowers and intermediates. Makes you drool for an unstayed rig, don't it?

Once you are happy with the rig, the turn-buckles, and for that matter all other sharp surfaces, must be bound with PVC sticky tape. Sailmakers know only too well the damage caused to expensive sails by unnoticed corners and pins in the rig.

One final point to remember: Wire rigging and even rod rigging, does stretch. The rig is nicely set up now, but it will need reworking two or three times an average season, so check regularly.

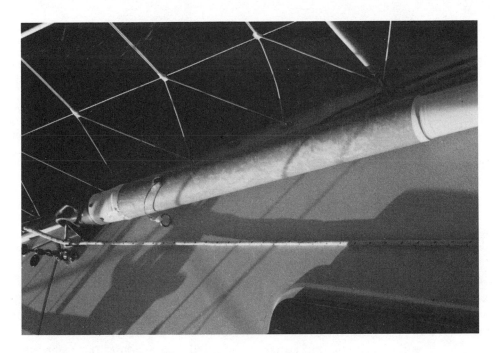

A layer of heavy elkhide on the spinnaker pole will not only protect the pole when it crashes against the pulpit or stanchions, but it will also give the foredeck crew a much less slippery grip.

An extremely civilized and long lasting method for securing ratlines to the shrouds. The metal sleeve is swedged onto the shroud and with the aid of washers holds up the rung.

27

Running Rigging

After a year of use, most rope halyards—and if left outside, sheets as well—become so coarse and stiff from salt and dirt that one assumes they're ready for the garbage bin. Not so. The stiffness seldom indicates a hardening of the synthetic, but rather that it's so full of dirt and salt that it almost stands up on its own, just like a good pair of dirty jeans. If decently looked after, good dacron rope will last a long time.

The greatest enemy of rope is chafe. Be sure all halyards are secured with shock cords or lines to the rigging when not carrying a sail. Do these at the end of each sail, for even just a few hours of steady chafing against a sharp point or cotter key can do irreparable damage.

Don't leave lines thrown on deck for any length of time. Rain will wash dirt along the deck and the line will end up as a dam, collecting all sorts of grit between its fibers—grit that will abrade it from within and weaken the line.

To restore the much desired suppleness to hardened weathered rope, all you have to do is wash the thing in lukewarm water with a mild, bleachless detergent. Don't, however, just throw your lines into the washing machine, or the line will either hogtie the impeller and burn the motor to ashes, or it will tie forty-nine million knots in itself, so tightly that you won't get them apart even with a chainsaw. So. Lay up the line in figure eights, tie it off, and throw it into an old pillow case and tie it off too, then throw the whole thing into the washer. You will find it comes out clean and supple and fun to fondle.

When storing sheets, don't coil them into loops, for that can cause kinking which can damage the rope if the sheet is made taut in a hurry and the kink jams in a block. To help avoid kinking, form the line into a figure eight for storage, or flake it down on the deck. In both cases it will run free on demand.

All lines should have their ends whipped or they'll be hard to lead through eyes and blocks, and besides that they'll look like hell.

The longest lasting and also one of the most decorative is the Palm and Needle Whip. Here is how it's done: "Cut a length of yarn, and using a regular sailing needle, anchor one end to the rope with two stitches. Lay on a number of turns snugly, then thrust the needle through the middle of a strand and then worm the whipping back to the left side and thrust the needle through the next strand beyond. Now pull the twine up tightly and worm it back to the right side of the whipping, thrust the needle to the next strand and pull tight. Finally

Line ends should be whipped this well for longevity. Melting the end of a synthetic braid without whipping it is a temporary solution at best.

worm back to the left side again, and again stitch through the strand and tighten.'' So says Hervey Garrett Smith, and he ought to know. To make the whipping last, dab a bit of varnish over it when you're varnishing the boat.

Okay, what did I leave out? Oh yes, wire-to-rope joints. Check regularly for fishhooks. The macho way is to hold the wire loosely in your palm and pull the wire through. If you bleed, it's frayed. The blood will nicely mark the location of the fishhook. If you don't fancy bloodletting, especially

your own, then by all means use a paper towel to cover your palm. Frayed wire will pull a small chunk from the paper as it goes by, flagging the fray for you.

If you have rope and wire halyards, you will of course not be able to throw them into the washing machine—pillow case or no pillow case. Just get some warm water in a bucket and heave in some detergent, then do like the nice Portuguese washerladies do, get down on your hands and knees and scrub. It'll make you a bit more humble

Unless you whip the ends of your lines, they will soon all look like this. Try to reeve this *into a block or eye.*

If you have lapses of memory and can seldom remember which side of the mast carries which halyard, then you may be well advised to get different color braid to help you. If you still have trouble after all your sheets and halyards are color-coded, take up lawn bowling.

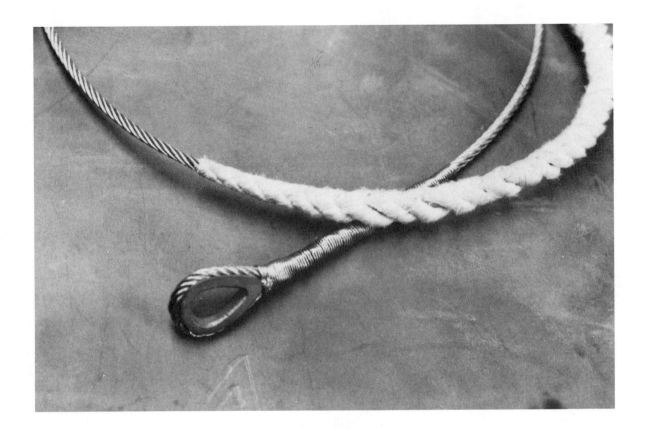

Check wire-to-rope splices for frayed wire. If you find a broken strand, then I'm afraid you'll have no choice but to replace the whole thing. See Checking Rigging *for details.*

28

Winches

Care and Service

I must say I'm amazed at how little attention is given to the average winch on the average sailboat (especially ours). Sadly many is the number of those who, although they have owned their boats for years, have never once taken their winches apart. That's nuts. The average two-speed winch is worth a small fortune nowadays and small neglects can lead to serious and expensive difficulties later on.

Winches work like dogs. A genoa sheet load on a forty foot cruising boat can be 1,000 pounds. If you don't believe me, just take the leward sheet off the winch in the next good blow and hold it tight. Didn't know you could fly, did you, Elmer?

Under normal cruising conditions, where the boat is in regular daily or bi-daily service, each winch should be lightly oiled and greased once a month.

Twice during a season, during which they undergo use as above, they should be stripped, cleaned and re-lubricated.

At the end of each season—and many recommend before the start of the next season—winches should be stripped, cleaned, thoroughly checked for damage and lubricated.

The exterior of winches can use some care as well. All winches, whether chrome or anodized aluminum or stainless steel, should be washed down regularly with mild detergent, then chamoised dry. Stainless and chrome can have stains removed from them with a non-abrasive liquid cleaner. Keep all polishes and abrasives away from anodized aluminum.

A spares kit is available for most winches containing things like pawls, springs, washers, etc. These should be aboard if a long cruise is undertaken, and most definitely before you start a major end-of-season teardown.

The tools you'll need are basic although they vary slightly from manufacturer to manufacturer. For example, with some Barlow winches you need a hex wrench and spanner—which they supply with the winch—to open, whereas with some Lewmars you just need a screwdriver. Beyond that you'll need nothing but some light machine oil—do not use detergent motor oil for it will eat into bronze or brass parts in the winch—some good quality marine grease, and a clean *non-fluffy* rag. I stress that because it's too easy to get a piece of fluff caught between the bearings, causing them to jam, not only

All you'll need to clean your winches is some diesel fuel, a brush, some lubricant and a rag. Oh yes, don't forget to get a small cookie tin to put all the mysterious parts into, so you can kick them overboard all at once instead of piece by piece.

small tidbit. Put a drop of oil between the grip of the handle and its stem to reduce friction and increase efficiency. Ardent racers use handles with ball bearings in them, so the least you can do is plop a drop of oil into yours now and then.

reducing the efficiency of the winch, but also severely wearing away the exposed side of the non-turning needle.

Locking winch handles should also be greased to avoid wear and have them function safely. A

Servicing A Winch

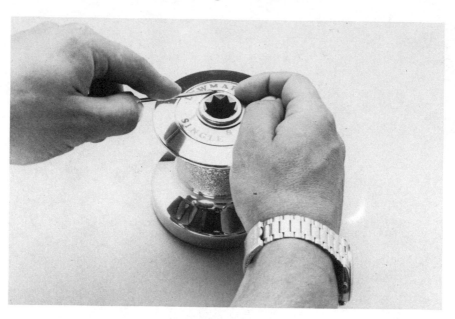

Either a clip or an Allen screw inside the hole to the handle will release most winch drums.

Lift off the drum, then remove washer and roller bearings. Put all pieces in a safe place, like a small pan, so they don't roll overboard.

Remove all parts, and lay them out in sequence. This will help you enormously during reassembly.

Wash all parts, bearing and drums included, in kerosene. Dry with a non-fluffy cloth. Fluffy cloths may shed and block the bearings.

Grease all parts, including bearings, lightly. Reassemble winch in reverse sequence. If you have parts left over, then you win the "Elmer of the Day" award. Try again.

TYPICAL SINGLE SPEED WINCH

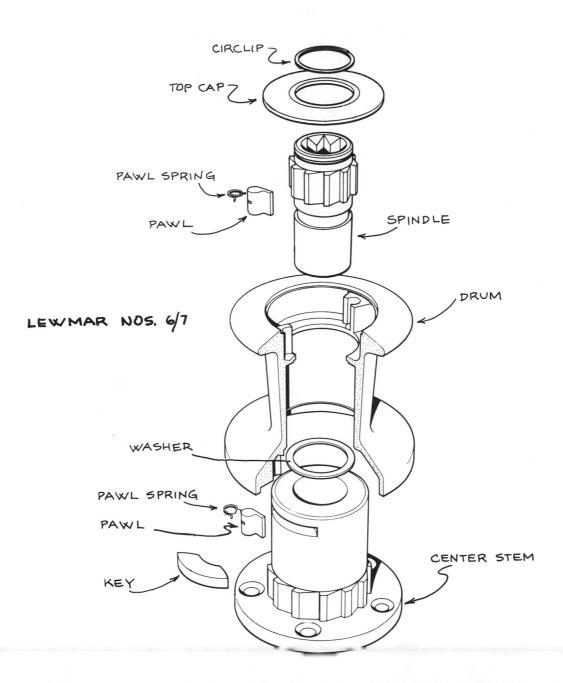

CIRCLIP

TOP CAP

PAWL SPRING

PAWL

SPINDLE

DRUM

LEWMAR NOS. 6/7

WASHER

PAWL SPRING

PAWL

KEY

CENTER STEM

TYPICAL TWO SPEED WINCH

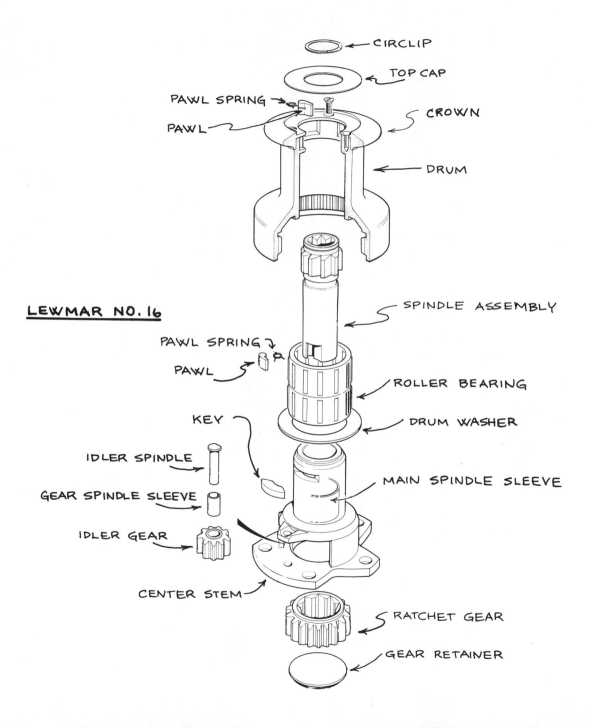

CIRCLIP

TOP CAP

PAWL SPRING

CROWN

PAWL

DRUM

LEWMAR NO. 16

SPINDLE ASSEMBLY

PAWL SPRING

PAWL

ROLLER BEARING

DRUM WASHER

KEY

IDLER SPINDLE

MAIN SPINDLE SLEEVE

GEAR SPINDLE SLEEVE

IDLER GEAR

CENTER STEM

RATCHET GEAR

GEAR RETAINER

Installing a New Winch

When you change winches, you'll probably need to drill a new set of holes. Be sure to get the new holes as far from the old ones as you can unless they match the old ones exactly. For a little extra strength fill the old holes with epoxy filler. If you are mounting the winch onto a fiberglass coaming, have the backing plate made larger than the last one to distribute the load somewhat past the old perforations. To fit a new winch follow this sequence.

a) Remove winch drum.

b) Locate the winch base to get the best support, remembering that "to avoid overrides, lines leading to winches should strike the winch drum at least five degrees below a line perpendicular to the winch axis. *Never* lead a line to a winch from above perpendicular to the winch axis. The further away from the winch the lead is, the more the winch will have to be tilted back away from the load to avoid overrides." That from Gary Mull, N.A.

c) Mark location of bolt holes, then remove winch.

d) Drill the bolt holes.

e) Wipe everything with acetone, then put bedding compound on the underside of the winch making sure that each bolt hole will be bedded but also making sure that no goop gets into the gear spindles.

f) Bolt winch into place, progressively tightening the bolts in a clockwise direction. Clean off surplus bedding compound and refit the drum.

g) Spin.

29

Sails

New sails cost a fortune. Mainsails of 7 or 8 ounces run $6 a square foot, genoas of 5 or 6 ounces $4 a square foot and spinnakers only about $1.50 but don't forget they're big. For a forty-foot boat you'd have no problem spending $10,000 for a suit of four new sails. What I'm trying to say is, it would behoove you to protect your sails with as much ferocity and indulgence as you can muster, for a very small amount of continued carelessness can lead to a lot of expense in a very short time.

The following guide for sail care was prepared by North Sails, one of the most respected names in sailmaking. There are no difficult or painstaking steps to follow—all that's required is a little thought and care. And who among us couldn't use a bit of that.

Storing Sails

When not in use, your sails should be stored *dry and folded* in their sailbags, much as they were when you received them.

Don't fold them on the same creases every time or you will have eight or ten *permanent* creases instead of many light ones, which generally shake out in a few minutes.

Store a spinnaker dry and loosely stuffed—in the case of a larger sail—in its turtle or folded in its envelope bag.

Don't store spinnakers wet for any length of time, as darker colors will bleed into lighter ones and dampness will promote the growth of mildew.

Damage Prevention

1. Direct sunlight
This is one of the worst enemies of Dacron and nylon sails. Sunlight will eventually rot the cloth. Therefore, roller furled genoas and mainsails must be covered if left up or on the boat.

2. Chafe
Chafe will cause sails to tear. It can be prevented by covering any part of your rig, which constantly rubs on sails, with leather or tape. This is especially important when using nylon sails such as spinnakers.

Check your boat over for untaped cotter pins, sharp corners on fittings, unprotected burrs, screw heads, etc. and tape them.

Remember to check the front of the mast carefully. The genoa drags across it every time you tack.

Never let the running backstay rub against the lee side of the mainsail.

Be careful not to drag sails over nonskid decks—that's like sanding them with good sandpaper.

Use genoa turtles to store racing genoas.

3. Dirt abrasion

Grit in dirt performs the same function as sandpaper. It will cause threads to part and eventually the sail will tear. You can prevent dirt build-up by wiping shrouds, taking care not to lower sails onto a dirty deck, and keeping sails away from greasy fittings.

4. Abnormal cloth wear

This can be caused by leaving sails up and flapping in the breeze when it's not necessary. When you are at the dock for lunch, etc., lower your sails. Don't luff head to wind with a large genoa. In heavy wind keep the main trimmed enough to eliminate flogging.

5. High temperatures

Heat can cause the bolt-rope to shrink and damage the cloth. Avoid storing your sails in places like a car trunk when the car is parked in the sun.

Common Causes of Sail Failures

1. Bloopers

These usually are ripped by dropping them over the bow into the water; a) when being set, b) when they collapse behind the main, or c) when being doused in a fresh breeze. When hoisting the sail, hoist extra high, let the sail fill, then ease the halyard to its normal position. Keep one man at the halyard to hoist the sail clear of the water until it collapses. This is especially important in rough seas. Use a takedown retrieving line rigged from

the blooper tack over the bow pulpit and aft near the mast, to control takedowns in rough water. Be sure the bow pulpit and bow lights can't catch the blooper.

2. Spinnakers

Usually fail from use in too much wind or rip on sharp objects on the bow or things like wrist watches. Explosive refilling after a collapse is also a problem. Three-quarter-ounce material has a high probability of failure at 15 knots apparent wind. One and one half ounce chutes usually fly well above 10 or 12 knots apparent wind.

3. Genoas

These most often split or tear when backed against a spreader. The principal problem is usually inattention by the crew or helmsman. Here are some good rules to follow:

a) If you are the jib sheet tailer, watch the sail at the spreader at all times. *Do not* let the spreader poke into the genoa. Be especially careful whenever the helmsman inadvertently luffs up. If the jib backs against the rig, it may split. Ease it before it is hard on the spreader. On a tack be sure to cast off early enough and when trimming after a tack, be careful not to overtrim.

b) If you are steering, be very careful never to back the genoa against the rig.

c) Be sure the spreaders are well protected with leather covers sewn over the ends and all corners and sharp spots are taped. Don't use wheels, rollers or pads that have the effect of extending the spreader tip beyond the line of the shroud. The less protrusion the less damage.

d) Inspect stitching of seams and leech in spreader areas periodically.

e) Have spreader patches installed as soon as possible if necessary on your boat, but remember even with patches the sail will fail if it is backed hard on the spreaders.

Another common cause of genoa failure is the

MAINSAIL

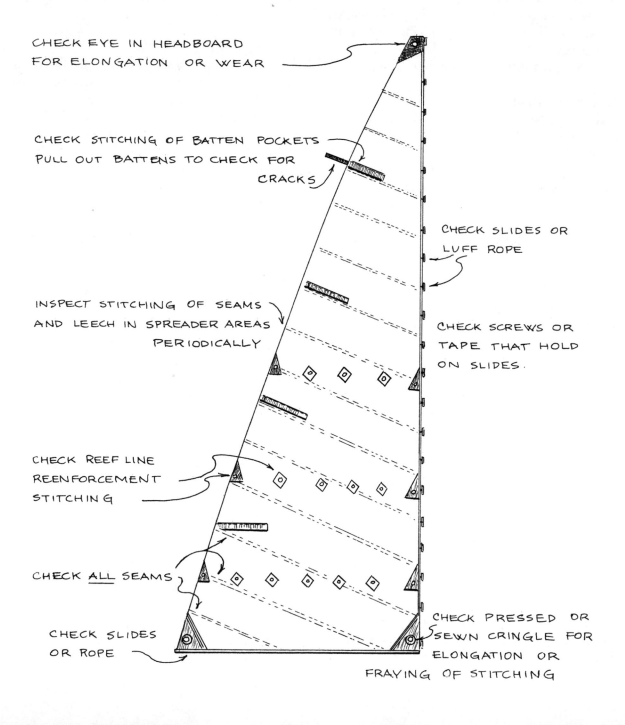

CHECK EYE IN HEADBOARD
FOR ELONGATION OR WEAR

CHECK STITCHING OF BATTEN POCKETS
PULL OUT BATTENS TO CHECK FOR
CRACKS

CHECK SLIDES OR
LUFF ROPE

INSPECT STITCHING OF SEAMS
AND LEECH IN SPREADER AREAS
PERIODICALLY

CHECK SCREWS OR
TAPE THAT HOLD
ON SLIDES.

CHECK REEF LINE
REENFORCEMENT
STITCHING

CHECK ALL SEAMS

CHECK SLIDES
OR ROPE

CHECK PRESSED OR
SEWN CRINGLE FOR
ELONGATION OR
FRAYING OF STITCHING

HEADSAIL

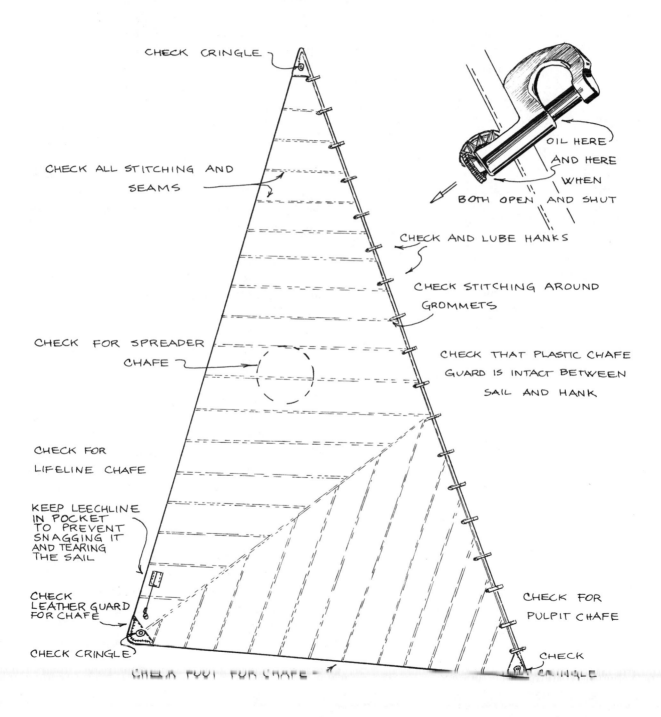

CHECK CRINGLE

CHECK ALL STITCHING AND
SEAMS

CHECK FOR SPREADER
CHAFE

CHECK FOR
LIFELINE CHAFE

KEEP LEECHLINE
IN POCKET
TO PREVENT
SNAGGING IT
AND TEARING
THE SAIL

CHECK
LEATHER GUARD
FOR CHAFE

CHECK CRINGLE

CHECK FOOT FOR CHAFE

OIL HERE
AND HERE
WHEN
BOTH OPEN AND SHUT

CHECK AND LUBE HANKS

CHECK STITCHING AROUND
GROMMETS

CHECK THAT PLASTIC CHAFE
GUARD IS INTACT BETWEEN
SAIL AND HANK

CHECK FOR
PULPIT CHAFE

CHECK
CRINGLE

leech cord catching in the rigging during a tack. Keep the leech cord tucked away in its pocket— not flying free. Cut the cord reasonably short, but remember the cord will shrink during the first season at least nine inches in forty feet.

Genoa luff tapes are often ripped during the hoist with a slot luff, if the sheet is trimmed too soon. The sheet trimmer must wait for the bow man to give the word to trim. The cunningham and reef tack line on genoas must be rigged to pull parallel to the headstay or forward of parallel, otherwise luff tapes will be ripped. Be sure the feeder and stay segments are rounded and have no sharp edges or corners.

4. Mainsails

Battens are broken and pockets torn by letting the sail flog. Always trim enough to settle the sail and prevent hard flogging of the leech.

Unreefing with the points tied in is a fairly common mistake. Use orange sailstops for ties. That way you will see them before it's too late. When reefing or unreefing, always get the luff tight before outhauling and trimming, or luff slides may be torn off or the luff rope ripped out of the groove or off the sail.

Permanent Cloth Damage

Stretching and deterioration of sailcloth is caused by two things:
a) Overloading the sail. *Do not exceed wind ranges recommended by your sailmaker for each sail.*
b) Flapping and flogging. "Flutter" fatigue degrades cloth at an extremely rapid rate. *Never let your sails flog unnecessarily.*

Cleaning

Clean only when necessary.

To remove surface dirt, hose your sails off with fresh water at the dock. Should your sails get so dirty that you absolutely can't stand them, soak them in lukewarm water with a mild soap or detergent and rub the dirtiest areas gently with a sponge or soft brush to loosen the dirt. Rinse thoroughly with fresh water. After hosing or washing sails it is best to dry them on the boat by going sailing with them up. This will help prevent the bolt-rope from shrinking. If this is not possible, they can be spread out on a lawn, but don't let them flap in the breeze and do not dry sails in the sun for extended periods. *Never put sails in a washing machine or a dryer, and donts' dry clean or iron them.* (Iron them!? Now *that* would win the *Elmer of the Century* award!)

1. Rust stains

Soak the stain in oxalic acid—use rubber gloves and put a plastic sheet under the sail so you don't eat up the floor. When the stain is out, wash the area thoroughly with fresh water to remove the acid. You can purchase oxalic acid at a hardware or paint store. *Do not use on nylon sails.*

2. Oil and grease

Major oil and grease stains are practically impossible to remove. For minor stains you can try Perchlorethylene. Immerse the stain in cold chemical and try using a blotter behind the sail. This chemical can be purchased at a dry cleaning supply house.

3. Mildew

Clorox—a 5% solution of sodium hypochlorite—will bleach out light stains. If you want a stronger solution you can purchase Chemex—which is a 15% solution of the same chemical—at a dry cleaning supply house. *Be sure to use them cold and do not use on nylon sails. Rinse the area thoroughly with fresh water.*

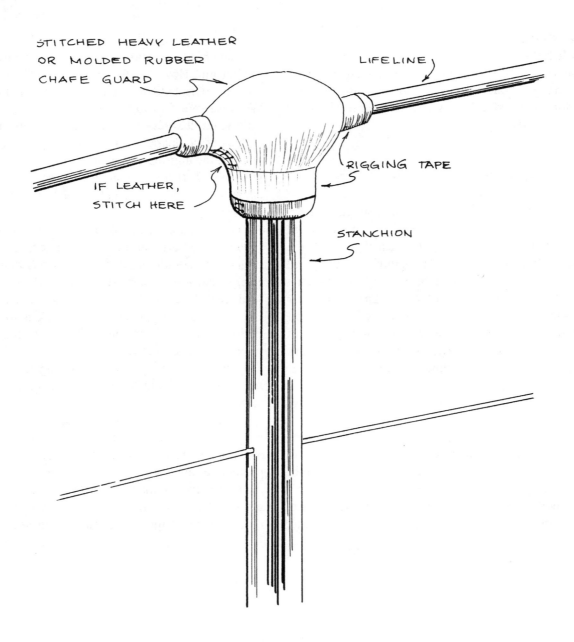

STITCHED HEAVY LEATHER
OR MOLDED RUBBER
CHAFE GUARD

LIFELINE

IF LEATHER,
STITCH HERE

RIGGING TAPE

STANCHION

Not only will a guard on top of your stanchion save your sails from tearing, but it will also reduce the number of enormous charley horses you get when you go crashing against a stanchion.

4. Blood

Wash the spot immediately in cold water. For old stains try Clorox (cold) if you're desperate, but don't get your hopes up. Again rinse the area thoroughly with fresh water. *Don't use Clorox on nylon sails.*

When Damage Occurs

Should you poke a hole in your sail, first assess the damage. Holes the size of an ice pick point aren't serious unless they are near the edge of the sail. They can be repaired temporarily by using sail repair tape or by placing a piece of duct tape on each side of the sail over the tear. Large tears near the edges or corners of a sail or near a batten pocket should be repaired properly. If in doubt check with your sailmaker. It is always much easier and less expensive to repair a small tear than a split panel.

Seams

As mentioned earlier, seams can be a sail's weak link. To provide additional protection, a product called Tuff Seam can be used to protect the vulnerable stitching. Tuff Seam is a transparent, flexible plastic that is *painted* onto a seam as a liquid and hardens to provide exceptional resistance to abrasion. How effective is Tuff Seam? We have a little experiment we like to show customers. We take a seam a foot long and paint half of it with Tuff Seam, leave half of it untreated. Then we rub a piece of sandpaper over the seam. In five or six strokes, the unprotected seam is abraded through, while the Tuff Seam-treated seam can withstand a hundred strokes or so, and seems little the worse for wear.

The most important aspect of maintaining sound sails is a keen eye out for small problems and implementing solutions to prevent serious damage. Every "blow out" starts at a weak point in a high load area of the sail. It can appear as chafed stitching, a small tear, puncture, or weak hardware. Periodically inspecting your sails for even the most minor tears and chafed areas is important. Using self adhesive dacron is a simple, strong, temporary solution and should be an essential part of any repair kit.

In conclusion, the more sails are cared for, the longer they will last. Annual professional service will remove the deepest salt, and provide the best preventive maintenance. By protecting sails from the destructive elements and taking care of potential problems as they occur, one is assured of a much safer and more pleasant sailing season.

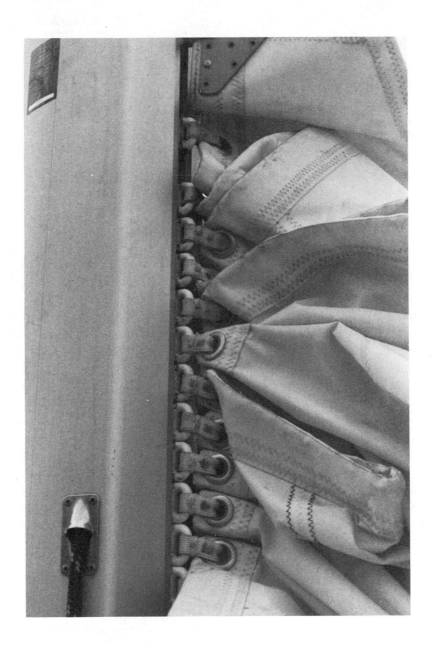

30

Frozen Fasteners

Nothing, I repeat, *nothing* will piss one off more royally than encountering a frozen bolt during an emergency repair. I mean there you are in the bloody engine room hanging from the exhaust pipe like some poor demented sloth, smiling to yourself at how well you're doing in spite of the fact that most of your body fluids have drained down to your head, when WHAM! You run unexpectedly into a frozen bolt. Well thank you very bloody much!

Some people caution strongly against resorting to brute force at such a time. I agree. You should sit down calmly and think through all the alternatives, consider special options and when you're through, *then* grab the biggest sledge hammer you can find and beat the rotten sonovabitch 'til it's just a pile of filings. Now *that* felt good, didn't it, Elmer?

If you don't have enough room to swing the sledge, you'll have to resort to more boring methods.

First, take a small hammer and give the thing a few taps. If that doesn't work, try to get some rust release stuff onto the threads somehow. You will immediately ask, "How?" and I'll immediately answer, "That's a good question."

If there is a washer under the bolt, you can drill right through the edge of it in a couple of places and squirt the rust release in through the holes. If there is no washer, drill right into the bottom of the head of the bolt and squirt through there. Let the stuff soak in, then give it a few more taps and try again. If the bugger still doesn't come, wipe off all the rust release, and if there is no danger of fire nearby, get a torch and heat up the bolt, then let it cool. Repeat this a few times. As it expands and contracts it might break the seal.

If absolutely nothing works, then you might as well give the bastard a great big yank and snap the head right off. You'll have to drill the thing out anyway and if you go and break the head off, not only will you feel a little better, but you'll also have a bit less metal to drill through. Drill straight down the center of the bolt and then tap in an extractor. This is a tapered tool akin to a tap, threaded in reverse to a normal thread, so that when it goes tight, it will begin to unthread what's left of the frozen bolt.

If the bolt is not horribly frozen but you have rounded off the head, the methods shown in the drawings can be tried. If nothing works, use dynamite. Don't forget to plug your ears.

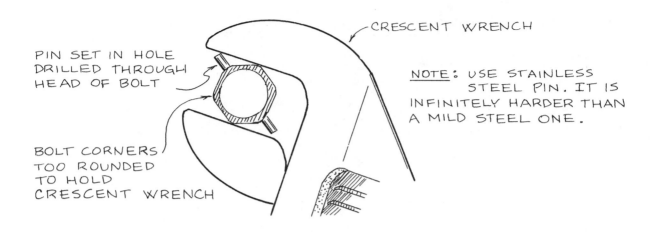

CRESCENT WRENCH

PIN SET IN HOLE
DRILLED THROUGH
HEAD OF BOLT

NOTE: USE STAINLESS
STEEL PIN. IT IS
INFINITELY HARDER THAN
A MILD STEEL ONE.

BOLT CORNERS
TOO ROUNDED
TO HOLD
CRESCENT WRENCH

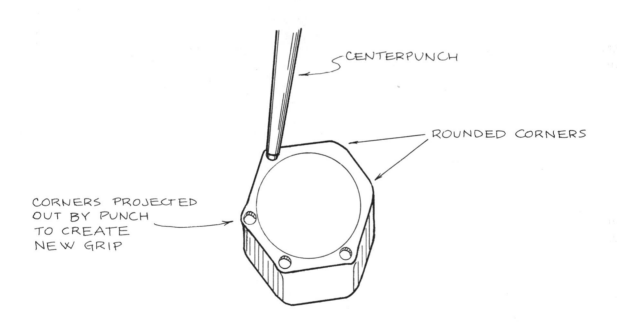

CENTERPUNCH

ROUNDED CORNERS

CORNERS PROJECTED
OUT BY PUNCH
TO CREATE
NEW GRIP

Few things make you want to go out and commit mass slaughter as much as a rounded bolt or nut. Yet the fault is seldom in the fastener—you have either used the wrong tool to start with and thus rounded the points, or you've let the fastener corrode to such an extent, that even a wrench made out of velvet would have done the damage. Anyway, to get it out you will have to somehow recreate some points for the wrench to grip. The above methods have been known to work.

EXTRACTING A BROKEN FASTENER

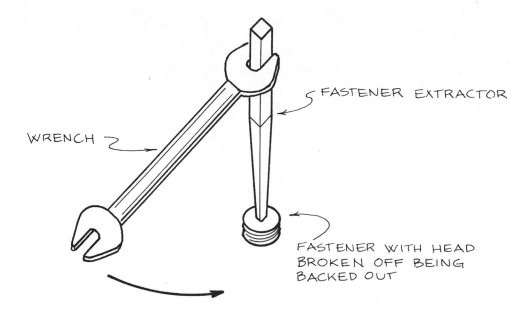

FASTENER EXTRACTOR

WRENCH

FASTENER WITH HEAD
BROKEN OFF BEING
BACKED OUT

① DRILL SMALL HOLE INTO FASTENER
② TAP EXTRACTOR INTO HOLE
③ BACK OUT FASTENER WITH WRENCH

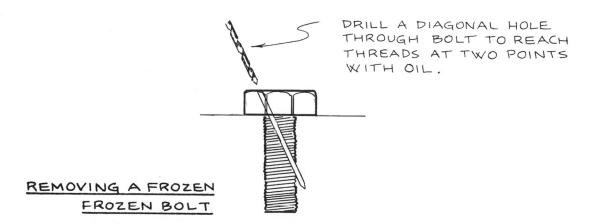

DRILL A DIAGONAL HOLE
THROUGH BOLT TO REACH
THREADS AT TWO POINTS
WITH OIL.

REMOVING A FROZEN FROZEN BOLT

VARIOUS SCREW AND BOLT HEAD SLOTS

ALLEN

SLOTTED

PHILLIPS

ROBERTSON

USE ONLY STAINLESS STEEL OR BRONZE FASTENERS ABOARD.
ANYTHING ELSE WILL BE CHEWED TO A PULP BY THE SALT AIR.

NUTS

LOCKWASHER

SELF-LOCKING NUT

WING-NUT

MACHINE SCREWS

ROUND HEAD

OVAL HEAD

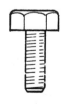
HEX HEAD

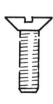
FLAT HEAD

Notes

SECTION THREE

BELOWDECKS

31

Binoculars

Care

It might sound exaggerated to say that your binoculars may one day save your life, but I can attest that they may. One night in a blow, I almost took a shortcut through the middle of a Virgin Island reef, but the binoculars showed me a thin line of white foam between the swells and we pulled away just in time. Without binoculars we would have been a landmark by now.

So. Take good care of your binoculars. Avoid great changes in temperature. If you have them outside in a freezing night and bring them into a hot cabin, condensation can build up inside them.

Never put away binoculars that have been exposed to rain, mist or fog without first wiping them dry.

Keep all lens surfaces clean. Most good lenses have a coating that allows the lens to transmit more than 99 percent of available light and this coating can be affected by things like salt, dust, and oil from fingerprints. If any of the above is left on the lens for a prolonged period, it could permanently adhere to the surface.

Cleaning

Use only lens cleaning tissues and a good lens cleaning fluid. Camera stores have them and optical stores have them and they don't cost much and they last forever—go get them.

To clean a lens, blow all the dust off it first. Just blow—don't spit. Then roll a single tissue into a cylinder. Moisten only the tip of it with lens cleaning fluid, then starting at the center of the lens, rub gently in a circular motion toward the edges.

If salt air or salt spray has gotten on your binoculars, don't put them away without flushing them with fresh water first. If you have rubber casing—as you should to absorb shock, keep out moisture and keep the buggers from sliding all over the place when you put then down for a tenth of a second—then pull back the rubber that surrounds the lens and flush out beneath it. Now clean as discussed before.

CLEANING BINOCULARS

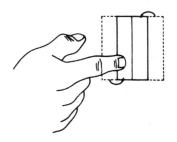

TAKE A SINGLE SHEET OF LENS CLEANING
TISSUE AND FOLD IT TWICE.

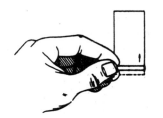

ROLL IT INTO A CYLINDER.
BLOW AWAY ANY DUST FROM THE LENS.

MOISTEN THE TIP OF THE CYLINDER
WITH LENS CLEANING FLUID. STARTING
IN THE CENTER OF THE LENS, RUB
GENTLY IN A CIRCULAR MOTION TOWARDS
THE OUTSIDE.

REPEAT THE LENS CLEANING PROCEDURE
UNTIL THE LENS IS CLEAN.

The lenses of a binocular are as delicate as—and infinitely more important to the ship's survival than—the lenses of a camera. Treat them with at least as much care. Always keep them covered when not in use; rinse them if salt spray has gotten on them; and clean them as shown above, on a regular basis.

32

Clocks and Barometers

Clocks

Care of these is so obvious that if I hadn't buggered up our very own clock by doing a bull-in-the-china-shop routine, I wouldn't even mention anything here. But I did, so I am.

When winding, don't wind until you're blue in the face, just until the thing seems to be giving resistance.

When setting the clock—on most marine clocks you do this by taking off the front lens and moving the minute hand manually—*don't* just grab the hand any old place and spin it like a roulette wheel. Place your finger gently near the *hub* of the minute hand and rotate it slowly. Use *only* the minute hand to set a clock, for on most clocks the two hands are friction fit, and if you try to rotate the hour hand, you might change its adjusted position in relation to the minute hand and possibly cause some maladjustment of the friction fit.

Be *very* careful not to bend the hands. I swear some of them are made of lukewarm butter.

Most brass clock and barometer cases come coated with a clear lacquer that will protect them for years *unless* you in your wisdom remove the lacquer with abrasives or metal polishes. So leave them alone.

The Ships Bells

Living aboard a ship by the ship's bell code has been practiced for hundreds of years. A ship at sea requires a constant watch throughout twenty-four hours. Traditionally the crew was divided up into two watches—port and starboard—with each watch standing three watches a day. To rotate watches from day to day to inflict much needed variety into a long voyage, dog watches of two hours each were stuck into the late afternoon and early evening. To keep everyone aboard aware of the time, the ships bell was struck by the watch officer at half-hour intervals.

8	bells	12:00	4:00	8:00
1	bell	12:30	4:30	8:30
2	bells	1:00	5:00	9:00
3	bells	1:30	5:30	9:30
4	bells	2:00	6:00	10:00
5	bells	2:30	6:30	10:30
6	bells	3:00	7:00	11:00
7	bells	3:30	7:30	11:30

The Watches

Barometer

In spite of what you may have been led to think, a barometer's main function is not to tell you whether it's sunny outside or not. What it does do is measure atmospheric pressure or the weight of the air surrounding it. Variation in atmospheric pressure at a fixed altitude—like sea-level—is usually an indication of a coming change in the weather. This is what the barometer does—it indicates changes in the weather twelve to twenty-four hours in advance.

To make note of the change without the added chore of recording it in writing, get into the habit of setting the *dead hand* each morning to the existing pressure. Then as the day and night progress, you will be able to notice the change and evaluate it.

At sea level, normal atmospheric pressure is approximately 29.92 inches or 1014 millibars. The average variation in pressure normally encountered is 1 to 1½ inches either way from the average. That's to put it mildly. Generally speaking if the barometer is below 28 inches you had better ready the storm anchor and the rosary.

33

Ventilation

If not properly ventilated, a wooden boat can rot into a pile of damp pulp, and a fiberglass boat can, at worst, lose its plywood bulkheads, and at best smell like a mushroom cellar. Thus, ventilation should not be thought of just as a matter of comfort when you are aboard, but should be amply provided when the boat is left to fend for itself.

Conversely, good locked-boat ventilation is important not only for when the boat is empty, but also during the time when you have to batten down the hatches in a storm but still want to keep breathing down below.

Anyway, the minimum number of vents on any boat is four good-sized cowls. Don't try to argue by saying that you have opening ports, because opening ports are closed during rainstorms and storm storms, and few things are as perfect a trigger for seasickness as a nice stuffy cabin reeking of sweat and the smell of cooking combined. There, you see? It's enough to turn your stomach just reading about it. So ventilate. And of course most ports are closed when the boat is left for the winter, when ventilation is the most important.

We have, unfortunately, underventilated *Warm Rain*, having placed one vent over the galley and another over the head, for although these two do wonders for the middle portion of the boat, they do sweet zip in the ends. Hence, we forever have a few specks of mildew in the engine room from the hot engine, and in the forepeak—where we sleep in port—from the hot Candace. When the mildew blooms, you'd swear you were making love in some old dungeon, which is great for a bit of variety, but depressing when mushrooms start to sprout between your toes.

The big problem of course is putting an effective vent on the foredeck, in a fashion that will not impede sail changing and anchor handling. Perhaps the solution is to put a deck fitting right into the deck without a dorade box, and have the cowl in it only when in port. When under sail, the screw-in flush-fitting cap would take its place.

You will notice that I have cautiously avoided the low profile mushroom type vents and with good reason. In a test that Nicro Fico did on two of its own products, a cowl vent was tested against a mushroom vent in similar conditions and the cowl vent was found to move roughly *six times more air* than the mushroom vent in five knots of wind. Now this ratio was smaller when the windstrength increased and the two vents came close to their capacity, but unless one lives in the trades, one cannot count on average winds much over five knots, hence the performance of a vent in light winds—

Now this *is what I call proper ventilation. With four good cowls like this, you can create a veritable hurricane below deck. Note also the acres of white acrylic in the hatches and the dorade boxes. They'll let in so much light, you'll have to wear sunglasses down below every time the moon is full.*

which are even lighter in protected harbors with boats all around, and lighter still when the boat is covered for the winter—is all important.

The most perfect solution to winter storage problems may just be a new piece of gear from Nicro Fico. This is one of the afore-dreaded mushroom vents *but* with a giant difference; it has in it a small fan and a tiny solar collector to power it. This little beast moves 1,100 cubic feet of air an hour, which is about as much as a cowl vent would move *if* the breeze were a steady 10 knots, and *if* the cowl was facing right into it. A more ideal solution for the winter months when the boat is abandoned, I have not seen before.

As for cowl vents, they should be set facing in opposite directions for the winter months, for in the northern hemisphere the winds usually blow

from two opposing directions, and this way the boat will be vented regardless.

For winter, the best way to have things not mildew in the boat is to take them home and stick them in the attic. That goes for sailbags and cushions and linens as well. Wipe and clean the boat thoroughly, for moisture and dirt love each other and create a perfect little haven for rot and mildew to start. Leave all locker doors open for the winter and pop all lids to help the air move about. If you can crack a hatch or two a bit, so much the better.

If you do get mildew, don't worry unduly. The stuff isn't carnivorous. Get some warm water and dump in some vinegar or bleach—depending on whether you want to smell like a swimming pool or a salad—and thoroughly wash and wipe dry the affected areas. Then for goodsake, *ventilate.*

This miniature beehive can be built on your aft deck with very little money or effort, to give your engine lots of nice fresh air and a plexiglass sliding door for a view.

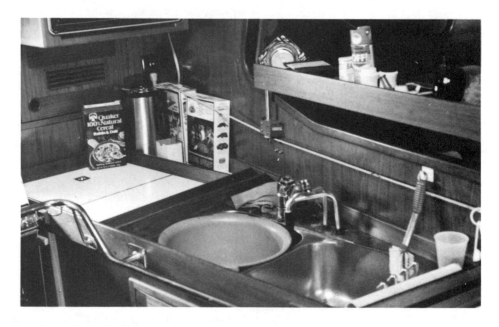

This is not *how you leave your boat for the winter. What we see here is a giant invitation to a mildew party. Heave all the stuff away or take it home or give it to the Salvation Army, but* get it out of there!

This *is how you leave your boat for the winter. Notice sails and bunk cushions gone from the forepeak, locker empty and locker door open for ventilation. Halt! Who left the kettle on the stove! Das ist nicht gut! Nicht gut!*

Ah, das ist ein sehr gut locker mit limberholes im der shelves, UND eine kleine Schnaps im der bottle. Sehr gut!

34

Freshwater Systems

Tanks

We sure take freshwater for granted in North America, and not until we go south or get off the continent do we begin to worry about what is in our glasses. Well, we should begin to worry a bit closer to home, namely in our water tanks.

If you do any cruising at all to remote places where you fill your tanks with well water, it's probably a good idea to treat it with a bit of pure household bleach. The recommended proportion is 1 teaspoon per 5 gallons of water. Let it sit for about ten minutes to give it a chance to massacre the bad guys.

If you find that your water has gone bad through sitting in the tank for some time, here is what you do: Drain off all the old water. You can try pumping it out—which will wear down either the battery or your arm—or you can do it the intelligent way, which is siphoning with a hose. Since most bilges are lower than the watertanks, this should be a snap. When the tank is empty, pour in some bleach—one cup of bleach for each 4 gallons of water—and refill your tank. Pump your pumps a few times so that you get some bleach-water into your pipes and your pump as well. Let it stand for four hours, then siphon tank dry again. Put in a few gallons of fresh water and then siphon that to rinse. Now fill with fresh water. If the thing still tastes like bleach, dump in some vinegar—one gallon of vinegar per 25 gallon tank—and let it slosh around for a day or two. Then drain and fill with fresh water. If it now tastes like vinegar, throw in a couple of gallons of olive oil and some basil and then you'll have yourself the world's largest reservoir of Italian salad dressing.

Anyway, if you're going cruising, take along some bleach. If nothing else, you'll have the whitest undies in the harbor.

Winterizing

The most idiotic thing I've ever heard of is people spending good money to buy antifreeze to put into their watertanks so the water won't freeze over the winter. I mean how Elmer can you get?! If you don't want the water to freeze in the tank, just drain the damned thing out! You'll have to drain the antifreeze out in the spring anyway so what's the deal? Not only is the stuff expensive, but it tastes awful *and* it's PINK!! JEEEEZUS!

Every water tank should have a nice big inspection hole in it through which you can reach in and clean the tank. If you make the hole big enough, you can crawl in there and close the lid when the wife puts her mouth on auto-pilot.

To insure that the water in the hoses and the pumps won't freeze, you can do two things. The first is to disconnect the check-valve—the thing that stops the water from draining back into the tank as soon as you stop pumping—and let the water drain back. To be sure you get it all, disconnect the hose at the pump and blow into it until it's empty. This will drain the water from the pump as well.

The second and easier method seems a lot more logical to me. Disconnect the hose at tank. Drain out all water. Stick hose into a bottle of tequila. Pump until first drop comes out of pump. Plug hose. In the spring, grab a lime and some salt, then lie on top of tank and put hose in mouth. Pull the plug. Swallow. To your hcalth.

Pumps

I'm not even going to begin to discuss pressure water systems and electric pumps here, because if you're too lazy to pump your water, you'll be much too lazy to look after your pump.

Hand pumps are another matter. Most of the good simple lift type—see photo—will work for a very long time without problems, becoming ornery only if left unused for a long time, This can result in parts drying out or forming just enough oxidation to make pumping nearly impossible. Ours froze up when we deserted them for a year while we lived in Paris, and since I didn't feel like taking them apart, I just rubbed a little olive oil onto

On a well-designed pump, you should be able to pull out all the guts by removing a single nut on the top and taking out the swivel pin from the pivot arm. Clean off interior deposits with warm water and baking soda. Don't Elmer around with scouring compounds or scrapers or solvents; you'll just bugger up the delicate fits or turn the rubber cylinder to mush.

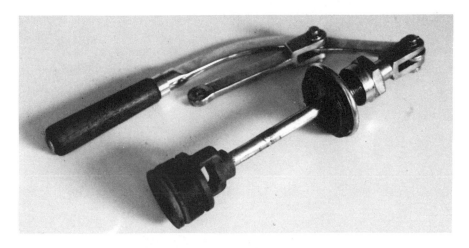

The simple but hefty interior of a water pump. If not ignored, it will give you good service for years. Don't let water sit in the pump over the winter. Take it apart as in previous photo, and dry it and lightly oil it with a film of olive oil and stick it under your pillow.

the shaft and shot a drop down into the pump, and after a few minutes of letting the oil soak around I gave it a couple of pumps, and the thing was better than it had ever been before.

If you don't like the taste of olive oil, you can use the anti-chap stuff you put on your lips. This is a good idea to do a couple of times a season anyway, just to make the use of the pump as effortless as possible.

If your pumps stop pumping and lubricants don't help, it means that either your waterline is crimped or you're out of water or something in your pump has failed. If it's the last, you'll have no choice but to take it apart and replace the failed part. A visual inspection will usually tell you what it is. One note. When reassembling a pump, *don't* crank everything ultra tight to prevent leaks. A better solution is to use white Teflon tape on all threaded fittings. Not only will this make the joint more leakproof with less tightening, but it will also be a help when you next want to take apart your pump, not only because the joint isn't as tight as it would have had to be without the tape, but also because the tape stopped the threads from corroding together.

Hoses

Good water hoses seem to last forever, but if you do have to change them, be sure you get only ones approved by the food and drug people, for these will be non-toxic and generally leave no flavor. When changing a water hose that has been in place for some time, you might have trouble pulling it off the fitting. Don't brace your feet and tug and pull. Heat up some water and pour it over the end of the hose. It will soften and become pliable and practically fall off. When putting clamps back onto a hose, don't pull them too tight or you'll cut right through the walls of the hose. Take it easy.

35

Galley Stoves

Oh boy. Talk about bad news. I don't do much of the cooking aboard—not because I'm macho but it's just that I'm a rotten cook—yet still I hate our galley stove from the bottom of my heart. It's a Shipmate kerosene stove, and I guess that's as good as you can get, but by God the sucker stinks and spurts and flares up and goes out and sometimes it gushes enough smoke that you'd think a bloody refinery was on fire. But I have to admit one thing, the sucker is safe. Once it did flare up with a five-inch flame, but that's minor when compared to some alcohol fires, and certainly minor when compared to a propane explosion which can, without blinking an eye, blow the deck clear across the bay.

So we live with it and cook with it when we can, and although Candace often screams in fury and threatens to assassinate me in my sleep unless I get her a propane stove, she quickly calms down when I offer to do all the future cooking, and goes back to the beast, mumbling something about how she'd rather cook on a candle than have that.

Anyway, there *are* a few things that you can do to your kerosene and alcohol stoves which will make them function better or at least bugger up less frequently.

First, you should probably realize how your stove works. Since both alcohol and kerosene burners have roughly similar pieces and modes of function, I'll just couple them together here.

Neither one actually burns the fuel itself but rather a *vapor* that is formed when the liquid makes contact with the *hot* burner. When I say hot, I mean *hot*, so the first priority is to preheat the burner sufficiently.

Preheating

Fill the preheating cups below the burner *completely*. For the kerosene, use the small plastic container that comes with the stove; for the alcohol, just pump up the pressure in the tank to between 6 and 7 p.s. and then open the handle and the cup will fill from the tank—and light them and wait until they are very nearly burnt off. Now turn the valve to *Clean* as far as it will go, but gently, otherwise you'll jam or break the little cleaning needle—see drawing—then turn it back about halfway or rather until the flame burns as blue and as free of yellow as possible.

Pressurizing

Having the tank at the proper fuel level and having the proper pressure in the tank will determine how well your flame will burn. Not only can your tank be too empty, but it can also be too full. Never fill tank more than three-quarters full or you won't have enough air in there to compress to keep pressure up. The pressure in an alcohol tank should be pumped to about 7, and kerosene near 10.

Neither should be pumped up with that hilarity of a pump they ship with your stove that takes eight thousand nervous little jerks to get the pressure up. Heave it. Then get yourself a valve from a bike tube and have it soldered into a washer and use the nut that came with the tank to thread it into place. Now when you want to pressurize, just screw a small bike pump to the valve and give it a few hearty ones and the pressure will be where you want it.

Fuel

For both the alcohol stove fuel and the kerosene pre-heating fuel, use only a good grade of denatured ethyl alcohol stove fuel. The Shipmate people warn against using "radiator antifreeze or any methyl alcohol as the burners will not operate properly and the vaporizers will clog." Not only that, but the bad stuff has a horrendously nauseating stench.

To tell whether the fuel you are using is all right, burn a bit of it in a clear dish. If some gooey stuff ends up at the bottom, get a cleaner fuel.

Kerosene fuel should be purchased with equal care. Do not use diesel fuel or even Number 2 Heating Oil. Good kerosene should be colorless like water. It might be a good idea anyway to install a little brass screen at the bottom of the funnel you use for filling the tank, for any little dirt can clog up the orifice of the burner.

REPLACE ORIGINAL JOKE OF A PUMP
WITH A BICYCLE PUMP.

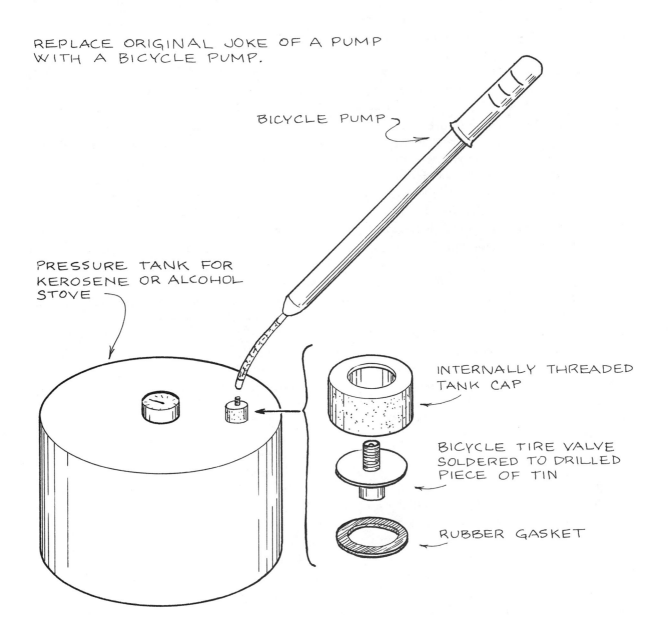

BICYCLE PUMP

PRESSURE TANK FOR
KEROSENE OR ALCOHOL
STOVE

INTERNALLY THREADED
TANK CAP

BICYCLE TIRE VALVE
SOLDERED TO DRILLED
PIECE OF TIN

RUBBER GASKET

CIVILIZING YOUR KEROSENE PUMP

Problems: Kerosene Stove

1. Yellow flaring flame

This usually happens very soon after you turn on the stove. It won't improve so you might as well turn it off. Don't mess with trying to clean it with the needle. All you'll get is a nice big stink when the flame goes out and the kerosene keeps flowing. The problem most often is that the burner *wasn't hot enough* to start with. Let it cool a bit, then refill the cup with alcohol, etc. If you don't let it cool first, the alcohol will just evaporate as soon as it touches the hot cup.

2. Fading flame

If the flame fades at any time, there are only two causes; one is low pressure the other a dirty nipple. The first you can fix by giving the pump enough pumps to get it back to 10. Below 9 you'll have a feeble flame. The second problem, dirt, can be remedied as follows. Light a match, and hold it close to the burner. Turn the handle to *Clean* and back again quickly. If the flame of the burner goes out, the match will relight it.

3. Pulsating flame

This is a true-blue bastard. If you don't fix it soon, the flame will blow itself right out. It happens because some little manifold in the back that is supposed to be full of air that acts as an air-cushion against pulsating, has had the air in it displaced by fuel. This problem can be minimized by releasing the pressure in the tank *as soon as* you stop using the stove, but it will occur no matter what you do. I'm not saying that to be mean, I'm just saying it so you won't feel betrayed when it happens.

The Shipmate owner's manual tells of three or four different things to do when the pulsating occurs, including things like turning the tank upside down or burning all fuel out of the tank or saying sixteen *Hail Mary's* and drinking a quart of water with your nose held shut. They're all too complicated and too slow. Here's what you do.

Shut off the stove. Get two small crescent wrenches—or wrenches that fit the brass fittings on the flexible coupling behind the stove—a tall but narrow cup that will fit behind your stove, and some paper towels. Next, unscrew the filler cap—release the pressure first or the cap will put a dent into the overhead—on the tank and put the funnel into the filler hole. Say one *Hail Mary*. Now tilt the stove forward so you can increase the space a bit behind it. *Don't* try it with just one wrench or you'll tear the coupling right out of the hose. Now *don't* pull the fitting apart until you have the cup under it. Okay, pull. You'll propably drip a bit, but then that is what the paper towels are for. Now, open the two burners to let air run back into the manifold as the fuel runs out. When no more fuel runs, re-tighten the fittings and *close* the burners. Dump the fuel you have in the cup back into the tank, close off tank and preheat burner, etc.

One tip. When you first notice the pulsating, don't shut the stove off in panic; finish cooking, the flame will probably be okay. When you're finished cooking, let the burner cool off a bit and then fix it. Saves burnt fingers.

4. Leaks

The only leak that's readily reparable is the one at the stuffing box. This you'll identify by a small flame at the stuffing box screw when the burner is on. Tighten with a crescent wrench until the flame goes out. If it doesn't, don't crank until you break something—replace the graphite packing.

If you have leaks anywhere else in the burner, I'm afraid that's bad news, for it will mean more labor and some parts. If it's leaking through the top, your needle might be broken or bent. You can remove the nipple with the special T tool that came

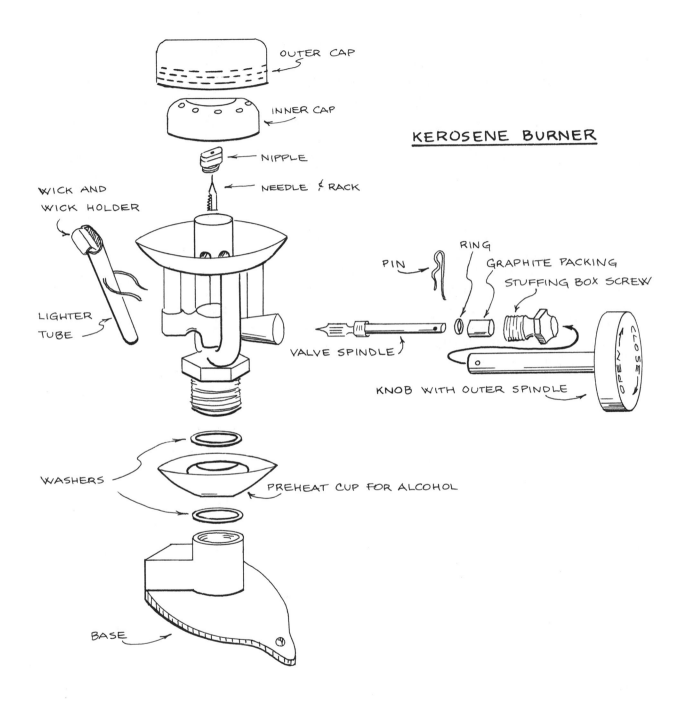

OUTER CAP

INNER CAP

KEROSENE BURNER

NIPPLE

NEEDLE & RACK

WICK AND
WICK HOLDER

PIN   RING   GRAPHITE PACKING
STUFFING BOX SCREW

LIGHTER
TUBE

VALVE SPINDLE

CLOSE   OPEN

KNOB WITH OUTER SPINDLE

WASHERS

PREHEAT CUP FOR ALCOHOL

BASE

WHEN TURNING KNOB TO "CLEAN" DON'T KEEP TURNING UNTIL YOU
BREAK SOMETHING. ALL YOU'RE TRYING TO DO IS DISLODGE SOME
DIRT FROM THE NIPPLE WITH THE NEEDLE.

with the stove, then turn the control knob counterclockwise until the needle and rack are free. Then stick a pencil eraser down onto the needle and lift. The needle and rack should come with it. Now loosen the packing nut and pull out the knob and valve spindle. Remove the spindle from the knob and replace the packing. Put the knob and valve spindle back in place and tighten the packing nut. Turn the knob to the *Close* position. Carefully push the new needle into the end of a wooden match stick. Put the needle and rack into the nozzle hole with the toothed side *facing* the valve spindle teeth and hold it in this position with a light downward pressure. Turn the knob towards the *Clean* position until there have been four or five clicks. Then turn the knob to the *Close* position. Remove the match and screw the orifice back into place. Check that the cleaning needle is correctly seated by turning the knob to the *Clean* position. The tip of the cleaning needle should be visible. Finally, replace the caps on top of the burner. What a production!!

If the burner leaks at the base, you'll have to take the whole damned thing apart and replace the washers at the base. Scrape off all of the old washers from the parts before you put the new washers on. When you reassemble, make sure the valve is aligned with the control knob shaft, otherwise you'll never get them together. Don't try to force the shaft into a non-aligned burner—it will put side-pressure on the packing box which will then leak forever.

5. Spare parts

Keep washers, packing, and spare rack and needle on hand. If you can afford one, keep a whole spare burner aboard. Replacing the whole burner is usually much easier than fooling around replacing one part at a time. Anyway, if one part if worn, the others can't be far behind.

Problems: Alcohol Stove

Much the same as above with regard to leaks. One caution: When using this stove, do not try to cook with too small a flame. These small flames can accidentally be blown out and the alcohol will continue to flow through the burner. When you go to relight, you'll have yourself a nifty bonfire. This is particularly true of the oven burners which cannot be readily seen.

A last caution: Alcohol ignites at a very low temperature. It can easily spill from the burner and flare up and look menacing, but it burns with a fairly cool flame and can easily be put out by water. What I'm getting at here is, if you see a flame, don't panic. I know of an accident in the Bahamas, where an alcohol stove flared up and the wife screamed and the husband jumped overboard and the boat burnt to the waterline. Stupid. Stay cool and put the fire out. Use water; it's a lot easier to clean up than the white soda dust of a fire extinguisher.

Propane Stoves

1. Precautions
Make out your will.

2. Safety
As if you didn't already know, propane is heavier than air and so if it leaks out of your stove, it will lurk in the bilge waiting for the first spark so it can explode and blow the whole show to Kingdom Come. There are a few precautions you can take.

The best way to avoid spills is not to have any gas in any part of the system but the tank itself unless the stove is being used. This would of course mean going to the tank each time to shut off the valve, which I know you won't do, and you know you won't do. So. The next best thing is to get

If you have a propane galley stove aboard, be sure you have one of these warning-light-cum-remote-tank-switches aboard to shut fuel off at tank when stove is not in use.

Don't try to cut copper tubing with a hacksaw or a chisel. All you'll do is flatten the pipe. Use a pipe cutter to make a perfect cut.

yourself a remote control solanoid switch—see photo. The red light on the panel tells you that the valve is open and there is gas in the system. When you throw the switch, the gas is shut off at the tank. To void the system, the best thing to do is to let the flame burn down with the main switch OFF but the burner still on. The difficulty with this is that you might forget to shut the *burner* off after it has gone out, and the next time you flick the main switch on, the gas will leak merrily from the burner. See, I told you to make out your will.

A weak part of this safety system is in the fact that it's electrical and thus can fail, as most electrical things tend to do sooner or later. So I just don't know what to tell you except to be very careful with everything you do with the stove.

3. Problems

As you may have guessed, the stove is virtually trouble free—you've got to get some reward for being willing to be blown to Hell—except for leaks. The valves on most stoves are pretty heavy-duty and simple and cheap, so if you find one feeling stiff, or mushy, or anything out of the ordinary, don't fool around trying to adjust it or fix it—get rid of it and get a new one.

The only other place the thing will usually leak is through the fittings. Make sure you have as few fittings as possible—one at the tank and one at the stove is ideal, with some delicate copper tubing in between. Check all couplings for leaks at least once a week. I know they were tight to start with, but boats vibrate and boats shake and couplings do loosen. To check them, don't try sniffing and don't try listening; get a cup of soapy water and a brush, and brush some on each fitting. If you see a bubble, you have a leak. Fix it by tightening.

Never tighten a coupling with a single wrench. You can twist the coupling right out of the tubing. Always use *two* wrenches, one on each half of the coupling, so there will never be any strain on the pieces beyond the coupling.

If tightening the coupling doesn't stop the leak then there is probably a problem with the flare in the tubing. The only way to fix that is to cut off the old flare as close to the end of the tube as possible, and re-flare the tube. Don't use a hacksaw to cut, for it can lopside the tube— use a proper little pipe cutter. Once you've cut the tube, look at the flare-nut itself to make sure it has no interior flaws that could have caused the leak. If it does, get a new one. Put it on the tube, then, using a flaring tool, put the tube into the proper-sized hole, tighten the wing-nuts to hold it in there tight, then bring down the flare and flare the tube. Now check the flare for any burrs, then tighten coupling and check with soapy water.

To limit the potential danger from spills, the tank must be located in a totally isolated compartment that has an overboard drainhole at its lowest point. Check the drainhole each time you check the coupling to make sure it's free and open. Good luck.

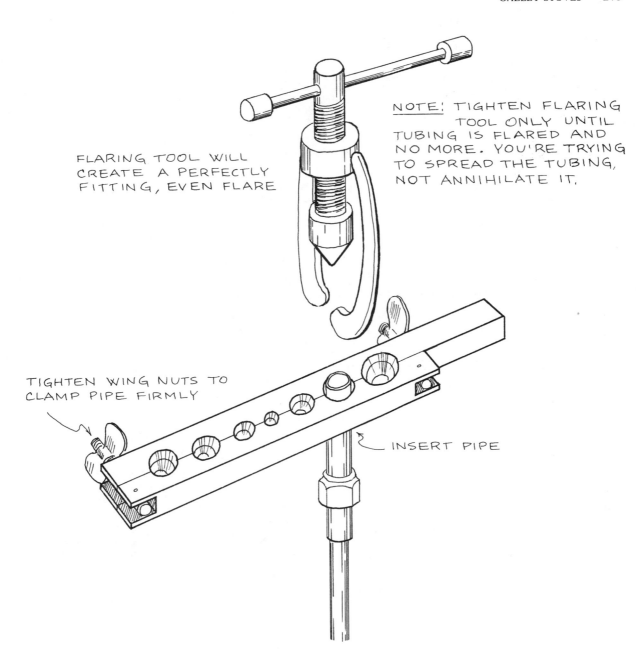

NOTE: TIGHTEN FLARING
TOOL ONLY UNTIL
TUBING IS FLARED AND
NO MORE. YOU'RE TRYING
TO SPREAD THE TUBING,
NOT ANNIHILATE IT.

FLARING TOOL WILL
CREATE A PERFECTLY
FITTING, EVEN FLARE

TIGHTEN WING NUTS TO
CLAMP PIPE FIRMLY

INSERT PIPE

THE PROPER FLARING TOOL

36

Refrigerators and Iceboxes

Refrigerators are so many in types and modes of function that it would be ludicrous—not to mention boring—to begin discussion of each, so let's just cover a few things that are fairly common to most units.

Defrost whatever you have as often as possible. Don't kid yourself into thinking that the coating of frost, because it's cold, cools the box as well as the plate itself does. Not so. The frost is pretty porous stuff, thus a fairly good insulator, as is ice—see Igloo—hence the unit has to work much harder, meaning it will use more of whatever makes it run, and meaning also that the working parts will wear out faster.

When cleaning a cold-holding plate, use warm water and bicarbonate of soda. Dry with a soft cotton cloth. Never use hot water. Never use cleaning products, for aluminum reacts with some, and never use anything sharp to scrape ice or crud away, for aluminum is also soft and you can damage it.

Check all wiring—if you have any—periodically, to make sure there is no corrosion. if you have copper tubing, check the couplings for leaks.

Iceboxes

Iceboxes are a different kettle of fish—and too often they smell like one—and need to be treated in a more simple but exhaustive fashion. The first thing to do is to keep the thing clean. If dirt builds up, then all the critters that reek will move into it and live happily ever after. Clean with warm water and soda as above, and as above, avoid use of sharp objects, especially if your liner is fiberglass, because every gouge will just become a nook for critters.

One of the worst smelling things in an icebox is the drain hose. This is where all the melt and dead-meat juices ferment with the spilled milk and the herring. Phew! Jamming a garden hose right to the drain fitting and turning the water on full blast will get the bulk of the stuff out, but there will still be a potent film of grunge left on the walls of the pipe. The only way to get that off is to plug the end of the hose that's in the bilge, and fill the pipe with a powerful mix of warm water and baking soda or bleach. Let it sit for a good hour or two, then repeat. The best way to prevent future build-ups is to flush the hose occasionally with warm water and soda. Leaving a box of open soda in the ice box is a rather feeble notion, for the stuff is sure to spill on the first hard heel, and sprinkle itself all over the food. Ever have a peanut butter and soda sandwich, Elmer? Yuk.

Whenever you leave the boat, even if only for a few days, *always* leave the icebox open to let the air circulate and stave off a mildew attack.

37

Interior Wood Maintenance

On most modern boats, interior wood consists of the bulkheads and some trim and sometimes some cabinetry and the cabin sole. On most production boats the common finish used is oil, not because it's exceedingly wonderful in any way, but just because it's quick and cheap and looks okay. I'm not saying there is anything wrong with oil, after all we have it all over *Warm Rain*, but most oils do turn hard after awhile, and sea rails and grab rails do get dirty, and the only way to clean them without raising the grain too much is by sanding and then re-oiling.

Bulkheads of course seldom get dirty but they too darken with age, until the wood eventually loses its warmth and becomes merely gloomly.

Cabin soles are almost universally oiled, although some are varnished which makes them rather slippery in rough weather when the cabin sole is usually awash with water that has sprayed in or has been tracked into the boat.

What all this rambling is leading to is this: When it's time to clean up all your wood in order to re-oil, *don't* re-oil—varnish instead. Belowdecks you can easily get away with two coats of varnish. We varnished a couple of areas that were constantly black from hand marks and grease marks like the galley and the companionway, and after five years I haven't once touched that varnish except to wipe

it with some warm water and dish soap.

When you are trying to clean teak belowdecks, always use a mild concoction of TSP and water—see *Cleaning Exterior Wood*—for not only will it get out the dirt, but it will also dissolve and remove the old darkened oil that was last put on.

Once the teak is thus cleaned, you'll probably find the grain a bit too high to look good under varnish, so it's best to sand everything down thoroughly with 100 grit and then varnish it.

Varnish will not only be infinitely easier to keep clean than oiled wood, but because it seals the wood completely, the natural lighter colors and the highlights of the grain will remain, making the boat look always fresh and "woody." Besides, because of its gloss, it will reflect light better and make belowdecks brighter. I saw a boat that was solid teak inside, first when it had two-year-old oil on the wood, and then a week later after it had been completely sanded down and covered with two coats of varnish. I promise you the effect was night and day. As soon as I can get off my butt, *Warm Rain* will get the same treatment.

For the intransigent who will continue to oil no matter what, wash down with TSP and use a good pure Tung oil—see *Oiling, Exterior*. It won't darken and it seals almost as hard as varnish.

38

Heads

Use

Ninety-nine out of a hundred times, the head will be plugged because something unmanageable will be heaved into it. The best simple rule to follow is: If you didn't eat or drink it—toilet paper notwithstanding—then it shouldn't be in the head. Now immediately the cry will go up, "Yes, but whatabout—" Forget it. No buts. No buts and no matches and no gumwrappers and no gum, and no paper towels and no dental floss and *no hair*! Some women are in the habit of combing their hair and then throwing all the hair they shed into the head. Forget it lady! On our boat we ask our friends not only not to throw hair into the head, but also to refrain from combing their hair belowdecks, period. Few things will clog up a bilge pump or a head pump faster than a nice clump of long, tangled hair.

Now I know that most of us conduct our conversations about heads with a blush and a dumb grin, and are often too embarrassed to mention anything about them to our guests, but I tell you Elmer, you better bring up the subject early or you'll soon be crouching in the head, elbow deep in shit.

While you are enlightening the guests, you might also enlighten them how to pump. Make sure they know how the valves work; how to flush and how to pump dry; and how many good pumps it takes, not just to clear the bowl, but to clear the discharge hose as well.

Care

Much as with the water pumps, a little lubricant on the pump shaft will make for easier pumping. If your head has a packing gland in it as most of them do, don't tighten it down too much or you'll find pumping more difficult and the packing will wear out easier.

If the packing leaks a bit, loosen off the nut and put in a bit of heavy waterproof grease—it will normally stop the leak.

It's a very good idea to flush the head out once in awhile with something like "Sea-Lube," for it will dissolve the salt well, and lubricate the inner parts. Pump the bowl dry, pour the recommended amount into the bowl, pump it a couple of times so that the whole inner pump is loaded with it, then let it sit overnight. If the head is slow to empty and you suspect it is plugged, for heaven's sake don't use any Drano or other liquid pipe cleaners. The stuff is horrendously corrosive and most heads have

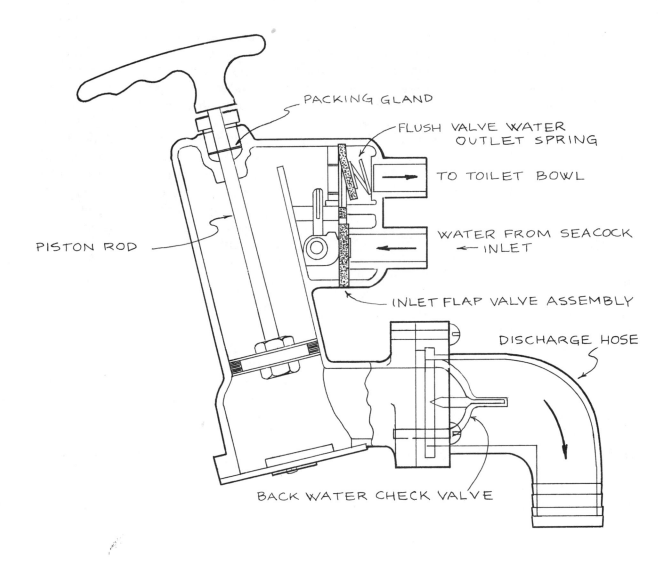

PACKING GLAND

FLUSH VALVE WATER
OUTLET SPRING

TO TOILET BOWL

WATER FROM SEACOCK
← INLET

PISTON ROD

INLET FLAP VALVE ASSEMBLY

DISCHARGE HOSE

BACK WATER CHECK VALVE

THE MYSTERIES OF A MARINE HEAD

some relatively fine pieces in them that could be corroded in short order.

If you are trying to eliminate built up odors, avoid corrosives such as Pinesol. Use bleach. It kills the algae which are most often the cause of the odor. To do a decent job, you'll have to disconnect the inlet hose from the seacock—use warm water to soften up the hose; it will come off more easily—and stick it right into the bleach bottle and pump the bleach into the bowl and the pump itself, from there. The algae are growing inside the inlet hose as well as the outlet hose and the head.

Repair

If the water is coming into the head faster than it's going out, there could be something lodged under the outlet flap valve. Don't panic. This happens all the time. Just shut off the inlet valve and pump hard a few times until the bowl is empty. If the problem persists, you may have a build-up of salt and goo under the valve. You'll have to take it apart and clean it or replace it. This is usually a simple job requiring the removal of a couple of screws. Before you install the new valve, scrape off any build-up around the valve base to insure perfect seating.

If the head is below the waterline, and the water level rises in the bowl when the boat is not in motion, then either the inlet or the outlet valve is not seating perfectly, This can be repaired by replacing the valves, but a more prudent thing to do—I would say mandatory on a shipshape yacht—is to install a vented loop into both the intake and the discharge pipes—see drawing. This will break any siphoning action, which, if the boat is left unattended may eventually cause it to sink.

If a head is clogged and whoever last used it swears on his mother's grave that nothing forbidden has been thrown in there, then your problem might be an overzealous application of toilet paper. Wait a bit to give the stuff a chance to loosen up,

then give the pump a few solid ones. If there is still no movement, then I'm afraid Elmer, it's time to bend our knees and do a little penance. First of all check the backwater valve—also known as a *Joker* valve. Some joke. Ha, ha. This is where things like matches and hairpins would be caught. If that looks okay, then check the piston on the pump, for it may no longer be in one piece. Usually it takes something major to stop a head completely.

I would say it's almost mandatory to have a decent gasket and parts kit aboard for a head. Why not? You'll need it sooner or later so you might as well have it ready. Few things can spoil a good cruise more than a faulty head, although the antics over the rail might be good for extended laughter.

Winterizing

If the boat is left in the water, the head must be properly winterized, for not only can the water in it freeze and cause damage to seals and pump and sometimes even crack the bowl, but if sea water is left in the system, you can have a horrendous build-up of algae in it, which will set off such an odor that when you next come aboard you'll think you just entered a rotten egg factory.

So. Close the inlet seacock and remove the hose as above, when getting rid of odors. Get a can of permanent antifreeze—it has to have a glycol base otherwise it may damage the parts—and stick the intake hose into it. Pump the fluid into the head until you are sure the whole system is full of it. You'll see it go through the bowl but give it a few pumps thereafter. Now close the outlet seacock as well. Leave it thus until the spring. Don't forget to grease the pump rod in the spring, for the antifreeze removes all lubricants.

If the boat is hauled for the winter, leave your seacocks open and pump the bowl as dry as you can. Then remove the drain plug at the bottom of

A VENTED LOOP TO PREVENT SIPHONING

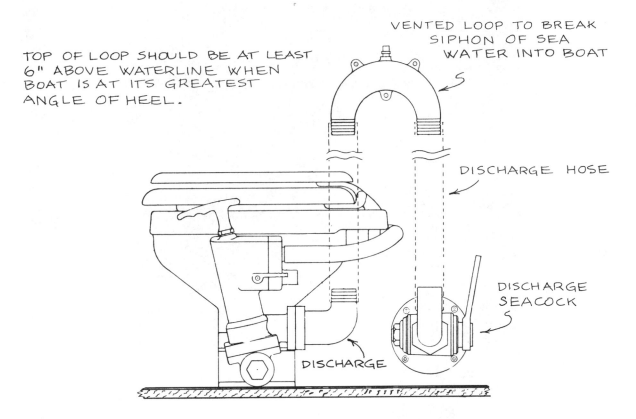

TOP OF LOOP SHOULD BE AT LEAST 6" ABOVE WATERLINE WHEN BOAT IS AT ITS GREATEST ANGLE OF HEEL.

VENTED LOOP TO BREAK SIPHON OF SEA WATER INTO BOAT

DISCHARGE HOSE

DISCHARGE SEACOCK

DISCHARGE

NOTE! PUT A VENTED LOOP ON INTAKE SEACOCK AS WELL.

the pump, so whatever water is left in the system can drain out. Leave as is and let it air. Dump a little lubricant—only the ones recommended for heads, not oils or kerosene or alcohol—to soften the dried parts. If you have the time or inclination, the last few days of winter would be a perfect time to take the pump apart and clean the valves and check the parts.

The more astute among you will have noticed a total absence of mention of electric grinder heads. This is no accident. I realize that they are more efficient when used in connection with holding tanks, for they seem to use somewhat less water, but then that is a tiny benefit compared to the problems they can be if they break down, and a miniscule benefit compared to the dread they put into the heart, as the grinder chatters and whirrs and slashes, mere inches from the jewels.

This is how the head should look for the winter—gone.

WINTERIZING THE HEAD

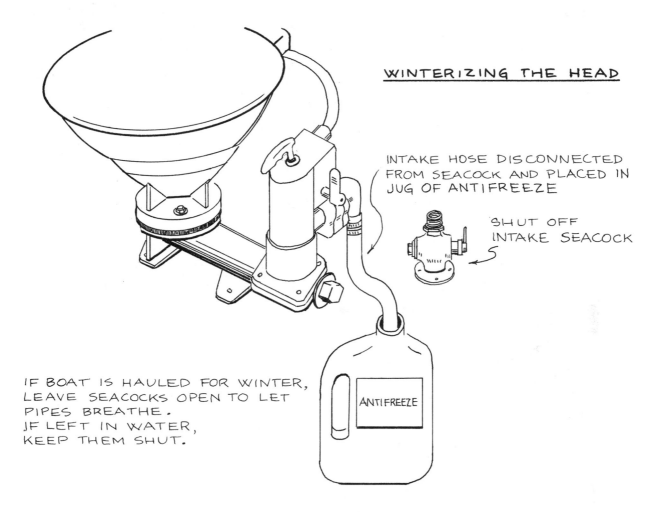

INTAKE HOSE DISCONNECTED FROM SEACOCK AND PLACED IN JUG OF ANTIFREEZE

SHUT OFF INTAKE SEACOCK

IF BOAT IS HAULED FOR WINTER, LEAVE SEACOCKS OPEN TO LET PIPES BREATHE.
IF LEFT IN WATER, KEEP THEM SHUT.

ANTIFREEZE

Don't forget to plug the end of the hose to keep out the ocean in case your seacock decides to pack it in.

39

Bilge Pumps

I dread putting bilge pumps in such an obscure place because they really should go right at the beginning of the book in all capital letters, for they are without doubt the most important pieces of equipment on board. Sadly enough they are often the most neglected ones. One well distributed book that claims to be a book of how to maintain sailboats, doesn't have a single word in it about bilge pumps. It makes one wonder if the simpleton who wrote it had ever in his life actually been on a boat.

Anyway. If you ever pay attention to the real stories behind boats sinking, you will all too often hear that a fairly minor leak became a maritime disaster because the bilge pumps were found to be "inoperative." How can that be? A decent diaphragm pump like a Whale or an Edson has barely a half dozen moving parts, of which almost every time a failure occurs only two are affected and, generally speaking, those two could have been kept in check without ever opening up the pump.

So, Elmers of the world, lend me your ears and you might save yourselves from becoming skippers of submarines.

Where and How to Install

a) One pump should be in the cockpit located so the helmsman can manage it while still managing the helm.

b) A second pump should be down below out of the weather, so located that a crew member can comfortably stand and brace himself and pump away until he's blue in the face. A very nice idea that I saw on a Swan was to put the pump just below the floorboards, enabling the man on the pump to stand upright and use a nice, long (about forty-eight inch) handle. This gives you so much leverage that you barely exert any pressure at all, save for the weight of your body. Shifting weight using your legs is a lot less exhausting than using your spaghetti arms and already aching back. Anyway, if you're lucky, you'll be in a good storm and you'll be thrown about so much that having the handle to hang onto will actually seem like a blessing. How is *that* for youthful insouciance!

c) The intake hoses must have screens on them to keep crap from plugging up the pumps. The

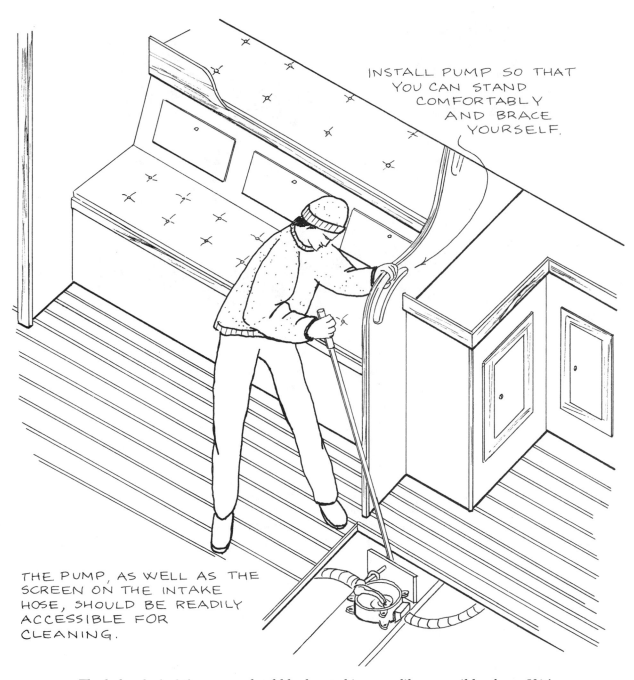

INSTALL PUMP SO THAT YOU CAN STAND COMFORTABLY AND BRACE YOURSELF.

THE PUMP, AS WELL AS THE SCREEN ON THE INTAKE HOSE, SHOULD BE READILY ACCESSIBLE FOR CLEANING.

The belowdecks bilge pump should be located in a readily accessible place. If it's put below the floorboards for aesthetic reasons, then be sure to keep your floorboards trimmed to a loose fit. It they're snug now, Elmie, just imagine how snug they'll be once you start taking on water and they swell.

A perfect place for a good bilge pump. Mounted just below the floorboards in the main cabin, it leaves room for the crew to pump comfortably while standing if you have a long lever about four feet in length. The way the pump is mounted, its sides can be readily opened for cleaning and servicing.

cross sectional area of the screen should be twice that of the hose, so that the effective intake area is not reduced.

d) The screens must be accessible in case *they* plug up.

e) The *pumps* must be accessible in case *they too* plug up. Accessible does not mean that you should be able to see them or touch them, but that you should be able to *work* on them.

f) The hoses, both inlet and outlet, should be as short as possible to reduce the friction in the system.

g) The hoses should be as straight as possible for the same reason. The Edson pump people say that "one right-angle connection is equal to the resistance of twenty feet of hose."

h) The discharge through-hull should be well above the waterline, otherwise the backpressure from the sea can greatly increase the amount of force necessary to pump the pump and the efficiency of the pump will thus be greatly reduced and you'll turn blue in the face infinitely sooner.

To me the ideal large pump to get is one like the Whale Gusher 25, for it has two large handwheels on either side of the housing, a quick turn on which opens up the whole pump, yielding ready access to the whole guts.

Maintenance

It's incredible how little coddling these pumps require. After ten years of use, our Whales have given us problems only once and that was after a long period of non-use. The thing that seems most common in causing pump failures is the fouling of the rubber valves or flaps. This tends to occur most frequently if there is an icebox draining into the bilge, which exudes more than its share of thick gooey stuff. Together with the salt crystals that are left behind, they create a heavy build-up at the hinged portion of the flap, stopping the flaps from closing completely and rendering the pump useless.

This need not occur. An occasional filling of the bilge with warm water and baking soda—cheap and available—which is then pumped into the pump and allowed to sit for ten minutes, will loosen most deposits, which can then be pumped out with the addition of more warm water. Don't use *hot* water for it tends to harden the neoprene or rubber flaps and drastically shorten their lives. I suppose you can use something like *Sea-Lube* which is a liquid thing put out by Wilcox-Crittenden to dissolve salt accumulation in heads. It'll save you heating up water. Big deal.

Once a year, the pumps should be disassembled—a big ten-minute job—and all goop cleaned out from all corners and nooks. Put a little Vaseline on the rubber parts to keep them soft.

If the valves seem to have hardened, for godsake change them—for a couple of dollars you can have peace of mind.

Some pumps, like the Whale 25, have a gasket around the hinged aluminum doors of either side. If this gasket is in any way crimped when the door is being closed, you can develop a slow but steady leak which can eventually eat a nifty little hole in the edge of the door, necessitating an expensive replacement, or resulting in pump failure.

Once a year, check all hose connections to make sure they are tight, and in areas where the hose is bent, check to make sure it has not collapsed. A hose that might be perfectly firm when new can develop fatigue under stress and collapse and cut off the flow of water.

A nice touch which should help to keep the pump clean, is to fill the bilge each time you fill your water tanks and then pump out the fresh water through the bilge pumps. If you have some baking soda aboard, pitch some in there now and give the pump a little thrill. It might save your life out of gratitude one day.

NOTE: THE MOST COMMON FAILURE IN BILGE PUMPS IS THE BUILD-UP OF GOO, CRAP AND CORRUPTION ON THE TWO FLAP VALVES (INTAKE AND OUTLET) PREVENTING THEM FROM CLOSING. IF THESE ARE CLEANED REGULARLY THE REST IS A PIECE OF CAKE.

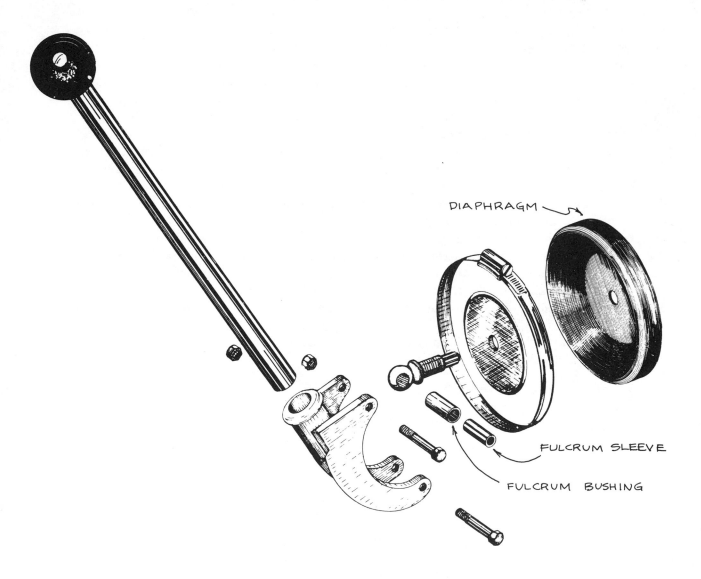

DIAPHRAGM

FULCRUM SLEEVE

FULCRUM BUSHING

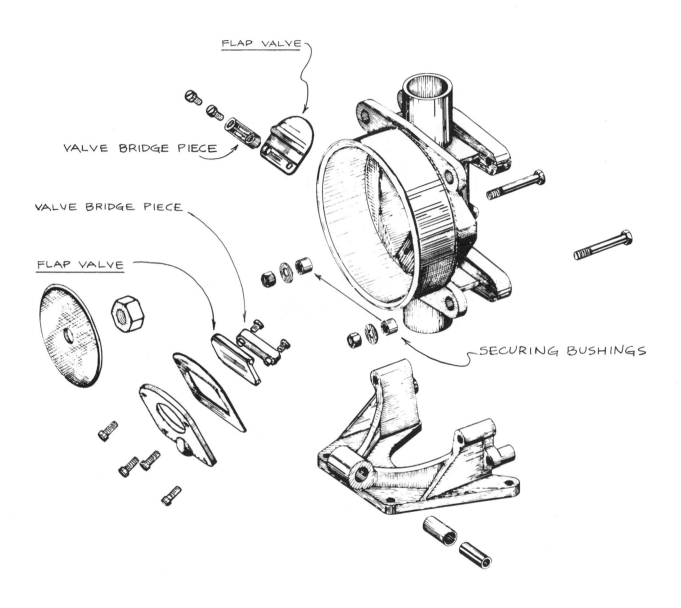

FLAP VALVE

VALVE BRIDGE PIECE

VALVE BRIDGE PIECE

FLAP VALVE

SECURING BUSHINGS

DIAPHRAGM BILGE PUMP

40

Electrical Equipment

I suppose we wouldn't even have this topic if it wasn't for the battery, so we might as well start with it.

Battery

I am probably as negligent as any of us with my batteries aboard and believe me I have paid the price in dollars and in time. To be able to maintain a battery in a marine environment, you have to start with a decent product. By that I mean you need to have a heavy-duty marine battery, not a little flimsy car battery, no matter how heavy-duty the manufacturer calls it. The differences are absolutely enormous so don't take this discussion lightly.

First of all, a good-sized marine battery will have a much greater amp-hour capacity than a car battery. To put it simply, it will have a greater reserve of power. Therefore, a 120 amp-hour battery will give you twice as much total power as a 60 amp-hour car battery.

Second, a good marine battery is designed to deliver power steadily over a longer period, whereas a car battery is designed to give you a great surge of power all at once to get an engine turned over and that's it. After the car engine is running,

a car battery goes back to sleep, for then the alternator takes over and provides the juice. On a sailboat the demands are usually quite different. Sure the engine has to be started, but unlike a car, much of the drain into radios and especially lights—both interior and anchor lights—occurs when the engine is no longer running. Unlike the car's demand, the sailboat's demand is a slow but steady one.

Third, a marine battery will have a much deeper recovery rate than a car battery. What that means is that a marine battery can be drained very deeply up to a couple of hundred times and it will still recover to complete health if recharged, whereas a car battery may last through but thirty discharges and recharges. In other words—car batteries are designed to run nearly fully charged most of the time, but good marine batteries are designed to be drained very deeply and then recharged, over and over again.

Don't ask me what the difference in construction is, for I don't know all the details, but I do know that a good 130 amp-hour battery weighs about three times as much as a car battery and is about four inches longer, so it must mean that there is a lot more lead in the thing, which in turn must mean that a much longer time must pass before it's

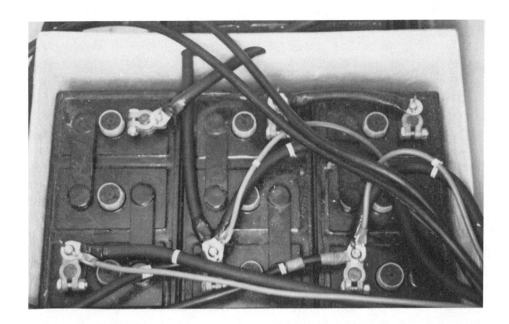

Batteries spew out all sorts of evil juices that eat wood and metal but have no appetite for fiberglass and some plastics. The case above is hand-laid-up fiberglass. Its bottom is bonded to a wood shelf to inhibit any movement. Notice how spotlessly maintained the terminals are.

For the home builder, a plywood box covered inside with a couple of laminates of fiberglass would be easier to make. Be sure to make your box good and sturdy; a battery flopping around in a seaway carries a lot of weight.

completely eaten away.

What all that means is, don't save money by buying a car battery. It simply won't last. I thought I'd beat the "marine" scam and slide by with a cheapo forty dollar heavy-duty car battery, but I've got to confess I didn't slide very far. After one year the battery was a doornail. On the other hand we have a good marine battery that is now in its sixth year and working fine.

Besides, a good marine battery has a very heavy duty case which can take the pounding and banging that a sailboat battery undergoes.

1. A few no-no's

a) Never break the circuit between the alternator and the battery while the engine is running. The master switch must *never* be switched off.

b) Never confuse the battery poles with one another. The poles are generally stamped with a plus and minus respectively. The minus pole must always be connected to the engine block.

c) If you have to use an outside battery to start the engine do it like this. Let the flat battery remain connected in circuit. Connect the outside battery to the flat battery, plus to plus, minus to minus. When the engine starts, disconnect the outside battery but never break the circuit to the flat battery.

d) Never use a rapid charger while the alternator is connected to the battery.

e) Always disconnect both battery cables before carrying out any work on the alternator.

f) If electric welding work is to be carried out on the engine or installation units, disconnect the charging regulator cables at the alternator and insulate.

g) Check V-belt tension and cable connections at regular intervals.

h) *Never* check a battery's water level by lighting a match and peeking into the holes, There are explosive hydrogen gases in there that can blow your moustache to the top of the mast.

2. Installation

How long a battery will last will be determined by where it is installed. If it's hidden in some obscure, hard to get at place, you can be pretty sure that it will never be checked for either charge or water level, at least not until it goes completely dead. So install it in a clean accessible place where the ventilation is good so the explosive hydrogen gases given off can escape, and where you can see and reach to refill the battery or clean terminals or whatever.

But don't have it too exposed. I once saw batteries at the bottom of a sail locker in the cockpit. That's madness. A wet sail bag or rain or spray can easily short the terminals causing an endless drain.

Keep the batteries as low down as you can for, a) they are heavy and b) there is less motion lower down.

Install batteries as close as you can to the engine so the cables can be short and there will be as little voltage loss as possible.

Just because the battery is as heavy as it is does not mean it's going to sit placidly where you put it. Quite the contrary. In a good seaway it will come adrift and, with its weight, destroy everything in its path. Spilled battery acid will then eat away whatever is still left in one piece. Hence the battery *must* be in an isolated box and it must be firmly lashed in place. The heavy plastic cases you can buy are good, and the tiedown straps that come with them are good, but some of the buckles and the thread they're sewn on with are bad news because they get eaten away by battery acid. So be careful what you buy. The box and all should be well secured. Strap everything to a bulkhead or the shelf the battery sits on. Built-in boxes made of plywood are ideal for they won't require any heavy strapping, but they must be lined with fiberglass or spilled acid will eat right through the wood.

A well laid out panel with a battery tester. This is handy to have belowdecks so you can see how much your lights and radios have drained the batteries.

3. Dual batteries

This is almost a must on a boat with interior electrical lights. Number 1 battery should be used only when starting the engine, and the other for accessories only, i.e., lights, radios etc. A good three-way switch must be installed with this system which enables you to run on battery 1, or 2, or ALL. Once the batteries are installed, for godsake mark *right on the battery* which is in fact Number 1 and Number 2, or you'll be like me, who after ten years still isn't quite sure which is which. Some people say that since the engine starter battery will be used much like a car battery, that a car battery will suffice. Maybe so. But it makes me feel good in

know I have a built-in spare if the need arises.

A good way to use the dual batteries is to use ALL for starting the engine. Once the needle on the battery charge indicator has climbed a bit, *shut off the engine* and switch the switch to Number 2. Then restart the engine. *Never* switch the switch while the engine is running, for you will short-circuit the regulator and it will then be ruined.

Once Number 2 is fully charged—remember this is the one that suffers the deep drain from reading lights and anchor lights—SHUT THE ENGINE OFF and switch to Number 1 only, then restart the engine.

4. Maintenance

This is so pitifully simple it almost hurts to say it.

a) Check the level of the water. It should never fall below the top of the plates, for then you'll have an uneven plate wear meaning shorter life. Ideally the water level should be checked every day, but we both know you'll never do that—I certainly don't—so have a little pity and do it at least once a week. Refill with distilled water, but don't overfill or the extra stuff will come squirting out when you put the caps on. One is supposed to use only distilled water to fill batteries because the minerals in tap water will accelerate battery demise. So it may behoove you to have a gallon of bottled water handy.

b) Keep the terminals and the top of the battery clean. Don't let anything build up on the battery for it can become a short between the terminals and drain the battery.

c) A couple times a year, remove the cable terminals and with a round file clean off all the built-up stuff inside the rings and with sandpaper clean off the battery terminals until they shine. Now dab a bit of vaseline over everything to fend off the corrosive fumes, then slip the fittings back on firmly and tighten them down. Now dab a bit of vaseline all over the terminal's top.

If the clamp won't slide off after you have loosened the nut, don't try loosening it by bashing away at the terminal with a hammer. If you do, you can very easily break the terminal right out of the casing. Take a screwdriver and pry the jaws of the cable ends open, then tap the cable very gently. It should come like a lamb.

5. Winterizing

At the Concordia yard, they pull the batteries out of every boat under their care and store them in a dry clean place. They also hook up trickle chargers to them—ones with an automatic shutoff so they don't overcharge—and in the spring, the batteries come out bursting with enthusiasm and juice. If you don't want to spend money on an automatic charger, just check the battery level with a hydrometer—one of those glass things with the rubber sucker on the end—and put the cheapo charger on for a day or two.

An added advantage to yanking the battery out of the boat is that thieves will have greater difficulty starting her up.

When storing a battery for the winter, keep it off a cement floor, for it appears that the electricity trickles away into the moist cement and into the ground, not only killing your battery but also electrifying the entire earthworm population of your yard.

Electronics

There isn't much you can do about looking after electronics except for keeping moisture out of them as best you can. Spraying a bit of WD 40 onto all cables and terminals will help. The single biggest thing you can do is to be sure they're installed well out of the way of spray and rain. When you inspect terminals and find a lot of corrosion, don't just clean them off and spray them and forget about them. The corrosion was there for a reason, so find out what the reason was and correct it.

Your next major contribution can be to remove everything, from radios to depth sounders—anything that moves—and keep them in a warm dry place over the winter. Not only will this foil thieves—they seem to seldom enter a boat that has been gutted but it will prolong the life of your instruments as well.

Things left aboard, like lights, should have the bulbs removed and the contact points sanded clean with 100 grit. Then they should be sprayed with WD 40 before being reinstalled again.

During the season check all connections and terminals once in a while—a poor connection can

If you're worried about your battery running low, you can install a few spares. Just kidding, Elmer. This is actually the winter storage room at Concordia. Notice that none of the batteries is directly on the cement floor, and all are hooked into automatic trickle chargers.

seriously damage an expensive instrument.

When winterizing instruments that have their own power, like radio receivers, hand-held compasses, etc., remove the dry-cell batteries from them and store them separately.

Repairs almost always have to be done by a professional, and the only thing you can do is to deter-mine whether the failure is actually in the instrument itself or in the electrical system. For this, get a small inexpensive multimeter which measures both voltage and ohms—resistance. The first is needed to find whether or not there is a live current in a wire, and the second to trace down corroded junctions and short circuits.

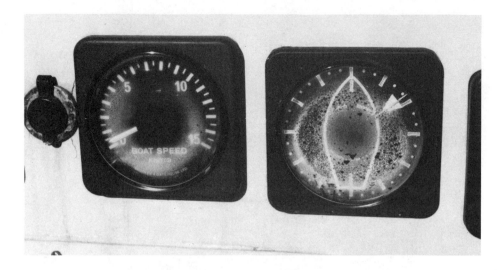

How to ruin your instruments on short order. These are best removed for the winter and stored somewhere dry. As for the summer, you'll have to make sure the joint between the instrument and whatever it's mounted on is perfectly caulked or gasketed.

Expensive electronics should be covered during short layups, with a moisture collector set near them. As for long layups, all the stuff should be taken out of the boat and stored at home.

Starters and Alternators

These generally need little active maintenance, but they both do show a grave disdain for water, so keep them out of the way of spray and drips. As for the ultimate in maintenance, let me tell you that the Concordia yard removes all starters and generators from boats under their care over the winter, and they clean and check them all, renewing brushes and solanoids as needed. Apart from that, they keep them in a dry place over the winter, away from cold damp air. Removing either of these is a rather simple job, usually no more than three bolts and a couple of wire connections per; the only problem that may be encountered is accessibility. If you can spare the time, by all means remove these when you lay up your boat, and if not, at least clean them and oil them and cover them snugly with a good oily cloth.

Wiring

If you have to do any wiring or rewiring on a boat, the proper way is to use crimped wire fittings on everything and then seal the ends of the crimp with solder to keep out corrosion. Never just twist a piece of multistrand wire under a terminal screw and call it good, for in a salty and humid marine environment this kind of connection is begging for corrosion.

To put on a crimp-type fitting, take a proper wire stripping tool, strip a bit more than ¼ inch from the end of the wire and slip on the fitting. If you stripped right, the wire should be just barely coming out through the plastic cover, or if you are using a butt connector, the wire should bottom out without any of it showing. Now, using the crimp portion of the tool—the jaws—press firmly until the jaws come together. If you don't want to bother soldering the ends, then seal them well with silicone sealer.

When installing a light fixture with loose wire tails, you can either solder the incoming wires to the lamp's wires or you can use some small Mars fittings. A well done Mars connection is almost as good as a soldered one if it's sealed off with silicone, and is much easier for the amateur to per-as good as a soldered one if it's sealed off with silicone, and is much easier for the amateur to perform satisfactorily. Be sure to strip about ⁵⁄₁₆ inch wire for a small Mars, and hold the two pieces to be joined firmly in your fingers with both ends exactly side by side. Now slip on the connector and twist firmly until you meet resistance. Give it a tug to be sure it took. Again don't forget to seal the base of the Mars with silicone sealer.

Soldering

If you must solder use rosin core solder *not* acid core solder. The trick to soldering is to get the wires hot enough to melt the solder *when it touches the wires. Never* try to apply solder to a joint by melting the solder with the iron and then dripping the molten bead onto the wires. That is totally futile. You will create what is called a cold joint that will come apart in no time.

You have to use care to get the wire hot enough without burning off the insulation. Get the solder to run in a nice, smooth-surfaced bead, then get the iron out of there or the bead will just run off. Let the wires cool before you test the joint. The best way to insulate a soldered joint is to use a "heat-shrink" tubing. This you can buy in different sizes and it is nothing more than its name implies—a piece of light plastic tubing that will shrink like crazy when quickly heated with a pocket lighter. Just clip off what length you think you'll need and slip it over the soldered joint—slip it over one of the wires in advance if you are doing a

FORK CONNECTOR

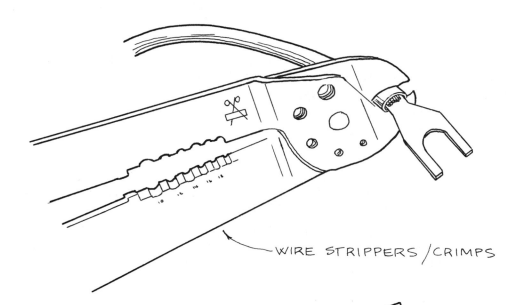

WIRE STRIPPERS/CRIMPS

SEAL OFF ENDS WITH
SILICONE SEALER TO
KEEP OUT MOISTURE

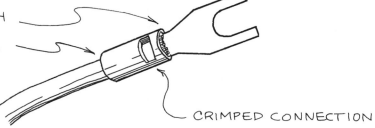

CRIMPED CONNECTION

MAKING A CRIMPED CONNECTION

THE WESTERN UNION SPLICE

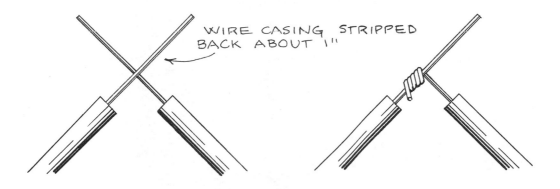

WIRE CASING STRIPPED
BACK ABOUT 1"

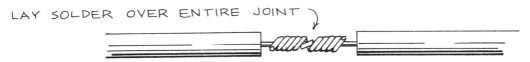

LAY SOLDER OVER ENTIRE JOINT

IF YOU'RE REALLY DEDICATED, PUT SOME HEAT-SHRINK OVER IT.

Elmer! Did you do this?

Don't install any toy lamps aboard a boat; leave them for the mobile home crowd. Junk is junk and it's guaranteed to break, fail or fall apart.

Western Union joint—making sure you cover all of the wire, then heat and watch it shrivel. Like magic.

Generators

Preventive Maintenance

a) Disconnect all wires from the unit.
b) Loosen and remove all mounting bolts.
c) Lift generator carefully from base.
d) When free, cover with a cloth so you won't be damaging any of the woodwork on your way out.
e) Go to the nearest lifeline.
f) Count to three, swing, and heave. Mind the splash.

This is an ultimate bit of preventive maintenance, for it will prevent me from having to row over to your boat and chop a hole in your hull with the largest size fire axe I could procure on short notice, all because your generator ran so flawlessly for five nerve-wracking mind-numbing hours, in some silent secluded anchorage that I spent weeks sailing to so I could listen to the birds and the rain and the wind.

Thanks, Elmer, I knew you had a soul deep down in there somewhere.

41

Outboards

I don't know much about these things except that they make a lot of noise in harbors and quiet anchorages, but they are nice to have when trying to explore distant backwaters that are too shallow to reach by sailboat. There are of course those of you who use outboards to power your sailboats by, and to those I say you're lucky devils, for if you get really annoyed with the thing all you have to do is undo a couple of bolts and heave. Hard to do with a 500 lb. diesel.

Anyway, since, as I said, I know little about outboards, I turned to the people who make the most reliable little ones—British Seagull. They furnished me with a wonderful handbook that reads as if it were written by a big-moustached schoolmaster with a hickory stick. It's full of good information and I know that not all things in here apply to all outboards, but it's just too much fun to read so here it is.

Starting and Running

If a clutch is fitted, always start the motor in the "free" drive or neutral position.

If the motor is fitted with a recoil starter, pull the cord slowly until you feel the pawls engage and then give the cord a firm quick pull to start the motor...return the cord slowly and allow it to retract fully into the starter before re-pulling.

Before attempting to start the motor insure the gear lever is in the neutral—i.e., central—position.

As soon as the engine starts, partially close the throttle control to avoid the engine's over-revving.

When selecting either forward or reverse gear, always keep the motor in the straight ahead position and the r.p.m. as low as possible.

Care should be taken when reversing as the underwater unit cannot tilt clear if an obstruction is hit.

Beware

1. Water in the fuel

Condensation may produce water in the fuel, and so sometimes when the tank is low, tip the contents out through the filler opening by turning the motor upside down, and refill with fresh mixture. Disconnecting the fuel pipe, and draining through the tap is useless as the tap filter will stop the water. It's wise, however, to disconnect and drain the pipe to clear out anything undesirable in the pipe itself.

2. Sand

If allowed to get into the motor, sand will cause expensive, and extensive damage. Don't lay the motor on the shore, or in the automobile with sand about...use a canvas cover to protect the power-unit.

3. Unorthodox inboard installations

Installing the motor inboard in a well or trunk is rather a touchy matter, for unless they are really well designed and properly ventilated, the motor can only breathe its own exhaust gases and die of suffocation!

Before Using the Motor

This little book is written to ensure that your outboard motoring is 100% pleasure, and if you abide by its advice you need have nothing to fear, even if you scarcely know a crankshaft from a connecting rod!

It requires no skill or mechanical ability at all to run a Seagull...there are hundreds of thousands of engines operating faultlessly day in and day out in the most unskilled hands. (So even the Elmerest among us have a chance.)

In many ways a motor is like a human being...normally it is fit and well, but it must have some essential things in life, and if it doesn't get them it falls sick.

Almost all the ailments attached to outboard motoring can be accounted for by the attitude of..."It doesn't matter...any old plug will do...any old fuel...any oil that's available...mixed in any proportions...no need to read the instruction, I know all about engines...never mind about fixing the engine on the boat properly, we're in a hurry...this'll do...that'll do," etc., etc.

Let us say at once, this will NOT do!

Your outboard doesn't ask for very much, and there's no difficulty in giving it what it requires...we don't write this book for fun...we do it because it's vital for your own pleasure, security and peace of mind.

And So...a Few Musts

a) Carry out meticulously the instructions which follow as regards gasoline and oil.
b) Don't use grease in the gearbox...use oil, and oil only.
c) Always use the right spark plug.
d) Don't dismantle unless absolutely necessary... due to the engine design, decarbonizing is unnecessary. If the engine is given its correct "food and drink" and the present of a new plug occasionally, it will require little further supervision.

Don't do your first run with a new engine under rush conditions in front of a large audience. For instance, avoid a vital trip catching the last tide in a small dinghy laden to the gunwhales with gear and people, in half a gale in the pouring rain. (How is *that* for a "for instance"!)

Choose fine weather conditions and, if possible, a seamanlike and mechanical companion...a quiet and secluded spot, where success or otherwise doesn't matter much. Take your time, and see that the engine is fitted exactly as laid down in the instructions.

If you run into trouble it's much more likely to happen on your first trip or two than any other time.

The engine is new and a little stiff...you haven't got the knack of pulling the starting cord...you're inclined to run the motor gently, when what it actually wants is plenty of hard running...so put in an hour or two, quietly, under ideal conditions to get the hang of things. After you've worked together for twenty hours, you will be astonished how the whole outfit...you included...really gets down to business.

Most outboards are designed for a rich oil mixture to provide not only unlimited life, but adequate oil protection from the internal corrosion always associated with the long periods of idleness inseparable from service at sea.

We do NOT recommend gently running in.

The bearings are so large, that under light loads, there is insufficient pressure and friction to polish up the internal surfaces to the extent necessary to obtain that ultimate first-class performance, which can be expected from these motors after fifty hours running.

So don't dawdle about with the engine when new...quarter to half throttle at least is a very good speed.

If you write to us for assistance...don't just say, "I can't make my engine go," that's useless!

Give us ALL the information you can, particularly as regards the type of boat on which the engine is used, and the way in which it is mounted. Describe exactly what happens and how the motor performs. Tell us what type of gasoline and oil you are using and ...more important than anything...let us have the *engine lettering and number.*

Fuel Mixture

Fresh fuel is essential...the use of stale, unfiltered fuel from dirty containers will cause endless trouble.

A light grade engine oil suitable for two-strokes should be *thoroughly* mixed with gasoline in a separate *clean* container. We recommend B.P. Super Outboard Motor Oil, Castrol T.T., Duckhams Outboard Two-stroke, Esso Aquaglide, Finamix, Mobilmix T.T., Shell Outboard Motor Oil, Texaco Motor Oil 2.T. Multiple viscosity lubricants such as SAE 20W-50 motor oils are not suitable. The correct ratio is one part of oil to twenty-five parts of gasoline (other engines differ). The oil proportion must not be cut below this,

irrespective of the claims made for some lubricants.

Propeller Spring Drive

The propeller drive is transmitted through a spring with a hook which engages with the propeller hub to lessen the shock from hitting any obstruction.

If, because of such an accident, the hook is straightened and the drive lost, the spring must be replaced. This only entails the removal of the spring retaining pin and washer, not the propeller. Always carry a spare spring.

Engine Mounting

In a small dinghy, send the crew forward to keep the stern high until the engine is running.

A transom angle of approximately ten degrees is best to insure that there is a free flow of water to the propeller.

Always fit the security bar and safety pin to avoid any possibility of the engine's becoming dislodged.

A warning. If the dinghy is to be towed in rough water we recommend that the motor be removed and stowed aboard the parent vessel. Similarly, if left unattended at congested steps, it is better to take the motor off the transom and stow it inboard for safety's sake.

For Auxiliary Power

On sailing craft using a rudder it is quite satisfactory to mount the motor away from the centerline, to one side of the transom.

Starting and Running the Motor, From Cold

a) See that the motor is free to swivel to permit steering.

b) Unscrew the air valve in filler cap one turn only, NOT to its fullest extent.

c) Open fuel tap.

d) Close choker shutter.

e) Open the throttle lever as far as it will go. When you have used the motor for some time, use any throttle opening that suits your particular motor.

f) Depress the flooding button on the carburetor to overflow the fuel, thus checking the supply.

g) Place the knot on the starting cord in one of the slots of the start-pulley-plate, and wind cord clockwise.

h) Put one hand on the fuel tank to prevent engine from tilting and, with the other, pull the starting cord firmly, horizontally, not violently, and the motor will probably start at the first or second attempt depending on the temperature.

In a few moments the motor will commence to run unevenly and show signs of getting rich, and then the choke shutter should be opened *gradually* to its fullest extent, that is to say wide and clear.

The speed can then be varied by opening or closing the throttle as desired.

To stop the motor, close the throttle fully and shut the fuel tap.

To Start the Motor, Hot or Warm

Proceed as before, but don't flood the carburetor or close the choke. Never continue pulling the starting cord with the choke shut, and if you suspect that you have got the engine over-rich the answer is: *fully* open the throttle, open the choke, shut off the fuel at the tap, and pull the starting cord until the engine, *after* three or four attempts perhaps, starts up.

When it runs, reopen the fuel tap and all will be well.

Water Pump and Cooling System

Don't run the boat in a few inches of water with the propeller churning up sand and mud.

This will obviously speedily clog up the water cooling system and stop circulation. *This must not happen.*

The engine can be run at slow speeds for a minute or two without the water flowing, providing the motor is then speeded up just sufficiently to circulate water for a brief period as a precaution.

When removing the engine from the boat—remember the silencer may be hot—stand the motor in a vertical position for a minute to drain before stowage.

Never tilt the engine beyond the horizontal until all the water has had time to drain from the circulating system.

Laying-Up Drill

Before laying up for a long period:

a) Flush the cooling system through with fresh water by applying a fresh water hose to the cylinder water outlet.

b) See that all the water is drained from the cooling system by standing the motor in a vertical position for a minute or two.

c) Drain the fuel line by dismantling the fuel pipe from the tank fuel tap. Get rid of stale fuel in the tank itself by opening the filler cap and turning the motor upside down.

d) With the spark plug removed and the throttle

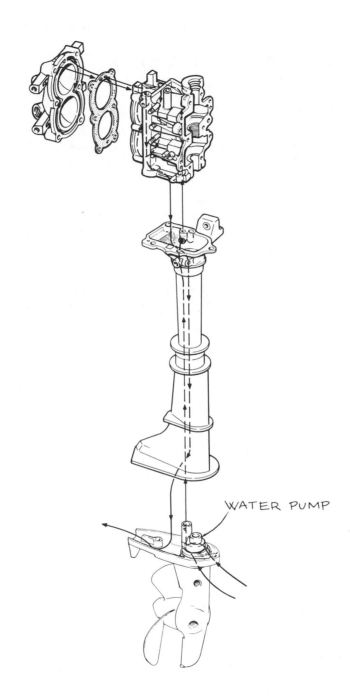

WATER PUMP

WATER FLOW DIAGRAM FOR A SMALL OUTBOARD ENGINE

fully open, inject a thin oil through the plug hole and carburetor induction. Spin the engine.

e) Replace the spark plug loosely to keep dust, dirt and damp out of the cylinder.

f) Oil the carburetor control at each end of the throttle cable and operate the throttle a few times.

g) Remove the high tension lead...dry and clean the black plastic terminal. Better still, fit a new high tension lead the following season.

h) Unscrew the oil filler plug in the gearbox. Drain, and refill with SAE 140 lubricant.

i) Thoroughly brush the external surfaces of the motor with thin oil after removing all salt deposits with fresh water.

j) When out of use, the engine should be stored *upright* (vertically) as on the boat and kept warm.

When bringing the engine into service, remove the spark plug and spin the engine to clear excessive oil before attempting to start.

Check the spark plug and replace if necessary. Before refitting, oil or grease the threads and insert the plug very carefully at the correct angle so that the threads are not crossed. Check and correct gap. Top up the gearbox.

Submersion

Should the motor at any time be dropped overboard...on recovery *immediately*:

a) Scrap all fuel...everywhere.

b) Flush the motor with fresh water. Dry thoroughly.

c) Inject thin oil through carburetor inlet and plug hole.

d) Get the engine started up again as soon as possible. It can be run out of the water...clamped on a bench for up to half a minute, but avoid engine "racing" by shutting down the throttle.

General Observations

If, after use in salt water, the engine is wiped over with an oily rag, it will be found that a protective skin will form over the gearbox, and the motor's appearance will be maintained.

Alternatively, a good way of maintaining the engine's appearance is to give the whole motor a couple of good coats of marine varnish, omitting the silencer.

On Boat Handling

See that your mooring buoy is a sensible one, with a really large, upright loop on it, big enough to slip your arm through. You want to be able to grab it by hand, if necessary, in rough water.

Have a short, handy boathook, no longer than necessary, with a really deep and big hook. The tiny double-hook showroom variety is useless when bouncing about in a small boat.

Always approach your mooring against the wind or against the tide, whichever has the most influence on the boat.

Do everything slowly, smoothly and deliberately.

Don't throw the tiller about and make tight turns...you don't DRIVE a boat...you HANDLE it, and you never see professional fishermen making an exhibition of themselves. They make everything look so easy...that's the measure of their skill.

When picking up the buoy, bring it right alongside, well within reach, and don't stop the motor 'til the last second. Otherwise you will lose way and control.

The most important thing is to get right up to your objective with motor running slowly, and don't stop it until you simply *must*.

Never go anywhere without a useful anchor and at least five fathoms of light but strong line so that if the engine hits a snag or stops for any reason through accident you can *stay where you are*, and not drift into trouble.

Also, always carry some effective means of attracting attention. It's surprising how tragedies can take place with lots of boats in the vicinity who have never noticed any trouble.

Lastly, remember that in any motor boat, however quiet, your voice can be heard much more clearly by surrounding craft than by your own companions. A suppose lly confidential and innocent comment about people or their boats may well become, unknowingly, a public broadcast. There's probably enough trouble awaiting you when you get ashore without adding to it!

Well, good luck, and fair winds and tides, and don't forget to attach a safety lanyard to the engine itself—NOT the boat bracket—as an added precaution against accident.

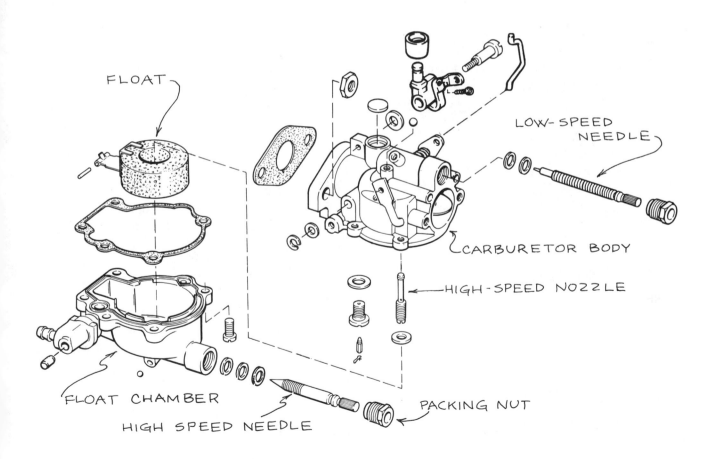

OUTBOARD MOTOR CARBURETOR

42

Diesel Engines

Use

I can give firsthand testimony that on a sailboat nothing will suffer more and cost more to repair than a diesel engine that has been neglected. The irony here is that with a diesel, neglect doesn't mean too much use and not enough care, but rather it means too *little* use and not enough care. A diesel engine, unlike most of us, thrives on work; the harder they're worked the happier they are, for then the temperature of the engine is at a good level with all things evenly heated and evenly working. On a sailboat, however, this is seldom the case, and often the more dedicated the sailor, the more his engine suffers.

My friend Rod Fraser, who runs a small marine engine shop in the boatyard next door, has been working on marine engines for over twenty years, and according to him, most good sailors are their diesel's worst friends. This is most evident in Fisherman's Cove, where wide open water is about a hundred yards away, and the winds are usually decent right off the cove's entrance, so most people—us included—run their engines about ten minutes total before they hoist the sails and shut the engine off. Now this is the worst thing you can do to a diesel; all you have done is run the engine

cold and built up only enough heat in it to thicken the condensation, which will then happily rust valves and springs and shorten the engine's life.

Most of you who own cars in a cold climate will know from firsthand experience that cars which run cold for short distances will have their highly vulnerable parts like mufflers rust out infinitely faster than cars that run mostly hot. Why should it be different with a diesel engine?

So. To make your diesel live happily ever after, NEVER run it for a short while. Letting it idle by the dock doesn't do much for it either, because for it to reach normal operating temperature it has to run for at least a half hour under a decent load and that means pushing close to hull speed at sea.

Now I am not for a minute advocating that we should all begin to motor around mindlessly just aiming and steering from here to there, but when we do run our engines we should *run* them and not walk them, otherwise we're better off sailing in and out of anchorages and in and out of docks— which is actually a really wonderful idea, for it's ten times more fun and ten times less stinky.

If you don't want to waste time at sea motoring, then the alternative is to run it at the dock *under load* while you're getting ready to go out. Check to make sure your docklines are secure, then put the boat in gear and work her up to 1600 r.p.m. I would *strongly* advise checking with the owner of your marina first, for he may disapprove of your towing his pilings and his wharves slowly out to sea.

Before Starting

Rod Fraser has a very firm belief—a boat should be treated like an *airplane*, not like a car. Those of you who fly know that that means checking everything from fuel and oil to ailerons and elevators. If the engine of your car fails, you pull up beside the road, but if the engine of your boat fails, particularly when you are going through a narrow tidal pass or over a breaking bar, or fighting off a lee shore in a gale, you can't just say; "Let's park here, Bertha, and go take the bus." So. Don't just Elmer down to your boat and turn on the ignition and pull away from the curb. First:

a) Check oil levels. An oil level below the lower mark will lead to bearing and piston ring damage, while oil level above the top mark leads to loss of power and overheating.

b) Check to make sure fuel petcock is open.

c) Check to make sure intake seacock is open.

d) If you have fresh water cooling, check coolant level.

e) Then switch on master switch to ALL.

Starting

I would not even mention this simple procedure had I not struggled getting our engine to start *the wrong way for four years*. Now that's enough to give me the *Elmer For A Day* award for at least a decade. So:

a) Make sure the boat is in neutral.

b) Set the throttle lever at the level your engine manufacturer recommends. Some, like Volvo, tell you to have the lever at half-throttle, while others, like BMW, need full-throttle. This depends on the engine cold-start system and at what point of the throttle it engages. So check your manual *and* remember what it says. I didn't bother, and for four years kept starting the engine without assistance of the cold-start switch. Dumb!!

c) Turn ignition key or switch on to check that all the warning lights for oil pressure, battery charging, light up.

d) Start the engine.
   NOW HOLD ON. Don't just walk away as if your job were done. It's not. If there are problems, now is the time to find them. *Not* when you are miles out to sea.

e) Look over the side to see if there is water coming out of the exhaust. All but a few boats have a wet exhaust system. If there is no water, shut the engine off immediately and investigate.

f) Check to see that battery warning light and oil pressure light went out. If the oil pressure light stays on, shut her down before you damage rings and bearings.

g) Open the cover to the engine compartment and have a look. What should you see? *Nothing* out of the ordinary, that's what. No water squirting, no fuel dripping, no fan belt shredding.

h) Listen! Listen for any knocks, taps, shrieks and howls—anything that would make you want to investigate. If you do hear or see something, for godsake don't pretend you don't. Like the barkers yell at the stripjoint doors on 42nd Street; "Check 'er out!"

Starting in Cold Weather

When starting a diesel with an electric starter, make sure you engage the "cold start" switch on your engine—how obvious can you get! Right?

Check your engine manual to see exactly how. If the engine is slow in starting, don't just keep pressing down on the start button or you'll wear the battery down. Give the thing about a minute to recover and then try again.

If you are hand-starting the engine, have all your decompression levers in their *decompress* position, and get the engine turning over as fast as possible, *then* shut each lever down one by one while still turning, until the engine kicks in.

Never race a cold engine; you could easily damage it.

Stopping

a) Let engine idle a few minutes to allow for cooling.
b) Always have the throttle lever in idle position.
c) Do *not* shut off ignition key, but engage kill switch—or lever—firmly until the engine stops.
d) Do not stop engine by opening the decompression levers.
e) Do not shut off ignition before stopping engine.
f) NEVER switch batteries while the engine is running. You will ruin the charging regulator immediately.

Fuel System

1. Dirt

Fuel injectors, because of their tiny orifices, are frighteningly sensitive to both dirt and air. A good primary fuel pump should be installed between the tank and the fuel pump on the engine. If you have two tanks, it may be nice to install one on each tank, so that if one fouls completely, the other will still work.

When buying fuel in foreign ports, take care to filter the fuel first. Taking a cheapo portable system with you would not be a bad idea. It may take up a little room, but that's peanuts compared to washing out all your fuel tanks, taking apart the fuel lines and washing, piece by piece, your filters and the fuel pump and the injectors.

If you could see what I filtered out of fuel in an unmentionable Mexican port, then you would immediately put four thousand filters between their fuel and your tank.

A good filter is a simple stainless box with different density filter screens set into three baffles—see illustration. It's important to have the screens vertically and set slightly above the bottom, for then the heavier particles of grunge will settle there without being forced through the screen, which can easily happen if a screen is installed horizontally and the fuel is splashed straight onto it.

2. Air

As for air, the most common culprit allowing air into the fuel system is you; or in our case, me. You will do it on purpose once a year while you are cleaning and replacing fuel filters, and you'll probably do it on an irregular basis by running out of fuel. Even though we keep an eye on our log and our engine hour meter to try to estimate how much fuel we've used, and even though we do scientifically measure the amount left in each tank with two bamboo chopsticks firmly duct-taped together, I still, on occasion, end up in the middle of nowhere, hanging upside down in the steaming engine room, bleeding all the fuel lines, after having sucked them full of air from a tank that has run empty. The best way to avoid running out of fuel is to refuel once the tanks fall to a quarter full.

3. Guck

There are two families of guck that help to foul injectors. The first is guck that comes from the breaking down of the diesel fuel, which will happen if the fuel sits a long time, and which will begin to happen on a small scale if the diesel sits for a

STAINLESS STEEL BOX WITH
THREE BAFFLES WITH SCREENS
OF VARYING DEGREES OF FINENESS

FILL HERE

LEAVE ENOUGH ROOM
BETWEEN SCREENS TO
ALLOW ACCESS FOR
CLEANING

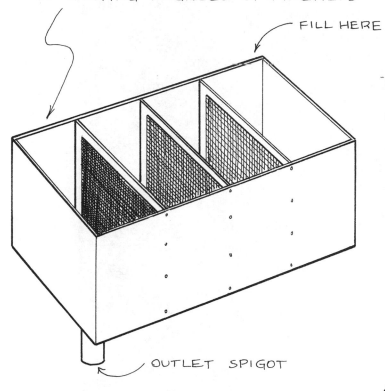

OUTLET SPIGOT

SPLASH-GUARD LIP

KEEPING DEAD THINGS OUT OF YOUR FUEL TANKS

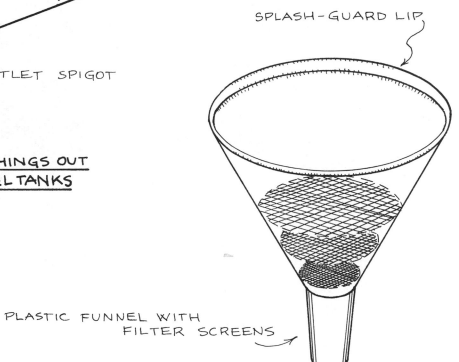

PLASTIC FUNNEL WITH
FILTER SCREENS

If you get into the habit of wiping down your engine at regular intervals, you will find most problems early and save yourself costly repairs and much frustration.

If you ignore and mistreat your diesel, you are guaranteed problems which a mechanic will be happy to repair at $35 an hour. Plus parts.

few months. The first thing to happen is that a very fine scum will form in the fuel which can coat, and hence foul, the injectors. If left to sit—depending on the quality—the fuel can form a muck a few inches deep and as thick as molasses.

To prevent this from happening, a good quality *fuel treatment* should be put into the fuel if it is left to sit more than a month or two. This will not adversely affect the performance of the engine.

The other type of guck that can frequent the fuel tank is a growth of algae, that can occur in the fuel if a slight amount of moisture is present. Moisture can form very rapidly in a tank through condensation. These critters can foul the injectors just as quickly as the guck that comes from the breakdown of the fuel.

To prevent the algae from growing, put a small amount of an additive into the fuel each time you fuel up. We have been using one called "Bio-Bor" for seven years, and have not had a problem yet. In the seven years, we have used a total of two dollars' worth of the stuff. Big deal.

Fuel Filters

1. Pre-filters and fine filters

These are the ones that normally come with the engine itself. One is normally built right into the fuel pump, while the other is a small independent filter, somewhat akin in looks to the regular free-standing filters with settling bowls. The fuel pump filters usually consist of a simple screen most of which can be removed and rinsed in clean diesel fuel and replaced. The cartridge type filters have to be replaced. This should be done at least once every season or after 100 hours of running the engine. Check in your engine manual first to find the filter, and second to determine what you have to replace. Some filters need to have their sealing rings replaced as well, while others are reusable. In either case, you should inspect the seals carefully

to be sure there is no damage. Use special care when fitting new rings or gaskets. It's useless to get a new ring and then destroy it immediately through sloppy installation which ends up pinching a groove or a nick into the delicate piece.

Before you dismantle a filter, use one precaution: Always wash down the exterior of the filter with a brush and some diesel fuel, then wipe with a clean cloth. Be thorough. It's silly to go to a lot of trouble to change a filter screen, only to end up scooping chunks of dirt into the filter itself, dirt which can then make its way into the system. Once the screen is removed, clean the inside of the container thoroughly.

There are new marine diesels whose fuel systems are self-bleeding and that's wonderful, but most of us mortals with older boats will have to bleed the system after cleaning the filter.

2. Extra filters

As I mentioned before, at least one of these critters should be fitted into every fuel system, for not only will it screen out particles and guck, but it will also collect whatever moisture may be in the tanks—from condensation or other sources—by gathering it in the settling bowl. These bowls are normally of glass, so you can see if any water has come into the filter. You can then drain out the water by loosening the drain cock or plug on the bottom of the bowl.

The filter element in the bowl itself will have to be changed every 100 hours of engine time. These elements are the paper absorbent type that actually soak up guck like a blotter, so there is no way of cleaning them; they have to be replaced.

Again, beware when putting back the gaskets.

Bleeding the Fuel System

As I mentioned above, some of the new engines do come with self-bleeding fuel systems; for us

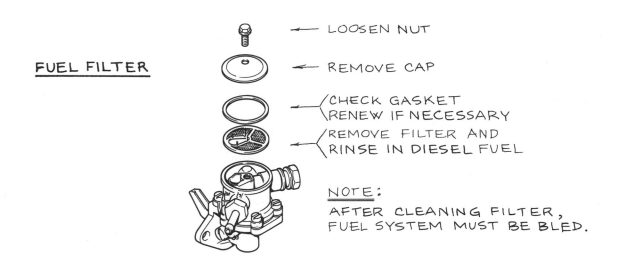

FUEL FILTER

← LOOSEN NUT

← REMOVE CAP

CHECK GASKET
RENEW IF NECESSARY

REMOVE FILTER AND
RINSE IN DIESEL FUEL

NOTE:
AFTER CLEANING FILTER,
FUEL SYSTEM MUST BE BLED.

Clean out the fuel filter every hundred hours. Wipe down the pump before you take it apart or you'll scoop more grunge into it than you're trying to get out. Rinse the screen in diesel fuel and wipe out the whole pump. Then re-assemble.

A good pre-filter in the fuel system is mandatory. The glass settling bowl in the bottom allows you to see and drain off any water that might have gotten into the system.

others we must bleed the system when we get air into it, either through filter changing or running out of fuel. Most engines vary somewhat in specific details of procedure, but generally speaking what you have to do is step by step get all the air out of the system, starting from the fuel tank and ending up with the injector pump or sometimes the injectors themselves.

The first thing to do is go over your whole fuel system and find out where everything is: filters, fuel pump, injector pump, so when you start to bleed you won't be scrambling back to your manual every five seconds.

a) Be sure you now have fuel in your tanks.

b) Open the petcock on the tank.

c) Go to the first filter/water separator in the line, and loosen the bleed-screw on the inlet side about three turns.

If the tank is *above* the filter so that the fuel runs down by gravity, then you can just sit and watch the fuel come out. Have a cup below it to retrieve it, or at least keep it from going into the bilge.

If the tank is *below* the filter, you'll have to have a little in-line primer pump at the tank like the ones found on portable outboard-motor tanks. The only other way of moving fuel through the line is with the manual lever on the fuel pump of the engine, but since this would mean sucking from the tank and hence the first filter, you will keep sucking more air into the system.

Anyway, pump or drain until the fuel coming out the loosened vent is pure fuel without any air bubbles. Then tighten the bleed screw.

d) Go to the outlet side of the filter and loosen the bleed screw there and bleed as before.

e) Go past the fuel pump on the engine to the bleed screw on the engine fuel filter, and loosen and pump and tighten as before.

f) Now go to the injection pump. If there is one bleed screw on it, loosen and bleed; if there are two, loosen and bleed the one closest to the tank—farthest from the injectors—first. *Always work on bleeding screws in sequence—from tank toward injectors.*

Now go start the engine. If it runs smoothly then you're fine; if not, you'll have to loosen the nut that attaches the fuel line to each injector, and bleed them. To save yourself the effort of pumping, just let the engine run while you bleed here, and let it do the pumping for you.

Do this injector by injector and in sequence as before. Do the injector closest to the injector pump first, and work toward the most distant.

Engine Oil

This is no place to be loose with your purchasing. Buy *only* oil that is recommended for rapid diesels. Don't pick up some third-rate stuff—it usually doesn't have the additives necessary for the high-compression diesels.

1. Checking the oil

The engine oil check should become a daily routine. It is best to perform this while the engine is warm, but I also do it before I start the engine to make sure the oil hasn't all drained out during the night. *Don't* rely on the oil pressure light or alarm to tell you what the level of the oil is. It won't. Regular pressure can often be attained with the oil level much below the acceptable minimum.

If you run the engine for an extended period, it's best to check the oil every eight hours. When I worked on the tugs that is what we did, and the diesel of a sailboat should be treated with no less respect.

The level of the oil should be right up to the second line *but* not over. Having too much oil in the case can be as bad as having too little. If you are near the bottom line, add a quart of oil.

A TYPICAL SMALL DIESEL OIL SYSTEM

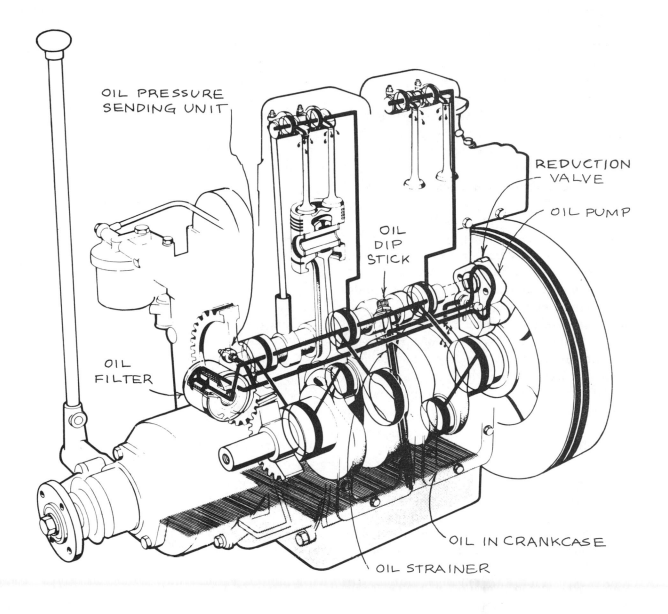

OIL PRESSURE
SENDING UNIT

REDUCTION
VALVE

OIL PUMP

OIL
DIP
STICK

OIL
FILTER

OIL IN CRANKCASE

OIL STRAINER

2. Changing the oil

Almost every manufacturer recommends changing the oil every 50 hours. When the oil is being changed, the oil filter should be changed also. I have tried changing the oil under all sorts of circumstances, and have found that it is about eight thousand times harder to change the oil in a cold diesel than a hot one. Here I am assuming that you have a normal sailboat installation which doesn't permit your getting anywhere near the drain plug, meaning you'll have to pump out the stuff through the dipstick hole.

The silly little pumps that are supplied for this purpose are an agony to use in the first place—ours leaks and squirts dirty oil everywhere—so don't make things worse by trying to pump thick, cold oil. Besides, cold oil will stay thick and remain on surfaces keeping the dirt with it.

Get yourself one or two, one-gallon plastic milk or water jugs. Most small diesels have a capacity of between two and six quarts. I say plastic jugs because first, the oil pump hose will be held fairly firmly by the narrow mouth of the jug, whereas with a wide-mouthed thing like a pail, the pressure of the pump will tend to kick the hose straight out and you'll have so much oil squirting around that you'll thing you've struck a well.

The second good reason for using plastic jugs instead of bowls or pails or pots and pans, is that they are disposable so you don't have to clean anything afterwards. And third, you can just screw the lid on a jug and heave it in the garbage without having to look high and low for a safe disposal site.

3. Oil filters

Some manufacturers say to change these at every one hundred hours—every second oil change—while others say each fifty hours—with every change of oil. But for the few bucks it costs, you might as well change the damned thing every time you change the oil, for then you won't have to remember whether you changed the filter the last time or the time before. Oil filters are generally of two kinds: the complete ones which you just unscrew and throw into the garbarge and replace; and the cartridge type which you take apart, remove the old cartridge and replace only it. Both must have the old ones out and new ones in place before the new oil is put in.

The complete ones are the easiest to change, but only it you have a filter strap. See photo. Remove the filter only after the old oil has been drained, and put the new one in place after having spread a bit of oil onto the new rubber sealer ring. Hand-tighten until the surfaces make contact, then give it another quarter turn. Don't overtighten or you'll have a hell of a time getting it off.

The cartridge type is no mystery. It usually has a center bolt that loosens the housing. But before you do that, clean thoroughly around the filter, just like you did with the fuel filter, to prevent any dirt from getting into the open filter and base. Next, empty the bowl and throw away the filter elements, then rinse and wash the bowl with a bit of diesel. Wipe the bowl clean. Check and, if necessary, replace the rubber sealing ring, then put it carefully in place, followed by the filter and the bowl. Tighten the bolt.

Now pour in whatever quantity of good diesel oil your engine takes, check the level, then start her up, run her for a bit and check the level again.

Air Cleaners

These are mostly the cartridge type which you have to simply take out and replace. Some are reusable and need only a bath in a bit of diesel fuel, then a quick soaking in engine oil, then draining off of the oil, before they can be put in place again.

CHANGING THE OIL FILTER

FILTER SHOULD BE RENEWED EVERY TIME OIL IS CHANGED.

OIL GASKET SLIGHTLY BEFORE INSTALLATION.

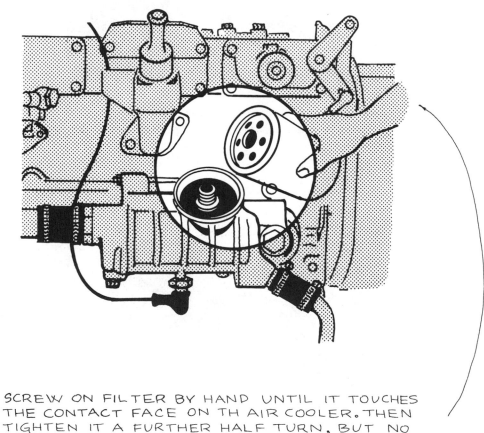

SCREW ON FILTER BY HAND UNTIL IT TOUCHES THE CONTACT FACE ON TH AIR COOLER. THEN TIGHTEN IT A FURTHER HALF TURN, BUT NO MORE.

If you're a dedicated skipper, you might fabricate a little stainless steel tray to sit under the oil filter so when you change the filter, you won't get any oil running down into the bilge.

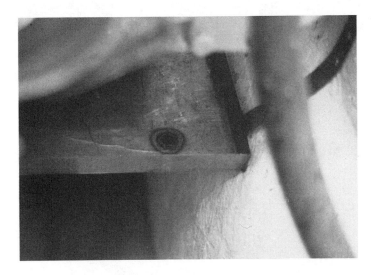

If you are a really *dedicated skipper, then you'll fabricate a pan to go under the whole engine. Note drainhole.*

V-Belts

These should be checked every fifty hours of running, for they can start to slip from either oil or from wear. Run your hand along the belt and check for cracks. Then check the pulleys. Check them for cracks, or grooves or bent walls. This last item might be best checked by sighting the pulley with the engine running, for then you will more easily notice if a wobble is present. If it is, you won't have much choice but to change the pulley.

The tension of the belts should be checked also. They should deflect about ¼ to ⅜ inch when pressed firmly, halfway between the widest span of pulleys.

To change the belt, just loosen all the bolts that hold the alternator—usually three including the adjustable arm—then remove the belt and replace it. Make sure you got the exact right size—*look* in your engine manual for measurement. Don't measure the old belt; it has probably stretched. After a new belt has been run in for a few hours, check the tension again, for new belts tend to elongate at first.

Oh yes, it shows excellent seamanship to always have a spare belt aboard.

To tighten a V-belt, just loosen the bolt in the slot of the bracket, lift alternator until the bolt is tight, then re-tighten bolt.

THE V-BELT

THE V-BELT TENSION IS CORRECT IF IT CAN BE
PRESSED DOWN 1/4 TO 1/2 INCH DEPENDING ON
DISTANCE BETWEEN PULLEYS.

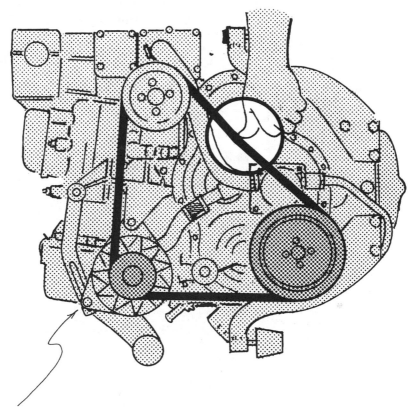

TO CHANGE BELT, JUST SLACKEN ADJUSTMENT
BOLT ON ALTERNATOR

This bizarre-looking gadget is a wrench to help you wrench off the throw-away-type oil filters. If you happen to overtighten a filter, I'm afraid you'll have no choice but to use one of these.

Tightening Cylinder Head Bolts

A number of diesel manufacturers recommend that the cylinder head nuts and/or bolts be tightened every 50 hours. If allowed to loosen unchecked, you could develop leaks and burns in the headgaskets.

The problem with checking these yourself is that you'll have to invest in a torque wrench—a wrench that tells you how much force or torque you're applying to the bolt. A torque wrench is a costly little beast—about $50—but it will easily amortize itself over the years if you consider that a couple of hours of a mechanic's time will cost you more than the price of the wrench. You'll be using it not only here, but also when tightening the retaining nuts on the injectors, something that comes up nearly every season.

Next, look closely at your manual to ascertain the *sequence and the amount of torque* the bolts require, and whether the engine should be warm

or cold. Don't take this lightly; pay close attention to all three. Some sequences are random, although generally they start at the center and work out. Nevertheless, follow the recommended sequence. As for the torque, some heads have combinations of bolts and nuts, and the torque required for these can vary as much as 200 percent. So read and heed.

One important point. Check the torque required for your bolts *before* you buy the tool. Some manufacturers use foot/pounds, other kilo/meters etc. Either have these translated to your wrench's reading or buy a wrench with the appropriate "language."

NOTE: Tightening the cylinder heads can change the amount of clearance in the valves, so couple these tasks each season, and follow each year's head-bolt tightening with checking of the valve adjustment.

Valve Clearances

The valves on diesels should be checked every time the head bolts are tightened, and adjusted every 100 hours or annually. If they are neglected and go out of adjustment, then at best they'll become loose and make a loud clattering noise; and at worst they can become too tight and overheat and either become deformed or burned. Keep the above in mind when adjusting your valves; never overtighten.

First and foremost consult your owner's manual to determine whether your particular engine needs to have its valves set with the engine *warm* or *cold*. This is not a quirk; even the most common engines such as Volvo and BMW require opposing conditions. Cold means not run for at least six hours, and warm means normal operating temperature.

Next, with the engine stopped, remove the valve covers. Now start with the first cylinder. Crank the engine until both valves *rock*, which means they're both partially open. Mark the flywheel with a pen or screwdriver at twelve o'clock or at whatever point the flywheel is accessible, then turn the engine *one complete revolution* so the mark is back in the same place. Now note from your owner's manual the setting for each valve—the inlet often varies from the exhaust—then check the valves with a feeler gauge. The valve clearance is considered to be correct if the feeler gauge of the proper size can be pulled through with just a slight resistance. If it's okay, move onto the next one; if it's off, then adjust it.

If the clearance is off, then take a screwdriver and the correct box wrench—don't fool here with a crescent wrench—and slacken the hex nut on one valve. Now, turn the adjusting screw with the screwdriver until you have proper clearance. Then tighten the hex nut.

Proceed to the next valve and the next cylinders and adjust the same way.

Lastly, put new gaskets onto the valve covers, set in place and tighten bolts. Run the engine for awhile to make sure the covers are tight and leakproof.

ADJUSTING VALVE CLEARACES

THE SCREW ADJUSTS THE VALVE SETTING
THE NUT LOCKS SETTING FIRMLY
THUS: HOLD SCREW, LOOSEN NUTS, ADJUST
    SCREWS, TIGHTEN NUTS

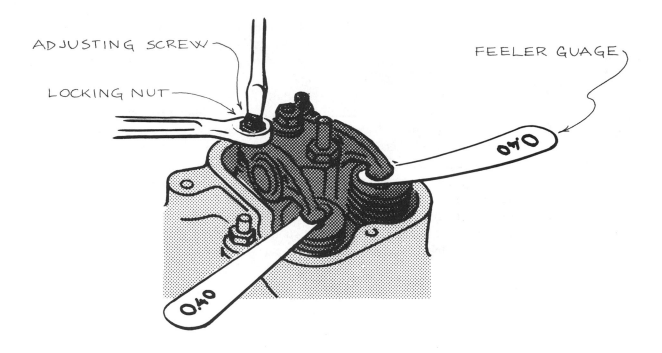

CLEARANCE IS SAID TO BE CORRECT WHEN
GUAGE ENCOUNTERS A SLIGHT RESISTANCE.

Checking the Injectors

Most people who really know diesels recommend that the injectors be checked and cleaned after every 100 hours of operation. This is not necessary on most workboats or boats that run hard and long for extended periods, but for sailboats, whose engine often runs cold and whose fuel often gets cold, injector fouling is a greater problem.

You will not be able to actually check the injectors yourself for that requires special high-pressure machinery, but you will have to be able to remove and reinstall them without buggering them up. So.

1. Removing
First of all clean everything around the injector: delivery pipe, cylinder head and the injector itself. Use a clean brush and some diesel. Then wipe dry.

Next, unscrew the clamp, the delivery pipe, and the leak-oil line from the injector. If you have little plastic caps to fit over the orifices, then fit them now; if you don't, use clean rags to cover everything and keep stuff from getting into the injector and the fuel line and the cylinder itself.

Next, remove the nuts on the yoke that holds the injector into the cylinder head and try to lift out the injector. Every time I tried to do this the thing stuck, but then who knows; you might get lucky. If the injector doesn't slide right out, don't try prying it straight up—you might damage it or simply waste time. Twist the injector back and forth—this is normally fairly easy; it not, use a wrench on the flat sides of the injector—and pull up on it at the same time. It'll come.

The tips of the injectors are delicate and expensive. Don't throw them around. Wrap them in rags and take them down to an injection shop—any decent-sized town will have one.

2. Fitting
First check to be sure the contact surface on the injector and the copper sleeve into which it slides are clean. If not, rub with a cloth and diesel fuel.

Push the injectors down into position and fit the yoke but do not tighten the nuts.

Connect the delivery pipe and return line. Make sure that everything aligns and that the cones are in the correct position. Don't forget to fit clamps in position as well. Tighten the retaining nuts on the yoke with the torque wrench. Look in the technical specs of your manual for correct torque—it should be around 15 foot-pounds.

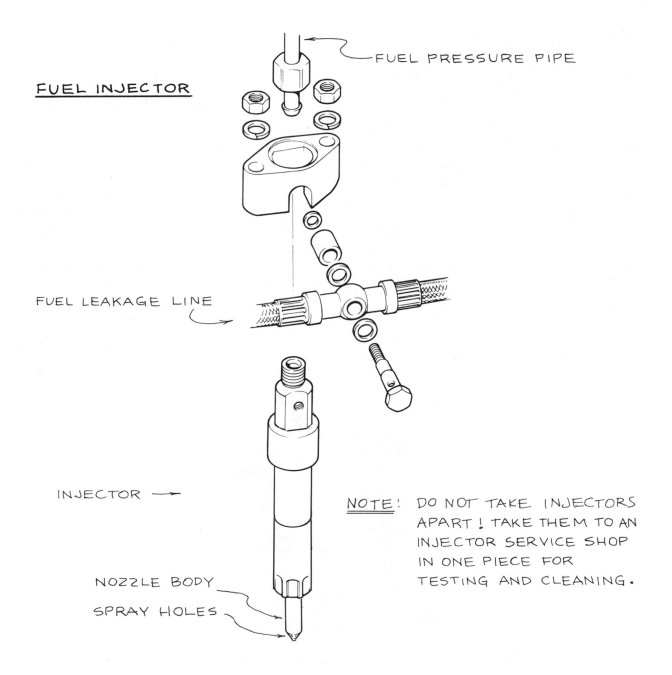

FUEL INJECTOR

FUEL PRESSURE PIPE

FUEL LEAKAGE LINE

INJECTOR →

NOTE! DO NOT TAKE INJECTORS APART! TAKE THEM TO AN INJECTOR SERVICE SHOP IN ONE PIECE FOR TESTING AND CLEANING.

NOZZLE BODY

SPRAY HOLES

Injectors should be removed every 100 hours for cleaning and inspection. Now I know you haven't the faintest how to clean and inspect these suckers, but at least you can take them out and lug them down to an injector shop and have them do it for you. Note a few important tips in text before you begin.

The Cooling System

Note: If you don't have a glass water-strainer between your salt water inlet and your waterpump, then get one and install it.

This is where the shit really hits the fan for, as Rod Fraser and most mechanics emphasize, most diesel problems emerge from some sort of failure in the seawater system. I completely agree, and I am the ultimate authority on the subject, having had the engine torn down on two separate occasions, both times because I was too stupid to recognize an early warning sign of impending doom. A couple of other times I avoided similar disasters by being quick and agile and brimming with fear.

The simplest failure that can occur is that the seals in the raw water pump fail through overheating, and water gets into the engine unnoticed and sits there and rusts the valve springs and freezes the valves and God knows what else. Now water pumps seldom overheat out of sheer boredom. They are most often aided by one of two causes; one, someone forgetting to turn on the seawater intake before turning on the engine, and the other is that somehow the intake got plugged up and no one noticed that there was no water coming in.

This situation is even worse on so-called "freshwater cooled" engines. One thing you should understand right away is that freshwater cooled engines use salt water to cool the fresh water—by means of a heat-exchanger—which makes them actually *more* vulnerable to this problem. To explain: The thermostat on a "freshwater cooled" engine is in the freshwater system, therefore the thermostat can read quite normally for a few minutes without *any* salt water passing through the system. Now, during these few minutes the engine itself can re-

A water filter between the intake seacock and the water pump on the engine is mandatory. It will in no way guarantee that the system won't get plugged up, but the large bowl on the bottom, in which incoming water circulates at a good speed, will mulch up things like seaweed and kelp which might otherwise foul your pump impeller. And if something like a piece of plastic does get sucked into the system, at least it will always stop at the filter so you'll always know where to look.

A SMALL DIESEL SALT WATER COOLING SYSTEM

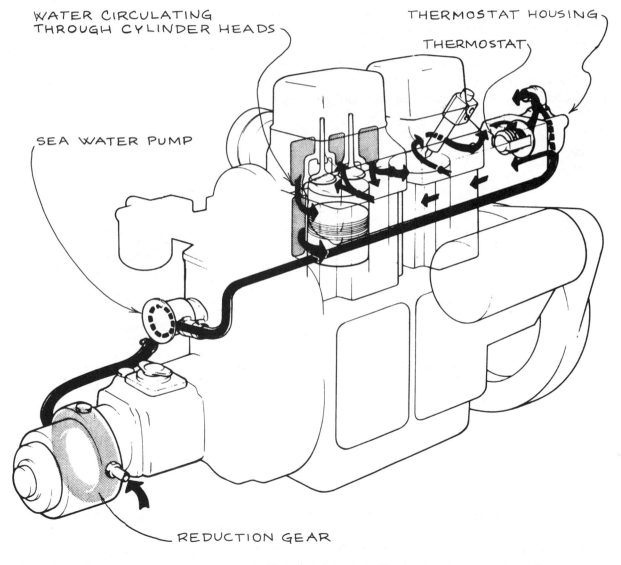

WATER CIRCULATING
THROUGH CYLINDER HEADS

THERMOSTAT HOUSING

THERMOSTAT

SEA WATER PUMP

REDUCTION GEAR

A WATER FILTER SHOULD BE PLACED BETWEEN THE INTAKE
SEACOCK AND THE SEAWATER PUMP.

main safe, BUT the neoprene impeller, now running dry in the saltwater pump, can overheat and be destroyed. Rod Fraser told me of an instance where not only did the impeller get cooked, but the exhaust got so hot without the water to cool it that the rubber hose burnt through and the boat caught fire.

So, now you can see why it is so important to look over the side at your exhaust through-hull when you first start up the engine. Of course underway you'll have to rely on other means of verification, for I know most of you won't bother sticking your heads over the sides every five minutes. I know I sure don't. On saltwater-cooled engines you can usually get away with looking at the gauge, but even that works on quite a delay, so the best thing to do, according to Rod, is to listen. An exhaust that has water in it will sound much smoother and quieter than one running dry which will have a throatier, hollower sound. If you don't know what that means in reality, then just listen for a change. When you hear it, shut off the engine and investigate.

The first thing to do is scoot below and put your hand on the saltwater pump; it it's hot, take off the cover and check the impeller. If it's at all damaged, replace it. NOTE: You should always have a spare impeller on board— see *Replacing Impeller.*

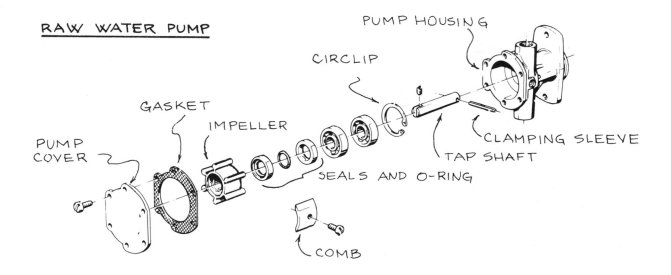

RAW WATER PUMP

PUMP HOUSING
CIRCLIP
GASKET
IMPELLER
PUMP COVER
SEALS AND O-RING
CLAMPING SLEEVE
TAP SHAFT
COMB

Take a good hard look at your water pump regularly. If you see any drips coming from the housing—some pumps have a weep hole on them—don't try to seal the leak from the outside with goop. The pump might be trying to tell you that a seal inside has failed. If left uncorrected, water can get into the engine and if that happens, Brother, you better get out your checkbook.

Next, you'll have to see what caused the problem. Check the glass bowl of the water-filter first—if you don't have one, install one—looking especially for a piece of floating plastic that could have been sucked into the system. Rod Fraser recommends capital punishment for all those who throw plastic bags and such into the sea. All I can say is that I'd gladly tie the noose.

If the bowl is fine, go out on deck and see if you can poke the boathook down around your intake through-hull. There might be a sheet of plastic or a bag stuck over it.

If you can't visually find the cause, you'll have to take the cooling system apart piece by piece. First shut off your intake seacock and pull off the hose between the seacock and the water filter. Blow into it as hard as you can. If there is no blockage, move along hose by hose toward the engine pump. If you can't find any cause, start the engine up again for a minute and see if water now comes out the exhaust through-hull. You may have unwittingly unblocked the thing or removed the floating plastic from the intake. If there is still no water, then hoist the sails and start sailing. The thing is a *sail* boat after all.

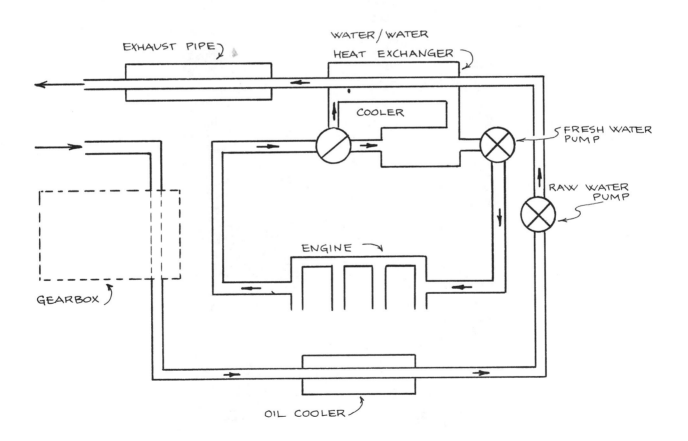

MARINE DIESEL ENGINE COOLING SYSTEM

Replacing the Pump Impeller

The impeller is made of neoprene rubber and, as mentioned above, it can be damaged by overheating. To replace it, first shut off the intake seacock, then remove the cover from the seawater pump. If you have to pry it off, do it with care so that you don't damage the gasket under it.

Now, using two screwdrivers, pry the impeller off the pump shaft. Be sure to put something under the screwdrivers to protect the impeller housing.

On some engines the shaft will slide out slightly from the pump and that's to allow you access to a bolt retaining the impeller. Check your manual if in doubt.

With the impeller out, clean the impeller housing. Slightly oil the shaft and the new impeller before installation. Install the impeller with the blades going against the direction of rotation. If the housing gasket is damaged, replace it.

To get at your raw water pump impeller, just remove the plate held by the six screws—one is hidden. Remove impeller as shown in drawing.

CHANGING THE RAW WATER PUMP IMPELLER

EXTRACT THE IMPELLER GENTLY. IT'S A
GOOD IDEA TO USE SOMETHING UNDER THE
SCREWDRIVERS TO PROTECT THE HOUSING.

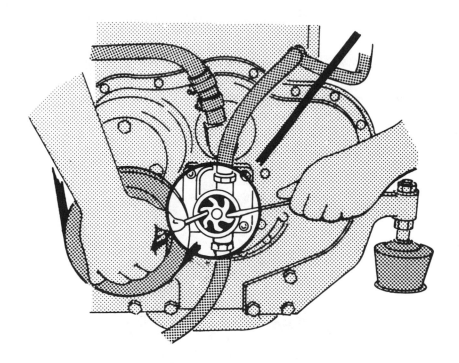

CHANGE IMPELLER IF ANY CRACKS IN IT ARE
VISIBLE. IF THE ENGINE HAS BEEN RUN
WITHOUT WATER FOR MORE THAN JUST A
FEW MINUTES IT'S A GOOD IDEA TO CHANGE
THE IMPELLER EVEN IF THERE IS NO VISIBLE
DAMAGE.

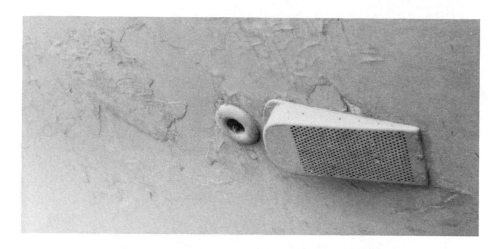

When you put a screen over your engine cooling-water intake, do put the screen over the intake, *not* beside it. *And when you get a screen, get the smallest possible, not one that's large enough to filter Niagara Falls. I mean if you really want to slow down your boat, just throw out your anchor.*

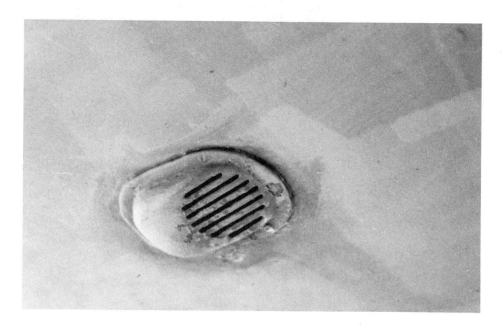

This is a little better—it's only twice the size of the intake—but it still sets up a goodly drag.

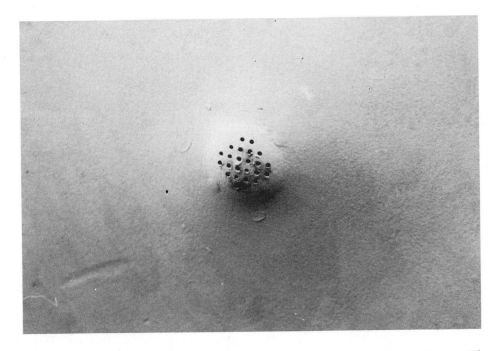

Now we're talking slick. This beautifully faired-in screen I found on a Swan. What else is new?

Hoses

If I would have to pick the weakest part of any sailboat, one that can lead to its sinking faster than anything else, I would pick the hoses. A failed water hose in either the cooling system or the head or the galley sink, will let the ocean gush in under enormous pressure and fill the boat to a point of no return in no time. No manual bilge pump could possibly keep pace, at least not with me yanking feebly on it.

For a long time I assumed that unless a hose was cut, it would last forever, but I've learned over the years that hoses—especially rubber ones—harden with age particularly if effected by heat, and become brittle and crack and can literally come apart when exposed to the vibration of a diesel engine. Once a hose becomes so weak, it takes very

little to break it, and when one considers how much awkward crawling is done in a tight space like an engine room where hoses are often kneeled on and stepped on and crunched against hard things, then one at once becomes more aware of the vulnerability of such hoses and the importance of their upkeep.

So. When a hose is first installed, one should be sure that it is made fast with nylon ties to as many places as possible to avoid chafe and shaking. If a chance of chafe still exists, then a larger-sized rubber hose should be slipped over the hose to be protected, acting much as a simple chafe-guard would over a dockline. When tightening a hose clamp, do be careful not to overtighten, for the clamp can easily cut into the hose, thereby drastically reducing the strength of its walls.

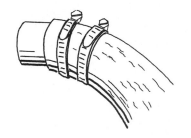

BEND HOSE TO CHECK FOR
BRITTLENESS

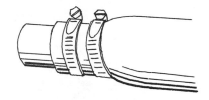

IF HOSE FEELS SOFT OR LOOKS
SWOLLEN THEN THE WALLS HAVE
FATIGUED. CHANGE IT.

CHECKING HOSES FOR
BREAKDOWN OF WALLS

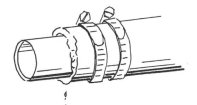

IF THE RUBBER STARTS
TO CRUMBLE THEN
ITS DEAD. CHANGE IT.

With the above precautions taken, there is little left for you to do on a new hose but to check periodically for chafe. Once the hoses begin to age, however, the best thing to do is to get into the habit of wiping the whole engine room and in the process all the hoses. When doing so, give the hoses a squeeze along their whole length and check for softened areas, and look for bulges, and inspect for cracks, especially at the hose ends where the pressure of the clamps creates a graver possibility of failure. If a hose feels soft but shows no failure on the outside, don't assume that the hose is still good to use, for it's usually the inside walls that begin to break down first when subjected to the heat of the cooling water, and not only will the walls thus become weak, but they may begin to crumble and release all sorts of bits of broken stuff into the cooling system, causing havoc around the pump and around small openings.

Once any of the above symptoms are discovered, don't hesitate, for heaven's sake. Change the hose! It only costs a few dollars and you'll have one thing less to worry about.

A TYPICAL SMALL DIESEL FUEL SYSTEM

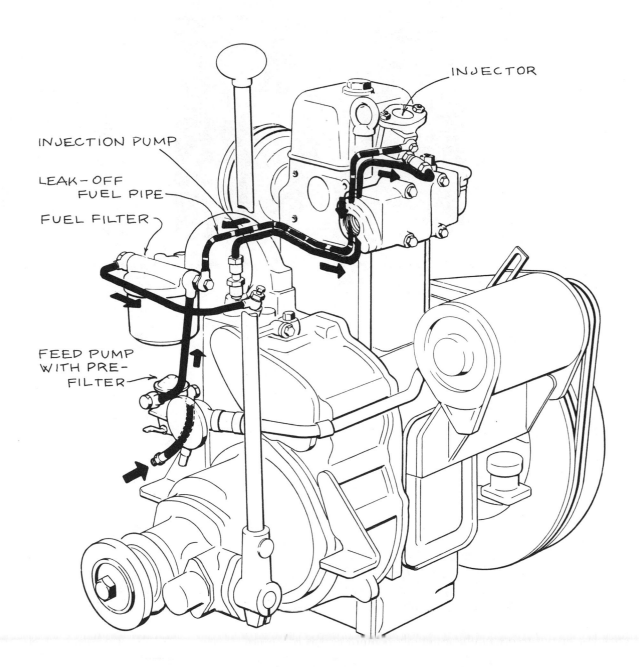

INJECTOR

INJECTION PUMP

LEAK-OFF
FUEL PIPE

FUEL FILTER

FEED PUMP
WITH PRE-
FILTER

Any place where a hose of tubing might be chafed or crushed, a piece of hose should be tie-wrapped around it as a guard.

Engine Controls

The exposed ends of the control cables should be checked and lightly greased after every 50 hours of running time. Check also pins and cotter keys for looseness and for wear, and if you find some, don't hesitate to replace the part. Make sure all control cables run free with the minimum amount of bend especially in the last two feet before the exposed ends, for the cable ends may then bind against the housing and cause premature wear or even a sharp crimp which could lock up the controls.

With the new adjustable mounts, an engine is easily re-aligned. The engine is lowered or raised by the two nuts on the bolt and the third nut on the wrench.

The Coupling

If the coupling between the gear box and the drive-shaft is allowed to go out of alignment, then not only will your cutlass bearing wear out in an inordinately short time—necessitating expensive repairs—but the vibration set up by the misaligned shaft will rattle and shake everything in the boat and cause fatigue and wear in the most unsuspected of parts. So, check your coupling for alignment at the beginning of each season. Loosen the nuts on the coupling and check the spaces between the two faces with a feeler gauge. On a four-inch diameter coupling the maximum difference should be $\frac{4}{1000}$ of an inch. If your coupling is of a different diameter, allow $\frac{1}{1000}$ per diameter inch. Any more than that will cause excessive vibration. To re-align the shaft, raise, lower, or shift sideways your engine mounts. Most of the newer ones are adjustable by means of two sets of nuts on the mounting bolt. See photo.

The Stuffing Box

The stuffing box should not be touched until it develops a steady drip. When it does, get out your big pipe wrenches and give the nut a slight turn. After a few hundred hours, the packing gland inside the box will have become so worn and compressed that you will have no choice but to change it.

First you will have to remove the old packing that's squished into the sleeve of the stuffing box. I have never done this, but Rod tells me that it *must* be done with a special pulling tool—an inexpensive thing that looks like a corkscrew. He has tried many things over the years and none of them worked and some of them even broke and stuck in the sleeve. So don't skimp—get the tool. And while you're at it, buy some new packing. But before you rush off you'd better read the following—it's enough to stagger the mind.

To determine what size packing you'll need, you will have to physically measure the space between the wall of the stuffing box and the shaft. When you remove the nut to do this, water will start coming into the boat. Don't panic. Just get the measuring done and then put the nut back on. Now comes the good part. Say you measure ¼ inch space, well, now you go to your marine hardware store and tell the man that you want some $\frac{3}{16}$ inch packing, because you see, the box that says $\frac{3}{16}$ on the outside, actually has ¼ inch packing inside it. Get it? If that isn't the epitome of stupidity, I don't know what is. If the stuff is in bulk in a store, then measure the thing to be sure it's the right size for your space. Don't forget to buy the pulling tool to get the old stuff out.

Now comes another little quirk. Until I met Rod Fraser, I was told by all who work on boat engines that the packing must be wrapped overlapped on the shaft and then slit with a razor blade to get a good snug fit. Well now along comes Rod and tells me that you should cut your rings of packing—you cut independent rings and stack them, with each joint staggered 120 degrees from the last one to prevent leaks—actually *shorter* then a tight fit by *the cross section of your packing material.* In other words, if your packing material is ¼ inch, then you wrap the packing around the shaft and cut it ¼ inch short of a perfect fit. This, he tells me, is to allow for the expansion of the packing once water gets at it. If the packing has no room to expand, then it will simply expand by cutting a groove into the shaft itself. Well, I must say it makes sense, and he has been doing it for twenty years and it has worked for him, so who am I to question it.

So cut your rings and grease them slightly—they'll slide easier into the sleeve—then put them nicely in place, and gently pull the nut tight over them. Tighten by hand until snug, then give it a quarter turn and lock the locking nut.

Laying Up for Short Periods

If the boat is not to be used for a few weeks, it is strongly advised that the engine be run *hard* under working loads for at least a half an hour every fourteen days. If the layup is for a couple of months, and there is no chance of frost and no chance that the engine will be run, then a few short preventive steps should be taken to prevent the engine parts from corroding and seizing up. Now this is no idle bull. I myself thought this to be paranoidal overkill. Only after I started my engine following a three-month layup, only to hear the most horrendous bloody racket you ever heard, then finding that it was time to pay a few hundred dollars to replace bent rods caused by corroded valves, did I actually become a steadfast believer.

So.

a) Run the engine until it's warm, then shut it off

and pump all the oil out of the engine and reverse gear with the help of the heinous little scavenging pump we talked about before.

b) Fill up the engine and reverse gear with a rust inhibiting oil until the level reaches the bottom mark of the dipstick. Good inhibiting oils are Exxon Rust Ban, Shell Ensis Oil 20, or corresponding oils of other makes.

c) Drain the fuel out of the fuel filter, and loosen the tank-end of the flexible fuel line that leads to the fuel pump. Place the end of the hose into a quart can containing ⅓ inhibiting oil and ⅔ regular diesel fuel.

d) Vent the fuel system and start the engine. Run it at rapid idling until about a half pint (¼ liter) has been used up from the can. Then shut off the engine.

The inhibiting oil in the fuel will now protect all interior engine parts from corrosion.

e) Shut off the intake seacock—might as well shut them all off while you're at it,

Winter Layup

This is serious business. We once left the boat inadvertently over a winter—ended up staying in Paris six months longer than we thought we would—and came back to frozen pumps, and cracked headgaskets and blown head plugs, and rusted valve springs and gummed up injectors; a $1,000 oversight in all, so I know whereof I speak.

1. The cooling system

a) Close intake seacock. Drain off all raw cooling water from the exhaust manifold and the engine. Most saltwater cooled engines have individual drain cocks for each cylinder, as well as one for the manifold and exhaust.

b) Mix about 4 gallons (18 liters) of fresh water with ½ gallon of rustproofing agent like Exxon Cutwell 40, or Shell Donax C, or similar,

in a good-sized bucket. Always add the oil to the water, not the other way around. I have no idea why, but that's what the man says so do it. Stir well.

c) Lead hose from saltwater pump and drop it into the bucket. Now turn on the engine and run it until all the water is gone from the bucket. Keep stirring the goop while the engine runs. This will have formed a protective oil film in all the cooling chambers and channels. Remember not to let the engine run dry or you might damage the impeller.

d) Now drain all water from the engine through the drain cocks in the block and the plug in the exhaust. The stuff you ran through was just to coat the parts—it was *not* an antifreeze. Take off the saltwater pump cover and let the water drain out here too. Remove impeller and store it at home. Put the cover back and put in the bolts so you don't lose them. Reconnect all the original hoses.

e) On freshwater cooled engines, follow up by winterizing the freshwater half of the system: Drain whole system and replace with anti-freeze.

2. Injectors

Pull each injector as described before, and spray or put in about a teaspoon of inhibiting oil into each cylinder. Then turn over the engine several times to get the oil to coat everything, then replace injectors and set with torque wrench as described before.

3. Air cleaners and exhaust through-hull

Plug the air cleaners and the exhaust through-hull with rags to keep cold moist air from getting into engine. Don't forget to remove all this parapheralia before you start up the engine in the spring. Plug tank vent while you're plugging, to keep moisture out of the fuel.

4. Engine exterior

Clean all of engine and gearbox with diesel fuel and a rag and remove any chipped paint, then wipe with acetone and repaint to prevent any future rust. Oil all raw metals.

Lubricate all control cables, steering cables, and linkages.

5. Battery

As mentioned in electrical section, remove, top off and store in a dry warm place. Not on a concrete floor. Recharge regularly. See *Battery*.

Now this *is shipshape.*

Maintenance Schedule

We have already talked about what should be done before starting the engine each day, so let's go on with the less frequent tasks.

Every 50 hours or annually.
a) Change engine oil and filter.
b) Change oil in reverse gear.
c) Check V-belt and pulleys.
d) Clean raw water filter.
e) Clean fuel filter, (at fuel pump).
f) Clean battery terminals.
g) Check and lubricate steering and engine controls and cables.

Every 100 hours or annually.
a) Clean injectors.
b) Tighten head bolts.
c) Check valve clearances.
d) Change fuel filters.
e) Clean air filters.
f) Tighten fuel lines.
g) Check all hoses.
h) Tighten hose clamps.
i) Check electrical connections.

Ditto.

A FRESHWATER COOLED DIESEL ENGINE WITH HEAT EXCHANGER

OIL CIRCUIT

A. FROM ENGINE BLOCK
A.a. COLD – THROUGH OIL FILTER
A.b. WARM VIA THE HEAT
     EXCHANGER THROUGH THE
     OIL FILTER
B. OIL THERMOSTAT
C. OIL FILTER
D. TO ENGINE BLOCK

RAW WATER CIRCUIT

I.   FROM RAW WATER VALVE –
     GEARBOX
II. THROUGH OIL/WATER HEAT
     EXCHANGER
III TO RAW WATER PUMP
IV   THROUGH WATER/WATER
     HEAT EXCHANGER
V   TO EXHAUST PIPE JACKET

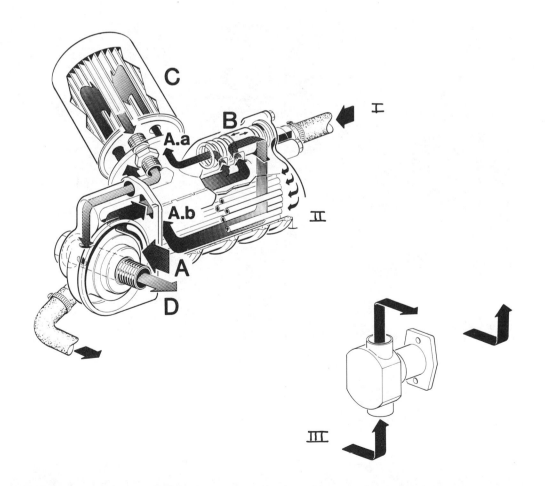

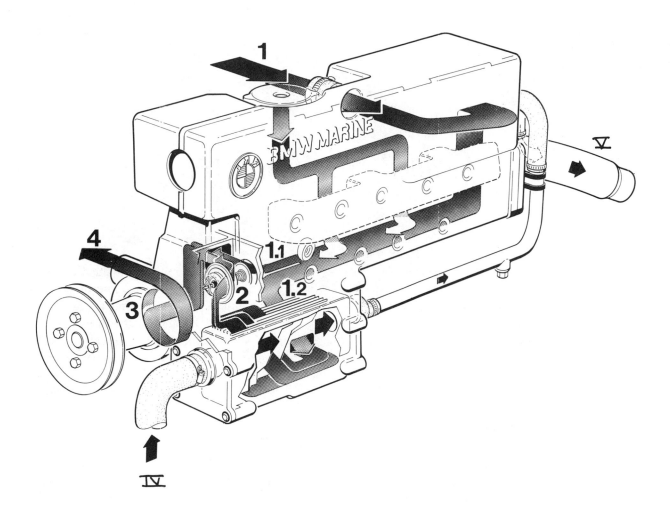

FRESH WATER CIRCUIT

I.   FROM ENGINE BLOCK
I.I COLD - TO THE FRESH WATER PUMP
I.2 WARM — VIA THE HEAT EXCHANGER TO
     THE FRESH WATER PUMP
2.   THERMOSTAT
3.   FRESH WATER PUMP
4.   INTO ENGINE BLOCK

43

Gasoline Engines

These things tend to frighten me to death, not just because gasoline fumes explode so readily—I have seen too many boats burned to the waterline from fires started by gasoline—but also because they are dependent on fickle electrical parts, which tend to be a problem once exposed to the corrosive salt environment a sailboat normally lives in. Apart from that they have carburetors which have to be fooled with, carburetors which contain jets that can get plugged, and floats that can get stuck or holed or corroded, any of which means an engine that won't run.

With these small points in mind, I cannot discourage the use of gas engines too much and if you are considering installing one because it's cheaper to buy than a diesel engine, then why don't you consider forgetting it, and do what the Pardeys and hundreds of others do—go without an engine altogether.

For those of you who still have old Atomic Fours and the like, I suggest that instead of spending money on the next overhaul, try to get hold of a small recondiitoned diesel. It might cost a bit more but you might live a lot longer and a lot more happily.

Until then though, here are a few things that you can do to keep your engine running safely and reliably.

Most of the things mentioned in the diesel section, with the exception of a couple of obvious things like fuel injectors and bleeding the fuel supply, apply here, so follow the suggestions contained therein. The only thing that is basically different is the tune-ups you will have to perform on a gasoline engine, tune-ups which involve valve adjustment, ignition and timing, and carburetion.

Valve Adjustment

This has to be done first. It is much the same with gas as with diesel engines, except that it should be performed here when the spark plugs are out for inspection to make it easier to turn over the engine and stop it exactly where you want it.

Carburetors

Carburetors have always been a mystery to me. I did once have an old Porsche with a bizarrely convoluted set of carburetors whose linkages and fittings were so worn that I would have to make adjustment about every twenty blocks, and I did then fiddle and fumble with some sort of success, but I must admit my actions had no pattern or logic, I just twisted and yanked and poked enough to keep the sucker going. It was then I learned to fear and hate all carburetors and I have not been able to make friends with one ever since.

Anyway, from what I've found out, it seems most carburetors on small sailboat engines are pretty straightforward things, and there are only a couple of things that you can normally adjust with any success so we might as well cover them.

1. Adjustment

The first and simplest thing to adjust is the idling. The screw for this is usually found in the linkage where the throttle cable joins the carburetor body. Idling on most engines should be set around 600 rpm in neutral or to run about a minimum of 650 rpm in forward. To get the optimum idling speed and optimum performance, you'll have to have an ideal mixture of gas and air. This you set by turning the slow speed needle valve on the carburetor. See your manual for location. The needles are threaded and normally work in the fashion of a screw; turning to the right—clockwise—will tighten the screw and make the mixture leaner and turning it counterclockwise will loosen the screw or make the mixture richer. So. First of all run your engine until it reaches normal operating temperature. Then run it at a low speed—700 to 800 rpm—and adjust the needle until the highest consistent rpm is achieved. Allow 15 seconds after each adjustment for the engine to respond. After final adjustment is completed, turn the needle counterclockwise ⅛ turn to prevent engine from being too lean at slow speeds, particularly in neutral. Lastly reduce engine speed and turn idle adjustment to allow engine to run at minimum speed of 650 rpm in forward gear.

2. Cleaning, inspection and repair

First, inspect all hoses and clamps and replace if need be. Dismantling the carburetor is done on an annual basis at the Concordia yard, and that sounds like a good idea if it is to remain reliable throughout the season.

To inspect and clean the carburetor, you will first of all have to take it apart. Take it apart and lay it out on the Sunday paper so you'll remember where all the pieces belong. The best thing to use for cleaning out the built-up gum inside is gasoline and a clean brush. If you are going to use the very strong carburetor cleaner, make sure you don't get it onto the delicate float, inlet valve or any plastic or electrical parts. The best thing to do then is to put the parts in a shallow tray and spray down everything with aerosol type carburetor cleaner. This stuff is vicious so use goggles to protect your eyes. Use the brush on stubborn parts. To clean out the internal passages use the long plastic nozzle that comes with the cleaner to duct the spray. It's best to use compressed air to blow the parts clean and dry, for rags may leave lint behind that can clog up the fine passages in the reassembled carburetor. Be sure all particles of gaskets are removed from gasket surfaces. If gaskets must be scraped, be sure not to damage the surface of the carburetor where the gaskets fit.

When installing new parts from a carburetor rebuild kit, inspect gaskets and compare to original gaskets to insure all holes are correctly punched. Also, inspect new gaskets for any loose fibers or crumbs of gasket material.

Inspect float and arm for wear or damage. If the float has become oil-soaked, discard it and get a new one. Check float arm wear in the hinge pin and float valve contact areas. Replace if necessary. Inspect float valve, float seat, and needle valves for grooves, nicks or scratches. If you find any, replace the part. These are critical pieces working with critical tolerances so don't start fooling around with files or grinding stones trying to reshape things.

Ignition and Timing

Here is where most of the problems begin, but fortunately this portion can be easily worked on by even the most simple of minds among us.

1. Spark plugs

Pull out the spark plugs and check them one by one, noting which belongs to which cylinder. The condition of the plug will pretty much tell you how the engine is running and what problems it may have.

a) A clean well-burning plug will have a light gray color and will be pretty much intact.

b) A carbonned up plug will have soot-like black deposits, indicating too rich a mixture, or too much idling and not enough hard running.

c) An oily black plug tells you that oil is getting past worn or cracked piston rings or past the intake valve guides. Don't fool yourself by putting in a "hotter" plug. The engine will run better for a short time but it tends to pre-ignite and hurt the engine, and it will burn a lot of oil, sometimes so much oil that you may run dry on a long run and damage the rest of the engine. You need a ring job. This is expensive and time consuming, and may be a perfect opportunity to turn the old dear into an anchor for the mooring.

d) Colored powdery deposits from white through red are usually from additives. You can't make adjustments for these.

e) Burnt or blistered insulator and electrode burnt to a wedge, indicate among other things, either too lean a fuel/air mixture, or over advanced ignition timing.

Unless the plugs are in near perfect condition, chuck them and replace them with new ones. If they seem okay, rub them with a wire brush and put them back in. Don't forget to set the gap. Check your manual for that.

2. Spark plug wires

The wires and especially their casings break down with time. At each tune-up, check each wire for cracks and check the ends for corrosion. Most mechanics recommend that you replace the whole shooting match every two years. It's only wire and it can often be bought as a complete pre-made harness for your specific engine.

3. Distributor

Take off the distributor cap and check all terminals for wear and build-up. Clean with a small file if build-up is bad. Wipe the whole cap clean to avoid any stray paths for the current.

Next pull the rotor out and clean the tip with a very fine file. Now look the breaker points over carefully. Open them slightly with a screwdriver to see if there is any buildup. Clean with a pass of a nail file. Now let them close and check for any misalignment of the two points. They should meet surface to surface one directly lined up to the other. If the points look burnt or worn or if anything seems amiss, heave it and get another one. Be sure the new points align well. If not, you can bend the moving portion slightly to correct.

Next, go look in your manual to see what the opening gap for the points should be, and grab your feeler gauge and then come back. Bring a beer.

Okay. Now crank the engine either by hand—using the flywheel—or with the starter, until the cam hits the highest spot and the points open to the maximum. Now loosen the adjustment screw and set the gap with the feeler gauge according to the book. Tighten screw.

Put everything together the same way you took it apart.

Timing

You've all seen mechanics fool around with the little light that flashes off and on, as the engine turns over. What they're doing is trying to set the spark—a flash is given off by the light upon firing—with a notch on the flywheel which the light then lights up for you to see. To match the flash of light and the notch, you loosen the nut or bolt holding the distributor, and gently *turn* the distributor until you match the flash with the gash. Now tighten the distributor where it sits. Neat, right?

Now if you think you got lost back there somewhere, don't worry, because you have to go and buy a timing light anyway and the instructions come with it.

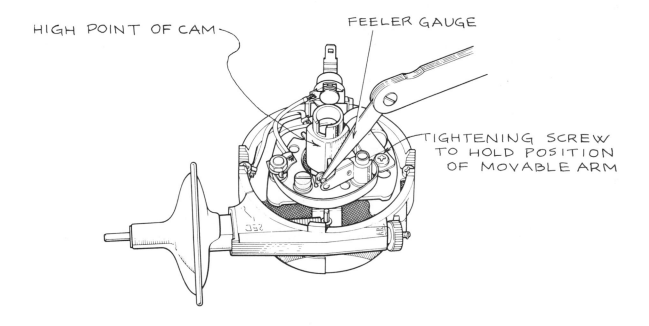

HIGH POINT OF CAM

FEELER GAUGE

TIGHTENING SCREW TO HOLD POSITION OF MOVABLE ARM

A LUCAS DISTRIBUTOR
(THEY ALL LOOK MUCH THE SAME)
HAVING THE GAP SET

44

Steering

For some reason most people are as afraid of their steering systems as they are of engines. That is truly sad, for the common steering system isn't much harder to understand than the average bicycle.

The important thing is to have a good look at it first; crawl in there and see just what does what, so that if an emergency arises—and if the steering goes you can usually treat it as a small emergency—you won't fall into a state of chaotic panic, but instead will smartly pop the emergency tiller in place, then make the necessary repairs to your steering without interrupting your cruise. Sounds easy, right?

The key here, as with most things aboard, is maintenance. If the whole system is kept well oiled and lubricated, and the parts inspected for wear and weakening—especially the sheave mounting brackets and cable ends and the stops—then one should encounter few major surprises unless one is incorrigibly unlucky.

Maintenance

The Edson Steering people, who are one of the most respected names in the manufacture of steering components, were kind enough to furnish the following material on steering maintenance.

The bearings in the sheaves should be checked and oiled monthly. While you're down there, check all mounting bolts, nuts, clevis pins and cotter keys.

The wire rope, the roller chain, and the pedestal shaft bearings should be checked and lubed annually.

On an extended voyage where the steering is constantly working, the system should be inspected daily and lubricated weekly.

To properly maintain the moving parts in the top of the pedestal, it is necessary to remove the compass and its cylinder. For proper alignment when re-installing the compass, place three or four lengths of tape on the pedestal and compass as shown. Slit the tape when removing compass, align the strips of tape when re-installing the compass for visual compass re-alignment. Your compass *must* then be checked for accuracy. Lubrication of needle bearings should be done by squeezing Teflon lubricant into the holes located on top of the bearing housings inside the pedestal bowl. Spin the wheel when squeezing the lubricant in to make sure the entire bearing is serviced. Winch grease or water pump grease can be used as an alternative, but don't let the bearings run dry. Do not over grease as it will run onto the brake pads. Oil the

BEFORE DISMANTLING
THE BINNACLE TO
SERVICE THE STEERING
SYSTEM, PUT TAPE
OVER COMPASS JOINTS

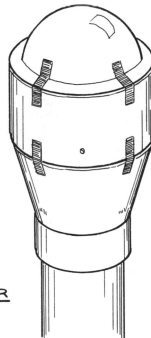

SLIT THE TAPE WHEN
REMOVING COMPASS
THEN REALIGN THE
STRIPS OF TAPE WHEN
RE-INSTALLING IT.

OVERLAPPING TAPE FOR
COMPASS ALIGNMENT

chain with #30 weight motor oil. Do *not* grease chain as it does not penetrate the links.

Inspect the condition of the wire, tension of the wire and lightly oil. Place about five layers of Kleenex on the palm of your hand, squirt oil on the tissues and lightly oil the wire. This will lubricate the strands and will also *flag* a broken or hooked strand by tearing off a small section of tissue. If you do have a wire break, replace the wire immediately—be careful, or you might get deep and painful cuts. Replace the wire after five years. If still good, keep the old wire on board as a spare. To check for proper wire tension, lock the wheel in position by using the pedestal brake, or by tying off the wheel. Cable tension is best when you cannot move the quadrant or drive wheel by hand with the wheel locked in place. Overtightening will greatly reduce the sensitivity of the system.

It must be emphasized that all on board must be familiar with the care and operation of the steer-

STEERING WIRE ADJUSTMENT

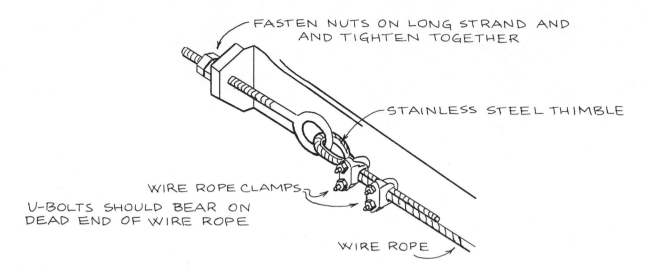

FASTEN NUTS ON LONG STRAND AND AND TIGHTEN TOGETHER

STAINLESS STEEL THIMBLE

WIRE ROPE CLAMPS

U-BOLTS SHOULD BEAR ON DEAD END OF WIRE ROPE

WIRE ROPE

* NUTS SHOULD BE RE-TIGHTENED AFTER INITIAL LOAD.
* SPACING BETWEEN CLIPS SHOULD BE SIX TIMES THE ROPE DIAMETER.

ing system and engine controls. One person must be assigned the job of maintenance and must be thoroughly familiar with the operation and intent of all the equipment. If at any time your steering system makes strange noises or reacts differently than it has previously, you must find the causes immediately and correct the problem.

Screws, nuts, bolts as well as clevis and cotter pins that are part of the steering system, engine controls, or pedestal accessories must be checked regularly for tightness and wear. Failure to inspect all steering parts, engine controls and pedestal accessories may cause loss of control or failure of the engine or steering system. All boats *must* have an emergency tiller or its equivalent, and all on board must be familiar with its location and operation. An emergency tiller drill is just as important as a man-overboard drill and must be regularly conducted.

On a new boat and at least once a year, inspect

STANDARD STEERING SYSTEM SERVICING

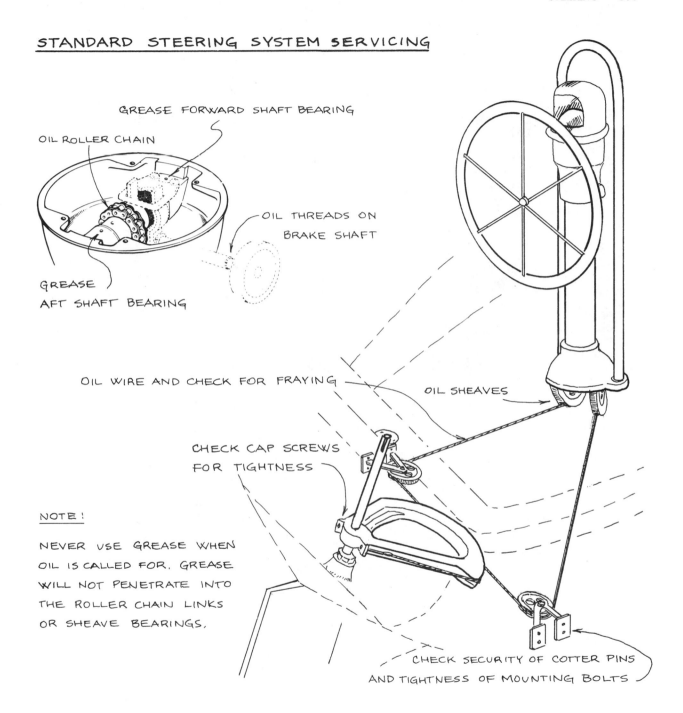

GREASE FORWARD SHAFT BEARING

OIL ROLLER CHAIN

OIL THREADS ON
BRAKE SHAFT

GREASE
AFT SHAFT BEARING

OIL WIRE AND CHECK FOR FRAYING

OIL SHEAVES

CHECK CAP SCREWS
FOR TIGHTNESS

NOTE!

NEVER USE GREASE WHEN
OIL IS CALLED FOR. GREASE
WILL NOT PENETRATE INTO
THE ROLLER CHAIN LINKS
OR SHEAVE BEARINGS.

CHECK SECURITY OF COTTER PINS
AND TIGHTNESS OF MOUNTING BOLTS

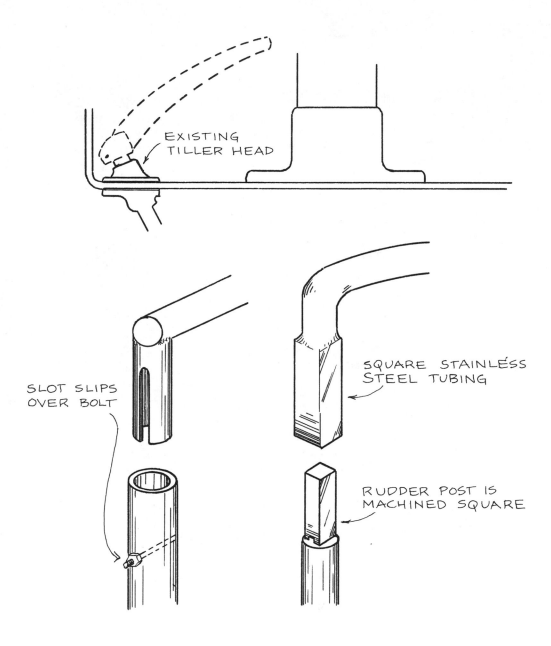

EXISTING
TILLER HEAD

SQUARE STAINLESS
STEEL TUBING

SLOT SLIPS
OVER BOLT

RUDDER POST IS
MACHINED SQUARE

I don't care how reliable you deem your steering system to be, you'd have to be a complete Elmer to go sailing without an emergency tiller system.

the system when under a strong load. On a calm day and under power, go away from the other boats and with the person who is assigned the maintenance watching from below, put the wheel hard over at full throttle. The maintenance man should watch carefully for all parts of the system bending, distorting, creaking, or giving any indication of failing if placed under a heavy load for a period of time. If for any reason, something did fail or needs adjusting, the day is early and you will have plenty of time.

When leaving your boat at her mooring or slip, make sure that your wheel is properly tied off. Do *not* leave the steering system to free wheel.

The pedestal exterior should be cleaned with detergent and water. Do not use acetone and/or any other strong solvents as they may damage the finish.

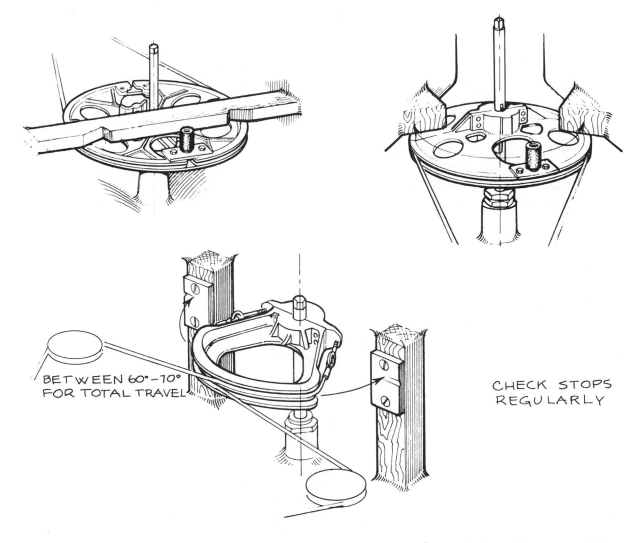

BETWEEN 60°-70° FOR TOTAL TRAVEL

CHECK STOPS REGULARLY

THREE TYPICAL RUDDER STOPS FOR STEERING SYSTEMS

45

Tools

Buy the best. I've said in *From a Bare Hull* to get the best tools you can, for they will last a long time and be ready and able whenever you need them, and if that was true for boatbuilding—most of which is done on dry land and close to repair shops— then it's quadruply true for maintenance, most of which is done close to corrosive salt water and sometimes as far away as Pango Pango.

Wrenches, Pliers, etc.

1. Crescent wrench

This is an abominable tool. I have used various ones for twenty years, and I'll be damned if I can figure out which way you turn the gnarly screw thing on the bastard to loosen it, and which way to tighten it. This is especially a thrill when you don't quite have a view of the nut you're working on, and just when you think that a tiny bit tighter setting will get the jaws just right, you turn the bloody screw and turn and turn waiting for the jaws to touch, only to look and realize that they're open wider than the jaws of a crocodile trying to eat a hippo.

But all that aside, you will need a six-inch long one, for it's awfully handy when you're at the top of the mast or wedged into the engine room with the correct wrench out of reach.

Get the best quality whose jaws don't sway from side to side, and whose screw turns smoothly.

I have seen a lot of damage done to boats by this tool and it was seldom the tool's fault—blame usually lay with the Elmer using it. If the jaws are left just a bit too loose, I guarantee you will round the nut or the bolt quicker than you can say "Elmer Fudd." Look closely to be sure you have the jaws perfectly tight *and* that the jaws are set dead-flat against the sides of the nut or bolt head, and *not* wedged half-assed from one point to another. Be especially careful when working with bronze nuts or bronze turnbuckles, for they are softer than stainless and will round very quickly.

2. Box and fork wrenches

The best set of tools to get is the combination wrench whose one end is a *box* and the other a *fork* of the same size. The box with its six or twelve points is the safest wrench to use, for it will grip all six sides of a bolt or nut, whereas the fork will grip but two. Of course you will not be able to use a box wrench for turnbuckles or fittings with hoses on them. There you'll need the open fork.

The miserable crescent wrench. Don't use it on vital nuts and bolts for it rounds them too easily. Great for tightening handles on buckets.

The combination fork and box wrench—lower tool—is the most versatile and safest wrench to use. The small ratchet wrench above it is great too, but you'll go broke buying all the different sizes.

A set of sockets is almost a must for working on the engine. Be sure to get the extension shown for hard-to-reach places. (What place on an engine isn't hard to reach?)

3. Socket wrenches

These are the fastest wrenches to use, but they are even more limited than a box wrench, for they can only handle nuts if the body of the bolt protrudes no more than the depth of the socket. If that sounds as weird to you as it does to me, then read it again; Candace says it makes sense. Sort of.

The most invaluable service the socket can render is the reaching of otherwise inaccessible nuts with the aid of a three- or four-inch extension. Be sure to get one.

Big Bertha. She's big and heavy and ugly but you'll need her to tighten the nut on the stuffing box.

4. Pipe wrench

As heinous as these tools are, for they are awkward and heavy and start to rust the second they smell salt water, I just don't know how you can set sail—especially for a cruise—without one, for the stuffing box and through-hull nuts can only be tightened with these and nothing else. For the stuffing box you will actually need two or you'll torque the thing right out of the hull if you try loosening or tightening the nut without holding the part that's usually glassed into the hull.

Get the smallest ones that will do the job.

You'll need a set of Allen wrenches. Get ones that are pinned together as above or you'll be playing Pick-up Sticks forever.

5. Allan wrenches

These are the things that look like bent nails with six sides. They serve only limited use on winches and engines, but boy when you need them, you need them. Get some. Unless you enjoy playing Pick-up-Sticks, get the kind that looks like a pocket knife with a bunch of different sizes attached.

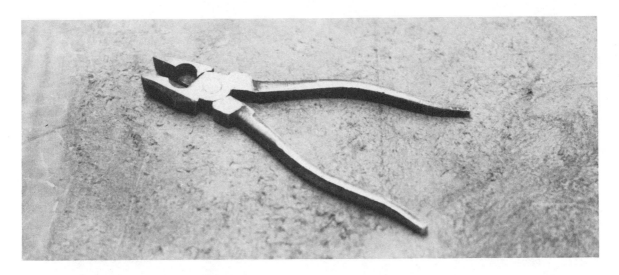

This kind of pliers you'll seldom need on a boat. The adjustable jaw kind are much better. Unfortunately I don't happen to have a picture of one so you'll just have to use your imagination.

6. Pliers

The adjustable kind are very versatile, but therein lies their greatest fault, for they are too tempting to use in places where a wrench of the proper size is called for. But they are far too convenient to pass up just for that. Resist *all* temptation to use them on nuts or bolts.

Channel locks make very good small pipe wrenches. Again observe their limitation—in this case, size—and don't try to use them on a nut that is too large, for you will grip only a part of it (barely), and you will readily ruin the corners when you slip.

Vice grips we have not had aboard *Warm Rain* since building her, and I don't think we've missed them. If you can think of some use for which adjustable pliers are unsuitable, then by all means get some.

Needle-nose pliers are handy when working with wiring and gnarled cotter keys.

7. Cable cutters

If the mast goes overboard, the rigging will keep it next to the boat, and in a good seaway it will bash the hell out of the hull. With cable cutters, you can cut the bugger loose in no time. Get one that will definitely cut through your size of rigging. Don't leave port without it.

8. Wire strippers/crimps

You'll have to have one of these. It's almost impossible to do decent wiring without one.

Cable cutters are a must for anyone who sails his boat hard—or dumbly. If the mast goes overboard, it can quickly damage the hull unless the shrouds are cut and the rig set loose.

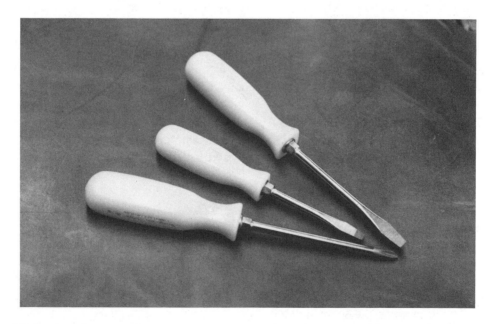

Make sure the screwdrivers you get are good quality or they'll round and bend in no time.

Screwdrivers

1. Combination screwdriver

This is the critter whose hollow handle holds every conceivable type of bit, which makes it as handy as hell, for all the bits are always at your fingertips except when you turn it upside down with the bottom open, in which case all the bits will be all over the floor. Don't laugh this off as being an unlikely occurrence. It's not. I once did it three times in one day, after which Candace immediately enrolled me in *Stupids Anonymous*.

Get ones that are of good heat-treated steel, for the cheapos are so soft that their tips will bend twisting the navel out of an orange.

2. Standard screwdrivers

A set of at least three straight-bit screwdrivers will be needed aboard. A fairly stocky four-inch blade with ¼ inch tip will be good to get into most small areas. Be sure the tip is so thick that it fits snugly into a number ten screw head, for on a boat these tend to be the most common. You'll also need a small fine screwdriver for electronics and instruments, as well as a large one with a good broad, grabable handle for stubborn screws, like the ones tapped into aluminum masts and booms tend to be.

You will also need a couple of Phillips screwdrivers, small and large. If you get the combination driver mentioned above, you won't need to buy these separately for there'll be a couple of bits in there. If you are building anything new or rebuilding something, try to use Phillips screws. The screwdriver is much less likely to slip out of these than out of a straight bit.

A Robertson screwdriver—the one with the square tip—is rarely needed. Besides, your combo will take care of it.

Screwdrivers, as everything else on a boat, should be of the highest quality. If they are, they will last a lifetime.

Measuring Tools

1. Tapes

The standard metal slide-out tapes are great to have around the house, and are even of use aboard when tuning the rigging or measuring for awnings and such, but they have a very short lifespan aboard because once the edges of the tape lose their coating, the metal of the tape rusts frighteningly quickly. If you are determined to have one aboard, keep the tape well oiled by running it through an oily rag, and store it wrapped in a cloth. Even then there is little guarantee that it will ever come out of its little house again.

2. Folding rules

The fine wooden folding extension rule, made of good hardwood, and having solid brass hinges, is perhaps the best measuring tool aboard. It won't rust, it won't crack easily, it makes exact measurements, it acts as a good straightedge, and last but not least, it *floats*. Get one.

3. Squares

For any small woodworking you might do, you'll need a small finishing square. Historically the best squares were fitted with rosewood handles and there are a good number that follow that tradition. The best kind have the arm secured to the handle at four points, and have brass face plates and brass facing strips on the handle's sides. Good ones cost about $10, great ones about $20.

You will have to have a bevel square aboard as well. This is the thing that lays out angles. Again the good ones have rosewood handles and brass fittings.

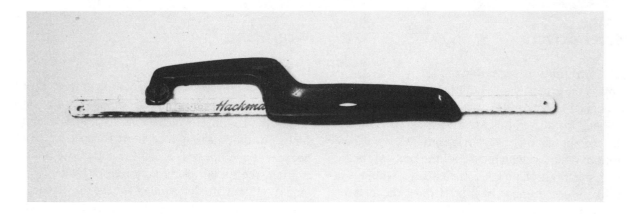

A clever handle for a hacksaw blade that lets you cut in awkward places.

Saws

1. Wood saws

A finished boat is not a construction site so you won't need any big mean saws around. I can't for the life of me think what you'd use a ripsaw for— the coarse cutting ones, whose hooked teeth stick out slightly sideways from the blade—unless you plan on cutting firewood.

In contrast to ripsaw teeth, crosscut saw teeth are filed to cut with their edges and shaped with no hook to prevent snagging on wood fibers. A good twelve-inch backsaw—cross-cut teeth—with a stiff reinforced blade and sturdy handle, will do nicely for most small jobs aboard. With their sixteen or so teeth per inch, they cut very accurately and very cleanly. Keep the blade lightly oiled and well sharpened to give it longer life. For true blade protection, sew a case out of good stiff canvas with a tie at the end to tie through the handle. This will keep out some of the humidity and protect the blades from being nicked and dulled by other tools.

2. Hacksaws

A good hacksaw is a must on a boat for cutting screws, bolts, chain, etc. Very few hold the blade stiff enough, which is why most metal cutting looks like it was done by a butcher. A wobbling blade also dulls more quickly. Mercifully the Garrett Wade catalog carries a beauty. Their new design with a tightening lever is said to give absolutely positive high tension control. It costs $20, but might be well worth the price.

3. Saber saws

On occasion it's handy to have a saber saw on board, but the cheap ones are worse than nothing and the really good ones that cut with acccuracy and have a decent life span cost over $100—the best you can get, a German Bosch, costs $250—and every time you want to use one you have to find an AC plug, and by then you would have cut the thing ten times over with a handsaw.

Planes

A regular plane is too awkward to use for most small projects. Get a little block plane that requires only one hand, leaving the other one free to act as a vise. The body is only about six inches long which means it will fit into most awkward places. Where even this plane doesn't cut quite close enough to the end, use a Sur-Form. That's the thing that looks like a small plane but has a thousand tiny blades instead of one. Actually it's a glorified lemon-rind grater. Keep the blade sharp.

A few hints: Plane with the grain. Look at the side of the stock and you'll see which way the grain runs. If you go against the grain, you'll lift out small bits of wood and the surface will end up rougher than before.

When planing end-grain, push the plane one way to the middle of the board only; then repeat this process going in the other direction. This prevents splitting the board at the edge.

Rasps and Files

For small trimming you'll need to have a good rasp and some files. A shoe rasp is ideal. It has no handle so it takes up little room, and it has four different cutting surfaces on a single tool, which is very handy indeed. It has a coarse and a medium rasp, and a coarse and a medium file.

The only other thing you might need around is a round file for smoothing holes, and a small saw file—triangular blade—for sharpening your saw. Forget the other oddities; you'll never use them.

Chisels and Knives

You have to have chisels. A good one-inch one is a must and a small ¼-inch one is nice to have

around. Get ones with replaceable ends so that if you hammer the hell out of them, you will be able to replace just the end and keep the rest.

Never cut anything but wood with a wood chisel. Do *not* use it to scrape old paint or glue or to open cans or pull nails. When not in use, wrap it in a piece of canvas and stow with care.

For cutting metal, get a small cold-chisel.

A good working knife is a must aboard, and for all-around use it's mighty hard to beat a Swiss army knife that doubles as a screwdriver and corkscrew and bottle opener and nailfile and toothpick and eyebrow plucker. If only it could cook.

Drills

Don't get a brace-and-bit. It's harder to stow than a frozen giraffe, and there is seldom enough space aboard to use it. Get one of those nifty hand drills that has a coffee grinder handle. Get one with a nice big chuck like ⅜ inch to make it usable with large bits. Get a good one.

Any good electric drill is nice to have aboard. You will wear through your palm before you'll drill through a piece of metal with a hand drill, and electric drills also set screws and can be used for buffing and can also take a small grindstone or wire brush or a small sanding disk. Get a good one like a Milwaukee or a Makita. If you're thinking of getting a cheap one, forget about it. Go buy a couple of jugs of rum instead; it's a much wiser investment.

Clamps

Have a couple of four-inch clamps aboard, not just to hold glued joints while the glue sets, but also to clamp pieces securely while they're being drilled or sawed.

Drill bits. Get a good set and keep them dry or they'll rust and go dull in no time and they're not easy to sharpen.

One four-inch C-clamp and one smaller one will be handy to have aboard.

If at all possible, every boat should have a small bench vise built in somewhere. Anywhere out of the way is fine. Failing that let me tell you about one of man's great inventions—the Multi-Angle Swivel Vacuum Vise. It weighs only five pounds and grips firmly to any smooth non-porous surface with its vacuum-cup base. To attach, you simply apply pressure and turn a lever. It creates a strong gripping vacuum. Don't be a sceptic; it works. We lifted 400-pound windows with these suckers when we built our house. This thing also swivels 360 degrees and tilts 90. The hardened jaws have a V-groove for round work, and another nice touch—slide on rubber jaws to protect delicate work. Get one. It's made by General and it's in the Garret Wade catalogue for $36.

Sanders

If you have lots of varnishing to do, you'll have to get a small block sander. The good ones are made by Rockwell and Makita and Milwaukee. The best ones are the one-handed ones. Get one with a high rpm motor (over 10,000) for then the orbits it creates will be so fine you'll never see them. The square sanding pads on these extend past the frame so you can get right into corners and up to edges. Regular sheets of sandpaper fit these perfectly if a full sheet is quartered. It's only about $70 and that's a steal. Sands ten times faster and more evenly than my right hand. It also gives great massages. Use fine grit.

Hammers

Get a small four-ounce plastic mallet or hammer or whatever you want to call it. This is the tool you'll use to discover delaminations in your fiberglass hull or rot in your wood one.

Get a regular hammer too, to check your bolts. Claw hammers are seldom needed and they tend to mar things around them. One with a flat peen instead of a claw might be handier.

Toolbox

Make one. I've tried plastic fishing tackle boxes and they're pretty feeble, for none is built to carry the weight or the bulk, so the fittings crack and bend. The best tool box is the traditional ship-wright's box made of wood. The one improvement these need is a hinged lid so things don't spill on a heel. Use decent wood and fine brass fittings and glue a piece of carpet onto the bottom and have it come up the sides a bit as well, to protect any surface you might be putting the box onto. They look so damned good they'll make your tub feel like a ship.

Find a nice secure place for it, out of the way of moisture.

If you have lots of wood to varnish, get a block sander. It will save you days and days of labor.

A ball peen hammer will have infinitely more uses aboard than a claw hammer.

A rattail brush with its fine bristles is an ideal boat sweeper, for it picks up even the smallest speck of sand and grit.

Just because a wire brush is worn down, that's no reason to throw it away. As long as you see the wires, keep it. (I don't know what for, but you must have had it around for a reason so you might as well keep it.)

When you're using wood screws, always pre-drill the hole one size smaller than your screw. Without pre-drilling you can easily split the wood.

Masking tape is one of the most useful things aboard, but if misused, it's a menace. Never leave masking tape on for more than a day, especially on surfaces exposed to the sun. The glue will stick like crazy and the paper will break down, and you will spend fifteen years taking off a four-inch piece.

A small vise would be a true dream to have aboard. Always pad the jaws so you don't damage the piece you're working on.

Handy tools for rope work and sail repairs. Do have a ball of treated marlin aboard. It smells as rich as a Conrad novel.

The cutters in the photo you will seldom use—your wire strippers will have a cutter in them—but the stubby screwdriver is a godsend for tight places.

This is the ideal wood glue aboard a boat. It's very water resistant—but not waterproof—yet it's easy to use and clean up, and *makes a hell of a strong joint.*

A SHIPSHAPE TOOL BOX

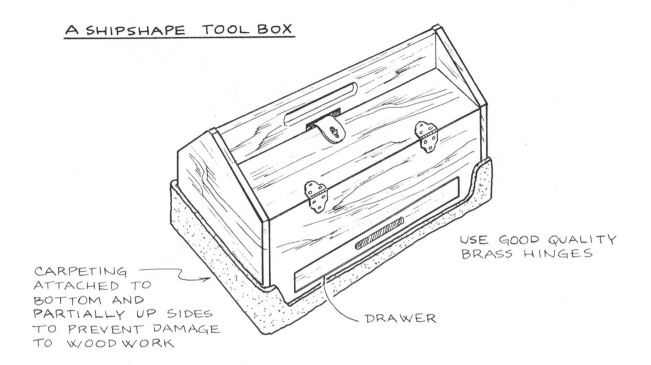

CARPETING
ATTACHED TO
BOTTOM AND
PARTIALLY UP SIDES
TO PREVENT DAMAGE
TO WOODWORK

USE GOOD QUALITY
BRASS HINGES

DRAWER

*Whenever you use varnish, filter it first to get out the little bits of crud and harden-
ed varnish. You can use the thing shown, or your lady's nylon stockings.*

Ropework like this is not only beautiful but on the shaft of a boathook it is eminently useful as well, for it gives you a good solid non-slip grip. This is important when fending off, for it can make the difference between damaging the boat or skimming safely by.

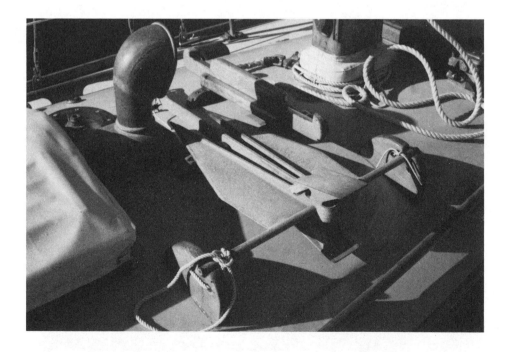

Two good examples of a shipshape yacht. First the anchor is neatly chocked and made fast so it won't cause damage in a seaway, and second, the varnished skylight is protected by a well-fitting cover secured by a drawstring.

An automatic fire extinguisher—heat activated—is an excellent choice for an engine room. If you have to get into the room to activate an extinguisher, you'll be letting in a lot of air to fuel the fire.

This chafe could have been largely prevented by having the snapshackle, that was set in the rail, tied to the lifeline above it to keep it from flopping and chafing.

A mast collar in impeccable condition. It will keep all water from entering belowdecks as well as prevent rot that can set in-between a poorly fitted collar and the mast. For a perfect seal, a bead of silicone has been run around the top of the collar. This should be checked and renewed regularly.

And a shipshape bung for a shipshape tender allows rainwater to be drained out without having to turn the tender over.

The circular-wicked kerosene lantern with a large reflective hood gives the most light of any non-pressurized lamp. The wick itself must be kept even all the way around or you'll get sooting and less light.

A shipshape and very pretty tender for a boat over forty feet. Note centerboard for sailing, dual oar positions, nicely spliced painter with chafe preventer on metal ring, and the canvas covered rubber fender tacked to the gunwale to protect the mothership's topsides. Note also good wide floorboards. Some people mistakenly take these out of their tenders to reduce weight. That's bad. Great loads will then be placed on individual planks from people stepping into the tender. The floor-boards help spread the loads over the ribs, saving the planks.

Worksheet

The Concordia yard was good enough to make an estimation of what it takes to keep one of their Concordia yawls in top shape. The following is a list of the hours required annually for each task. Remember, this is a 39-foot full-keeled wood boat, and I am using it as an example of the absolute maximum amount of work that could be needed. If you have a fiberglass boat, leave out things like the brightwork, and figure out the amount of hours for the rest of the work in proportion to the size of your boat.

Bottom: Sand, paint two coats.
        Sand, paint boot-top, one coat.
        Red-lead keel prior to painting.   28 hours.

Topsides: Sand and paint two coats.   25 hrs.

Brightwork: Sand and varnish two coats.   50 hrs.

Deck: Sand and paint one coat.   12 hrs.

Cabin: Clean and paint bilges.   3 hrs.

Spars: Sand and varnish—two coats.   25 hrs.

Standing rigging: Minor maintenance.   3 hrs.

Running rigging: Grease winches, oil turnbuckles.   6 hrs.

Engine: Winterize; overhaul starter, alternator, commission engine, change oil etc.   17 hrs.

Plumbing: Disconnect for winter, check toilet pumps, hook up for spring, etc.   10 hrs.

Step spars and rig: Unrig and re-rig.   24 hrs.

Total…190 hrs.

46

Rigging Guide

by Gary Mull, N.A.

Introduction

The purpose of this guide is twofold: First to help the owners of new and used boats determine which of a wide variety of running rigging systems is most appropriate to their boat, their crew and how the boat is used. Second to help owners without engineering backgrounds or long experience with sailboat rigging select gear and equipment which is appropriate, in terms of size, function and strength, to the system they wish to use.

Many new boats are sold with only the basic equipment necessary to get the boat out on the water. Often the owner wishes to modify the basic hardware and rigging to suit his specific racing or cruising requirements. Many times after buying a used boat, even one several years old, the owner finds himself faced with a deck layout which at best makes the boat hard and unenjoyable to sail, and, in the extreme, dangerous to the people aboard.

There are as many different ways of rigging a boat as there are boats and sailors who own them. It simply is not within the scope of this guide to show every possible deck layout. Instead, I have broken the deck hardware and rigging into a number of systems, e.g. mainsheet, traveler, jibsheet, etc., and then given examples of a number of successful variations of each of these systems.

Working with the individual boats, with known restrictions of deck, cabin top, and cockpit details, the reader will be able to choose for himself the type of system best suited to himself, the boat, and how he plans to sail her.

Even though each boat may require a different deck layout or equipment, there are certain rules which should be universally applied, regardless of the size, type, or use of the boat.

All leads must be *fair*. Blocks should *always* be sited so that lines entering and leaving the blocks should have the minimum fleet angle possible, but in no case more than 10 degrees. See diagram.

Running rigging should *never* cross. A corollary of Murphy's Law is that, if two pieces of running rigging cross, there will inevitably be a foul.

Boats are symmetrical, winches are not. Therefore, in locating winches, remember that lines lead onto the winches in a clockwise direction, This will ordinarily mean that winches have to be displaced either fore and aft or athwartships to get fair leads for both tacks.

Nearly all horn cleats today are mounted improperly. The cleat should be rotated

FLEET ANGLE

NOT TO SCALE

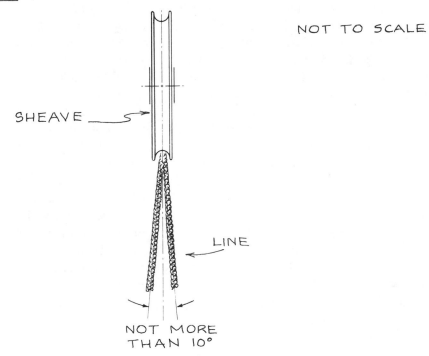

SHEAVE

LINE

NOT MORE
THAN 10°

WINCH/CLEAT ANGLE

NOT TO SCALE

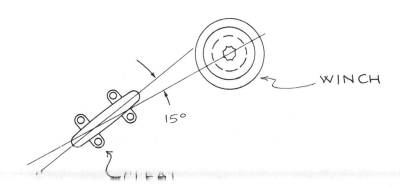

WINCH

15°

CLEAT

counterclockwise about 15 degrees from the axis of a line drawn from the winch center to the cleat so that the cleat is "open". See diagram.

In order to avoid overrides, lines leading to winches should strike the winch drum at least 5 degrees below a line perpendicular to the winch axis. *Never lead a line to a winch from above perpendicular to the winch axis!* The further away from a winch the lead is, the more the winch will have to be tilted back away from the load to avoid overrides.

In general, a non-swiveling block is better than a swiveling block. Swivels tend to wear more quickly and they also can contribute to a line winding around itself.

Finally, never use gear of doubtful strength. The possible saving in cost of weight over properly sized equipment simply isn't worth the risk to yourself or friends.

Most designers and builders rely on a combination of experience and good memory to know what has been used in the past and how it has worked out. This method is generally successful as long as they're working in familiar territory. However, for the non-professional, or the designer or builder working on a boat outside previous experience, this can degenerate into little more than guesswork.

In my design office we have developed, from designing a wide variety of boats, sailing experience in all conditions, plus feedback on a tremendous range of sailing hardware from all over the world, some rather complex empirical curves and formulae for establishing the loads of various pieces of running rigging. These have proven to be quite accurate over a wide range of types and sizes of boats. Working with each specific design, we can make corrections for the aspect ratio of the foretriangle or the mainsail, stability and displacement of the boat, and specific wind speeds in which we are interested. Then, depending upon whether the boat is to be used as a long distance family

WINCH/LINE LEAD ANGLE

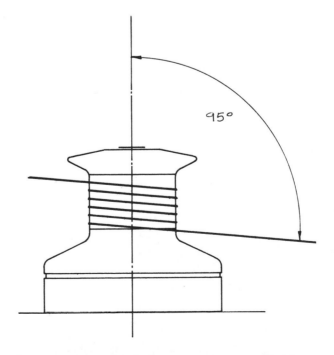

NOT TO SCALE

95°

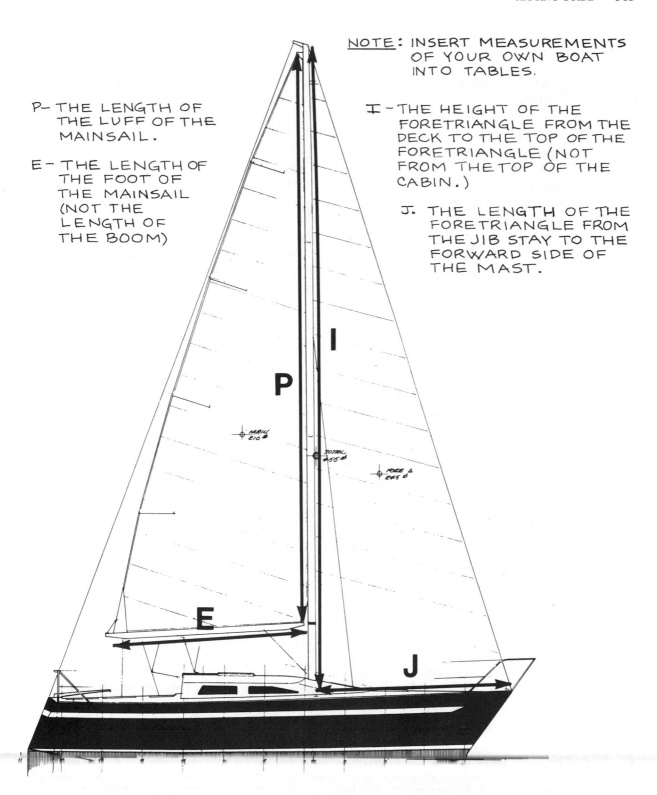

NOTE: INSERT MEASUREMENTS OF YOUR OWN BOAT INTO TABLES.

P— THE LENGTH OF THE LUFF OF THE MAINSAIL.

E— THE LENGTH OF THE FOOT OF THE MAINSAIL (NOT THE LENGTH OF THE BOOM)

I— THE HEIGHT OF THE FORETRIANGLE FROM THE DECK TO THE TOP OF THE FORETRIANGLE (NOT FROM THE TOP OF THE CABIN.)

J. THE LENGTH OF THE FORETRIANGLE FROM THE JIB STAY TO THE FORWARD SIDE OF THE MAST.

cruising boat or a very sophisticated racing boat such as a Six Metre, we can work with safety factors to produce the results needed.

The design loads used to develop this guide have proven satisfactory in my office for a tremendous number of boats of various types. However, no empirical method is fool proof! Many factors affect the loads and strengths of rigging and fittings. This is a guide only and is not to be considered an assumption of responsibility by Nicro Corp. or Gary Mull. After going through the tables in this guide the owner is cautioned to make certain that all of his equipment is in proper working order, that all lines are in good shape, shackles are properly aligned with their loads, and that good seamanship and sensible judgement are exercised at all times. The final and sole responsibility for safety aboard rests with the skipper.

In order to make this guide useful for a broad variety of sizes and types of boats, it has been necessary to assume an "average" boat and forego a bit of mathematical sophistication. The information given here has been developed through the use of our design curves and formulae and will work for the vast majority of cases. However, for boats with very high sailplan aspect ration, very heavy displacements, or very high stability, if would be well for the user to go *one size larger* in running rigging and fittings. Likewise, cruising boats may want to go a size larger to allow for wear or possible lack of maintenance due to being away from home port. Racing boats will sometimes want to use larger sheaves to reduce running friction. ULDB's may be able to use slightly lighter gear but this must be done with caution and awareness of possible danger to personnel as well as the boat. Multihulls are not covered in this guide.

Halyards and Related Hardware

To determine the appropriate wire or rope size, measure the height of the triangle from the deck to top of the foretriangle: Call this "I". Measure the luff length of the mainsail. Call this "P". Enter the table with I, for jib, spinnaker and topping lift, P for main, and read directly what size wire halyard to use.

Halyard sizes shown here assume clean, undamaged, 7x19 galvanized or stainless steel wire rope. Rope tails are usually twice the diameter of the wire. Tail splices should be carefully made, using a minimum of four tucks with the core and four tucks with the cover. A properly made tail splice will develop sufficient strength to carry the load of the halyard.

Enter the table for halyard shackles with the wire size and read directly which shackle to use. Take care to make certain that the head cringle of the jib or spinnaker and the hole in the headboard of the main are large enough to accept the shackle selected.

Enter the table for halyard lead blocks with the wire size and read directly the desired halyard lead block, fairlead block, or gang-fairlead block required. Note the breaking strength shown for the blocks for each wire size. Care must be taken not to exceed these limits. It is also wise to try to locate halyard lead blocks so that the crew is not in line with the load in order to avoid the possibility of being hit with a broken halyard or block.

For cruising boats or others where low maintenance and long wear are desired, use the next larger wire size and select blocks accordingly. On racing boats, one size larger block will often be desirable from the standpoint of reduced friction and ability to adjust halyards under high load.

TABLE FOR HALYARD SIZES

I or P	MAIN HALYARD	JIB HALYARD	SPINNAKER HALYARD	TOPPING LIFT
20′	1/8″	5/32″	3/16″	1/8″
25′	1/8″	5/32″	3/16″	1/8″
30′	5/32″	3/16″	7/32″	5/32″
35′	5/32″	3/16″	7/32″	5/32″
40′	3/16″	7/32″	1/4″	3/16″
45′	3/16″	7/32″	1/4″	3/16″
50′	7/32″	1/4″	9/32″	7/32″
55′	7/32″	1/4″	9/32″	7/32″
60′	7/32″	1/4″	9/32″	7/32″
65′	1/4″	9/32″	5/16″	1/4″
70′	1/4″	9/32″	5/16″	1/4″
75′	1/4″	9/32″	5/16″	1/4″
80′	1/4″	9/32″	5/16″	1/4″
85′	9/32″	5/16″	3/8″	9/32″
90′	9/32″	5/16″	3/8″	9/32″
95′	9/32″	5/16″	3/8″	9/32″
100′	9/32″	5/16″	3/8″	9/32″

NOTE: For rope spinnaker halyards and rope topping lifts, use rope diameter twice wire diameter shown.

Mainsail Control

Mainsail shape is as important to cruising boats as it is to racers. A main with too much draft, (see diagram) draft too far aft, or a tight leach, causes bad weather helm and cranky handling as well as poor speed and pointing.

The following mainsail controls are covered in this guide:

Main Halyard
Cunningham
Outhaul
Flattening Reef
Reefing
Main Sheet
Vang
Traveler

1. Main halyard

It is helpful to have a mark on the halyard that will tell the winch handler when the sail is at full hoist. For a racing boat, "full hoist" positions the top of the headboard at the lower edge of the mandatory black band. In this position, in very light wind, the sail should have no vertical wrinkles. For a cruising boat you should get a full hoist in about 15 knots of wind. If your main won't hoist as noted above, it is short on the luff and you should discuss this problem with your sailmaker. Main halyard wire diameter, shackle, and lead blocks are specified later.

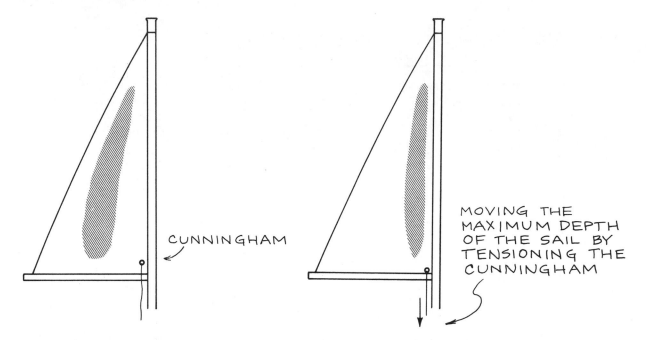

CUNNINGHAM

MOVING THE
MAXIMUM DEPTH
OF THE SAIL BY
TENSIONING THE
CUNNINGHAM

2. Cunningham

This is a small tackle, usually 3:1 or 4:1 fixed to a cringle in the luff of the main about 3% of P above the tack on boats with fixed goosenecks. It is used to stretch the luff, much as downhauling a sliding gooseneck, to keep the sail camber from drifting too far aft in a breeze. A good guide for adjustment is to haul down on the tackle until all horizontal wrinkles in the luff have disappeared. Ease it off for broad reaching and running.

3. Main outhaul

This is a small tackle, usually fitted internally in the boom, attached to the clew or to an outhaul car. It is used to stretch the foot to control mainsail shape. For a racing boat the clew should come out to the black band (the edge of the leach just inside the *inboard* edge of the bank) in about 8 knots of wind. A cruising boat should get full outhaul in about 15 knots. If your main won't outhaul like this without stretch wrinkles along the foot, it is short and you should take it up with your sailmaker. A good guide for adjustment is to outhaul to remove any vertical wrinkles in the foot in light to moderate

winds. In more breeze continue to outhaul to flatten the sail. Remember to stay inside the black band if you are racing. Ease off the outhaul reaching and running and in light air to increase sail draft.

4. Flattening reef

This is normally found on racing boats, but many cruiser-racers are being fitted with flattening reef systems lately. A very strong cringle is built into the leach about 3% or 4% of P above the clew. A wire, similar to a secondary outhaul is shackles into this cringle and led into the body just aft of the black band. This line usually leads out the forward end of the boom just aft of the gooseneck. The line is then taken to a lead block on deck, and thence to a winch. The use of the flattening reef is virtually self-explanatory. In light to moderate winds, the normal outhaul is used to adjust sail shape by outhauling to flatten the sail camber as the wind increases. However, at some point the hauling is permitted while racing. At this point the flattening reef is used to continue flattening sail camber. Remember you aren't allowed to pull the flattener beyond the black band either!

5. Reefing

Reefing is simply reducing the area of a sail. For mainsails there are two basic methods of reefing: Roller reefing and "slab" or "jiffy" reefing. I avoid roller reefing because of problems it creates in maintaining proper sail shape, and because of the possible liability of a mechanical system which might break down. The term "jiffy" was coined by a yacht broker to convince novice sailors that reefing isn't beyond their capabilities. "Slab" reefing describes what's happening quite accurately so I use this term. You're simply reefing a "slab" of mainsail at the foot.

The size of the "slab" determines the amount of area reduction. Usually the first reef is between 10% and 20% of the mainsail area. A usefule rule of thumb is that a 10% reduction in area requires a slab about 5% of P above the boom. A 20.0 reduction, a 10% slab, etc. Usually the second and third reefs are the same spacing up the luff of a bit longer. Make sure a reef doesn't come just above a batten as this will certainly result in a broken batten. Your sailmaker or designer will work this out for you.

A set of reef points consists of a grommet in the luff (the luff cringle), a grommet in the leech (the leech cringle), and a few smaller grommets across the sail between the two cringles (reef point grommets).

To reef, you need either a hook on the mainboom gooseneck for the luff cringle or use the "cunningham" tackle. You'll also need a leech cringle outhaul for each reef set-up.

The action goes like this:

a) Set-up the boom topping lift, if there is one.
b) Ease the vang.
c) Ease the mainsheet.
d) Lower the halyard till the luff cringle is on the hook or otherwise firmly secured at boom level.
e) Re-hoist the halyard with luff tension.
f) Outhaul the leech cringle.
g) Ease the topping lift.
h) Sheet in the main.
i) Re-set the vang.
j) Gather in the loose slab ("bunt") and tie up neatly with the reef points.

Remember outhauling the leech before setting-up tension on the halyard can rip the sail.

At the end of a reef you have a smaller version of the full sized main and all the shape adjustments can and should be made to get the mainsail looking right. Use the halyard to stretch the luff to keep the mainsail camber forward. Use the leech cringle outhaul to control flatness.

6. Mainsheet

This is the primary mainsail control and is used to restrict the movement of the mainboom in the horizontal plane.

Explanation of tables for mainsheet systems.

Measure the length of the foot of the mainsail and call this "E". If the mainsheet block(s) are attached near the end of the boom, use "End-Boom" data. If the block(s) are attached in the middle of the boom, use "Mid-Boom" data. For locations inbetween, judgement may be used, but remember that it is better to be on the safe side and use "Mid-Boom" data.

To find the required purchase ratio of End-Boom mainsheet tackles, divide the mainsail area by 50 for racing boats and by 25 for cruising boats. (For Mid-Boom mainsheets use 25 and 13 respectively). If the answer is 6 or less use that figure as the required purchase area. If the answer is greater than 6 a winch will be required.

Mainsheet diameter is usually determined by handling rather than by strength. As a guide, take the mainsail area and divide by the mainsheet purchase, times the winch power—call this the "size factor". Use the table below to find the mainsheet line diameter.

7. Boom vang

This is used primarily to control mainsail leech

MAINSAIL REEFING

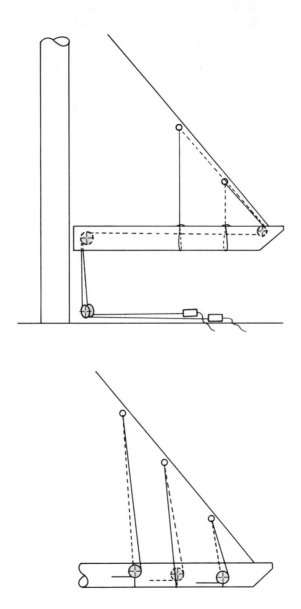

NOTE:
LOCATE BLOCKS SO THAT WHEN SAIL IS REEFED, THE LINE
THROUGH THE LEACH CRINGLE TO THE BLOCK LEADS AFT ABOUT
45°. THIS IS VERY IMPORTANT TO GIVE BOTH OUTHAUL AND
DOWNHAUL LOADS TO THE LEACH. LOCATING THESE BLOCKS TOO
FAR FORWARD, WILL RESULT IN EXTREMELY BAD (TOO FULL) MAINSAIL
SHAPE.

SIZE FACTOR

END BOOM	MID-BOOM	DIAMETER
50	25	3/8"
100	50	7/16"
200	100	1/2"
300	200	9/16"
400	300	5/8"

shape and "twist" by exerting tension on the leech.

To windward in light air, little or no vang load is needed. The traveler will be to windward of centerline and the end of the boom on centerline or just slightly to leeward. This will put a bit of "twist" in the main to account for wind shear in light air. As the wind increases, wind shear is less and you'll need less twist. Ease the traveler to leeward a bit and increase vang load progressively till in very strong winds, the traveler is well to leeward and the mainsail is "de-powered" or "boarded-out" with no leech twist.

Off the wind the vang keeps the boom from lifting in order to maintain power in the main. A bit of twist is still called for in light to moderate breezes.

When jibing the vang keeps the boom from "skying" but in very strong winds, ease the vang a bit before the jibe to avoid breaking the mast.

8. Mainsheet traveler

This is used to allow light leech tension and "twist" in light air by taking the traveler to weather of centerline in conjunction with no vang load and light mainsheet tension. This allows the boom to be on centerline but the leech can twist off a bit in the upper part of the sail.

In a breeze higher vang loads in conjunction with the traveler let to leeward, and heavier mainsheet load, allow the entire sail to be flatter and "de-powered" or "feathered". In gusty conditions

the traveler may be "played" out in a puff-back up in a lull.

Jib Sheets

Jib sheets are probably the singlemost important piece of running rigging, other than halyards, on the boat. Their location and adjustment can affect the performance of a boat tremendously. To start off with, the sheeting angle for your boat should be carefully checked. For large headsails, racing boats today are using anywhere from a seven to eight degree sheeting angle. Cruising boats can very comfortably use ten degrees. In fact, because of the size and location of cabin houses, chainplate location, spreader length etc., many cruising boats can't even attain ten degrees. However, owing to the shape of boats, a simple solution for a cruising boat with too wide a sheeting angle is to use a headsail with a much higher clew so that the sheeting point goes further aft on the boat, and thus the sheeting angle narrows naturally. For the method of laying out sheeting angle, refer to the diagram and table. It is also wise to check with your sailmaker before installing new track. For smaller headsails, those that sheet somewhere in the vicinity of the shrouds, the sheeting angle should be about eight degrees in moderate air and can be opened up top around twelve degrees or so in a breeze. Basically, if you are in light air and

TABLE FOR JIBSHEET SIZING

I	JIB SHEET DIA.
20′	1/4″
25′	5/16″
30′	5/16″
35′	3/8″
40′	7/16″
45′	1/2″
50′	9/16″
55′	5/8″
60′	5/8″
65′	3/4″
70′	3/4″
75′	1″

TABLE FOR SHEET & GUY SIZES

I	SPIN GUY DIA.	SPIN SHEET DIA.
20′	1/4″	1/4″
25′	5/16″	1/4″
30′	5/16″	5/16″
35′	3/8″	5/16″
40′	7/16″	3/8″
45′	1/2″	7/16″
50′	9/16″	1/2″
55′	5/8″	9/16″
60′	5/8″	9/16″
65′	3/4″	5/8″
70′	3/4″	5/8″
75′	1″	3/4″
80′	1″	3/4″
85′	1″	3/4″
90′	1″	3/4″

SHEETING ANGLE

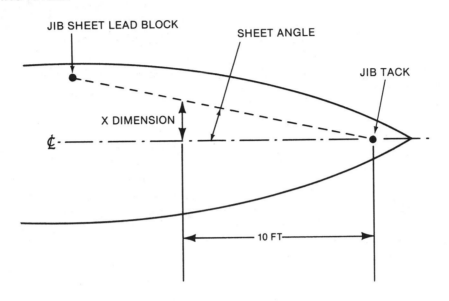

SHEET ANGLE	X DIMENSION
7°	14-3/4″
8°	16-7/8″
9°	19″
10°	21-1/8″
11°	23-3/8″
12°	25-1/2″
13°	27-3/4″
14°	30″
15°	32-1/8″

smooth water, you can sheet in closer, that is, with a narrower sheeting angle, and do quite well. For stronger winds and lumpier seas where you need more "punch", open up the sheeting angle several degrees and let the boat foot. As far as the fore and aft location of the sheet is concerned, the optimum position of the sheet is such that when the boat is headed gently up into the wind the sail luffs along the entire length of the luff. If it luffs at the head sooner, mover the sheet forward a bit. It if luffs at the foot sooner, move it aft a bit.

Staysails

All of the suggestions about jibs can be taken for staysails as well. It should be noted that in the table for halyards sizes and halyard shackles the topping lift sizes have been sized so that they can be used for staysail halyards as well.

Spinnakers

Generally, the spinnaker halyard should be hoisted right to the top. There used to be a theory that on reaches the head of the sail should be lowered a bit to get it away from the mast, but newer sail cuts of spinnakers seem to need this less and less. Off the wind, particularly in strong breezes, having the head of the spinnaker below maximum hoist will tend to allow the spinnaker to oscillate and cause severe control problems. See table for the size of the spinnaker halyard and halyard shackles.

Racing boats today generally use wire halyards while cruising boats tend more toward rope halyards. On long distance ocean races, rope halyards are still favored by many.

Spinnaker Pole Positioning

The best way to think of the adjustment of a spinnaker pole is as a method to position the tack of the spinnaker. First of all, since it is better to have the tack of the spinnaker as far away from the boat as possible, keep the pole perpendicular to the mast. The general guide of having the pole horizontal only works when the boat is relatively upright. if the boat is heeled at all, make sure the pole is perpendicular to the mast rather than parallel to the water. Next, since most spinnakers are designed symmetrically, the tack of the spinnaker should be the same height as the clew. Adjust the pole both with the topping lift as well as at the inboard end to get the tack and the clew of the spinnaker at the same height. Refer to table for the size of spinnaker pole topping lifts and snap shackles.

The spinnaker pole afterguy, together with the foreguy, position the pole in the fore and aft direction. In general, it is best to have the spinnaker pole aft as far as possible, without the chute collapsing all the time. Always keep the foreguy tensioned against the afterguy and topping lift so that the outboard end of the pole is positioned rigidly. Allowing the spinnaker pole of bounce around makes trimming the chute nearly impossible. Refer to table for the size of afterguys and afterguy snap shackles.

Spinnaker sheets do the same thing for spinnakers that jib sheets do for jibs. However, because of the cut of most spinnakers, the optimum sheeting point is generally such that the sail breaks first in the upper third of the luff. Trim the sheet in just enough to keep the shoulder slightly curling but never breaking.

Appendix

Block Loading Factors

The load on a block depends on the tension of the line passing through the block and the turning angle involved. The chart shows the block loading factor for some common angles, from 0° to 180°, and the resulting load on the block if line tension is 100 lbs. (45kg). Maximum loading for an application determines the block strength required.

	Turning Angle	Block Loading Factor	Block Load [Based on 100 lbs. (45kg) Line Tension]
A	0°	0	0 lb. (0kg)
B	30°	.518	51.8 lbs. (23.5kg)
C	45°	.767	76.7 lbs. (34.9kg)
D	60°	1.000	100.0 lbs. (45.45kg)
E	90°	1.414	141.4 lbs. (64.3kg)
F	120°	1.732	173.2 lbs. (78.7kg)
G	135°	1.846	184.6 lbs. (83.9kg)
H	150°	1.931	193.1 lbs. (87.8kg)
I	180°	2.000	200.0 lbs. (90.9kg)

A
0 lbs. (0kg)
100 lbs. (45kg) 100 lbs. (45kg) 0°

B
51.8 lbs. (23.5kg)
100 lbs. (45kg) 30° 100 lbs. (45kg)

C
76.7 lbs. (34.9kg)
100 lbs. (45kg) 45° 100 lbs. (45kg)

D
100 lbs. (45kg)
100 lbs. (45kg) 60° 100 lbs. (45kg)

E
141.4 lbs. (64.3kg)
100 lbs. (45kg) 90° 100 lbs. (45kg)

F
173.2 lbs. (78.7kg)
100 lbs. (45kg) 120° 100 lbs. (45kg)

G
184.61 lbs. (83.9kg)
100 lbs. (45kg) 135° 100 lbs. (45kg)

H
193.1 lbs. (87.8kg)
100 lbs. (45kg) 150° 100 lbs. (45kg)

I
200 lbs. (90.9kg)
100 lbs. (45kg) 180° 100 lbs. (45kg)

Line Breaking Strengths

To use this table, each box contains the breaking strength expressed in pounds and kilograms (in parentheses); the shaded portion of each box gives the weight of the line per 1,000 feet (330 meters) in pounds and kilograms (in parentheses).

DIAM. (mm)	1/16 (1.5mm)	3/32 (2mm)	1/8 (3mm)	5/32 (4mm)	3/16 (5mm)	7/32 (5.5mm)	1/4 (6mm)	9/32 (7mm)	5/16 (8mm)	3/8 (10mm)	7/16 (11mm)	1/2 (13mm)	9/16 (14mm)	5/8 (16mm)	3/4 (19mm)	7/8 (22mm)
1 × 19 STAINLESS STEEL	500 (227)	1200 (546)	2100 (955)	3300 (1500)	4700 (2136)	6300 (2864)	8200 (3727)	10300 (4682)	12500 (5682)	17500 (7955)	22500 (10227)	30000 (13636)	36200 (16455)	47000 (21364)	67500 (30682)	91400 (41545)
	8.5 (4)	20 (9)	35 (16)	55 (25)	77 (35)	102 (46)	135 (61)	170 (77)	210 (95)	300 (136)	400 (182)	530 (241)	640 (291)	825 (375)	1190 (541)	1620 (736)
7 × 7 STAINLESS STEEL	480 (218)	920 (418)	1760 (800)	2400 (1091)	3700 (1682)	5000 (2273)	6400 (2909)	7800 (3545)	9000 (4091)	12000 (5455)	15600 (7091)	21300 (9682)	26600 (12091)	32500 (14773)	45500 (20682)	60200 (27364)
	7.5 (3)	16 (7)	28.5 (13)	43 (20)	62 (30)	83 (39)	106 (50)	134 (63)	167 (79)	236 (110)	342 (155)	440 (200)	550 (250)	680 (309)	970 (441)	1320 (600)
7 × 19 STAINLESS STEEL	480 (218)	920 (418)	1760 (800)	2400 (1091)	3700 (1682)	5000 (2273)	6400 (2909)	7800 (3545)	9000 (4091)	12000 (5455)	16300 (7409)	22800 (10364)	28500 (12955)	35000 (15909)	49600 (22545)	66500 (30227)
	7.5 (3)	16 (7)	29 (13)	45 (20)	65 (30)	86 (39)	110 (50)	139 (63)	173 (79)	243 (110)	356 (162)	458 (208)	590 (268)	715 (325)	1050 (477)t1430 (650)	
DACRON							1650 (750)		2550 (1159)	3700 (1682)	5000 (2273)	6400 (2909)		10000 (4545)	12500 (5682)	
NYLON							1650 (750)		2550 (1159)	3700 (1682)	5000 (2273)	6400 (2909)		10400 (4727)	14200 (6455)	

COMMON PAINT FAILURES
CAUSES AND SOLUTIONS

Failure	Identification	Cause	Correction
Flashing	Non-uniform sheen is noted in irregular areas.	Caused by inadequate and non-uniform priming and resultant loss of vehicle into substrate.	Properly prime and seal all surfaces uniformly before applying finish coat.
Lapping	Uneven color or sheen differences in dried paint film.	Caused by waiting too long before painting back into wet edge. Fast setting paints. Improper ventilation when painting causing fast setting. Painting hot surfaces. Using fast evaporating thinners.	Paint large areas without stopping. Leave good wet edge, film thickness, make breaks only at hatches, ports, windows or angles. Avoid hot drafty ventilation. Don't paint in direct sunlight. Don't use fast evaporating solvents.
Crawling	Paint fails to form continuous film on the surface and shrinks, shrivels up, or bubbles while still wet.	Water, wax grease and silicone lubricant will cause this condition. High gloss surfaces which have not been sanded or roughed will also cause it.	Wash surface clean of wax, grease and oil, and sand or buff down glossy surfaces before painting. Avoid use of silicone lubricants in painting areas.
Wrinkling	Film in drying stages shrinks into tiny crests and valleys in irregular pattern.	Caused by poor application, with extra thick film being deposited in irregular manner. Surface film dries faster than under film, thus shrinking and forming wrinkles. Rapid temperature changes from warm, direct sunlight to colder temperature, starts surface dry and then slows down drying of underfilm.	Observe proper rule of application and paint under correct temperature and weather conditions. Add a small amount of thinner, if paint is heavy in body.
Loss of Adhesion	Peeling, stripping or flaking of paint from under surface.	Inadequate priming. Excess moisture. Improper or excessively thinned primers. Knots or sap streaks which bleed out wood resin. Painting over gloss enamels or hard varnished surfaces, Painting over dirt, grease and oil.	Use correct system of coating. Eliminate moisture. Use good primer and avoid excessive thinning. Sand or roughen up gloss of original surface before painting. Remove contaminants.
Alligatoring	Cracking of paint film which grows larger as paint ages, with paint adhering tightly by with irregular fissures over painted area.	Application of a hard-drying paint or enamel over a soft-drying undercoat. Top coat shrinks as it dries and pulls away from soft-drying undercoats.	Select correct system of paints and be sure primer or undercoat is dry.
Checking	Slight V-shaped breaks appear in paint film.	Due to uneven shrinkage through the cross section of a coat of paint, this is caused by poor pigment and oil combinations in the paint.	Use reliable paint formulated with correct pigment and oil combinations. Do not add additional materials upsetting the paint's composition.
Slow Dry	Paint takes too long to dry to a firm non-sticky film.	Grease, water, and wax will slow down the dry of paint. Combination of low temperature and humidity will also slow down the dry of paint, as well as applying the paint too thick.	1. Remove all grease, water and wax when preparing the surface. 2. Do not paint in cold weather and excessive humidity. 3. Apply thin coats.

Cracking and Scaling	Cracks cut through to under surface and paint curls up around the edges, eventually losing all adhesion and scales off.	Usually due to a combination of following causes: thick paint films with brittle undercoats, surfaces not receptive to successive coats of paint, poor wood like yellow pine, high interior moisture content, and poor grade paint materials.	Correct causes and use reliable paints.
Blistering	Formation of bubbles on surface of the paint.	Nearly always caused by moisture from within forcing paint film away from wood or substrate. Also caused by painting in hot sunlight on overheated surfaces, and by using quick dry enamels which surface-dry fast trapping solvents. Paint applied in excessively thick coats often blister when subjected to high temperatures.	Eliminate the source of moisture. Avoid painting in hot sunlight and on surfaces which are over-heated. Avoid practice of applying paint in heavy coats.
Lifting	Wrinkling of top coat or lifting of undercoat. Like the action of a solvent paint remover.	Caused by softening of undercoat by the solvents in top coat. Often due to too short a drying time interval between coats, adverse drying conditions, and use of inordinately strong solvents in top coat.	Provide longer drying time between coats, and good drying conditions.
Chalking	Formation of small particles like dust on the surface.	Deterioration of surface of paint film which produces excessive erosion due to poor choice of vehicle and pigments by the manufacturer.	Choose yacht enamels formulated with proper pigments and the correct combinations of vehicles and pigments to get the desired effect.
Yellowing	Yellowing of white paints.	Caused by certain gases, cleaning agents, cooking, ammonia washes, and by poor selection of pigments and vehicles.	Current causes due to environment and exposure, and select finishes with best non-yellowing properties.

TROUBLESHOOTING POLYURETHANES

SYMPTOM	PROBABLE CAUSES	POSSIBLE CURES
Orange Peel	- Tack coat viscosity too heavy. - Dry time between coats too short. - Spray pressure too high when applying second coat. - Waxes or mold releasing agents not thoroughly removed. - Spray gun nozzle held too close to wet tack coat. - Proper barrier coat primer not applied. - Moisture on surface when spraying.	- In most cases INTERTHANE PLUS must be sanded smooth and repainted. - Buffing is rarely effective in these cases.
Cratering, Fisheye	- Surface porosity underneath the INTERTHANE PLUS.	- If problem is severe, surface may require sanding and repainting.
Sags, Runs	- Spray gun held too close or too long. - Paint film too thick. - Tack coat too dry to support second coat.	- Use proper spray techniques.
Blistering, Peeling	- Moisture trapped in wood, primers, gelcoat and driven to the surface by sun and heat. Solvents trapped in paint film due to poor drying conditions. Improper surface preparation causing poor adhesion.	- Scrape or sand out the infected areas and rework when clean and dry with the appropriate system.
Loss of gloss, premature dulling	- Paint film too thin. - Too much solvent reducer added to INTERTHANE PLUS. - Moisture deposit on wet paint. - Improper scouring of the glossy surface with an abrasive or harsh chemical reducer.	- Gloss may be temporarily restored with waxing - Repainting of area may be required.

PROCEDURE FOR CORRECTING RUNS AND SAGS

As with all polyurethanes INTERTHANE PLUS should be applied in multiple thin coats. When applied in heavy coats, runs and sags may appear due to the thin nature of the coating. The following procedure has proven successful in correcting runs and sags:

1. Sand smooth with 600 grit wet or dry.

2. Sand with 3-M 2021 IMPERIAL FINE PAPER.

3. Use medium grit rubbing compound (Automotive Type) with buffing machine.

4. Use polishing compound (Automotive Type) with buffing machine.

5. Wax.

NOTE: Due to the change in the integrity of the paint film which may take place as a result of this process, the buffed area may not maintain the same level of gloss as long as the remainder of the boat.

GLOSSARY OF TERMS
USED IN
MARINE PAINT/COATING APPLICATIONS

This glossary is a compilation of terms commonly used in the marine painting field, with generally accepted definitions of those terms. Although many of the terms used are generally understood, some are interpreted in several different ways; others are not commonly used because of lack of clear definitions. The purpose of this glossary is to eliminate misunderstanding resulting from conflicting interpretations of these terms.

A

abrasion resistance — resistance to mechanical wear.

abrasive — the agent used for abrasive blast cleaning; for example, sand, grit, etc.

absorption — process of soaking up, or assimilation of one substance by another.

accelerator — catalyst, a material which accelerates the hardening of certain coatings.

acid number — a numerical index of free acid in an oil or resin.

acrylic resin — a clear resin polymerized from acrylic acid and methacrylic acid.

activator — catalyst or curing agent.

adduct curing agent — a curing agent combined with a portion of the resin.

adhesion — bonding strength; the attraction of a coating to the substrate.

adsorption — process of attraction to a surface; attachment, the retention of foreign molecules on the surface of a substance.

air cap — (or air nozzle) perforated housing for atomizing air at head of spray gun.

air drying — dries by oxidation or evaporative drying by simple exposure to air without heat or catalyst.

air entrapment — inclusion of air bubbles in paint film.

airless spraying — spraying without atomizing air, using hydraulic pressure.

aliphatic hydrocarbons — "straight chain" solvents of low solvent power, derived from petroleum.

alkali — caustic, inorganic compounds which release hydroxyl groups in aqueous media.

alkyd resins — resins prepared by reacting alcohols and acids.

alligatoring — surface imperfections of paint having the appearance of alligator hide.

ambient temperature — room temperature or temperature of surroundings.

amine adduct — amine curing agent combined with a portion of the resin.

amines — organic substituted ammonia; organic compounds having an NH2 group.

anchor pattern — profile, surface roughness.

anode — the electrode of an electrolytic cell at which a net oxidation reaction occurs. In corrosion processes, the anode is the electrode that has the greater tendency to go into solution.

B

barrier — shielding or blocking device.

base — refers to the larger Volume size of a two-part catalyzed system — usually the non-catalyst. May also refer to any bare surface to be painted.

binder — resin; film former; vehicle.

bituminous coating — coal tar or asphalt based coating.

blast angle — angle to nozzle with reference to surface; also angle of particle propelled from wheel with reference to surface.

blast cleaning — cleaning with propelled abrasives.

bleeding — surface floatation of color from under coats.

blistering — bubbling in dry or partially dry paint film.

blooming — whitening, moisture blush; blushing.

blushing — whitening and loss of gloss due to moisture; blooming.

body — viscosity; middle or under (coat).

bonding — adhesion.

bounce-back — spray rebound.

boxing — mixing by pouring from one container to another.

bridging — forming a skin over a depression.

brittleness — degree of resistance to cracking or breaking by bending.

brushability — ease of brushing.

bubbling — a term used to describe the appearance of bubbles on the surface while a coating is being applied.

C

catalyst — accelerator; curing agent, promoter.

cat-eye — hole or holiday shaped like a cat's eye; cratering.

cathode — the electrode of an electrolytic cell at which a net reduction reaction occurs. In corrosion processes, the cathode is usually the area that is not attacked.

cathodic protection — corrosion prevention by sacrificial anodes or impressed current.

chalking — powdering of surface.

chipping — (1) cleaning steel using special hammers. (2) type of paint failure.

chlorinated rubber — a particular film former used as a binder, made by chlorinating natural rubber.

cleaner — (1) detergent, alkali, acid or other cleaning material; usually water or steam borne. (2) solvent for cleaning paint equipment.

clean surface — one free of contamination.

coal tar — black residue remaining after coal is distilled.

coal tar epoxy paint — paint in which binder or vehicle is combination of coal tar with epoxy resin.

coal tar urethane paint — paint in which binder or vehicle is combination of coal tar with polyurethane resin.

cobwebbing — premature drying causing a spider web effect.

color-fast — non fading.

color retention — ability to retain original color.

compatibility — ability to mix with or adhere properly to other components.

convertor — that which causes change to different state; catalyst; curing agent; promoter.

copolymer — the type of antifouling paint that has its major biocide chemically linked to the binder rather than physically added to it.

corrosion — decay; oxidation; deterioration due to interaction with environment; eaten away by degrees.

coverage — milage, usually in square feet per gallon for a given dry film thickness.

cracking — splitting; disintegration of paint by breaks through film.

cratering — formation of holes or deep depressions in paint film.

crawling — shrinking of paint to form uneven surface.

cross-linking — a particular method by which chemicals unite to form films.

cross-spray — spraying first in one direction and second at right angles.

curing — setting up; hardening.

curing agent — hardener, promoter.

curtaining — sagging.

D

deadman valve — shut-off valve at blast nozzle, operated by remote control.

decorative painting — architectural painting; aesthetical painting.

degreaser — chemical solution (compound) for grease removal.

delamination — separation of layers.

dew point — temperature at which moisture condenses.

diffusion type antifouling — organotin containing antifouling paints. The organotin is physically added to the binder and slowly diffuses through the coating once the paint is in the water.

dry film thickness — (d.f.t.) — the film thickness of paint after all of the solvent has evaporated from the wet paint.

dry spray — overspray or bounce back; sand finish due to spray particle being partially dried before reaching the surface.

drying time — time interval between application and final cure.

dry to handle — time interval between application and ability to pick up without damage.

dry to recoat — time interval between application and ability to receive next coat satisfactorily.

dry to touch — time interval between application and tack-free time.

dulling — loss of gloss or sheen.

E

electrolysis — decomposition by means of an electrical current.

electrolyte — a substance which disassociates into ions when in solution or a fused state and which will then conduct an electric current. Sodium chloride and sulfuric acid are common examples.

electrostatic spray — spraying in which electric charge attracts paint to surface.

emulsion paint — water base paint with an emulsified resin vehicle.

enamel — pigmented varnish; any hard, glossy coating.

epoxy resins — film formers usually made from bisphenol and epichlorohydrin.

epoxy amine — amine cured epoxy resin.

epoxy adduct — epoxy resin having all of the required amine incorporated by requiring additional epoxy resin for curing.

epoxy ester — epoxy modified oil, single package epoxy.

erosion — wearing away of paint films; heavy chalking tends to accelerate erosion.

ester — reaction product of alcohol and acid; an organic salt.

extender — filler.

external mix — spray equipment in which fluid and air join outside of aircap.

F

fadeometer — device for measuring color retention or fade resistance.

fading — reduction in brightness of color.

fallout (spray) — overspray.

false body — thixotropic.

fanning (spray gun technique) — arcing.

fan pattern — geometry of spray pattern.

feather edge — tapered edge.

filler — extender; bulking agent; inert pigment.

film build — dry thickness characteristics per coat.

film former — a substance which forms a skin or membrane when dried from a liquid state.

film integrity — degree of continuity of film.

film thickness gauge — device for measuring film thickness above substrate; dry or wet film thickness gauges are available.

fineness of grind — measure of particle size or roughness of liquid paint; degree of dispersion of pigment in the binder.

fingers (airless) — broken spray pattern; fingerlike.

fire retardant paint — a paint which will delay flaming or overheating of substrate.

fish eye — see cratering.

flaking — disintegration in small pieces of flakes.

flammability — measure of ease of catching fire; ability to burn.

flash point — like the lowest temperature at which a given flammable material will flash if a flame or spark is present.

floating — separation of pigment colors on surface.

flooding — see floating.

fluid tip — orifice in gun into which needle is seated.

fogging — misting.

force drying — acceleration of drying by increasing the temperature above ambient temperature accompanied by forced air circulation.

fungicide — a substance poisonous to fungi; retards or prevents fungi growth.

G

galvanic corrosion — corrosion of dissimilar metals in electrical contact.

generic — belonging to a particular family.

gloss — sheen; ability to reflect; brightness; lustre.

gloss retention — ability to retain original sheen.

grit — an abrasive obtained from slag and various other materials.

H

hardener — curing agent; promoter; catalyst.

hardness — the degree a material will withstand pressure without deformation or scratching.

hiding power — ability to obscure substrate.

high build — producing thick dry films per coat.

holiday — pinhole; skip, discontinuity; voids.

holiday detector — device for detection of pinholes or holidays.

hydrophilic — having an affinity for water; capable of uniting with or dissolving in water.

hydrophobic — having an antagonism for water; not capable of uniting or mixing with water.

hydroxyl — chemical radical —OH; basic in nature.

I

impact resistance — a measure of resistance to a blow; ability to resist deformation from impact.

incompatibility — inability to mix with or adhere to another material.

inert pigment — a non-reactive pigment; filler.

inflammability — measure of ease of catching fire; ability to burn; use of the word flammability is preferred to inflammability due to the possible misinterpretation of the prefix "in" as a negative.

inhibitive pigment — one which retards corrosion process.

inorganic — containing no carbon.

inorganic coatings — those employing inorganic binders or vehicles.

intercoat adhesion — the ability of each coat of paint to stick to the preceding coat.

intercoat contamination — presence of foreign matter between successive coats.

internal mix — a spray gun in which the fluid and air are combined before leaving the gun.

intumesce — to form a voluminous char on ignition; foaming or swelling when exposed to flame.

iron phosphate coating — conversion coating; chemical deposit.

isocyanate resins — resins characterized by CNO grouping; polyurethane resins.

K

KTA Panel — a proprietary paint test panel with unique configuration and markings.

ketones — organic solvents containing CO grouping; commonly used ketones are acetone-dimethyl ketone; MEK-methyl ethyl ketone; and MIBK-methyl isobutyl ketone.

kreb units — units of viscosity.

L

lacquer — coatings that dry by solvent evaporation.

leaching — the process of extraction of a soluble component from a mixture with an insoluble component by percolation of the mixture with a solvent, usually water.

leafing — orientation of pigment flakes in horizontal planes.

lifting — softening and raising of an undercoat by application of a top coat.

M

MEK — see methyl ethyl ketone.

MIBK — see methyl isobutyl ketone.

mandrel test — a physical bending test for adhesion and flexibility.

mil — one one-thousandth of an inch; 001".

milage — coverage rate; square feet per gallon at a given thickness.

mill scale — oxide layer formed on steel by hot rolling.

mill scale binder — gray oxide layer between mill scale and steel.

mineral spirits — aliphatic solvent with solvency similar to turpentine.

miscible — capable of mixing or blending uniformly.

misses — holidays; skip; voids.

mist-coat — thin tack coat; thin adhesive coat.

monomer — composed of single molecules; a basic chemical used to make polymers.

mud-cracking — irregular cracking as in a dried mud puddle.

N

nonflammable — incombustible.

nonvolatile — solid; non-evaporating; the portion of a paint left after the solvent evaporates.

O

oil modified polyurethane — similar to alkyd technology, but generally have better abrasion resistance and drying qualities.

opacity — hiding power.

orange peel — dimpled appearance of dried film; resembling orange peel.

organic — containing carbon.

osmosis — transfer of liquid through a paint film or other membrane.

oxidation — combination with oxygen; drying; burning; rusting.

P

PVA — see polyvinyl acetate.

PVC — see pigment volume concentration or polyvinyl chloride.

pass (spray) — motion of the spray gun in one direction only.

passivation — act of making inert or unreactive.

peeling — failure in which paint curls from substrate.

phenolic resins — particular group of film formers, phenolformaldehyde type.

pH value — measure of acidity or alkalinity; pH 7 is neutral; the pH value of acids ranges from 1 to 7, and of alkalis (bases) from 7 to and including 14.

pickling — a dipping process for cleaning steel and other metals; the picking agent is usually an acid.

pigment grind — dispersion of pigment in a liquid vehicle.

pigments — solid coloring agents.

pigment volume concentration (pvc) — percent by volume occupied by pigment in dried film.

pimpling — small blisters resembling "goose pimples."

pin-holing — formation of small holes through the entire thickness of coating; see cratering.

polymerization — formation of large molecules from small ones.

polymer — the product of polymerization; large molecules.

polyurethane — a wide range of possible binder systems with unique qualities. The aliphatic type is used for the highest quality marine enamels.

polyvinyl acetate (PVA) — a synthetic resin used extensively in emulsion (water) paints; produced by the polymerization of vinyl acetate.

polyvinyl chloride (PVC) — a synthetic resin used in solvent type coatings and fluid bed coatings, produced by the polymerization of vinyl chloride; PVC is also used in emulsion (water) paints.

porosity — hole; degree of integrity or continuity.

pot-life — time interval after mixing during wjich liquid material is usable with no difficulty.

preventive maintenance painting — spot repair painting; touch up or full coats of paint before rusting starts.

profile — surface contour as viewed from edge.

profile depth — average distance between tops of peaks and bottom of valleys on the surface.

R

reactor — the catalyst or cross-linker, which causes two-part systems to cure when added to the base.

red label goods — flammable or explosive materials with flash points below 80 F. (26.7C).

reflectance — degree of light reflection.

resin — a material, natural or synthetic, contained in varnishes, lacquers, and paints; the film former.

S

settling — caking; sediment.

shade — degree of gray tone in a color.

shelf life — maximum interval in which a material may be stored in usable condition.

silicone alkyd — an alkyd modified with silicone resin which enhances gloss retention.

skinning — formation of a solid membrane on top of a liquid.

skips — holidays; misses, uncoated area; voids.

solid — non-volatile portion of paint.

solids volume — percentage of total volume occupied by non-volatiles.

soluble matrix type antifouling paint — an antifouling paint containing resin as a binder. The solubility of the binder serves to release the biocide which is usually cuprous oxide.

solvent — a liquid in which another substance may be dissolved.

spray cap — front enclosure of spray gun equipped with atomizing air holes.

spray head — combination of needle, tip, and air cap.

spray pattern — configuration of spray, gun held steady.

spreading rate — coverage, mileage, usually at specified dry thickness.

substrate — surface to be painted.

synthetic — manufactured; not occurring naturally.

T

tack — degree of stickiness.

tails (airless spray) — finger-like spray pattern.

thermoplastic — mobile or softens under heat.

thermosetting — becomes rigid under heat and cannot be remelted.

thixotropic — false-bodied; a gel which liquifies with agitation but gels again on standing.

tipping off — slightly dragging a brush over a wet painted or varnished surface to smooth it from brush or roller marks or to break small bubbles in the wet film.

tooth — profile; mechanical anchorage; surface roughness.

two-component gun — one having two separate fluid sources leading to spray head.

U

underatomized — not dispersed or broken-up fine enough.

V

vehicle — liquid carrier; binder; anything dissolved in the liquid portion of a paint is a part of the vehicle.

vinyl coating — one in which the major portion of binder is of the vinyl resin family.

vinyl copolymer — resins produced by copolymerizing vinyl acetate and vinyl chloride.

vinyl resins — a particular group of film formers; see PVA and PVC.

viscosity — a measure of fluidity.

viscosity cup — a device for measuring viscosity.

voids — holidays, holes, skips.

volatile content — percentage of materials which evaporate.

W

wash primer — a thin inhibiting paint usually chromate pigmented with a polyvinyl butyrate binder.

water blasting — blast cleaning using high velocity water.

water spotting — a surface defect caused by water droplets.

weatherometer — a testing device intended to stimulate atmospheric weathering.

weld slag — amorphous deposits formed during welding.

weld spatter — beads of metal left adjoining a weld.

wet edge — keeping the paint wet enough when it is applied by brush so it can be brushed back into without showing lines of demarcation from one painted area to the next.

wet spray — spraying so that surface is covered with paint that has not started to dry.

wet film thickness — (W.F.T.) the thickness of paint when it is first applied before solvent evaporation takes place.

whipping (spray gun) — arcing, waving.

Z

zinc silicate — inorganic zinc coating.

zinc yellow — zinc chromate.

Glossary of Terms

A

ABX – A grading system for plywood indicating that one side is flawless (A) and one side is good, but perhaps seamed or patched (B) and the laminating glue is resorcinal (exterior grade) (X).

Acetone – A very combustible, fast evaporating cleaning fluid for cleaning surfaces. The only thing that will dissolve and clean polyester resin.

Acid Brush – A small inexpensive brush of about ½ inch bristle width with a tin handle; ideal for gluing or cleaning.

Accordion Hose – A flexible rubber hose used to act as a flex unit between a deck fill and tank.

ACX – Same as ABX except the second side holes and flaws are *not* repaired (C).

Aft – Toward the rear or stern of a boat.

Aloft – Upon the mast or rigging.

Ammeter – An indicating gauge that reflects the amount of amps being drawn.

Amp/Hrs. – A rating which reflects the number of amps per hour a device draws or charges.

Anchor Light – An electric or kerosene 'white' light placed in the rigging during overnight anchoring to advise other boats.

Anchor Roller – A stainless steel or bronze roller over which anchor-chain commutes.

Anchor Windlass – A mechanical winch, manual or electric, which aids in hauling anchors and chain.

Anemometer – An instrument used to measure wind speed.

Aqualift – An exhaust system, usually a small cast iron unit attached directly to the engine.

Arbor – An attachment used with a drill motor; supports hole saws of different sizes. Usually has a drill bit inserted throughout its center. center.

B

Backstay – The wire rope giving aft support to the mast.

Back-up Plates – Reinforcing plates, usually steel or brass, used when bolting through vulnerable material such as wood or fiberglass.

Baffles – Structural partitions in fuel and water tanks that restrain liquids from gaining momentum during violent boat movement.

Baggywrinkle – Fluffed, short rope ends fabricated to prevent sails from chafing on shrouds.

Ballast – High density weight (lead, steel, or cement) carried in the lower part of a vessel to give her stability and enable her to right herself.

Band Saw – A large saw with a flexible, thin loop of a blade, used to cut curves or fine finishing angles.

Bar Clamp – A very long adjustable clamp of 24 inches or more used to clamp large pieces.

Barograph – A barometer equipped with a moving graph that records barometric changes.

Battens – Flexible plastic fiberglass or wood strips utilized in a reinforced pocket in the leech of a sail, used as an aid to properly set a sail with a roach.

Battens Pockets – Reinforced sheath on the leech of the sail that houses battens.

Battery Box – A protective box, usually plastic, which protects the battery from external damage and also accumulates battery spillage.

Battery Cables – High output cables (usually #4 or lower gauge) that connect the battery with the alternator or generator.

Battery Straps – Strong non-corrosive straps used to lash a battery to its shelf or support to keep it from damage.

Beam – The widest dimension of a vessel.

Bedlog – A set of raised tracks upon which the main hatch slides.

Berth – A bunk or any sleeping accommodations of a vessel.

Berth Rail – A trim piece that keeps berth cushions in place.

Bevel – The act of cutting to a taper.

Bevel Square – An adjustable tool which with two arms and a wingnut can be used to duplicate or record angles.

Bilge – Area of the boat below the cabin sole utilized for tanks, storage, etc.

Bilge Pump – A high capacity manual or electric pump used to pump out bilge water.

Bilge Pump Strainer – A strainer or sieve (hopefully brass) attached to the lower end of a bilge pump hose needed to keep flotsam and jetsam from clogging the pump.

Binnacle – A housing for compasses.

Bobstay – The stay from the tip of the bowsprit to a fitting at the waterline, counteracting the pull of the forestay.

Boiler Punchings – Steel punchings, usually scrap, which because of their small size (thus high density) are commonly used as ballast.

Bolt Rope – Roping around the edge of a sail needed to take the strain off the sailcloth.

Boom Bail – A 'U'-shaped bracket screwed to booms through which blocks and lines can be led.

Boomgallows – A standard support upon which the boom rests when the sails are stored.

Boomkin – A horizontal extension off the stern of the boat used to accommodate a backstay if the main or mizzen boom length demands.

Boomvang – A rope and block mechanism which controls the upward movement of booms.

Bowsprit – A horizontal extension off the bow of the boat used to accommodate the headstay if the size of the headsails demand.

Bos'ns Chair – A canvas sling used for hoisting one up the mast.

Boot Stripe – A painted stripe above the yacht's waterline to catch oil or dirt; or just for esthetics.

Bridge Deck – A narrow part of the deck between the cockpit and the companionway or cabin.

Bulkheads – Usually structural partitions of a boat. Solid dividers, e.g. lazarette bulkhead, chain locker bulkhead, engine room bulkhead.

Bull-Nose – (a) to round off a sharp edge; (b) a concave bladed router bit used to round off a sharp edge; (c) the rounded edge itself.

Bullseye – A high strength plastic eyelet that can be secured to the deck to aid in fairleading lines.

Bulwarks – Raised portion of deck that follows the sheer line, usually used for protection of crew and equipment.

Butt Connector – A metal press fitting that unites two wires end to end without complex splicing.

C

California Reefing – Same as slab and jiffy reefing.

Cam Cleat – A piece of deck hardware consisting of two cogs between which line will pass in only one direction.

Cap Nut – A finishing nut with one side sealed off.

Car – A moving fitting attached to a traveler to which a block may be attached.

Carriage Bolt – A smooth-headed bolt with square shoulders to keep it from turning.

Catalyst – A chemical activator for an otherwise inactive substance.

Caulk – To drive cotton line into the seam of a wood planked vessel.

Ceiling – The lining which keeps things from touching the inside skin of the hull.

Center Bond – The laminations uniting two halves of a twin molded hull.

Center Punch - A pointed tool for making marks on wood or metal.

Charley Noble – A through deck fitting (usually with cap) for a stove pipe.

Cheek Block – A fixed pulley which is attached to a boom, etc. on its side.

Chicken Head –A metal fitting at the top of a mast to which are secured the shrouds, stays and sheaves.

Chocks – Blocks of wood or metal on the deck which act as pads for deck equipment such as a dinghy, spinnaker pole, etc.

Chronometer – A very accurate clock used for navigation.

Circular Saw – Also known as skill saw; a small electric saw with a rotating circular blade.

Clam Cleat – Similar to a cam cleat, but without moving parts.

Clamping – Mechanically holding two parts together.

Cleat – A T-shaped piece of hardware, usually of wood or aluminum attached to the mast deck or caprail for securing items.

Cleat Stock – Square cross-sectioned strips of wood used to join perpendicularly uniting pieces of plywood.

Clevis Pin – A stiff piece of metal rod which secures a joint (e.g. toggel and turnbuckle).

Clew – Lower aft corner of sail.

Clipper Bow – A bow that has a forward curve.

Club Footed Jib – A self-tending jib whose foot is attached to a boom at the clew rather than being free flying.

Coaming – Side of cabin, cockpit, etc.

Cockpit – The sunken area of a deck in which the helmsman and passengers sit.

Cockpit Sole – The floor of the cockpit.

Cold Chisel – A very hard chisel for cutting metal.

Companionway – The entrance by which you pass through when going below from topsides.

Companionway Ladder – The steps in the companionway leading below.

Compression Tube – A reinforcing tubing welded into aluminum mast, through which a bolt passes. It prevents the walls from collapsing.

Countersink – To set the head of a screw or bolt below the surface; tool used for this purpose.

Cunningham Hole – A hole and cringle in a sail used to tighten or stretch the luff.

Cutter – A single mast vessel with two headsails.

D

Davit – An overhanging fixture from which a dinghy is supported.

Deadeye – Old-fashioned method of rigging adjustment used in combination with lanyards. Replaced by modern turnbuckles.

Dead Light – A non-opening piece of glass in deck, cabin atop, etc. for light.

Deck Beams – Athwartship beams that support the deck.

Deck Bridge – The piece of decking between the cockpit and companionway entrance.

Deck Cap – A metal cap that fits over a deck-pipe to prevent water from entering boat.

Deck Fill – A metal deck fitting with screwdriver top through which water and fuel can be administered to tanks below decks.

Deck Pipe – A metal deck fitting through which chain is fed below.

Displacement – Very close estimate of the vessel's weight.

Dolfinite – A very oily bedding compound best used on fiberglass to wood or wood to wood joints.

Dove-tailing – A very positive method of corner joints for wood, using intermeshing wedge shapes of each wood as fasteners.

Dove-tail Saw – A very stiff-bladed hand saw with well reinforced blade for very accurate cutting.

Dowels – Wood turnings used as a common attachment, usually to join boards on end.

Downhaul – Line used to pull down sails. Commonly used in reference to a moveable gooseneck on tracks.

Draft – The vertical distance from waterline to lowest point of keel.

Drop Boards – Removable boards that slide into gallows, usually to shut off companionway opening.

Drops – Wood 'doors' usually below cushions that cover access holes to stowage below.

D-Shackle – A 'D'-shaped shackle with threaded pin.

E

Echo Sounder – A fathometer.

Elbow Catch – A spring-loaded catch for cabinet doors, usually hidden and accessible through a finger hole.

Engine Pan – Usually a fiberglass molding bonded to the hull. The engine mounts fitted onto its shoulders. Below the pan catches oil drippings.

Epoxy Glue and Resin – A high strength synthetic adhesive that will stick anything to anything.

Eye – A closed loop in wire-rope or line.

Eyeband – A fitting on the tip of the bowsprit to which the forestay, bobstay and whiskerstays are attached.

Eyebolt – A bolt with an open loop for a head.

Eyelets – Brass loops sewn into sails for reef points, etc.

F

Fairlead – A fitting which alters the direction of a line to keep it from fouling.

Fathom – 6 feet of measure.

Feather – To even two levels into each other.

Feeler Gauge – Small metal sheets of given thickness used to measure fine spacings; e.g. coupling to engine alignment.

Fender – A bumper or rubber guard hung from the boat's sides.

Fiddles – Wood or metal guardrails along the perimeter of counters, tables, etc. that keep items from falling.

Flare – Outward curve of a vessel's side. To widen or ream the end of a pipe for coupling purposes.

Flathead – A bevel-shouldered screw.

Flex Coupling – A rubber fitted unit uniting the engine with propeller shaft. The rubber acts as an absorber of engine vibration.

Flex Mounts – Rubber fitted engine mounts that prevent transmission of engine vibration to the hull.

Flux – A cleaning paste used on surface just before soldering.

Foot – The bottom edge of a sail.

Footpump – A water pump operated by foot.

Fore and Aft – In direction of centerline. Stern to bow.

Forecastle – The forward-most accommodations.

Forefoot – The underwater part of the bow from the forward part of the keel to the foremost part of the waterline.

Forepeak – Generally same as forecastle.

Forestay – The forward-most mast supporting rigging.

Fork Wrench – Open ended wrench.

Freeboard – Vertical distance from waterline to sheer.

Fresh Water Cooling – A closed water system which circulates through the engine block to cool it. The fresh water is in turn cooled through a heat exchanger by circulating exterior water.

G

Galley – A boat's kitchen.

Gallows – Boom gallows.

Galvanize – A zinc coating put on steel to protect it from corrosion.

Gate Valve – A conventional shut-off mechanism for water and fuel flow.

Gelcoat – A very hard outer coating (usually color pigmented) of a fiberglass boat.

Genoa – A headsail filling the entire fore triangle and more.

Gimbals – A swivel arrangement by which stoves, tables, compasses, etc. are allowed to remain level in spite of the boat movements.

Gooseneck – A swivel fitting that holds the boom onto the mast.

Grabrail – Holed handrail on deck or inside a boat.

Graphite – A mineral base lubricant.

Grinder – A term used sometimes for a belt sander.

Grommet – A brass eye sewn into a sail.

Guard – An adjustable metal fence on a table saw, running parallel with the blade.

Gudgeon – A hull fitting into which the pintle of the rudder fits.

Gypsey – A wheel on the windlass notched for rope.

H

Hack Saw – A very fine tooth bladed saw (the blade is removable) made for metal cutting.

Halyard – Lines used for hoisting sails.

Halyard Winches - Winches with a drum for wire or rope used to aid in hoisting the sails.

Hank – The attaching clip of a sail that holds it to the stay but allows it to slide up and down

Hasp – The hinged part of a fitting that combined with an eye and padlock completes a locking unit for hatches, doors, etc.

Hatch – An access hole in the ship's deck; also the cover for this hole.

Hatch Coaming – Built up buffer around a hatch opening to keep out water intruding under the hatch.

Hatch Cover – A fixed housing under which a hatch slides.

Head – The toilet of a boat.

Headsail – Sails such as jib, genoa, staysail, set forward of the mast.

Heat-Exchanger – A cooling unit of an engine which allows circulating raw water to cool captive fresh water.

Helm – Tiller or steering wheel.

Hex (Head or Nut) – A six-sided nut, or six-sided bolt-head.

Hobby Horse – The pitching of the bow and stern of a boat about its athwartship axis.

Hold Downs – Straps of steel or nylon used to fasten tanks to shelves, floor timbers, etc.

Hole Saws – Circular heavy walled saw blades of infinite diameters used in conjunction with a drill motor to cut holes.

Hose Barb – A tapered fitting with terraced ridges that allow a hose to slip on but not off.

Hose Clamp – An adjustable stainless steel ring used to fasten hoses to fittings.

Hose Ties – Plastic ties with a barbed tongue and eye used to fasten hoses to bulkheads, sole, etc.

House Pipe – A fitting in the bulwarks through which mooring lines or anchor lines are led.

I

Inboard – Toward the centerline.

Injectors – The device on a diesel engine which turns the fuel from liquid to vapor.

Intermediates – Stays that support the mast at a point between the spreaders and masthead.

J

Jack Stays – Spreader lifts.

Jam Cleats – A small cleat with general shape of a mooring cleat but one end is tapered so the line can be wedged with a single run; used for sheets where quick release and quick making-fast is necessary.

Jib – The foremost headsail.

Jiffy Reefing – A method which quickly hauls the luff and leech of the mainsail down to the boom by means of lines and blocks.

Joiner – A mechanical table plane for dressing wood surfaces.

K

Keel – The fore and aft underwater members which stabilizes the boat's direction and prevents leeway.

Ketch – Twin masted sailboat with the main forward of the mizzen and the mizzen forward of the stern post.

Key Hole Saw – A very narrow bladed hand saw with one end of the blade unsupported, used for hole or curve cutting.

Kill Switch – A control mechanism on a diesel engine that shuts it off by cutting off fuel supply.

King Plank – The central plank of a deck.

Knot – A vertical speed rating – 1 nautical mile = 6,080 ft./hr.

Knotmeter – A boat's speedometer.

L

Lag Bolt – Square headed wood screw.

Lay Up – The laminations of fiberglass.

Lazarette – A stowage compartment in the aft-most section of a vessel.

Lead-Fish – Large lead castings used for ballast.

Lead-Pig – Small (1016-10016) lead castings used for ballast.

Lead-Chot – Very small lead chunks used for ballast.

Leeboard – Canvas or plywood slabs used to keep a berth's occupant in the berth in spite of the vessel's roll.

Leech – Aft edge of the sail.

Leeway – Sideways movement of a vessel.

Lifelines – The lines attached to the stanchions providing a 'railing.'

Limber Holes – Holes in bulkheads that allow drainage from one compartment to another.

LOA – Length Over All (not including bowsprit or boomkin or aft hung rudder).

Locker – A stowage compartment.

Log – A mechanical device that records the distance the ship has moved relative to water.

Lowers – The lower shrouds.

Lubber Line – Mark on a compass corresponding to the boat's center line.

Luff – Forward edge of sail.

LWL – Load Water Line – length of hull at marked waterline.

M

Machine Screw – A fine threaded, slot headed fastener made to be used with a tapped hole.

Mainsail – Fore and aft sail attached to aft part of main mast.

Make Fast – To attach or secure a line.

Marine Eyes – The looped fitting over a shroud.

Mast Head – Top of the mast.

Mast Step – A fitting on deck or below onto which the foot of the mast is fitted.

Mat – An unwoven fiberglass material made up of randomly layered short fibers.

Miter – To cut on an angle.

Miter Box – A wood or metal frame which is used with a hand saw to cut material at a given angle.

Miter Gauge – The sliding fitting on a table or band saw against which the piece of wood is laid to assure a straight cut. The gauge itself is adjustable to any angle required.

Mish-Mash – A mixture of polyester resin and fibers of asbestos or fiberglass combined to make a thicker putty-like adhesive.

Mizzen – Fore and aft sail attached to aft part of mizzen mast.

Mizzen Mast – The aft mast of a yawl or ketch.

Molding – Trimming pieces of wood or plastic that hide joints or mistakes or both.

Mooring Cleat – A large deck cleat to which mooring lines are attached.

N

Negative Roach – A battenless, hollow-cut cruising mainsail.

Non-Skid – A high friction surface for deck and cabin top.

O

Open End – A type of mechanic's wrench.

Outboard – Away from center line.

Outhaul – The gear used to stretch the foot of sail along the boom.

Oval Head – A screw with a head of that shape.

Overhang – Stern or bow of hull extending past the LWL.

Overhead – Inside cabin top.

P

Pad Eye – A through bolted deck fitting to accommodate blocks, lines, etc.

Pan Head – A type of screw with a head shaped like the bottom of a cooking pan.

Pennant – Short length of wire to which head-sails are attached.

Pet Cock – A small 90 degree turn off-on valve ideal for fuel switch off.

Pilot Berth – An elevated single berth.

Pinrail – A rack that houses belaying pins.

Pintle – Rudder fitting that fits into gudgeons to form hinge.

Pitch – Sticky wood rosin.

Plastic Resin Glue – A powder base mixed with water that forms a very strong water resistant glue.

Plug – A tight fitting wood dowel used to fill screw head holes.

Plug Cutter – An attachment for a drill motor that cuts plugs.

Plug Remover – Any sharp tool to split an inserted plug and take it out.

Polysulfide – An unbelievably effective totally waterproof sealing-bedding compound.

Polyurethane Foam – A tight-celled polyester resin resistant insulation.

Poop – An overtaking sea swamping the aft deck and/or cockpit of vessel.

Port – Left side of vessel facing forward.

Portlight – A small cabin side window.

Preventer – Another name for a boomvang.

Pull Rings – Flush fitting swivel rings used to lift hatches.

Purchase – The lines and blocks used to gain mechanical advantage.

Q

Quarter Berth – Usually an excellent sea berth located in the aft quarters of the ship.

Quarters – The sections of the vessel from amidships to bow or amidships to stern.

R

Rabbet – A groove cut in a plank.

Radio Coax – Radio antenna wire.

Railstripe – A color line along the sheer.

Rake – Fore and aft inclination of mast, stern-post, etc.

Ratlines – Horizontal ropes or strips of wood between shrouds forming a ladder.

Rat Tail – Faired or feathered rope end.

Raw Water Cooling – An engine cooling system that circulates exterior water directly through the block.

Reaching Pole – A light boom for keeping light wind sails full.

Reef – To shorten sails.

Reef Points – Grommets or ties for shortening the sail.

Resorcinal Glue A two-part completely water-proof glue.

Roach – The outward curve added to a sail to increase its belly.

Rope Tail – A nylon end on a wire halyard.

Roving – A very heavy woven fiberglass material.

Rubrail – Bumper strip of wood or metal on the beams.

Rudder Preventer – A strip between hull and aft-hung rudder that keeps lines from catching on rudder.

Run – To sail before the wind.

Running Rigging – Sheets, halyards, etc., i.e. moveable rigging.

S

Sail Track – A track on the mast or boom into or onto which the sail slides are fitted.

Salon – Main living area in vessel.

Samson Post – Strong post in foredeck used as a hitch post for anchor line and mooring line.

Schooner – A rig that sports a smaller mast ahead of the main mast.

Scupper – An opening in the bulwarks allowing deck-drainage.

Scribe – To reproduce the curve of a surface onto another surface by using a compass with pencil.

Seacock – A 90 degree shut-off valve used on through-hull fittings.

Seakindly – having characteristics which respond well to any sea condition.

Searail – Fencing along table, cabinetry, etc. to guard items from falling.

Seating Cleat – Shelving upon which drop boards sit.

Section – Lines of a vessel as if cut in half looking fore and aft.

Set – To hoist sail.

Shaft-Log – A bearing supporting fitting guiding the propeller-shaft through the hull.

Shank – The shaft of the anchor.

Sheer – Curve of a gunwale.

Sheet – A rope used to trim sails.

Sheet Metal Screw – Heavy threaded self-tapping screw.

Shrink Tubes – Plastic tubing slipped over wire splices then shrunk by heat to seal the splice.

Shroud – Wire rigging giving the most athwart-ship support.

Silicone Seal – A quick drying non-hardening sealing compound.

Slab Reefing – Jiffy reefing.

Slides – Metal fittings that hold a sail onto the sail track.

Sloop – Single masted rig with single headsail.

Snap Shackle – Hinge bar shackle.

Sole – Cabin floor,

Sole Timber – Floor supporting beams.

Spinnaker Car – A moveable fitting that attaches the spinnaker pole to the spinnaker track.

Spinnaker Pole – A light spar that keeps the clew of the spinnaker well out helping fill the sail.

Spinnaker Track – A track attached to the mast over which the spinnaker car slides.

Spreader – A strut on a mast giving rigidity to rigging.

Spreader Lifts – Wires that keep spreaders in position.

Stanchions – Steel poles attached to deck or bulwarks to support lifelines.

Standing Rigging – Permanently attached wire stays and turnbuckles supporting the mast.

Starboard – The right side of a vessel facing forward.

Stay – A wire rope supporting the mast fore and aft.

Staysail – A triangular hanked sail.

Staysail Pedestal – A deck mounted base footing the staysail boom.

Stops – Moveable fittings on a track that keep a block in place.

Storm Jib – A very small, heavy clothed heavy-weather headsail.

Storm Trysail – Very small heavy clothed heavy-weather sail to replace mainsail.

Stuffing Box – A fitting at the shaft-log preventing the entry of water.

Sump – The lowest point in the keel where water collects.

Swedge – Method of attaching, by pressure, fittings onto a wire rope.

T

Tabernacle – A large deck bracket that houses the foot of the mast and the pin which allows it to be lowered.

Tack – The lower forward corner of a sail.

Taffrail – A rail around the stern – usually decorative if you like that sort of thing.

Tang – A metal fitting on mast or hull to which rigging is attached.

Tender – Given to heeling, antonym of 'Stiff.'

Terminal Blocks – An electrical, insulated block with fittings to unite wires.

Thimble – A round or heart-shaped metal eye chafe protector around which rope can be seized.

Tiller – A bar attached to top of rudder used for steering.

Toggle – A swivel fork uniting the turnbuckle to the chainplate.

Topping Lift – A line supporting aft end of a boom.

Transducer – A fathometer through-hull fitting.

Transom – A chopped stern, opposite of double-ender.

Traveller – A moveable attachment that allows control over movement of the boom.

Tumble-Home – Inward curve along the sheer line of some vessels.

Turnbuckle – Adjustable attachment uniting rigging to hull fittings.

U

Upper Shroud – That part of the rigging going to the mast head which provides athwartships support.

V

Vang – A rope controlling upward movement of a boom.

Vented Loop – A bronze fitting with a valve that prevents siphoning of water into appliances below the waterline.

W

Waterline – A horizontal line at the point of designed displacement.

Water Separator – A filter that takes water from diesel fuel by gravity.

Water Strainer – A filter for incoming raw water.

Whiskerstay – Standing rigging which prevents athwartships movement of bowsprit or boomkin.

Winch – A mechanical aid made up of a drum and pin and gears to aid in hoisting and trimming sails.

Winch Bracket – A fabricated mount for sheet winches.

Winch Pad – A welded pad on a mast serving as a base for a halyard winch.

Windlass – A winch to haul up anchor and anchor chain.

Y

Yankee Jib – Large foresail, its size between a working jib and genoa.

Yaw – To change bearing from side to side – unable to maintain course.

Yawl – A twin-masted rig, the mizzen being stepped abaft the sternpost.

Index